Monetary and Financial Systems in Africa

Aloysius Ajab Amin
Regina Nsang Tawah • Augustin Ntembe
Editors

Monetary and Financial Systems in Africa

Integration and Economic Performance

Editors
Aloysius Ajab Amin
Clayton State University
Morrow, GA, USA

Regina Nsang Tawah
Bowie State University
Bowie, MD, USA

Augustin Ntembe
Bowie State University
Bowie, MD, USA

ISBN 978-3-030-96224-1   ISBN 978-3-030-96225-8 (eBook)
https://doi.org/10.1007/978-3-030-96225-8

© The Editor(s) (if applicable) and The Author(s), under exclusive licence to Springer Nature Switzerland AG 2022

This work is subject to copyright. All rights are solely and exclusively licensed by the Publisher, whether the whole or part of the material is concerned, specifically the rights of translation, reprinting, reuse of illustrations, recitation, broadcasting, reproduction on microfilms or in any other physical way, and transmission or information storage and retrieval, electronic adaptation, computer software, or by similar or dissimilar methodology now known or hereafter developed.

The use of general descriptive names, registered names, trademarks, service marks, etc. in this publication does not imply, even in the absence of a specific statement, that such names are exempt from the relevant protective laws and regulations and therefore free for general use.

The publisher, the authors and the editors are safe to assume that the advice and information in this book are believed to be true and accurate at the date of publication. Neither the publisher nor the authors or the editors give a warranty, expressed or implied, with respect to the material contained herein or for any errors or omissions that may have been made. The publisher remains neutral with regard to jurisdictional claims in published maps and institutional affiliations.

This Palgrave Macmillan imprint is published by the registered company Springer Nature Switzerland AG.

The registered company address is: Gewerbestrasse 11, 6330 Cham, Switzerland

Foreword

The *Monetary and Financial Systems in Africa: Integration and Economic Performance* comes at a critical time when several efforts are underway to expand monetary arrangements in the region. The African Continental Free Trade Area (AfCFTA) came into force on 1st January 2021 and is expected to eliminate many tariff and other trade barriers. The kickoff of AfCFTA was preceded by the recent ECOWAS' failed attempt to conclude the establishment of its long proposed single currency, the Eco. As a result, the proposed West African Monetary Zone (WAMZ), which includes Anglophone countries, is now being finalized. The East African Community (EAC), which was dissolved at independence in that part of the region, is now being fast-tracked, while the South African Customs Union (SACU) is considering the inclusion of the Common Market Area (CMA) and other SADC members. These unions are pillars on which an African single currency, envisioned at the creation of the Organization of African Unity and fully embraced by its replacement, the African Union, is expected to be established.

The above activities come to add to other long-standing monetary union arrangements, including the CFA franc zones – the West African Economic and Monetary Union (WAEMU) and the Central African Economic and Monetary Union (CEMAC) and the CMA in Southern Africa. The new monetary arrangements are expected to provide additional potential for increased trade, competitiveness, greater employment, poverty reduction, and economic growth. There are, however, several challenges associated with African economic and monetary integration, and these include the relatively less developed financial infrastructure and the large variations in monetary and fiscal policies of the countries.

This book discusses monetary policy, delving into inflation-targeting and evaluates monetary policy effectiveness in stabilizing prices as well as the effect on other macroeconomic, welfare conditions and economic growth. It presents an in-depth analysis of regional integration, regional monetary and financial integration bringing out the sticky issues that constrain regional monetary integration, while providing suggestions on how to overcome them. The book provides solid analysis of previous monetary arrangements, including CEMAC (BEAC), CMA, ECOWAS, and EAC highlighting their success, challenges, and prospects in implementing monetary integration in Africa.

The book undertakes theoretical and empirical analyses of financial integration and economic performance, monetary unions and trade competitiveness, and capital markets. It also evaluates progress of the African Monetary Union project. Despite the important challenges highlighted, the authors are hopeful that monetary integration in Africa is achievable within a reasonable period as financial technological revolution transforms financial institutions.

African Research Universities Alliance   Ernest Aryeetey
Accra, Ghana

Preface

The book analyzes Africa's monetary and economic integration issues with the main aim of deriving appropriate monetary policy. It provides a valuable contribution to the knowledge base for policymakers, academicians, and the general public in the theory and practice of monetary and financial institutions under existing monetary regimes and their impact on economic performance. The analysis of issues is country-specific, sub-region-specific, and continental as a whole. The book also focuses on several issues: price stability, high employment, financial markets and financial institutions stability, interest rate stability, foreign exchange market stability, and economic growth. Formulating and implementing a sound monetary policy to complement fiscal policy is key to achieving economic goals. The continent continues to deal with various socio- economic issues despite its extraordinary wealth in human and natural resources.

For long African countries have tried to create a single currency as they see the huge benefits of a monetary union. But the prospect for the successful adoption of a common currency in Africa faces many challenges. Africa inherited different monetary and financial systems. For instance, the banking systems do not function in the same way. The banking system in West African Economic and Monetary Union (WAEMU) countries follow their French colonial heritage while non- WAEMU countries adhere to their British heritage. They produce different outcomes. Even having a single currency like the ECO currency has seen many twists and turns, putting into focus the France-Afrique relationship. The CFA franc zone with the institutional rigidity, foreign reserves restriction, lack of monetary policy, and exchange rate policy inhibit the economic development in the zone. However, there are lessons to learn from the CFA franc zone monetary unions, which have a long history.

African countries are taking necessary steps towards having monetary integration at sub-regional and continental levels. This has become more important as the digital revolution is transforming financial institutions. The aim is to have a single continental currency—the newly launched African Continental Free Trade Area (AfCFTA). AfCFTA is a precursor of the African Monetary Union. The authors present and analyze the prospects and conditions for successfully building African Monetary Union since monetary policy affects economic growth directly and indirectly through the transmission mechanism of credit to the private sector that promotes economic growth. At the same time, the key to the success of the proposed African single currency is to work towards the convergence criteria, including political and macroeconomic stability, but more importantly, having a prudent and responsible macroeconomic policy with a robust policy of credit access expansion.

Bowie, MD, USA
Morrow, GA, USA

Regina Nsang Tawah
Aloysius Ajab Amin
Augustin Ntembe

Contents

Part I Introduction   1

1 Introduction and Background: A Historical Perspective of
   the Role of Financial Institutions in Africa's Development   3
   Aloysius Ajab Amin, Regina Nsang Tawah, and
   Augustin Ntembe

Part II Country Monetary Policy Issues   41

2 Monetary Policy and Price Stability in Ghana's Fourth
   Republic: Have the Dues Been Paid?   43
   Abdul-Aziz Iddrisu and Imhotep Paul Alagidede

3 Monetary Policy Impact on Macroeconomic Performance
   in Tanzania: Empirical Approach   63
   Jehovaness Aikaeli

4 Effects of Monetary Policy Transmission on Economic
   Growth in Sierra Leone   81
   Elkanah Faux

Part III Regional Financial Sector Issues   95

5 The Monetary Union and Economic Integration: Challenges of the Creation of the West African Single Currency, Eco   97
Mohamed Ben Omar Ndiaye

6 The Political Economy of a Monetary Union in ECOWAS: The Case of the ECO Currency   123
Rachael Ntongho

7 The Effects of Minimum Bank Capital and Governance on the Financing of the EMCCA Economies   143
Issidor Noumba and André Arnaud Enguene

8 Facts and Prospects of Monetary Union in East Africa   169
John Sseruyange

9 The Development Cost of Maintaining Price and Economic Stability in Central and West African CFA Franc Zone   185
Aloysius Ajab Amin

10 Banking Development in West Africa   217
Regina Nsang Tawah

11 Capital Markets Development and Economic Growth in North Africa   239
Augustin Ntembe, Aloysius Ajab Amin, and Regina Nsang Tawah

Part IV Continental Monetary Policy and the Financial Systems — 259

12 Economic Performance Across Monetary Unions in Africa — 261
Joseph Onjala

13 Capital Markets' Development: Are African Countries Lagging? — 283
Thaddee M. Badibanga

14 African Monetary Unions and Competitiveness — 315
Oluremi Davies Ogun

15 Financial Institutions Versus Trade and Infrastructural Development in Africa — 343
Bruno L. Yawe, J. Ddumba-Ssentamu, Yusuf Kiwala, and Ibrahim Mukisa

16 Prospect of Economic Unions on Intra-regional Trade in Africa — 369
Grace Nkansa Asante

17 A Single Currency for Africa: Challenges and Possibilities — 395
Augustin Ntembe

Part V Conclusion: The Way Forward — 419

18 Conclusion: Currency Regimes and Monetary Integration in Africa, the Way Forward — 421
Regina Nsang Tawah, Augustin Ntembe, and Aloysius Ajab Amin

Index — 435

CONTRIBUTORS

Jehovaness Aikaeli School of Economics, University of Dar es Salaam, Dar es Salaam, Tanzania

Imhotep Paul Alagidede Wits Business School, University of the Witwatersrand, Johannesburg, South Africa
Institute for Indigenous Intelligence, Nile Valley Multiversity, Johannesburg, South Africa

Aloysius Ajab Amin Clayton State University, Morrow, GA, USA

Grace Nkansa Asante Department of Economics, KNUST, Kumasi, Ghana

Thaddee M. Badibanga Bowie State University, Bowie, MD, USA

J. Ddumba-Ssentamu School of Economics, Makerere University, Kampala, Uganda

André Arnaud Enguene University of Yaounde II, Yaounde (Centre), Cameroon

Elkanah Faux Bowie State University, Bowie, MD, USA

Abdul-Aziz Iddrisu Department of Banking Technology and Finance, Kumasi Technical University, Kumasi, Ghana
Wits Business School, University of the Witwatersrand, Johannesburg, South Africa

Yusuf Kiwala School of Business, Makerere University, Kampala, Uganda

Ibrahim Mukisa School of Economics, Makerere University, Kampala, Uganda

Mohamed Ben Omar Ndiaye Institut des Politiques Publiques, Universite Cheikh Anta Diop, Dakar, Senegal

Issidor Noumba University of Yaounde II, Yaounde (Centre), Cameroon

Augustin Ntembe Bowie State University, Bowie, MD, USA

Rachael Ntongho University of Manchester, Manchester, UK

Oluremi Davies Ogun Department of Economics, University of Ibadan, Ibadan, Nigeria

Joseph Onjala Department of Economics and Development Studies, University of Nairobi, Nairobi, Kenya

Abban Stanley Department of Economics, KNUST, Kumasi, Ghana

Regina Nsang Tawah Bowie State University, Bowie, MD, USA

Bruno L. Yawe School of Economics, Makerere University, Kampala, Uganda

Abbreviations

ACC	Actual Cost of Credit
ADF	Augmented Dickey-Fuller Test
AEC	African Economic Community
AERC	African Economic Research Consortium
AfCFTA	African Continental Free Trade Area
AFDB	African Development Bank
AGOA	African Growth and Opportunity Act
AIC	Akaike's information criterion
AMU	Arab Maghreb Union
APEC	Asia-Pacific Economic Cooperation
ARDL	Autoregressive distributed lag
ARIA IX	Assessing Regional Integration in Africa Nineth Edition
ARII	African Regional Integration Index
ASEAN	Association of South East Asian Nations
AU	African Union
AUC	African Union Commission
BAO	Banque d'Afrique Occidentale
BBWA	British Bank West Africa
BCEAEC	Central Bank of the States of Equatorial Africa and Cameroon
BCEAO	Central Bank of West African Countries
BCEAO	WAEMU Central Bank/ Central Bank for Francophone Countries in West Africa
BD	Banking Development
BEAC	Bank of Central African States
BEER	Behavioral Equilibrium Exchange Rate

BF	blended finance
BOG	Bank of Ghana
BOP	Balance of Payments
BOT	Bank of Tanzania
BSL	Bank of Sierra Leon
CB	Central Bank
CBM	Minimum Bank Capital
CBWA	Central [Federal] Bank of West Africa
CCT	Level of Corruption
CCT	Short-Term Loans
CE	Credits to Economy
CEMAC	Central Africa Economic and Monetary Community
CEN-SAD	Community of Sahel-Saharan States
CEPU	Credit to Public Enterprises
CET	Common External Tariff
CFA	African Financial Community
CFA	Communauté Financiere Africaine or African Financial Community
CFAF	Communauté Financiere Africaine Franc or French Colonies of Africa
CLT	Long-Term Loans
CMKTOCGDPR	Change in market capitalization to change in GDP ratio
CMT	Medium-Term Loans
CNR	Credit to Non-Resident
COBAC	Central African Banking Commission
COMESA	Common Market Easter and Southern Africa
COMESA	Common Market for Eastern and Southern Africa
CPI	Consumer Price Index
CRDT	credit
CSP	Credit to the Private Sector
DFTP	India's Duty Free Tariff Preference
DR	Discount Rates
EAC	East African Community
EAC	East African Community
EACB	East African Currency Board
EACSO	East African Common Services Organisation
EAHC	East African High Commission
EAMU	East African Monetary Union
EBA	European Union's Everything but Arms
ECA	Economic Commission for Africa
ECCAS	Economic Community of Central African States
ECO	ECOWAS Currency

ABBREVIATIONS xvii

ECOWAS	Economic Community of West African States
EFTA	European Union Free Trade Association
EMCCA	Economic and Monetary Community of Central Africa
EMCP	ECOWAS Monetary Cooperation Program
EMU	European Monetary Union
ER	Exchange Rate
ETLS	ECOWAS Trade Liberation Scheme
EU	European Union
FCFA	Franc of the French Colonies of Africa (Franc des colonies francaises d'Afrique)
FDI	Foreign Direct Investment
FEO	Foreign Exchange Operations
FMOL	Fully Modified Ordinary Least Square
FPE	Final Prediction Error
FSAP	Financial Sector Assessment Program
FSDP	Financial Sector Development Plan
FTA	Free Trade Area
GAFTA	Greater Arab Free Trade Area
GARCH	Generalized Auto Regression Conditional Heteroscedastic
GCF	Gross Capital Formation
GDP	Gross Domestic Product
GDPPC	Gross Domestic Product Per Capita
GMM	General method of moments
GNI	Gross National Income
GNP	Gross National Product
GSS	Ghana Statistical Service
HDI	Human Development Index
HQIC	Hannan and Quinn information criterion
IBRD	International Bank for Reconstruction and Development
ICA	The Infrastructure Consortium for Africa
ICEMGD	International Conference on Economic Management and Green Development
ICMA	international Capital Market Association
IDS	Institute for Development Studies
IFS	International Financial Statistics
IGAD	Intergovernmental Authority on Development
IIP	International Investment Position
IMF	International Monetary Fund
INF	inflation
INTR	interest rate
INTRATE	interest rate
IP	Political Instability

IPS	Im-Pesaran-Shin
LAC	Latin America and The Caribbean
LLC	Levin-Lin-Chin
MENA	Middle Eastern and North African countries
MK	Market Capitalization
MPC	Monetary Policy Committee
MPR	Monetary Policy Rate
MRU	The Mano River Union
MTM	monetary transmission mechanism
NASSIT	National Social Security and Insurance Trust
NBAA	National Business Aviation Association
NBER	National Bureau of Economic Research
NFA	Net Foreign Assets
NSE	Nairobi Stock Exchange
NYU	New York University
OAU	Organization of African Unity
OCA	Optimal Currency Area
ODA	Official Development Assistance
OECD	Organization for Economic Cooperation and Development
OHADA	Organisation for the Harmonisation of Business Law in Africa
OIC	Organization of Islamic Countries
OLS	Ordinary Least Square
OMO	Open Market Operation
PDC	Private Domestic Credit
PME	Small and medium enterprises
PPI	Private Participation in Infrastructure
PPML	Poisson Pseudo Maximum Likelihood
PPP	Purchasing Power Parity
REC	Regional Economic Communities
REER	Real Effective Exchange Rates
REPO	Repurchase agreement
RFI	Resource Financed Infrastructure
RGDP	Real Gross Domestic Product
RIGE	Revue Internationale de Gestion et d'Economie
RIR	Real Interest Rate
RLS	Recursive Least Squares
RSE	Rwanda Stock Exchange
SACU	Southern Africa Customs Union
SADC	Southern Africa Development Community
SBIC	Schwarz's Bayesian information criterion
SCF	Supply Chain Finance

SMCTOGDPR	Stock market capitalization to GDP ratio
SMTR	Stock market turnover
SPV	special purpose vehicle
SSA	Sub-Saharan Africa
SVAR	Structural Vector Autoregressive
SVEC	Structural Vector Error Correction
SVECM	Structural vector error correction model
TB	Trade Balance
TEG	Total Effective Rate
TVSTTOGDPR	Total value of stocks traded to GDP ratio
UCAD	University Cheikh Anta Diop
UEMOA	West African Economic and Monetary Union
ULC	unit labor cost
UMA	Arab Maghreb Union
UN	United Nations
UNCRD	United Nations Centre for Regional Development
UNCTAD	United Nations Conference on Trade and Development
UNDP	United Nations Development Programme
UNECA	United Nations Economic Commission for Africa
US	United States
USA	United States of America
USD	United States Dollar
VAR	Vector Autoregressive
VEC	Vector Error Correction
VECM	Vector error correction model
WACB	West African Currency Board
WACH	West African Clearing House
WAEMU	West African Economic and Monetary Union
WAMA	West Africa Monetary Agency
WAMZ	West African Monetary Zone
WAMZ_WNGA	WAMZ without Nigeria
WDI	World Bank World Development Index
WGI	World governance indicators
WP	Working Paper(?)
WTO	World Trade Organization
WWF	UN World Wide Fund

List of Figures

Fig. 1.1	Monetary and financial systems. (Source: Constructed by authors)	5
Fig. 2.1	Inflation and broad money growth (1991–2002)	47
Fig. 2.2	Reserve money and monetary aggregates (M2)	48
Fig. 2.3	Inflation rates (trend) under monetary and inflation targeting regimes	50
Fig. 2.4	Output growth under the monetary and inflation targeting regimes	53
Fig. 2.5	Output growth and unemployment under the monetary policy regimes	56
Fig. 2.6	HDI under the monetary policy regimes	57
Fig. 3.1	Inflation and GDP growth rates, 1980–2019. (Source: Bank of Tanzania annual reports, 2017/18 & 2018/19)	65
Fig. 3.2	Interactions between monetary variables and real output	70
Fig. 3.3	Monetary policy impulse response functions from SVEC model	76
Fig. 4.1	Relationship between monetary aggregates and real GDP growth. (Source: Created by author from World Development Indicators, 2021)	83
Fig. 8.1	Official exchange rate (LCU per US$, period average) except South Sudan. (Source: World Development Indicators, 2020)	175
Fig. 8.2	Interest rate spread (%) in EAC and WAEMU countries. Notes: The left panel shows interest rate spread in the EAC countries excluding Burundi and South Sudan, while the right panel shows interest rate spread in WAEMU member countries. (Source: World Development Indicators, 2020)	177

Fig. 10.1 Domestic credit to private sector as percentage of GDP. (Source: Based on data from IMF International Financial Statistics *, Regional averages exclude high-income countries) 220

Fig. 10.2 Bank liquid reserves to total assets ratio. (Source: Based on data from IMF International Financial Statistics *, Regional averages exclude high-income countries) 222

Fig. 10.3 Commercial bank branches per 100,000 Adults. (Source: Based on data from IMF Financial Access Survey. *Regional averages exclude high-income countries) 223

Fig. 11.1 The market capitalization of listed domestic companies (% of GDP). (Source: World Development Indicators, 2021) 247

Fig. 12.1 The conceptual framework of potential relationship patterns between financial Integration, economic Integration, capital accumulation, trade, and economic performance. (Source: Kizito Uyi Ehigiamusoe & Hooi Hooi Lean, 2018) 262

Fig. 12.2 (a) Trends in GDP growth rates across Africa's regional economies, 1990–2019. (b) Trends in average gross domestic product (2011 PPP$) 1990–2018. (Source: World Development Indicators and other sources) 273

Fig. 12.3 (a) Trends in gross domestic product per capita (2011 PPP$) 1990–2018. (b) Trends in GDP for Africa's regional economies, (2011 PPP) 1990–2019. (Source: World Bank, World Development Indicators, Various years) 275

Fig. 12.4 Trends in exports and imports as % of GDP, 1990–2018. (Source: World Development Indicators and other sources) 276

Fig. 12.5 Trends in Net FDI inflows among Africa's regional economies, 1990–2018 276

Fig. 12.6 Trends in HDI scores among Africa's Regional Economies, 1990–2018. (Source: World Development Indicators and other sources) 277

Fig. 13.1 Stock market capitalization of listed domestic companies-to-GDP ratio (1990–2019) 296

Fig. 13.2 Number of listed domestic companies (1990–2019) 300

Fig. 13.3 Stock market capitalization of listed domestic companies—2010 constant billion US$ (1990–2019) 303

Fig. 14.1 (a, b, c) Real effective exchange rate (1999=100). (Source: IFS online database) 333

Fig. 14.2 (a, b, c) Exports of goods and services as a percentage of GDP (1999=100). (Source: WDI database) 335

Fig. 14.3 (a, b, c) Exports-import ratio (1999=100). (Source: Computed from WDI database) 337

Fig. 14.4	(a, b, c) Index of technological development (1999=100). (Source: Computed from WDI database)	338
Fig. 15.1	Letters of credit. (Source: World Trade Organization (2016))	346
Fig. 15.2	Share of African trade (exports and imports) to China, European Union, and United States. (Source: Nyantakyi and Drammeh (2020))	349
Fig. 15.3	Digital adoption—Business sub-index (DIA) by region. (Source: Nyantakyi and Drammeh (2020))	350
Fig. 15.4	The relationship between the business digital adoption index and the average values of funded and unfunded trade finance assets in Africa (2014 and 2016). (Source: Nyantakyi and Drammeh (2020))	350
Fig. 15.5	Constraints to trade finance supply in Africa. (Source: Nyantakyi and Drammeh (2020))	351
Fig. 15.6	Sources of infrastructure financing in Africa in 2018, commitments in US$ million. (Source: OECD/ACET (2020))	363
Fig. 15.7	Investment by sector in Sub-Saharan Africa (US$ million): 1990–2019. (Source: https://ppi.worldbank.org/en/snapshots/region/sub-saharan-africa)	364
Fig. 16.1	The trend of exchange rate volatility and intra-regional trade on ECOWAS sub-region from 2000 to 2017	378
Fig. 16.2	The relationship between exchange rate volatility and intra-trade in SACU. (Source: Authors)	384
Fig. 17.1	African regional economic communities. (Source: de Melo & Brown, 2018)	399
Fig. 18.1	One monetary and financial system. (Source: Authors' construction)	432

List of Tables

Table 2.1	Descriptive statistics on the inflation rate	50
Table 2.2	Descriptive statistics on GDP growth	53
Table 2.3	Descriptive statistics on the unemployment rate	55
Table 2.4	Descriptive statistics on HDI	56
Table 2.5	Income distribution and poverty	58
Table 2.6	Poverty at national and regional levels	59
Table 3.1	Long-run parameters identification by Johansen normalized restriction	75
Table 3.2	Forecast error variance decomposition of the policy variable and price level	77
Table 4.1	Monetary aggregates in Sierra Leone	83
Table 4.2	ADF unit test results	90
Table 4.3	Relationship between RGDP and monetary aggregates, 1981–2019	91
Table 5.1	ECOWAS macroeconomic indicators	99
Table 5.2	The situation of the ECOWAS convergence criteria	104
Table 5.3	Total number of convergence criteria (primary and secondary) fulfilled per country in ECOWAS	105
Table 5.4	Net gains or losses in terms of prosperity resulting from the addition of countries one by one to the West African Economic and Monetary Union (percentage of GDP)	117
Table 7.1	Definitions of variables at stake and data sources	155
Table 7.2	Descriptive statistics	156
Table 7.3	Matrix of correlation coefficients	157
Table 7.4	Stationarity tests	160
Table 7.5	Effect of CBM on the actual cost of credit	160

Table 7.6	Effect of CBM on the term structure of loans	161
Table 7.7	Effect of CBM on economic agents in need of finance	161
Table 8.1	Average inflation (%) in East African community excluding South Sudan	178
Table 8.2	External debt accumulation in EAC countries excluding South Sudan (% of GDP)	179
Table 8.3	Banks with cross-border operations in the EAC	181
Table 8.4	Interregional trade in East Africa excluding South Sudan and Tanzania (% of total exports)	182
Table 9.1	The CFA franc (CFAF): Creation and changes	190
Table 9.2	CEMAC: Selected economic and financial indicators, 2012–2020	194
Table 9.3	UEMO: Selected economic and financial indicators, 2012–2020	194
Table 9.4	CEMAC and UEMOA: Production and trade structure: Primary and commodity exports 2020	197
Table 9.5	Banking sector and MFIs in Gabon 2000–2020	203
Table 10.1	Variables, definitions, and data sources	228
Table 10.2	Regression results for domestic credit to the private sector	230
Table 10.3	Regression results for claims on central government	230
Table 10.4	Regression results for commercial bank branches per 100,000 adults	231
Table 10.5	Regression results for bank liquid reserves to bank assets ratio	233
Table 11.1	Real GDP (constant 2015 US$) and GDP growth (annual %), 2006–2020	241
Table 11.2	The market capitalization of listed domestic companies (% of GDP)	248
Table 11.3	Listed domestic companies, total	249
Table 11.4	Stocks traded, turnover ratio of domestic shares (%)	251
Table 11.5	Stocks traded, total value (% of GDP)	251
Table 11.6	Ng-Peron unit roots test	252
Table 11.7	Cointegration test results: Dependent variable: $\Delta lnRGDP$	252
Table 11.8	Estimated long-term spillover coefficient (Dependent variable: $lnRGDP$)	254
Table 11.9	Estimated short-term spillover coefficients (Dependent variable: $\Delta lnRGDP$)	254
Table 11.10	Markov switching regression model	255
Table 12.1	A summary of the RECs	266
Table 13.1	African countries' economic performance (1990–2019)	290
Table 13.2	Classification of selected countries by income groups	294

Table 13.3	Trend line regression of the stock market capitalization of listed companies to GDP ratio (1990–2019)	298
Table 13.4	Stock market capitalization of listed companies in Mutefu	304
Table 13.5	Trendline Regressions of Market Capitalization and GDP (1990–2019)	305
Table 13.6	Effort in stock market capitalization (1990–2019)	306
Table 13.7	Correlation coefficients between economic growth and stock markets' development (1990–2019)	309
Table 15.1	Classification of the degree of the capital intensity of infrastructure and public works	352
Table 15.2	Taxonomy of instruments and vehicles for infrastructure financing	354
Table 15.3	Comparing definitions of blended finance (BF)	362
Table 15.4	Investment by sector in Sub-Saharan Africa (US$ million): 1990–2019	364
Table 16.1	Descriptive statistics for ECOWAS	379
Table 16.2	Currency union effect on trade	380
Table 16.3	Trade creation-trade diversion	382
Table 16.4	Trade potential in the ECOWAS sub-region	383
Table 16.5	Descriptive statistics of data for SACU	383
Table 16.6	Proposed common currency on trade	386
Table 16.7	Trade potential in SACU	388
Table 17.1	Membership in regional communities	400
Table 17.2	African Union trade by economic regions-imports (millions USD)	407
Table 17.3	Overall Regional Integration Scores Ranks	411
Table 17.4	Monetary Integration in African: Overview	413
Table 17.5	Intra-regional economic trade in total African trade (2016)	414

PART I

Introduction

CHAPTER 1

Introduction and Background: A Historical Perspective of the Role of Financial Institutions in Africa's Development

Aloysius Ajab Amin, Regina Nsang Tawah, and Augustin Ntembe

INTRODUCTION

Many African countries inherited monetary regimes and financial institutions from their previous European colonial powers or based on monetary institutions created by the colonial authorities. After independence, most African countries introduced central banks and currencies, a vital sign of sovereignty and development. Since then, there has been a series of institutional changes and developments in the monetary and financial systems, and they did so to ensure the achievement of their development goals. The changes in the monetary and financial systems have varied across the

A. A. Amin
Clayton State University, Morrow, GA, USA
e-mail: AloysiusAmin@clayton.edu

R. N. Tawah • A. Ntembe (✉)
Bowie State University, Bowie, MD, USA
e-mail: RTawah@bowiestate.edu; nntembe@bowiestate.edu

© The Author(s), under exclusive license to Springer Nature Switzerland AG 2022
A. A. Amin et al. (eds.), *Monetary and Financial Systems in Africa*, https://doi.org/10.1007/978-3-030-96225-8_1

continent. However, some countries have maintained a stable level of prices and stability in their financial markets. In contrast, others have had price volatility caused by external and internal shocks and by the types of monetary regimes and policy structures. Nevertheless, there has been no autonomy in monetary policy issues since some countries still maintain strong economic, political, monetary, and financial connections with previous colonial powers as is the case with the CFA franc countries (Masson et al., 2015).

During the colonial period, the monetary and financial systems operated under fixed exchange rate regimes, with more regulation and control of banks. Most countries have passed through fixed exchange rate regimes with stricter regulations and control of the financial sector, especially the commercial banks, to flexible exchange rate regimes with less control and regulations. Others have suffered from high level of inflation and shifted to less regulated and reformed financial sectors. Because of the flexible exchange regimes, governments tend to finance fiscal deficits through the domestic financial sector. There are still monetary exchange rate unions operating in the continent, including the franc zones of Central and West Africa and the Common Monetary Area of Southern Africa. However, they seem to operate differently with different outcomes.

The main objective of the African Union has been to promote regional integration as a tool for economic development, with improvement in welfare and governance. Thus, the question becomes whether the existing monetary unions should be expanded to promote regional integration and growth and, if so, how? Extending them would depend further on how the long-existing unions have influenced intra-regional trade, fiscal discipline, and terms of trade. Some of the monetary regimes have performed well in terms of having low and stable inflation but poorly in terms of diversifying, changing the production structure, and transforming the economies to broad-based industrialization and development. It is noteworthy that monetary and financial systems across Africa are indispensable in changing the structure of the economy's structure and enhancing economic growth.

The financial system has a set of financial institutions that are capable of transforming the economy. As a set of complex institutional entities and markets, they mobilize financial resources for investment and facilitate the financing of profitable activities. Financial institutions diversify loan risks by pooling a range of risk profiles and making loans with various terms. The intermediaries transform short-term liabilities into assets of several maturities. Hence, using financial resources from savers to borrowers, financial intermediaries make capital accessible to investors and promote economic growth and development.

COMPONENTS OF MONETARY AND FINANCIAL SYSTEM

Depending on the organization of the economy, the financial system can function through markets, central planning, or a mixture of markets and central planning. African countries have a mixture but most are market oriented. The financial system has multiple components which are unique with respect to the different economies. We can identify the following main component of a financial system – (i) Financial institutions, (ii) financial markets, (iii) financial services, (iv) financial instruments or financial assets, (v) money, (vi) regulatory agencies, and (vii) central banks (Fig. 1.1).

(i) Financial institutions like banks offer a wide range of products and services and mediate between investors and borrowers. They muster savings, raise financial resources or assets such as deposits, loans, and securities. Their primary role is mediating between suppliers of financial resources and those demanding financial resources. This role entails diversifying and managing risks. They are also non-bank financial institutions, including insurance companies, microfinance and credit associations, and finance and loan

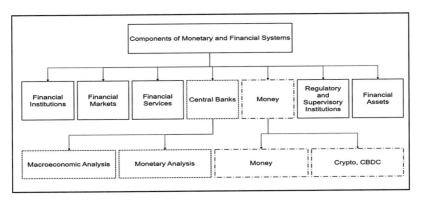

Fig. 1.1 Monetary and financial systems. (Source: Constructed by authors)

companies. Microfinance institutions in Africa provide savings, and these savings are transformed into investments. They absorb financial shocks and protect economies from financial shocks. However, weak regulation of this sector can worsen the financial system's instability.

(ii) Financial markets comprise lenders, borrowers, and investors negotiating with other transactions. The traded goods are some form of money, cash, credit, the value of real assets (equity), future income potential claims, and some derivative instruments according to the demand and supply. In general, financial markets function within a government regulatory framework that sets guidelines for transactions. Financial markets are settings or forums where two parties- sellers and buyers-cooperate or interact to buy, sell, and trade in financial assets. The asset price is the outcome of the interaction between supply and demand. The primary markets are usually referred to as new issues like stocks, bonds, and other financial assets. Moreover, the secondary market is the transactions in financial assets already issued. Generally, financial markets have four units- capital market, money market, credit market, and foreign exchange market. Financial markets create and transfer financial assets. In financial markets, as opposed to real transactions, no money is directly involved during the exchange process. But the transaction process used financial assets like services and products, loans, and deposits. They make money payments in the future, with interest and dividends paid periodically.

(iii) Financial services. Many businesses comprise the finance sector, including asset and liability management companies such as banks, credit unions, credit card companies, stock brokerages, investment, and insurance companies. They also support the acquisition and efficient use of investment funds or financial resources.

(iv) Financial instruments or financial assets are products traded in financial markets. These products include bonds, money, stocks, mortgages, equity shares, debentures, and insurance. In addition, credit seekers and investors demand a range of securities, deposits, and loans.

(v) Money is the basis of the financial system. Generally, money as a medium of exchange and payment should be acceptable to both the buyers and the sellers. The concept of money evolves in terms of its stability and reliability. The changes depend on technology

1 INTRODUCTION AND BACKGROUND: A HISTORICAL PERSPECTIVE... 7

and the financial system. However, money has four key functions: medium of exchange, unit of account, store of value, and standard of deferred payment. This last function underscores the importance of the stability and reliability of money. Financial and Digital technology generates and innovates various forms of money and transforms currencies- cryptocurrencies. The nature of cryptocurrencies with Central Bank Digital Currency poses challenges yet has potential benefits (Appendix 1). Hence, we need a robust, coordinated regulatory framework.

(vi) Regulatory and supervisory. The regulation of financial systems is necessary because of the importance of financial systems' direct impact on consumer protection, real assets, and economic performance.

Regulatory agencies are a crucial part of the financial system. They supervise and regulate the financial institutions' activities. The governments create regulatory agencies that evaluate the system and enforce guidelines to ensure the best practices in the system. They regulate and control the movement of financial resources in the system. The agencies supervise each institution of the system and safeguard the public's money and investment. Hence, the regulatory and supervisory agencies play a vital role in functioning of the financial system and sector. Thus, the system tends to have a high level of regulations and supervision because there is substantial information asymmetry between sellers and buyers of financial services and assets. Therefore, there are possibilities of huge losses for both individuals and businesses who may not absorb the losses. So, the system also merits a high level of consumer protection. Besides, banks are closely connected to other financial institutions, especially with paying financial contracts and asset markets that depend on trust, settlement systems, and credibility. As a result, the financial system is susceptible to instability that can significantly impact the real sector or real activity. Moreover, because of the importance of finance in the market economy, the state has to be involved in the financial sector to accomplish broad societal goals such as fighting criminality- imposing rules against ransom, money laundry, and other harmful activities.

Suitable sound supervisory and regulatory policies promote financial stability, such policies comprise capital adequacy requirements, provisions for financial institutions disclosure, and requirements for effective risk management schemes. These policies provide a framework and a conducive environment for financial institutions to function and promote a stable financial system for improved economic performance. The system also comprises sets of rules, regulations, and practices for its proper functioning. The institutionslenders, and borrowers perform consumption and economic activities in a conducive environment. The institutions in the financial system decide which projects to finance, who finance the projects, and on what terms. Each system has a unique regulatory framework provided by the government or government agencies.

An important aspect is that the regulatory and supervisory bodies protect and ensure financial stability and efficiency. Finance ministries and competent agencies promote financial efficiency, although the government can also assign financial and regulatory powers to the Central Bank. However, there may be the issue of conflict of interest. Whatever the case, the government, should never compromise the central bank's independence and the goal of maintaining price stability.

(vii) Central bank is not market-based; it is established and protected by legislation with a legal monopoly status of producing banknotes, cash, and other means of payments and transactions. A central bank is fundamental to the financial system and government functions. The central bank formulates the economy's monetary policy. It regulates member banks, primarily commercial banks, responsible for the flow of money and credit through offering credit and deposits facilities. The central bank's monetary policy influences the supply of money to the economy. Central banks ensure that the money supply does not grow too fast to cause inflation and not grow too slow to impede economic growth. It aims to keep at stable prices and keep unemployment low.

Central banks can take a two-pronged approach to manage financial, monetary, and macroeconomic aggregates. Traditionally, the central bank's rationale has been monetary policy, regulation of the financial system with its primary functions as a government's banker, the issuer of currency, banker's bank, lender of last resort, and controller of credit. However, the central bank also develops the financial system and promotes economic development. These roles are in addition to their prudential, regulatory, and monetary roles. Thus we can have two broad objectives of the central bank: monetary stabilization and developmental objectives. These two objectives are in the statutes of the central banks. Nevertheless, the two African CFA franc zone central banks do not state the developmental objectives.

The two-level strategy mentioned earlier is at two levels of analysis of macroeconomic developments: The first level is the comprehensive (economic) analysis of the country's economy and global financial markets. The second level is the monetary analysis. From an in-depth analysis of factors related to inflation and the money supply developments, the central bank implements monetary policy decisions. Hence knowing how the economy operates is crucial because, from the available economic developments, central banks generally appraise the effects of future threats to price stability.

The central bank utilizes monetary policy procedures and instruments to attain its price stability objective. In the medium term, the central bank targets the interest rate level of the money market needed to sustain price stability. The first strategy analyzes the economic and financial variables that involve short and medium-term implications for price stability. Note that Central banks regularly study activities in the real economy and the changes in wages, the fiscal sector, prices and costs, exchange rates, the consumer with business confidence, and critical financial market indicators both national and global. The second strategy concerns the study of monetary aggregates and factors relating to the money supply to maintain price stability in the long term. An in-depth study of monetary and lending developments enables understanding and addressing inflation risk consequences on economic growth.

These two-pronged approaches provide a detailed study of the economic, financial and monetary, developments in the economy. The in-depth analysis empowers the central bank to set significant rates to promote the country's price stability. Hence, the two-pronged approach is the core of monetary policy strategic pillars of the central bank. Many African central banks have adopted this stance.

Market-Based and Bank-Based Financial Systems

The effectiveness of the regulatory, legal, and policy framework is vital for the proper functioning of the financial system to channel financial resources into productive uses (Demirgüç-Kunt & Levine, 2001). The literature brings out two types of financial systems, the market-based and the bank-based financial system. In the bank-based system, the banks play a dominant role in savings mobilization, capital allocation, controlling firms with the managers' investment decisions, and offering risk management tools. At the same time, the market-based system is predominantly securities markets. Banks obtain savings from the firms and exercise corporate control and ease management risk. In a bank-based financial system, the functioning of the economy depends on the performance of the banking institutions. The savers direct their savings to productive use through, intermediaries such as banks, mutual and pensions funds, savings, and microfinance institutions(MFIs). The bank provides loans to borrowers to generate financial and economic power. The stock markets have limited financial ability and have less influence on economic trends.

The lenders and borrowers interact directly, a situation very common in developing countries. Given the importance of bank credit in economic development, many developing countries have directed scarce resources (credit) into socially productive sectors. Interventions sometimes at concessional rates have included credit guarantees, preferential loans, refinancing schemes, bank quota, and development finance lending. Programs like these have been fundamental in developing financial deepening and economic development in South Korea. Also, on a theoretical basis, Chakraborty and Ray (2006) demonstrated that a bank-based financial system does much better in creating a higher investment and income per capita, and reducing income inequality. The system has a more enabling environment for broad-based industrialization.

In the market-based system, financial markets offer money to governments and companies in bond and stock markets and money markets for short-term securities and foreign exchange and derivatives. Households as savers are the sources of funding in the market-based financial system. Savers direct their financial resources through insurance, pension, and mutual funds. With the market-based financial system, the stock market generates much financial power such that the economy depends on the stock market's performance. As a result, the economic trends depend on the stock market's performance, and the wealth generated is unequally distributed. Wealth tends to shift from individuals to individuals, with some gaining and others losing. In advanced economies, the economic system is based on stock markets. Although consumers search for non-banking sources to finance their projects in this financial system, and the private sector competes with the government for bank sponsorship, the banks tend to alter their interest rates and other activities to compete in the market.

The legal regimes differ in these two systems. The market-based financial systems seem to be more prevalent in countries with common law tradition, low corruption levels, high accounting standards, and robust shareholder rights protection such as in the United States and England. The government usually sets and implements laws in the civil law system in the bank-based financial system such as in Germany and Japan. Between these two systems, which is better, would depend on the economy and the legal system under which the financial system operates. The proper and well-performing legal and financial institutions are critical in promoting economic growth since both systems are conducive for growth. In general, the economy's performance depends on the efficiency of the financial and legal systems or institutions. The bank- based system performs better than the market-based in terms of per capita income, income distribution, investment, and promotion of industrial development. High-income countries tend to have market-based systems with more active and efficient stock markets than banks.

Having the two systems together strengthens and diversifies the financial systems to provide a greater and deeper pool of financial resources, and at the same time, give the users better access to various financial resources. The banking system can always provide options for funding and capital market liquidity being alternative funding sources (Chakraborty & Ray, 2006; Levine, 2002). This ability is essential as is observed in the Central and West African franc monetary system which is more dominated than the much less developed market- based system (Allen et al., 2011; Kangami, 2019). Kenya has one of Africa's most developed stock markets. Nevertheless, the banking sector in Kenya dominates the financial system.

Furthermore, commercial banks carry out many activities with the capital markets to diversify their portfolios. Diversification benefits the banking sector and the economy (Osoro & Osano, 2014). The high-income countries continue to deepen their financial institutions and markets, with more deepening occurring in the market based than in the banking sector (Beck et al., 2009). As countries grow, wealthy financial intermediaries like banks and stock markets develop and become more efficient and active. However, in the present state of financial development in Africa, relatively less developed financial systems tend to be associated with countries having the French civil law tradition, limited capital markets and banking systems, and weak accounting standards (Demirgüç-Kunt & Levine, 1999; Beck & Levine, 2002; Kangami, 2019).

Diversified Financial System

The continent has a diversified financial system (Allen et al., 2011) except in the CEMAC and UEMOA – the CFA franc zones where the stock markets are still developing, with just a handful of registered firms. Firms find it less advantageous to register in the CFA franc zone's embryonic stock markets. Instead, firms turn to the mainly foreign banking sector for credits. Bank credit is a vital instrument igniting economic growth and directing credit to enhance economic transformation, and economic diversification. Japan, Taiwan, and South Korea implemented programs that supported SMEs to strengthen export growth. In the case of India, credit policy was extended to the rural regions of the country through the expansion of bank branches to the disadvantageous areas of the country (Burgess & Pande, 2003). As is the case in India, governments in Africa can direct credit to critical economic sectors that generate broad-based growth with employment. The absence of financial resources or credit has been an important reason for the persistence of poverty across many African countries. Empirical evidence from countries shows how concerted effort to make credit accessible to the poor has reduced poverty and promoted economic growth (Burgess and Pande 2003, 2004).

Channels of Transmission

The economy's monetary policy transmission mechanism channels include interest rate, exchange rate, credit, expectation, and asset price channels. The monetary policy transmission mechanism (links)works through the financial markets such that there are links between monetary variables (interest rates, exchange rates, and quantity of money) and economic aggregates (employment level, price level, and GDP). The links are also between the quantity of money (M) and price level (P); and the link between investment (I) and interest rates (r). For instance, an increase in money supply reduces the interest rate (the price of capital). As a result, the transmission encourages investment spending in various projects that increase the output and employment. Sheefeni (2020) studies monetary policy's transmission mechanism in the Namibian economy. Using a structural vector error correction model, he analyzed the transmission monetary policy in Namibia with aggregate money supply, output, price level, and repurchase (repo) rate. The results showed that money supply incorporates information of the monetary policy transmission mechanism process with other factors in the output responses other than the prices and repo rate. Nevertheless, output rose with unanticipated money supply shocks. Hence, Sheefeni found the money channel to be important in increasing output.

Within the banking system, we can identify two types of channels – (i) the balance sheet channel, which affects the balance sheet of the households and firms, and (ii) the bank lending channel, which directly affects economic activities. These two channels are different due to the asymmetric information problem and transaction costs in credit markets, especially lending to the poor. Mwabutwa et al. (2016) examine the responses in output and price level from the exchange rate, bank rate, and credit shocks in Malawi. The output growth with structural changes in the economy is consistent with economic theory predictions. The credit market was vital in contributing to economic growth. The Central Bank can influence lending by using monetary instruments. The size of the bank is essential in financing its lending activities because the monetary policy is more effective if it finances its total expenditure. However, some borrowers find credit inaccessible because of asymmetric information problems in the credit markets, and the banks are the only sources of borrowing. Firms can borrow from financial institutions or the public by issuing bonds, but these types of options are inaccessible to many borrowers. Small firms that make up most of the private sector in African countries have limited access to financial institutions and even more limited access to the bonds and capital markets.

The broad credit or balance sheet channel operates within the asymmetric information problem like the bank lending channel. Still, the channel also depends on the business firm's net worth and the adverse selection and moral hazard problems. The larger the firm's net worth, the less severe is moral hazard and adverse selection problems when the bank lends to the firm. Firms with small net worth also have less or no collateral and higher possible losses due to adverse selection. Low net worth increases the adverse selection problem and reduces lending and business financing.

Also, low business net worth (small business equity) raises the moral hazard problem, with small equity business owners having fewer stakes in the business and taking riskier projects.

The riskier the project, the less likely it would be to pay back the loan, so a decrease in net worth reduces lending and investment activities and consequently reduces growth. Monetary policy can affect exchange rates and, in turn, affects aggregate output through imports and exports. For instance, an increase in money supply results in a decline in interest rates. With the decrease in interest rates, assets denominated in foreign currencies become more attractive than domestic currency deposits. As a result, exports become cheaper than imports, increasing net exports and consequently GDP, which operates through the exchange rate channel.

When the inflation rate increases, financial markets expect interest rates to increase and stabilize inflation allowing the central bank to use interest rates to moderate the changes in the price level. In addition, the central bank may use the monetary policy tool to give economic agents confidence and certainty in expectations on the economy's outlook to maintain its credibility. For instance, when economic agents expect monetary policy to be expansionary with a fall in interest rates and an increase in money supply, they would expect an increase in the price level. Nevertheless, the market expectation of inflation would mean increases in interest rates. Therefore, expectations have implications on the extent of the interest rate response. In this situation, monetary policy can create an expectation of inflation that results in the interest rate influencing the output. This point underscores the importance of the role of monetary policy in the financial sector. The monetary authorities use the interest rate and quantity of money to attain full employment and economic growth at stable prices.

The key role of the financial sector is to allocate financial resources into productive uses and investments. The performance of the financial sector affects the performance of the economy. For instance, with stock market booms, people tend to spend more; and when the stock markets perform poorly, as in a recession, people cut down their spending. In a boom, the economy creates economic activities and increases employment. People are willing to save part of their income, and firms are eager to acquire investment loans. Hence, the linkages go both ways (Mordi, 2010); Abeygunawardana et al. (2017) examine how the monetary policy shocks affect prices, interest rates, and output in the Sri Lanka economy. They found that the relationships conformed with the theoretical and empirical literature. However, the economy has a large informal sector and shallow financial markets, with relatively inflexible interest rates responses to deposits and loans. The large informal sector and shallow financial markets weaken the transmission mechanism resulting in market failures that can be resolved through government intervention.

What are the policy objectives of financial stability, financial efficiency, and price stability? Price stability is when the general price level is accurately stable, and the inflation rate is acceptably stable and low. In such a state, the nominal aspects of transactions are no concern for economic decisions. However, there is no clear consensus on the composition and choice of the items in measuring the price index; since there are issues relating to the correct quantity, the operative price stability target, the suitable time horizon for maintaining price stability. African central banks tend to aim at having yearly increases relatively low. For example, the CFA franc zone central banks aim at maintaining the annual rate at 3% compared to the rate maintained in the European Central Bank, since the CFA franc is tied to the euro and related to other arrangements made with France.

Financial stability is a state where the financial system can contain shocks and resolve financial imbalances for the conceivable future. Therefore, it is crucial to maintain and protect the financial system's resilience to risks and susceptibilities. Moreover, it diminishes the probability of shocks to the system, hampering the intermediary allocating savings to profitable investments.

Maintaining financial stability entails finding the sources of risk and susceptibility, evaluating the financial system relating to its role of efficiently allocating financial resources between investors and savers, and appraising risk pricing and management. The economic crisis resulting from financial problems can come from inadequacies in capital allocation, risk pricing, and management deficiencies. These inefficiencies can provide room for exposure, weaken future financial system stability, and hamper economic stability. Therefore, of great importance is monitoring financial stability systemically and comprehensively because many central banks treat financial stability mandates partly by issuing periodically public reports.

Financial efficiency is when the available resources (in the financial system) are apportioned at the lowest cost to the highest valued investments. In general, efficient financial systems are where information is readily available and distributed, and markets are not only competitive, but also resolve conflicts through market contracts. So, financial efficiency reduces the gap between the lending and borrowing rates and the spread of risks-borrowing costs. In addition, reduction of transaction costs, improving competition, increasing innovation, financial market integration, and transparency all promote and strengthen financial efficiency. Financial efficiency and financial stability are closely linked and interconnected.

Why is the Central Bank (CB) interested in an efficient and stable financial system? (1) The CB's mandate requires the CB to maintain price stability, contribute and support financial efficiency and stability by encouraging a well-functioning payment system, supporting efficient prudential supervision of credit institutions, and ensuring a stable financial system. In keeping with the norms of a competitive open market economy of efficiently allocation resources. (2) Price stability, financial stability, and financial efficiency complement each other. They have such close complementarities, the CB allocates substantial resources to study the developments in financial markets and situations for financial efficiency and stability. Especially The economic and monetary analyses, which provide inputs for decisions related to financial stability and monetary policy.

Most CBs have the power and tools to safeguard price stability. However, there is no clarity in the tools and powers of the CB to ensure financial efficiency and stability. Maintaining price stability is a necessary and precondition for financial stability and financial efficiency. CB monetary policy's objective of maintaining price stability contributes to the efficient operation of the real economy and economic growth. Price stability protects the households' disposable income and purchasing power through monetary policy intervention. Consumers can easily discern relative prices with stable prices since rapid changes in prices blur relative prices and the value of goods and services. Furthermore, economic agents tend to attach inflation expectations to price stability, such that adverse supply shocks like the rise in oil prices are expected to be short-lived and reduce the impact of inflation. At the same time, the CB has more room to respond to those types of shocks.

Price stability removes uncertainties and distortions resulting from inflation and contributes to financial efficiency and financial stability: – Price stability (PS) decreases risk premia in interest rates. PS enhances transparency in price movements in financial markets, diminishes the probability of misperceptions on future assets returns, and reduces misalignment risks between economic fundamentals and assets prices, increasing stable and efficient financial markets. Through sustaining price stability, the monetary policy protects the borrowers and banks from likely problems in their balance sheets. Moreover, credible monetary policy attains price stability and prevents problems relating to moral hazards. Therefore, the credibility of the monetary policy is important for price stability and necessary for financial efficiency and stability.

Financial efficiency can also be a result of increased development in capital markets. As capital markets become highly efficient, they enhance how the CB conducts the monetary policy by improving the quality of information and making information easily accessible in the financial markets. High-quality and accessible information is essential for monetary policy because readily available financial indicators provide improved estimates of private-sector expectations and better uncertainties assessment on future changes, especially interest rates, inflation, growth, and profits. Financial efficiency and financial stability are essential for monetary policy conduct since these effects are considered in evaluating the stance of monetary policy.

The Soundness of Financial System

Financial institutions with inadequate supervision and regulation and the absence of transparency can always result in a financial crisis like the 1990s and 2008 world financial crises. The 2008 global financial crisis underscores the significance of effectively and systemically managing and monitoring risk. The financial institutions and markets provide a good framework for performing economic transactions and carrying out monetary policy. The financial institutions and markets channel savings into investment projects and promote economic growth and development. Hence, problems in the financial system can interrupt financial intermediation and weaken monetary policy effectiveness, aggravate economic recession, initiate capital flight with pressures on exchange rates. In addition, problems in the financial system can generate fiscal issues, which may also relate to bailing out distressed financial institutions. With the rapid growth of connectivity amongst financial institutions within and across nations, advancement in financial technologies, and rise of FinTech companies, closer trade and financial links among countries, financial shocks in one institution can spread or spill over to other institutions and across the country borders. Hence, well-regulated and well-supervised resilient financial systems are critical for financial and economic stability.

The Economy

In the tri-sector macroeconomic model, the African economy has three main sectors: Primary, secondary, and tertiary. The primary sector (raw material) involves producing raw materials, including agriculture, fishing, mining, oil drilling, and forestry products (lumber). In agriculture alone, for 2010–2018, output increased by 11% through production area expansion with farm labor increase excluding factor productivity increases. Demand for agriculture output increases due to a rise in population and an increase in income of consumers. Cash crops growth is an essential factor in agricultural output growth. Cash crops, including cotton, cocoa, tea, sugar, and Sesame, saw an average increase in world prices, but coffee saw a reduction in world prices (AGRA, 2020).

African farmers account for more than 60% of the population. However, agricultural productivity and yield are low due to small-scale production and the scarcity of seeds and inputs (equipment, seeds, fertilizers). Large-scale production and integrated value chain such as poultry in South Africa and horticulture in Kenya, productivity with export capacity could be sharply increased. However, in most African countries, the productivity level of agriculture is relatively low. Preferential trade arrangements result in African countries producing and exporting primary products with no value added (AGRA, 2020). Leaving the African countries less productive and less developed.

The reason is that African countries entered into various trade schemes such as (i) the European Union's Everything but Arms (EBA), (ii) India's Duty Free Tariff Preference (DFTP), and (iii) US African Growth and Opportunity Act (AGOA). These schemes generally provide low tariffs for the African cash crops and promote exports of raw materials at low productivity without promoting the production of manufactured goods or highly valued chain goods (AGRA, 2020). Yet, the African governments fail to negotiate better terms for the development of their continent. In addition, African governments do not seem to seek ways of diversifying their economies to broad-based industrialization.

The secondary sector transforms raw materials into goods. It produces and sells goods (furniture, clothing, equipment, and automobile). This sector manufactures goods within a subset of the industry, with the industry having a set of activities and manufacturing being a part of those activities. Sometimes manufacturing and industry are used interchangeably.

Manufacturing is a process in which inputs are converted into outputs for final use or other productive use.

The tertiary sector, commonly called the service sector, produces services, not end products. The service sector has intangible goods. It includes education/teaching, financial services (include many activities such as investing, banking, insurance), internet information technology, healthcare, and other activities that render services. Some economists think that a fourth sector – the quaternary sector-should include information technology, research and development, and activities at the high organizational decision-making level. Financial services as a component of the service sector play a vital role in the economy.

Importance of African Resources

With about 1.3 billion inhabitants, Africa has a young population, with more than 60 percent in the age group of 0–25, and by 2050, Africa will be 2 billion people. The world is aging, and Africa, with a growing young population, has the world's highest urbanization rate. Africa's labor force is expected to be larger than China and India by 2034. Africa has abundant resources both in human and natural resources. That would be about 20 percent of the world population, an impetus for development through economic transformation and diversification. Launching the AfCFTA would transform Africa into a vast trading block with enormous financial flows because Africa has enormous endowments in natural resources- minerals, vast forests, fisheries, and rivers.

For instance, Africa is the major cocoa producer, exporting over 70% of cocoa beans with less than 16 percent of ground cocoa, more than 300% per ton more valuable than the raw cocoa beans. Aquaculture and fisheries added value is estimated to be over US$ 24 billion alone. If the Agricultural sector were to be transformed to agro-allied industrialization, it would be worth over US$100 billion by 2025. This type of agricultural transformation can be a growth engine that generates non-agricultural employment, increases income, and reduces poverty (AfDB, 2018; Leke & Signé, 2020). A rapid technological change and economic transformation would create many opportunities for businesses and consumers.

Goal of Development

According to Seers (1969), the main goal of development is the progressive reduction and eventual elimination of poverty, unemployment, and inequality. Hence, a key objective of development economics is to develop strategies that remove people from poverty and generate economic growth. To achieve these objectives, economists have also viewed access to credit as an important means of production transformation, creation of employment, and poverty reduction (Bencivenga & Smith, 1991; Banerjee, 2001; Banerjee et al., 2002; Banerjee & Newman, 1993).

Much literature (Ustarz & Fanta, 2021; Omar & Inaba, 2020; Levine et al., 2000; Schumpeter, 1934) on the link between finance and development shows a positive relationship with finance influencing economic growth. This link also could be a bi-relationship with each influencing the other. Because credit market imperfection hinders economic development, public policy can address market failure that includes asymmetric information, transaction, distributional costs, moral hazard, as demonstrated in the Indian study.

Lessons from Indian Case Study

India and Africa have over a combined population of 2.6 billion people. The African Continental Free Trade Area (AfCFTA) makes Africa the largest free trade area in the world. Before the 2020 COVID-19 pandemic, the World Bank saw Africa as a region with the highest growth rate averaging about 6 percent. However, the high growth rate does not mean inclusive growth. A larger proportion of Africa's population is still living in poverty. The World Bank 2019 poverty rate estimates were about 36% (490 million people). India was also a fast-growing economy with a large skilled, diverse force. Yet, one of the poorest countries in the world, with 22 percent (270 million) of its population living below the poverty line according to the World Bank estimates. India has made significant progress in reducing poverty through multiple strategies, especially with the social banking expansion policy. Hence, Burgess and Pande's (2003, 2004) comprehensive study on India is important because of the background and scope. The study had a large population with almost a third of the world's poor mainly found in the rural region of India, with panel data set covering more than sixteen Indian states for the period 1961–2000. The social banking project expanded branches of banks to most remote areas of India. With the social objective of serving the poor population, the project transformed the lives of millions of Indians. To a more considerable extent, the results of this study could be enlightening, informative, and transferable to other countries. The India study established a causal linkage between financial credit and reduction in poverty which is a significant contribution to development economics. The government's objective of expanding and diversifying banking services was to promote industries and exports, enhance agricultural growth, and promote entrepreneurship with employment creation (Deaton & Dreze, 2002).

Pande et al. (2018) argued that because of defaults in payments, even in microfinance, loan payments should have regular payments to avoid default but with a strong association or correlation between credit and poverty reduction. Furthermore, they found benefits in flexibility in repayment periods because they reduced borrowers' stress by lowering the transaction costs with enabling environment for investment in economic activities.

Poverty Reduction and Development

Agriculture is linked with poverty, but bank branches expansion results in increased wages in agriculture and increased non-agricultural activities with economic diversification and economic growth. Without financial access and credit, many poor people would remain poor, especially in rural areas (Aryeetey, 2008). With the expansion of rural banks comes an increase in credit and savings in rural areas and increasing financial intermediaries in rural India. The addition of bank branches increases expenditure in education, health, and development projects/activities like agriculture, public works, irrigation, rural development, and community development projects. The study found that the policy-driven program did not only significantly reduce poverty, it also increased production. The effects included expansion in non-agricultural activities with employment and a general wage rise. In addition, credit offered by the banks was at lower interest rates than those offered by local money lenders- the banks offered cheaper credit that was not available before.

The expansion of financial activities suggested that poverty exists in rural areas because the population does not have access to finance projects or economic activities. What accounts for the reduction of poverty with other positive outcomes? First, commercial banks were pressured to expand their branches to the rural areas and at the same time coerced to lend to poor people, where banks were nonexistent. The state had the resources, legislative powers, and coordination advantages to solve market failure and get things done. Hence, the state's action gave access to the population that would not have had such access, but for the State regulations forcing the commercial banks to expand their operations to economically disadvantageous areas. Second, both landowners and landless households could obtain credit to finance their various projects. Third, with the availability of bank services, households could save money and accumulate capital to channel into productive activities. Such public programs were costly, but rural banks were not there in the business of making an immediate profit but were created to ensure accessibility to the rural population, poverty reduction, and the good of the whole economy (Morduch, 1999).

Initially, the social banking program was costly partly because of high transaction costs, loan default rates, and high subsidies in terms of low-interest rates. However, the government learned from the experience and made the necessary adjustments. The cost for bank system expansion into rural areas was much higher than having microfinance institutions in the remote regions of any country. Microfinance institutions (MFIs) are varied with one common idea of serving the poor, and they tend to have high transaction costs partly because of no collateral requirements. Yet, they still lend to poor households profitably. Many low-income households save when they have the opportunity (Morduch, 1999). Hence, both the banking sector and MFIs work together. The rural poor and the commercial banks benefited, with the economy being the primary beneficiary. Overall, the bank program generated poverty reduction activities, created development and growth, among other outcomes.

This program was financially inclusive, which meant households and firms accessed and used formal financial services. Financial inclusion has many aspects; for instance, households and firms have greater access to financial services like bank services that help grow the economy. However, expanding financial services must be accompanied by proper supervision to avoid risking financial stability (Sahay et al., 2015). Good supervision enhances financial stability with increased financial inclusion. And financial inclusion should expand beyond extending bank branches to other financial services such as automatic teller machines, increasing the variety of depositors, and reducing transaction costs. In addition, financial inclusion achieves many macroeconomic objectives. Hence, decision-makers see financial inclusion as a channel of improving livelihoods, eradicating poverty, and growing the economy.

Financial Constraint

One of Africa's most significant problems for industrialization is the shortage of finances besides the basic physical infrastructure. The private sector is vital for growth. However, small businesses cannot easily access credit to participate in private sector development and promote a well-functioning business environment. Small businesses have limited access to credits because of information asymmetries, moral hazard, lack of collateral and credit history, less developed financial markets, and oligopolistic banking system dominated by foreign banks (like in CFA franc zone countries) sizeable informal sector in the economies. The estimates of AfDB (2018) show that the SMEs face an estimated credit gap of over US$ 136 billion, apart from the reality that loans are mainly on short terms. With limited long-term loans, the AfDB estimates further show that less than 60 percent of the loans are short-term loans, and less than 2 percent of the loans offered for up to ten years as long-term loans as of 2018 (AfDB, 2018). To industrialize, African leaders must implement bold monetary and financial policies to address the poor infrastructure, including energy, road, education, and health (AfDB, 2017). No country has ever developed without having appropriate domestic industrial and trade strategies because there has never been anything like free trade (Chang, 2009).

CONCLUSION WITH POLICY IMPLICATION

With China's insatiable appetite for African raw materials, including oil, much of the proceeds have been used to increase nonproductive public sector expenditures and importation of consumer goods, all without increasing the labor force productivity nor improving Africa's production structure (Ademola et al., 2009; Signé, 2018). Such situations have to be reversed for the benefit of the African economy and people.

Much evidence shows that the poor have less financial access to productive economic activities, particularly in rural settings. Nevertheless, when the poor in urban and rural areas can accumulate some capital, such as savings, they have a greater opportunity to be lifted out of poverty and contribute significantly to expanding the economy. Bank branch expansion in India has produced substantial returns. However, this positive outcome cannot be limited to India, with a large population. Therefore, it is crucial to seek areas of intervention to create and adopt production activities that could generate structural change in production, inclusive economic growth with poverty reduction.

A strong collaboration of the central bank and the banking system can promote essential investment by providing credit to key driving sectors. However, it may be challenging for the central bank to direct credit to the disadvantaged industries because the gains are not visible in the short run but in the medium to long run. The monetary authorities tend to use interest rates as the monetary policy tool to signal the lending rates, but this should not be the only tool. There are other instruments the central banks can use, as seen in the Indian case. Because of the high information and transaction costs, the banks may not assess the risk profiles in setting the loan cost fully. In the long run, it is essential to nurture strong deep capital markets and create a conducive environment for liquidity at realistic rates. The economy would benefit much more from an efficiently functioning bank-based and market-based financial systems.

Africa must shift away from exporting raw materials or natural resources and importing manufactured goods to trade in highly valued goods of greater benefits to the continent. That is, industrialization with the exportation of manufactured goods is imperative, which would benefit the population, economy, and balance of payments. For instance, CEMAC incurred a deficit of over 2000 billion CFA francs in 2018 (BEAC, 2019) due to commodity price fall. Nevertheless, raw materials are a strong base for the continent's industrialization. A manufacturing sector is vital in terms of productive factors because it is the route to economic expansion with structural change and development. It generates employment and increases productivity. Africa has excellent manufacturing potential, which is not being well exploited. African policymakers should be more focused on Africa's industrialization because of its potential of bringing about continental prosperity. The financial and monetary policy is essential in this development strategy.

A Synopsis of the Rest of the Book

This book provides an overview of monetary and financial regimes or arrangements in Africa and assesses the effectiveness of the different monetary and financial systems on the development of African economies. First, it analyses in-depth monetary and financial institutions in Africa from a historical perspective and the conduct of monetary policies in each of the arrangements. Second, the book discusses monetary and financial-related issues and their impact on the economy and assesses the effects of the different approaches and monetary policies on the economic performance of member countries and regions. Finally, the authors propose a plan for monetary unions and regimes across the continent.

We organize the book of eighteen chapters into five parts. The rest of this chapter, part I, summarizes the book. Part II has three chapters dealing with Country monetary policy issues. Part III is in seven chapters covering regional financial sector issues. Part IV has six chapters that discuss continental monetary policy and the financial systems. Finally, part V has one chapter and discusses the way forward.

In Part II, with Three Chapters, the Authors Discuss Monetary Policy, Focusing on Inflation Targeting and Monetary Policy Transmission Mechanism to the Real Sector

In Chap. 2, Abdul-Aziz Iddrisu and Imhotep, Paul Alagidede examines the price stability as the core of monetary policy frameworks of central banks in Africa. They determine whether the price stability objective has been effective and how other macroeconomic and welfare conditions have fared as a consequence. Using Ghana as a case study of inflation targeting, they assess the price stability performance and other macroeconomic developments. The question of whether the intended objectives and actual outcomes are in sync. The inflation rate has been low and stable under the inflation targeting regime. However, the constant breaches of the publicly announced inflation targets dent the monetary authorities' credibility, shake the very foundation of the inflation targeting framework, and raise serious questions of the quality of the forecasting framework of the central bank and the nature of assessments that feed into the target determination.

Jehovaness Aikaeli, in Chap. 3, studies the monetary policy impact on macroeconomic performance in Tanzania, with a particular focus on price stability. The results show that monetary policy in the country is effective in terms of its single objective of price stability since both the SVEC impulse responses and error variance decomposition show that most of the variations in the price level resulted from the policy rate. Monetary policy has a significant impact on price developments to target inflation. The Bank of Tanzania influences macroeconomic performance in the country by setting and monitoring the implementation of the monetary policy in the country. Because of the relationship between the policy rate and price in the country, he demonstrates that Tanzania can successfully use inflation targeting as its monetary policy framework for better macroeconomic results.

In Chap. 4, Elkanah Faux examines the effects of monetary policy transmission on economic growth in Sierra Leone. He applies time-series data for 1980–2019 to estimate the strength of monetary transmission on real GDP. The author applies the Fully Modified Ordinary Least Square (FMOLS) regression. The estimation method solves endogeneity and serial correlation by allowing heterogeneity in long-run parameter estimates. The diagnostic tests for unit root and cointegration tests revealed cointegration among the variables indicating a long-run equilibrium relationship. The results from the study reveal the strength of monetary policy interventions in promoting economic growth, with increases in credit to the private sector being the critical transmission channel. Although the real exchange rate, inflation, and interest rate all had the expected negative signs, they are not significant except the real exchange rate. Thus, the chapter underscores the importance of expanding credit access.

Part III, in Seven Chapters, Analyzes Regional Issues Related to Regional Financial Systems and Integration

In Chap. 5, Mohamed Ben Omar Ndiaye analyzes the current economic conditions for the viability of the ECOWAS monetary zone, highlighting the situation of the various components of this monetary cooperation program. He discusses deterioration in the profile of macroeconomic convergence with a downward trend in the number of countries that had met all the criteria. Moreover, there is little progress in the harmonization of economic policies. As a result, the convergence of economic policies is weak and not accompanied by a real and effective convergence of the economies. Based on the cost-benefit analysis of participating in the monetary union project, he shows that the dynamic gains would outweigh the costs in the long run. Hence, for an effective monetary system, he suggests a consolidation of the economic union with an establishment of the fiscal union through the harmonization of fiscal policies, the unification of the banking system, solid institutional frameworks, and structural policies for productive transformation and value creation.

Drawing from political economy, Rachael Ntongho, in Chap. 6 discusses the single currency that is being created in the Economic Community of West African States (ECOWAS). The idea of a single currency called Eco was initiated in 2000 when the fifteen ECOWAS member states decided to create a single monetary union. After elaborate preparation to launch the Eco in 2020, Eco was appropriated by the French-speaking ECOWAS member states in 2019 to an outcry by the rest of the ECOWAS states. However, the outcry has prompted disapproval by non-French ECOWAS members states. The non-French ECOWAS countries seek a way forward for a unitary currency in the region after rejecting the Eco proposed by their Francophone counterpart. Ntongho identifies the reasons for the failure of ECOWAS to establish a single currency acceptable by all member states. The author further re-examines the France-Afrique relationship and suggests viable measures to rebuild trust among French and the other ECOWAS member states towards a single ECOWAS currency.

In Chap. 7, Isidor Noumba and André Arnaud Engine analyze the effect of minimum bank capital on the financing of the CEMAC economies over the period 1998–2016, using data from BEAC and COBAC. Commercial banks operating in that zone are reluctant to finance local small and medium enterprises (SMEs). In December 2019, SMEs received 14.6% of total loans, while big companies obtained 78%. So, their analysis is on the effect of the minimum bank capital on the real cost of credit, the credit term structure, and the various economic agents. Their findings, among other things, show that: (i) the minimum bank capital is positively and significantly linked to the total credits to the economy; (ii) the minimum bank capital is negatively associated with the short-run loans. The study suggests that regulatory authorities find ways of encouraging banks to increase the level of business financing sharply.

Looking at Facts and Prospects of the Monetary Union in East Africa, in Chap. 8, John Sseruyange explores how the East African Monetary Union authorities can successfully sustain the union. He examines the structural attributes of the East African Community member countries that can potentially affect the progress of the monetary union. The convergence of macroeconomic variables among member states is important, and the structural similarities are only exhibited at the inflation level. At the same time, countries diverge, among other things, in exchange rates, interest rates, banking, public debt sizes, and trade. Hence, the East

African Monetary Union member states need to coordinate and harmonize monetary and fiscal policies.

In Chap. 9 Aloysius Ajab Amin identifies and examines factors impeding the economic growth and development in the CFA franc zone countries. First, he traces the evolution of the CFA franc special arrangements between franc zone countries and France, and later through France with the euro. The arrangements superficially appear to give some advantages. Still, the institutional financial features embedded in the arrangements have not created more rapid and sustained growth in the CFA franc zone economies, despite its longevity. Important factors include institutional rigidity, foreign reserves restriction, lack of monetary policy, and poor governance. They have severely affected the different aspects of the CFA franc countries' economies, therefore leaving the zone under-developed. The policy implications are far-reaching.

Regina Tawah, in Chap. 10, presents the evolution of banking in West Africa. The study focuses on the West African Economic and Monetary Union (WAEMU) countries to their French colonial heritage and the origin of the non-WAEMU countries to the British heritage. The author overviews the sub region's financial development and analyzes the factors that determine financial development, focusing on the development of the banking sector. The analysis utilizes panel data on the WAEMU and non-WAEMU countries from 2007 to 2017 to estimate a fixed-effect model to determine the factors that account for changes in banking development. The results show that governance measured using the control of corruption, the rule of law, regulatory quality, and government effectiveness as indicators, GDP per capita, and the interest rate spread significantly determine banking development. The proxies for banking development include domestic credit to the private sector as a percentage of GDP, depositors with commercial banks per 1000 adults, bank liquid reserves to bank assets, claims on the central government is the percentage of GDP, and bank branches per 100,000 adults, informing on financial depth, financial access and stability.

Chapter 11 on Capital Markets development and economic growth in North Africa Augustin Ntembe, Aloysius Amin, and Regina Tawah investigate the financial development and relationship between capital market development and economic growth over 2010 to 2021 in North Africa. The study uses panel data to find a long-run cointegration relationship between real output growth and capital market development in Algeria, Egypt, Morocco, and Tunisia. The authors used the ARDL and the

Markov Switching Regression to find that capital market development measured with market capitalization is positively and significantly related to real GDP growth in the selected North African countries. The error correction term is negative and significant, indicating the subsequent corrections of the deviations of real GDP growth from the long-term value. The paper suggests the need for an expansion and enhancement of capital markets in financing the economies of the selected countries.

Part IV Is in Six Chapters Covering Continental Monetary Issues and Economic Performance

In Chap. 12, Joseph Onjala reviews i) the recent theoretical and empirical literature on the economic integration and economic performance nexus, and ii) discusses trends in the economic performance of the African regional economies by analyzing the financial integration and economic performance nexus. The results provide lessons for government and policymakers to facilitate better, more accurate, and informed decision-making around their participation in financial and economic integration. He ends up by highlighting the main challenges associated with monetary integration.

Thaddee M Badibanga discusses, in Chapt. 13, the limited African capital markets constrain Africa's development. The capital markets are underdeveloped. Although with great potential, they are experiencing severe problems, including low capitalization, low liquidity, and a shortlist of participating companies on the stock exchange. There is, therefore, an urgent need for the right policies to speed the development of capital markets. According to Badibanga, the most urgent ones emphasize the reinforcement of institutional capacity to enforce contracts and commercial regulations, the creation of electronic registry systems of property ownership, the support of monetary policy, the diversification of financial portfolio options, and the creation of secondary markets.

Chapter 14 deals with African Monetary Unions and Competitiveness, where Oluremi Davies Ogun analyses the international competitiveness of African countries in functional monetary unions with the analysis focusing on country levels as opposed to zone levels. He computed four indices of competitiveness (real effective exchange rate, export – gross domestic product ratio, export-import ratio, and technological development) for the countries and their Eurozone counterparts in a comparative context. He finds the African countries lagging the Europeans on the first three measures but outperforming the technological development index. Conditional convergence appeared thus satisfied, raising the hope for a brighter future.

Bruno L. Yawe, J. Ddumba-Ssentamu, Yusuf Kiwala, and Ibrahim Mukisa perform an important examination in Chap. 15. They examine the Addis Ababa Action Agenda on trade and the World Trade Organization. The study emphasizes the importance of trade finance on a healthy trading system in meeting the Sustainable Development Goals. One of the constraining factors for expanding trade within Africa and with the rest of the world is a trade finance gap which is estimated at US$ 82 billion in 2019. So they evaluate different ways of financing infrastructure – private financing, official development assistance, national development banks; resource financed infrastructure; public-private partnerships. Chinese funding for African infrastructure has been running at levels comparable to, or higher than, financing from all G7 members and multilateral development banks combined. Hence, the African Union or countries can set up a development finance institution to facilitate and support trade with infrastructure development. This solution should entail setting up rapid emergency facilities and risk mitigation instruments earmarked to support banks.

In Chap. 16, Grace Nkansa Asante and Abban Stanley look at Africa's meager intra-regional trade record despite many efforts to promote regional blocs and trade among these regional groups. In finding ways to facilitate trade, they estimate the effect of adopting a common currency on intra- regional trade in SACU and ECOWAS countries and investigate whether countries were overtrading or under trading among themselves. Adopting a common currency proved to unleash more trade potentials in the blocs. Distance negatively impacted trade two blocs and adverse effects in the ECOWAS bloc, but the exchange volatility positively affected trade in the SACU bloc. Their results further indicated that countries in the two blocs were under trading, but SACU had more trade potential than countries in the ECOWAS bloc. They suggest that ECOWAS countries continue to strive to achieve the nominal convergence that can enable them to adopt the common currency. At the same time, the SACU bloc is urged to pool more non-member countries into the SADC.

In Chap. 17, Augustin Ntembe discusses the African Monetary Union project and evaluates the progress in creating a single currency for Africa. He considers the benefits and costs of monetary union in Africa, with the prospect for the successful adoption of a common currency in Africa and challenges. The African Union strategy towards economic integration relies on integrating existing regional communities and creating new ones that inter-alia will merge into an African Economic community, creating an African Central Bank and a single currency. As with the European Central Bank and a single currency, the proposed African monetary integration will have extensive political and economic implications across Africa. Hence, he argues that African leaders' political stability and commitment are crucial to achieving the African single currency.

Part V has one chapter, Chap. 18, where the Ntembe, Tawah, and Amin conclude the volume by underscoring the critical ingredients for the African Monetary union as a way forward for An African Monetary Union.

APPENDIX 1 CRYPTOCURRENCY MARKET WITH CENTRAL BANK DIGITAL CURRENCY AND POTENTIAL REGULATIONS
ALOYSIUS AJAB AMIN

This appendix examines the nature of cryptocurrencies with Central Bank Digital Currency, potential benefits, and challenges. More importantly, explores the regulatory framework.

Introduction

The financial world is experiencing a historic financial upheaval through financial technologies and innovations. The introduction of cryptocurrencies like Bitcoin takes the headlines. However, more is still to come. Continuous advances in technologies would make an enduring impact on monetary and financial institutions and the economy. Money evolves from commodity money through paper or fiat to virtual currency. The recent introduction and rapid growth of cryptocurrency are magical. Virtual currencies are unregulated digital currencies, and the developer controls the process using algorithms under well-defined network protocols such as gaming network tokens (Prasad, 2021).

Cryptocurrency

Cryptocurrency is a virtual currency, crypto assets, digital currency, crypto tokens, and decentralized virtual currency. Cryptocurrency is a digital currency that uses cryptography to secure and verify its network. As cryptocurrency is virtual and digitally secured by cryptography, it is difficult to counterfeit. Cryptocurrency is decentralized networks on blockchain technology linked with a distinct network of computers. It produces open-source software over the internet on a peer-to-peer (P2P) network as a currency and payment system. Cryptocurrency is a digital currency that utilizes encryption procedures to create and manage monetary units and validate funds transfer. The downside of cryptocurrency includes high energy use in mining activities, criminality, and high price volatility.

The system facilitates direct transaction eliminating any intermediary like the financial institutions and the Central Bank. The system, therefore, operates utterly different from the traditional financial system- really opposite the functioning of the traditional system. Hence, the system does not fit into the existing legal system. The cryptocurrency involves many elements in the ecosystem (wallet service, exchanges, miners, merchants, users, and blockchain). It is a complex, decentralized, dynamic, and online system.

Blockchain is the technology that facilitates the creation of cryptocurrency and other products, particularly Bitcoin and Ethereum. Blockchain is like a decentralized ledger showing peer-to-peer (P2P) network transactions. Participants carry out transactions such as money transfer, voting, settling trade directly without any central clearing agency using this technology. Blockchain sharply reduces transactional costs and quickens transactions. In simplifying cross-border and remittance payments, it fosters financial inclusion, and it will continue to transform the payment infrastructure and increase employment and income.

Because there are many blockchain applications, PwC identifies five main categories: provenance, payments and financial instruments, identity, contracts, dispute resolution, and customer engagement. According to PwC Steve Davies, blockchain technology can boost the economy significantly and improve the organization's operations (PwC, 2020). Hence, blockchain potentials are well beyond cryptocurrency and Bitcoin.

Issues about the crypto ecosystem included identification, valuation determination, monitoring, and managing risks. For instance, how do we deal with these assets substitute domestic currency and do not evade exchange rate regulation with account management procedures. Hence, a global regulatory framework is necessary to provide and safeguard all risks and provide security and fairness in economic activities.

Central Bank Digital Currency

Digital currency is an electronic currency or cybercash. A Central Bank can issue and regulate a central bank digital currency (CBDC) that can substitute or complement the physical or fiat currency. Like cash and coins, CBDC is a Central Banks' liability and can also apply the similar blockchain technology used in Ethereum or Bitcoin. The digital currency is held in a digital wallet. It can be used as a means of payment on transactions and transferred globally with the digital currency wallet at little or no cost. The CBDC is a digital form of the Central Bank's physical currency; its value is fixed to the physical currency or fiat paper money. The central bank strictly controls the CBDC. Therefore, the CBDC is not a financial asset like the crypto-assets.

CBDC raises monetary policy, financial stability, central bank operations, payment systems, and legal issues. Since CBDC is novel and complex, rigorous analysis is necessary. There is the rapid introduction of various forms of CBDC in the world, rising from 21 percent in 2020, July to 36 percent in October 2021. The Central Bank of the Eastern Caribbean countries launched its CBDC in March 2021. The countries have started using the DCash system that provides transfers and payments in digital Eastern Caribbean dollar CBDC. While China studies the possibility of using blockchain technology, it is CBDC. Nigeria Central Bank introduced CBDC the "eNaira" in October 2021, as the second country after the Bahamas and the Eastern Caribbean countries. The eNaira applies the same blockchain technology as the bitcoin- stored in the wallets, for payment transactions, transfer digitally and at no cost to the parties involved. CBDC-digital form of cash is a direct liability on the central bank, and customers' deposits are a liability on financial institutions. Digital currency and virtual currency. Digital currency is centralized in a location -transaction within the network- can be regulated or not regulated and is available in electronic or digital form, while the virtual currency is not regulated but is controlled by its developer under a defined network protocol (Agbo & Nwadialor, 2020).

Benefits and Risks

As countries introduce many CBDCs, there are important questions about the international monetary system and cross-border payments. Moreover, there are potential risks and benefits and require greater cooperation among countries and relevant parties, including regulators, investors, academics, central bankers, and entrepreneurs.

The benefits of cryptocurrency include financial democratization, improvement of people's lives, poverty reduction through financial inclusion, expansion of financial access to savings and credit products with a wide range of options. In addition, savers and borrowers benefit from remittances.

With CBDC, the government offers a secure and liquid means of payment. As a result, individuals do not need to have bank accounts, with cash carry and use of cash diminished. The use of eMoney is essential, especially where banking sector penetration is nonexistent. For instance, about 36 percent of the adult population in Nigeria does not have a bank account. Accordingly, those with handheld devices like mobile phones can easily access the eCurrency (eNaira) and increase the number of persons having direct and effective money transfers, which increases financial inclusion. Similarly, the system reduces transaction cost and informality since the system provides more transparency in payments. This transparency may result from increases in the tax base.

The digital government currency in a domestic unit of account could compete with large firms issuing currencies with involvement in the payment system. It may even reduce the issue of private currencies. With CBDC, the government can strengthen the payment system and strongly regulate the issue of private currencies in the payment system.

CBDC may improve monetary policy transmission, especially with interest-bearing CBDC, which would be more responsive than cash to changes in the policy rate. Furthermore, Central banks may regard the Distributed Ledger Technology (DLT) based CBDC to pay for DLT-based assets or means of payment. In this case, DLT based currency would result in automatic payments- especially dealing with payment to payment. In many developing countries, there is a high cost of cash management, which depends on the country's geographic size and the accessibility of remote parts of the country. Hence, CBDC offers low-cost means of payment nationally. Still, it facilitates remittances across borders. For instance, remittances to Nigeria in 2019 amounted to $24 billion, with fees ranging between two percent and six percent. With the eNaira, the cost is drastically reduced.

As with all crypto-based technology, the introduction of CBDC bears sizeable risks. There are significant **risks** not even seen, and when they come could be harmful. Rapid financial market changes and technologies with financial platforms pose serious vulnerabilities. Digital and webbed based developments are exposed to technological vulnerabilities like hacking, thus posing a confidence issue with the issuing agency. As the government or Central bank issues CBDC, it enters into direct competition with other private sector financial institutions-competing in financial services with the private sector. CBDC can reduce financial confidence as people move their accounts into the CBDC digital wallets since they have accounts in the central banks. This situation can generate financial instability that the Central Bank tries to avoid.

CBDC may tend to reduce the intermediation role of the commercial banks since people may deal directly with the Central Bank, and commercial banks may have to raise interest rates on deposits to attract customers. Central Bank would have to be active in the payment value chain- a process involving many steps including customers interface, wallets building, transaction monitoring, keeping up with the technology, safeguarding against money laundering and terrorism financing, managing cybersecurity, and any risk against a currency like cyber-attacks. Any error on such fronts can damage the reputation of the Central Bank. Digital currency is extremely risky for the implementation of monetary policy. The issues include financial stability, integrity, cyber security, digital technology risks, operational risk, and resilience.

Synchronized Infrastructure

A considerable challenge is the significant necessity of public infrastructure investment to develop a solid synchronized infrastructure with expanding internet access to remote regions. At the same time, develop a computer and tech-savvy population. We can also note that these activities demand a high level of energy consumption in an environment with constant power shortages.

Legal Framework

The legal framework is crucial for the cryptocurrency world (Chainanalysis, 2020). Some countries carefully weigh these options (pros and cons of CBDC) and develop appropriate measures. Since countries are fast introducing digital currency and the digital currency may soon be in the mainstream.

Therefore, the authorities can address some of the risks by moving funds from bank deposits to eCurrency wallets in regular transactions and imposing balance limits to enhance the intermediary role of banks and other financial institutions. To address financial integrity, preventing money laundering and other criminal activities, the authorities can introduce a robust verification system with rigorous controls. Wallets holders must meet top-level identity verification standards. Then they can address cybersecurity risk with systematic IT security assessment.

Hence, the main challenging issues are (i) how to regulate the cryptocurrency; (ii) who should regulate and to what extent. The cryptocurrency involves many elements in the ecosystem (wallets, miners, merchants, users, and exchanges). Moreover, it is a complex, decentralized, dynamic, and online system (Eveshnie, 2019).

These new forms of money have to maintain trustworthiness, safeguard the wealth of customers/consumers, and be embedded in the rigorous legal framework- legal frameworks must not be fragmented- it must be comprehensive, consistent, coordinated, and continuously updating, noting the market structure, product characteristics, and public sector role.

References

Agbo, E. I., & Nwadialor, E. O. (2020). Cryptocurrency and the African economy. *Economics and Social Sciences Academic Journal, 2*(6), ISSN (5282-0053); p – ISSN (4011 – 230X).

Chainanalysis. (2020). *The 2020 Geography of Cryptocurrency Report analysis of geographic trends in cryptocurrency adoption, usage, and regulation September 2020.* Chainanalysis Market Intel | Blockchain analysis for cryptocurrency markets.

Eveshnie Reddy. (2019). *An overview of the regulatory developments in South Africa regarding the use of cryptocurrencies.* Juta, and Company (Pty) Ltd.

Nadarajah, S., Afuecheta, E., & Chan, S. (2021). Dependence between bitcoin and African currencies. *Quality and Quantity, 55,* 1203–1218. https://doi.org/10.1007/s11135-020-01051-0

Prasad, E. S. (2021). *The future of money: How the digital revolution is transforming currencies and finance.* Harvard University Press.

PwC. (2020). *Time for trust: How blockchain will transform business and the economy.* https://www.pwc.com/gx/en/industries/technology/publications/blockchain-report-transform-business-economy.html

REFERENCES

Abeygunawardana, K., Amarasekara, C., & Tilakaratne, C. (2017). Macroeconomic effects of monetary policy shocks. *South Asia Economic Journal, 18,* 21–38.

Ademola, O. T., Bankole, A.-S., & Adewuyi, A. O. (2009). China–Africa trade relations: Insights from AERC scoping studies. *European Journal of Development Research, 21*(4), 485–505. https://doi.org/10.1057/ejdr.2009.28

AfDB. (2017). *Why does Africa's industrialization matter? Challenges and opportunities?* https://www.afdb.org/en/news/01/28/2019-1407/why-does-africas-industrialization-matter-challenges-and-opportunities-724

AfDB. (2018). *Why does Africa's industrialization matter? Challenges and opportunities?* https://www.afdb.org/en/news/01/28/2019-1407/why-does-africas-industrialization-matter-challenges-and-opportunities-724

AGRA. (2020). *Africa agriculture status report. Feeding Africa's cities: Opportunities, challenges, and policies for linking African farmers with growing urban food markets* (Issue 8). Alliance for a Green Revolution in Africa (AGRA).

Allen, F., Otchere, I., & Senbet, L. W. (2011). African financial systems: A review of development. *Finance, 1,* 79–113.

Aryeetey, E. (2008). *From informal finance to formal finance in Sub-Saharan Africa: Lessons from linkage efforts.* Paper presented at the High-Level Seminar on African Finance for the 21st Century Organized by the IMF Institute and the Joint Africa Institute Tunis, Tunisia, March 4–5, 2008.

Banerjee, A. (2001). Contracting constraints, credit markets, and economic development. Mimeo MIT.

Banerjee, A., & Newman, A. (1993). Occupational choice and the process of development. *Journal of Political Economy, 101,* 274–298.

Banerjee, A. V., Gertler, P. J., & Ghatak, M. (2002). Empowerment and efficiency: Tenancy reform in West Bengal. *Journal of Political Economy, 110*(2), 239–280.

BEAC. (2019). *Rapport annuel sur l'exercice de l'année 1998–2018.*

Beck, T., Demirgüç-Kunt, A., & Levine, R. (2009). *Financial institutions and markets across countries and over time data and analysis* (Policy Research working paper 4943). The World Bank.

Beck, T., & Levine, R. (2002). Industry growth and capital allocation do having a market or bank-based system matter? *Journal of Financial Economics, Elsevier, 64*(2), 147–180.

Bencivenga, V., & Smith, B. D. (1991). Financial intermediation and endogenous growth. *Review of Economic Studies, 58*, 195–209.

Burgess, R., & Pande, R. (2003). *Do rural banks matter? Evidence from the Indian social banking experiment* (LSE STICERD Research paper No. DEDPS 40). http://sticerd.lse.ac.uk/dps/de/dedps40.pdf

Burgess, R., & Pande, R. (2004). *Do rural banks matter? Evidence from the Indian social banking experiment).* Available at SSRN: https://ssrn.com/abstract=502103

Chakraborty, S., & Ray, T. (2006). Bank-based versus market-based financial systems: A growth-theoretic analysis. *Journal of Monetary Economics, 53*, 329–350.

Chang, H.-J. (2009). *Bad samaritans: The myth of free trade and the secret history of capitalism.* Bloomsbury.

Deaton, A., & Dreze, J. (2002, September 7–13). Poverty and inequality in India: A re-examination, *Economic and Political Weekly, 37*(36), 3729–3748.

Demirgüç-Kunt, A., & Levine, R. (1999). *Bank-based and market-based financial systems cross-country comparison* (Policy Research working paper 2143). World Bank.

Demirgüç-Kunt, A., & Levine, R. (Eds.). (2001). *Financial structure and economic growth: A cross- country comparison of banks, markets and development* (Chapter 4). The MIT Press.

IMF. (2020). Monetary and capital markets: Special series on financial policies to respond to COVID-19.

Kangami, D. N. (2019). *Common currency intra-regional trade flows and economic growth: Evidence from CEMAC customs union.* D.Ph.D. Thesis, University of The Witwatersrand.

Leke, A., & Signé, L. (2020). *Spotlighting opportunities for business in Africa and strategies to succeed in the world's next big growth market.* McKinsey & Company. https://www.brookings.edu/wp-content/uploads/2019/01/BLS18234_BRO_book_006.1_CH5.pdf

Levine, R. (2002). *Bank-based or market-based financial systems: Which is better?* (Working paper 9138 NBER). http://www.nber.org/papers/w9138

Levine, R., Loayza, N., & Beck, T. (2000). Financial intermediation and growth: Causality and causes. *Journal of Monetary Economics, 46*, 31–77.

Mohanty, M. S. (2014). The role of central banks in macroeconomic and financial stability.

Mordi, C. (2010). The link between the financial (banking) sector and the real sector of the Nigerian economy. *Economic and Financial Review, 48*(4), 7–30.

Morduch, J. (1999). The microfinance promise. *Journal of Economic Literature, 37*(4), 1569–1614. https://doi.org/10.1257/jel.37.4.1569

Mwabutwa, C., Viegi, N., & Bittencourt, M. (2016). Evolution of monetary policy transmission mechanism in Malawi: A Tvp-Var approach. *Journal of Economic Development, 41*, 33–55.

Omar, M. A., & Inaba, K. (2020). Does financial inclusion reduce poverty and income inequality in developing countries? A panel data analysis. *Economic Structures, 9*, 37. https://doi.org/10.1186/s40008-020-00214-4

Osoro, J., & Osano, E. (2014). *Bank-based versus market-based financial system: Does evidence justify the dichotomy in the context of Kenya?* (Centre for Research on Financial Markets and Policy WPS/05/14).

Pande, R., Troyer-Moore, C., & Rigol, N. (2018). Financial inclusion *Evidence for Policy Design (EPoD), the Harvard Kennedy School.* https://epod.cid.harvard.edu/topic/financial-inclusion

Sahay, R., Čihák, M., N'Diaye, P., Barajas, A., Mitra, S., Kyobe, A., Mooi, Y. N., & Yousefi, S. R. (2015). *Financial inclusion: Can it meet multiple macroeconomic goals?* (Staff discussion notes No. 15/17). IMF.

Schumpeter, J. (1934). *The theory of economic development: An inquiry into profits, capital, interest, and the business cycle.* Harvard University Press.

Seers, D. (1969). *The meaning of development* (IDS Communication No. 44, 1969). Institute of Development Studies.

Sheefeni, J. P. (2020). Money channel of monetary policy transmission in Namibia. *Economia Internazionale/International Economics, 73*(1), 131–150.

Signé, L. (2018). *The potential of manufacturing and industrialization in Africa trends, opportunities, and strategies.* African Growth Initiative at Brookings.

Singh, R. J., Kpodar, K., & Ghura, D. (2009). *Financial deepening in the CFA franc zone: The role of institutions* (IMF working paper WP/09/113).

Ustarz, Y., & Fanta, A. B. (2021). Financial development and economic growth in sub-Saharan Africa: A sectoral perspective. *Cogent Economics & Finance, 9*(1), 1934976. https://doi.org/10.1080/23322039.2021.1934976

World Bank. (2020). Housing finance in the CEMAC region.

PART II

Country Monetary Policy Issues

CHAPTER 2

Monetary Policy and Price Stability in Ghana's Fourth Republic: Have the Dues Been Paid?

Abdul-Aziz Iddrisu and Imhotep Paul Alagidede

INTRODUCTION

Price stability continues to be at the center of monetary policy objectives of many central banks (Mishkin, 1996). Fiscal policy inconsistencies in many African countries, usually underpinned by political difficulties, have

A.-A. Iddrisu
Department of Banking Technology and Finance, Kumasi Technical University, Kumasi, Ghana

Wits Business School, University of the Witwatersrand, Johannesburg, South Africa
e-mail: abdul-ziz.iddrisu@kstu.edu.gh

I. P. Alagidede (✉)
Wits Business School, University of the Witwatersrand, Johannesburg, South Africa

Institute for Indigenous Intelligence, Nile Valley Multiversity, Johannesburg, South Africa
e-mail: imhotep.alagidede@wits.ac.za

placed a greater burden on monetary policy authorities to deliver price stability. Unsurprisingly, monetary policy frameworks in these countries have evolved in pursuit of price stability objectives, with some central banks such as the South African Reserve Bank and the Bank of Ghana taking a more austere stance on inflation management. Given the inflationary episodes in several developing countries and the apparent macroeconomic instability, the International Monetary Fund (IMF) proffered policy prescriptions on achieving single-digit inflation (Anwar & Islam, 2013) in these countries. However, the extent of the feasibility of the single-digit inflation prescription has been questioned in the literature, given the structure of these economies (Anwar & Islam, 2013). A more fundamental issue of whether the price stability objective has been served in these African countries remains an important question in the literature and policy circles. Importantly, whether the management of inflation in these African countries has provided the impetus for the much-needed economic growth and the distribution of the benefits thereof in alleviating poverty is even more critical, given the endemic poverty levels in the continent. Indeed, the question of whether central banks in Africa pursue monetary policy frameworks consistent with their fundamentals is even more pertinent.

Using the case of Ghana, an inflation-targeting country, we consider the promised price stability and its delivery record under the various monetary policy frameworks since the Fourth Republic and how other macroeconomic fundamentals and welfare indicators have fared. Although the works of Abango et al. (2019) and Quartey et al. (2017) are attempts at answering this question, the focus has solely been on price performance, with Quartey et al. (2017) leaning heavily on the current inflation targeting regime. Meanwhile, the achievement of price stability (albeit important on its own) is supposed to provide the impetus for economic growth and welfare, a fact recognized by the Bank of Ghana Act 2002 (Act 612) under section 3(2) of the Act. Therefore, to focus the analysis solely on price performance is to miss the point entirely.

Significantly, beyond comparing inflation performance over different regimes, the current study delves deeper into the assessment of inflation performance against the specific policy benchmarks such as the inflation targets instead of a blanket comparison of inflation rates between two or more regimes. Another novelty of the current study is the consideration of welfare dynamics at national and regional levels under Ghana's various monetary policy regimes. We employ the idea of a soft and hard nose monetary policy regime to delineate the actual outturn of monetary policy targets in the different regimes.

The choice of Ghana as a context of the current study holds policy relevance for many other African countries on the inflation management journey. Ghana adopted an inflation targeting regime as a sterner stand to stem the inflation tide under previous policy regimes but has struggled to achieve publicly announced inflation targets on a sustainable basis. Understanding the factors that underpin such struggles and the developments in the fundamentals of the Ghanaian economy holds vital lessons for other African countries. Unlike South Africa, another inflation-targeting country, the economic structure and fundamentals of the Ghanaian economy represent many African countries, making it an ideal case study and model for these economies.

We find that the inflation targeting regime delivered relatively lower and stable inflation than the monetary targeting framework. The frequent breaches of the publicly announced targets run counter with the credibility requirements and the expectation anchoring pillar of the very tenets and foundations of the inflation-targeting framework. The inflation targeting regime witnessed a somewhat volatile output growth trajectory, characteristic of the hard nose monetary policy regime. The distribution of the benefits of growth is largely skewed towards the rich than the poor. The poverty levels are, thus, alarming and the regional disparities even more worrying.

In the subsequent sections, we provide the monetary policy frameworks since the beginning of the Fourth Republic. The fundamental forces that informed the adoption of a particular framework are presented and analyzed, and the reasons for its eventual collapse are addressed. We look at the price stability performance under each monetary policy framework, using hard nose and soft nose as a framework. In the former, authorities have a more radical stance on inflation and would sacrifice growth for price stability, while the latter favors growth at the expense of inflation. Both work via the standard Philips curve that stipulates an inverse relationship between inflation and unemployment. We look at the factors that underpin inflation in each regime and the related policy responses and consequences. We then consider the performance of output under the various regimes and how that relates to employment dynamics, income distribution, and the performance of other welfare indicators.

Monetary Policy Frameworks Since 1993

At the dawn of the Fourth Republic, monetary policy in Ghana had evolved from direct credit controls and monetary management to a liberalized phase of monetary targeting framework. Before the dawn of the Fourth Republic, the direct control regime created a disincentive for financial intermediation, heightened cost of transactions, and occasioned resource misallocation in a manner that battered the Ghanaian banking system (Addison, 2001). Meanwhile, given the absence of a well-developed capital market, the same banking system was expected to carry the monetary policy impulses to the real economy and affect the price level.

The Bank of Ghana, under the new liberalized monetary targeting framework, targeted money supply (monetary aggregates) to achieve price stability. The belief that money underpinned inflation dynamics informed the strategy of the Bank of Ghana for the management of inflation. The framework for monetary management by the Bank of Ghana is comprised of three targets: the operating, intermediate, and ultimate target (Addison, 2001). Price stability, considered in the context of inflation rates, represents the ultimate goal. On the other hand, the supply of money constituted the intermediate target, which, until 1997, was measured as M2 (broad money). Thus, the Bank of Ghana achieves price stability by reaching the target for monetary aggregates. With the growth in foreign currency deposits in Ghana's banking sector, the Bank of Ghana switched to M2+ in 1997 to include deposits denominated in foreign currency (Addison, 2001).

In the wake of the financial sector liberalization and the departure from direct controls, the Bank of Ghana had to rely on an indirect instrument (operating target) that correlated strongly with monetary aggregates (the intermediate target) to achieve the money supply target and inflation eventually. Thus, the Bank of Ghana achieves the intermediate target by achieving the operating target. Initially, the net domestic assets of the Central Bank were deployed as the active target but subsequently replaced with reserve money (Addison, 2001).

An underlying assumption in the targeting of monetary aggregates in Ghana was the stability of the velocity of money and money multiplier. However, innovation in the financial sector, propelled by advancement in information technology, brought in its wake new financial products that progressively confounded the definition of money, destabilized the money demand function, and weakened the monetary aggregates-inflation

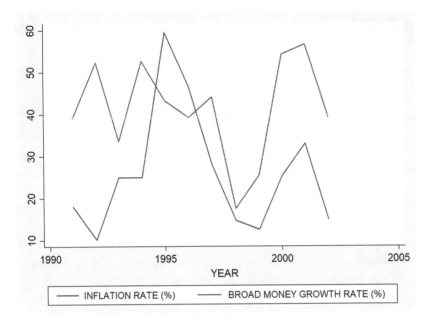

Fig. 2.1 Inflation and broad money growth (1991–2002)

relationship (Bawumia et al., 2008). As a result, as shown in Fig. 2.1, inflation rate and broad money drifted away substantially from each other over the monetary targeting regime. For instance, while inflation rose sharply to peak at 59.46 percent in 1995, broad money declined from 52.6 percent in 1994 to 43.2 percent in 1995. Essentially, the supposed intermediate target (monetary aggregates) was far from the eventual target (price stability), denting the appropriateness of the monetary targeting regime in delivering price stability in the country. Clearly, factors other than monetary aggregates underpinned inflation dynamics over the monetary targeting regime. From the relationship between the operating target (reserve money) and the intermediate target (broad money) in Fig. 2.2, we observe that they are equally adrift, raising the question of why it took the Bank of Ghana a decade to abandon the monetary targeting regime, or perhaps the technical assessment that informed the adoption of the regime in the first place.

Bawumia et al. (2008) show that demand for money in the late 1990s and early 2000 saw significant shifts in the wake of reforms and

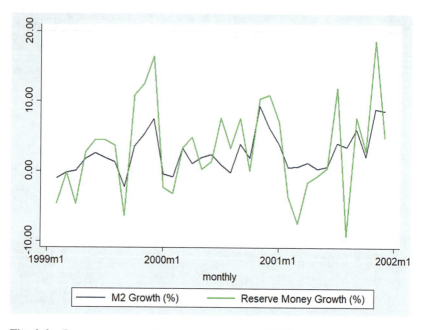

Fig. 2.2 Reserve money and monetary aggregates (M2)

liberalization of the country's financial sector, denting the long-held view of stability of the velocity of money and money multiplier. Indeed, inflation in the 1990s and early 2000 was a challenge in Ghana, reaching 59.46 percent in 1995 and posing substantial welfare and economic performance risk.

Under the monetary targeting framework, the apparent inflationary challenge prompted the Bank of Ghana to abandon that regime and adopt a hard nose monetary policy regime that focused heavily on inflation. Thus, the Bank of Ghana, in 2002, ushered in the inflation targeting framework, although the formal unveiling took place in 2007 (Quartey et al., 2017). The relative success of the inflation targeting regime in Canada, Finland, New Zealand, South Africa, the United Kingdom, and many other countries may have endeared the framework to Ghana. Accordingly, the Bank of Ghana, before the official unveiling in 2007, developed operational, institutional, transparency, and accountability structures (Quartey et al., 2017) meant to facilitate the smooth implementation of the explicit inflation targeting framework in 2007, a framework that remains operational to date.

The framework comes with it an explicit inflation target that is publicly announced, and the central Bank uses an interest rate to guide inflation and expectations to the announced target. Such a system then thrives on the Central Bank's credibility and ability to achieve the said target in a manner that builds public confidence and helps anchor public expectations. The Bank of Ghana operates through a short-term interest rate (Monetary Policy Rate), with the view to influence market interest rates, borrowing costs, economic activities, and the target inflation eventually. The Monetary Policy Rate (MPR) setting is informed by Bank of Ghana's judgment of future inflation trajectory and factors that could pose risks to achieving the publicly announced inflation target. This then places inflation forecasting at the heart of the Central Bank's policy decisions. The accuracy of the forecasts holds key to the credibility of the Bank of Ghana and its ability to anchor inflation expectations.

The current medium target inflation (headline) in Ghana is eight percent ± 2. The fiscal and monetary policymakers jointly determine this target. Having set the target, the instruments for its achievement remain the prerogative of the Bank of Ghana. Such independence is enshrined in the Bank of Ghana Act 2002 (Act 612), which laid the foundation for the operational autonomy of the Central Bank as a precursor to the launch of the inflation targeting regime. The authority to make monetary policy decisions under the inflation targeting regime rests with the Bank of Ghana's Monetary Policy Committee (MPC), which has seven members. Five members are drawn from within the Central Bank, including the governor who chairs the committee's proceedings. The other two membership slots of the committee are taken up by individuals from outside the Central Bank, with the Finance Minister entrusted with the appointment of these two individuals. The Bank of Ghana's MPC meets every two months. The typical duration of each of these meetings is two days which ends with a press conference on the third day regarding the monetary policy decision. Each committee member is entitled to a vote in determining the MPR, but a clear justification must accompany such a vote and stance by a member. The ultimate monetary policy stance of the committee is arrived at based on consensus (Bank of Ghana, n.d.). The subject of the next section is whether the inflation targeting regime has delivered superior price stability relative to the monetary targeting regime.

PRICE STABILITY PERFORMANCE UNDER THE MONETARY POLICY FRAMEWORKS

Given the overriding objective of price stability under the various monetary policy frameworks, we now assess the extent of success or otherwise on delivering that objective under the respective frameworks. Table 2.1 presents the descriptive statistics on inflation performance under the monetary and inflation targeting regimes. Figure 2.3 provides a graphical presentation of the inflation trend under both regimes.

Table 2.1 Descriptive statistics on the inflation rate

Policy Regimes	Mean	Minimum	Maximum	St. Dev.	Coef. of Var.	Obs.
Monetary targeting	29.87	12.41	59.46	14.90	49.88	9
Inflation targeting	13.95	7.13	26.68	4.70	33.69	17

Note: Data obtained from the World Bank's World Development Indicators. Coef. of Var. is the coefficient of variation. Obs means observations, and St. Dev. is the standard deviation

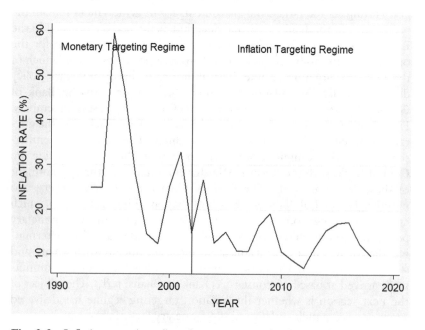

Fig. 2.3 Inflation rates (trend) under monetary and inflation targeting regimes

The relatively high inflationary episodes in the monetary targeting regime compared to the inflation targeting regime has been attributed to election-related fiscal profligacy (Alagidede et al., 2014; Adu & Marbuah, 2011), growth in money supply, and supply-side constraints (Adu & Marbuah, 2011), as well as volatility in output and food price hikes (Alagidede et al., 2014). We argue that a significant policy problem is the foundation of inflation management by the country's Central Bank under the monetary targeting regime.

As shown in the previous section, the inflation management plan was premised on the monetary phenomenon hypothesis, which has been far from reality. The monetary aggregates (the intermediate target) were far from the path of inflation (eventual objective); the operating target was equally at significant variance with the intermediate target. It then raises the question of whether periodic assessments were in place to monitor the trajectories of the operating target, the intermediate target, and the eventual price stability objective, and, if so, why it took a decade to realize the foundation of monetary and inflation management in the country was fundamentally flawed. As indicated earlier, periods of high inflation under the monetary targeting regime coincided with declines in monetary aggregates, implying monetary policy easing in inflationary periods.

The relative success in the inflation outcome under the inflation targeting regime, on the other hand, has been credited to the adoption of inflation targeting framework (Marbuah, 2011; Kyereboah-Coleman, 2012), and debt cancellations, foreign loans, and inflows of aid (Alagidede et al., 2014). Much as inflation management has been a relative success under the inflation targeting regime compared to the monetary targeting framework, it is important to analyze the performance of the former within its tenets and architecture. As indicated earlier, a target is publicly announced in an inflation-targeting framework, and the monetary policy authorities are expected to achieve this target. A failure to achieve the target impairs the authorities' credibility and shakes an important foundation of anchoring inflation expectations. Given such relevance, a determination of the inflation target must take the country's economic fundamentals into account. Therefore, we compare the inflation targets set under the inflation targeting regime with the various outcomes. When the explicit inflation targeting framework was unveiled in 2007, the target inflation range for the year was 7 percent–9 percent.

Meanwhile, the inflation outcome for 2007 was 12.7 percent (year-on-year). A target range of 6 percent–8 percent was set for 2008, yet the inflation outcome for that year was 18.1 percent (year- on-year), more than twice the upper band. In 2013, a target range of 7.5 percent–11.5 percent was set, and the year ended with an inflation rate of 13.5 percent (year-on-year). For 2014, the target range was set at 11 percent–15 percent, but inflation stood at 17 percent (year-on-year). A medium-term target range of 6 percent–10 percent was set since 2015, but the inflation outcomes have been 17.7 percent, 15.4 percent, 11.8 percent, and 9.4 percent in 2015, 2016, 2017, and 2018, respectively (year-on-year). The apparent reality is that the Bank of Ghana had missed the inflation targets in most cases. Although a target range of 7 percent–9 percent was set for 2007 when the explicit targeting started, the Bank of Ghana had an overly ambitious two-year medium-term target inflation of 5 percent, which has eluded the country just like the other targets. This raises fundamental questions about the nature of inputs and thinking that went into these targets over the years and whether the country's economic structure and fundamentals were considered. It also begs the question of whether these targets are driven by inner thinking or imposed from elsewhere.

Perhaps a more fundamental question is whether Ghana should be pursuing single-digit inflation given its economic fundamentals. Unfortunately, Ghana has persistently missed the target of a single digit due to many reasons, which include (1) the dominance of primary commodities in the country's export basket that suffers enormously from price volatility (2) the substantial exposure to imported inflation given the country's net importer status, (3) the frequent weakening of the country's domestic currency which fuels inflationary momentum, (4) the dominance of food in the consumption basket of Ghana (over 43 percent) which adds a layer of extreme volatility in the overall inflationary dynamics of the country, and (5) the 'perpetual fiscal deficit. Moreover, the single-digit inflation prescription by the IMF for developing countries under the Poverty Reduction and Growth Facility, which Ghana benefitted from, lacked concrete reasons mainly because of the structure of these economies (Anwar & Islam, 2013).

Another critical question in the light of the breaches, apart from considering the economic fundamentals in the target determination, is the quality of the forecasting framework of the Central Bank, which is supposed to inform money policy stance. The forecasting objectives are themselves questionable given the premise of an unrealistic target. In addition, the composition and weighting of the components of the CPI inflation basket itself are problematic. The CPI inflation baskets are infrequently updated. The situation is even dire in many countries in Sub-Saharan Africa, where surveys on households' budgets are infrequently undertaken to inform the adjustment of CPI baskets to keep pace with changing household consumption dynamics (Dabalen et al., 2016). The items in the basket are limited to a few urban areas, and the announced inflation does not represent actual price developments.

ECONOMIC GROWTH UNDER THE FOURTH REPUBLIC

Having considered the price performance of the respective monetary policy regimes, we now turn attention to the economic growth path over the period. First, we analyze the two main monetary policy regimes, with descriptive statistics and trends in Table 2.2 and Fig. 2.4, respectively.

Table 2.2 Descriptive statistics on GDP growth

Policy Regimes	Mean	Minimum	Maximum	St. Dev.	Coef. of Var.	Obs.
Monetary targeting	4.21	3.30	4.85	0.50	11.88	9
Inflation targeting	6.32	2.18	14.05	2.87	45.41	17

Note: Data obtained from the World Bank's World Development Indicators. Coef. of Var. is the coefficient of variation. Obs means observations, and St. Dev. is the standard deviation

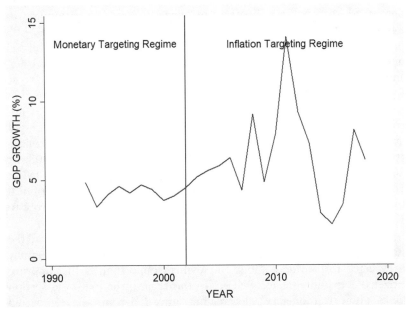

Fig. 2.4 Output growth under the monetary and inflation targeting regimes

Although the common denominator of the monetary and inflation targeting regimes has been price stability, the latter represents a rather austere stance on inflation (hard nose monetary policy), with implications for output dynamics under the two regimes. Relatively, output growth has been stable under the monetary targeting regime than the inflation-targeting framework. That is characteristic of the soft nose-hard nose monetary policy divide.

On the other hand, in the inflation targeting regime (hard nose monetary policy regime), the price stability objective is supreme and may come at the cost of output stability. Although the start of oil production contributed to the high growth rate observed in 2011 (14.05 percent), which represents an outlier, the period between 2005 and 2009, which also falls within the inflation- targeting period, equally saw explosive output growth. From output growth of 5.9 percent in 2005, it increased to 6.40 percent in 2006, dropped sharply to 4.35 percent in 2007, more than doubled to 9.15 percent in 2008, and almost halved to 4.84 percent in 2009.

The output growth trends under the two regimes also reveal the characteristics of standard Philips curve analysis. For instance, under the monetary targeting regime, output growth dropped from 4.85 percent in 1993 to 3.3 percent in 1994. In the standard Philips curve analysis, the drop in output growth implies an increase in unemployment, corresponding to lower inflation. Inflation did drop from 24.96 percent in 1993 to 24.87 percent in 1994, in line with the inverse relationship between inflation and unemployment. However, output growth rose to 4.11 percent in 1995, and inflation shot up to 59.46 percent. Fast forward, output growth rose to 4 percent in 2001 from 3.7 percent in 2000, and inflation increased to 32.91 percent in 2001 from 25.19 percent in 2000. The story is not entirely different under the inflation-targeting regime. When output growth increased to 5.2 percent in 2003 from 4.5 percent in the previous year, inflation increased from 14.82 percent to 26.68 percent in 2003. By 2007, output growth had dropped to 4.35 percent, and inflation fell to 10.73 percent in 2007. In 2008 when output growth more than doubled to 9.15 percent from 4.35 percent in the previous year, inflation rose to 16.52 percent.

Economic growth is beneficial when it helps transform the lives and the standard of living of ordinary citizens. The development of the economy is expected to provide copious employment opportunities that improve citizens' lives and enhance welfare. In this regard, the following section looks at how the monetary policy regimes' growth dynamics have impacted unemployment reduction and other welfare indicators.

Economic Growth, Income Distribution, Unemployment, and Welfare

The monetary targeting regime witnessed a relatively stable output growth, and the growth levels were lower than the inflation targeting regime. However, lower economic growth comes with the baggage of higher unemployment rates. Unsurprisingly, the unemployment rate under the monetary targeting regime was higher and more volatile than the inflation targeting regime, as shown in Table 2.3. Generally, periods of higher growth rates under both regimes have been accompanied by declining unemployment rates, and periods of sluggish growth have also witnessed higher unemployment rates, as depicted in Fig. 2.5.

Apart from unemployment, we also consider the welfare implications of the economic growth performance since the Fourth Republic. We rely on the Human Development Index (HDI) from the United Nations Development Programme (UNDP). The HDI incorporates measures of living standards, knowledge accessibility, and health. Specifically, it considers per capita income measured as gross national income per capita, life expectancy at birth, expected years of schooling, and mean years of schooling (UNDP, 2019). The index, therefore, covers three major aspects of welfare issues, such as good health, education, and living standards, making it ideal for our analysis. The HDI comes with four classifications that define the level of accomplishments of countries concerning the welfare measures. Each of these classifications is accompanied by a threshold. An index of 0.550 or lower is classified as low human development. An index that falls between 0.550 and 0.699 is regarded as medium human development. An index in the range of 0.700 and 0.799 is considered high human development, and an index above 0.800 is considered as very high human development (UNDP, 2019).

Table 2.3 Descriptive statistics on the unemployment rate

Policy Regimes	Mean	Minimum	Maximum	St. Dev.	Coef. of Var.	Obs.
Monetary targeting	7.78	5.28	10.36	1.84	23.65	9
Inflation targeting	5.72	4.16	8.34	1.14	19.93	17

Note: Data obtained from the World Bank's World Development Indicators. Coef. of Var. is the coefficient of variation. Obs means observations, and St. Dev. is the standard deviation

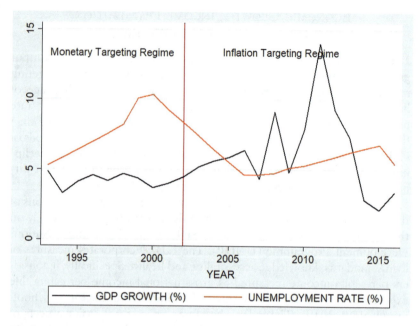

Fig. 2.5 Output growth and unemployment under the monetary policy regimes

Table 2.4 Descriptive statistics on HDI

Policy Regimes	Mean	Minimum	Maximum	St. Dev.	Coef. of Var.	Obs.
Monetary targeting	0.475	0.467	0.483	0.005	1.05	9
Inflation targeting	0.548	0.487	0.596	0.037	6.75	17

Note: Data obtained from the United Nations Development Programme. Coef. of Var. is the coefficient of variation. Obs means observations, and St. Dev. is the standard deviation

We start the analysis with the monetary targeting regime. The HDI over this period averaged 0.475, which is below 0.550 and thus regarded as low human development (Table 2.4). In other words, it reflects a lower standard of living, lower levels of education, and 'poor' health status or lower life expectancy at birth. Indeed, the maximum HDI recorded under the monetary targeting regime is 0.483, which is still below the threshold of 0.550. Although the inflation targeting regime also recorded an average HDI of 0.548, the period saw HDI levels classified as medium human

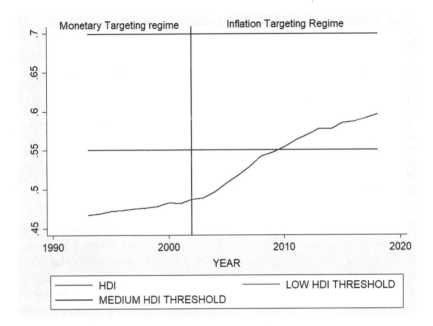

Fig. 2.6 HDI under the monetary policy regimes

development, especially from 2010 onwards (Fig. 2.6). This implies an improved standard of living, higher educational attainments, and improved health status or longer and healthier life than the previous regime. Although with substantial volatility, that is not farfetched, given the high growth levels recorded during the inflation targeting regime. However, it must be added that welfare initiatives relating to schooling and health, in particular, take time to materialize. Therefore, an improved HDI index in the current year may have taken initiatives in the prior years to achieve the current improved welfare.

The HDI, although a good gauge of welfare, is less informative in terms of the distribution of the wealth of the country. The living standard component (GNI per capita) in the HDI measure, in particular, obscures the nature of income distribution. We, therefore, consider more disaggregated data from the World Bank's World Development Index (WDI) in Table 2.5, which indicates the distribution of the benefits of economic growth of the country. Unlike other series, the disaggregated inequality data is not collected annually. Instead, the information is based on the

Table 2.5 Income distribution and poverty

Measures	1991	1998	2005	2012	2016
Income share held by highest 10 percent	30.1	29.6	32.7	31.7	32.2
Income share held by lowest 10 percent	2.6	2.2	1.9	2	1.6
Income share held by highest 20 percent	45.6	46.2	48.6	48.3	48.6
Income share held by lowest 20 percent	6.6	5.8	5.2	5.4	4.7
Poverty headcount ratio at US$1.90 a day	49.8	35.7	24.5	12	13.3
Poverty headcount ratio at US$3.20 a day	78.6	63.3	50.1	32.5	30.5
Poverty headcount ratio at US$5.50 a day	93.1	85.4	77.1	60.5	56.9

Source: World Development Indicators. The poverty headcount ratio is expressed as a percentage of the population

Ghana Living Standards Survey conducted by the Ghana Statistical Service in rounds and at distant intervals. The data collected during a particular round remains the official poverty and inequality data until the subsequent round. At the start of the Fourth Republic in 1993, the most recent data were the 1991–1992 survey of living standards in Ghana, which remained the official data until 1998–1999. The government conducted another round of surveys in 1998–1999. As Table 2.5 shows, income distribution has been skewed over the years in favor of the rich. Such gapping differences in income distribution are a sure recipe for entrenched poverty and endanger achieving the sustainable development goal of ending poverty of any form. Indeed, poverty levels were high, especially in 1991 and 1998, coinciding with the monetary targeting regime where economic growth was relatively low. Income distribution deteriorated even in the inflation targeting regime, where growth was somewhat higher. As the economy grew steadily, the associated income benefited the rich more than the poor. As a result, the rich increased their grip on the country's wealth, leaving the poor counting their losses in the sharing of the national cake.

However, based on the World Bank estimates, the observed poverty levels mask the worrying disparities in different parts of the country. To provide such insights, we look at the national level poverty lines and the regional differences in Ghana with data from the Ghana Statistical Service (Ghana Statistical Service, 2018). At the national poverty line of GHS 1314.00 per annum (equivalent to USD 231.75 per annum), 31.9 percent of Ghanaians were regarded as poor in 2005/2006, with substantial regional disparities in poverty levels. The three northern regions remain the poverty hotspots of the country. These three regions contributed a whopping 41.9 percent to the national poverty in 2005/2006. In extreme poverty terms, the three Northern regions contributed 59.1 percent to the extreme poverty levels observed in Ghana during 2005/2006. In 2012/2013, the percentage of Ghanaians regarded as poor reduced to 24.2 percent, out of which the three northern regions contributed 36.6 percent. However, the Volta region emerged as another growing poverty hotspot, contributing 12.1 percent to the national poverty level. In 2016/2017, poverty levels dropped marginally to 23.4 percent in Ghana. The three northern regions contributed 44.4 percent to the poverty levels, with the Volta region contributing 13.6 percent.

Whereas poverty levels are declining at the national level, regional disparities continue to magnify. The three northern regions and the Volta region have witnessed substantial deterioration in poverty levels over the years. These are regions with considerable rural settings, implying deplorable economic conditions for the rural folks. Indeed, poverty in rural Ghana, as shown in Table 2.6, has been high. The relatively better economic growth during the inflation targeting period has benefited the wealthiest and the urban dwellers more than the poor and the rural folks.

Meanwhile, the rural population in Ghana, until 2009, has been more than half of the national population, according to WDI data. In 2009, the

Table 2.6 Poverty at national and regional levels

	Percentage below the poverty line at GHS 1314 per annum			Percentage below the extreme poverty line at GHS 792.05 per annum		
Region	2005/2006	2012/2013	2016/2017	2005/2006	2012/2013	2016/2017
Upper West	89.1	70.7	70.9	76	45.1	45.2
Upper East	72.9	44.4	54.8	56.9	21.3	27.7
Northern	55.7	50.4	61.1	36.1	22.8	30.7
Brong Ahafo	34	27.9	26.8	13.7	6.6	8.7
Ashanti	24	14.8	11.6	9.8	2.9	1.6
Eastern	17.8	21.7	12.6	5.8	6	1.7
Volta	37.3	33.8	37.3	13.3	9	11.4
Greater Accra	13.5	5.6	2.5	5.2	1.5	0.0
Central	23.4	18.8	13.8	7.6	6.8	2.1
Western	22.9	20.9	21.1	6.8	5.5	2.3
Urban Ghana	12.4	10.6	7.8	5.1	1.9	1
Rural Ghana	43.7	37.9	39.5	23.4	15	15.6
National	31.9	24.2	23.4	16.5	8.4	8.2

Source: Ghana Statistical Service (GSS, 2018)

rural population in Ghana dropped to approximately half of the country's population (49.97 percent). However, as of 2018, the rural population stood at 43.94 percent of the total population, which is still substantial.

Conclusion and Policy Recommendations

The price stability objective continues to be the preoccupation of many central banks in Africa, including the Bank of Ghana. However, the extent to which that objective has been delivered remains an important question in the literature. Although the Bank of Ghana's monetary policy framework has evolved, price stability remains the common denominator. The question then is: have the dues been paid? We assess the price stability performance of the Bank of Ghana and other macroeconomic and welfare indicators since the Fourth Republic. We find that the inflation outcomes under the monetary targeting regime have been far from the price stability proposition. Indeed, not only was the intermediate target far from the eventual price stability objective, but the operating target and the intermediate target were equally far adrift.

On the other hand, the constant breaches of the publicly announced inflation targets severely blight the positives of relatively lower inflation outcomes for the inflation-targeting regime. The sheer frequency of such violations not only questions the nature of assessments that inform the determination of the targets, but it is also an indictment on the quality of forecasting that is supposed to inform policy stance. Indeed, the breaches endanger central bank credibility and ability to anchor inflation expectations which are at the core of the very foundation of the concept of inflation targeting. Price stability is undoubtedly noble, but an unrealistic target is counterintuitive and even more harmful. The inflation targeting regime witnessed a somewhat volatile output growth trajectory, characteristic of the hard nose monetary policy regime. The distribution of the benefits of growth is largely skewed towards the rich than the poor. The poverty levels are, thus, alarming, and the regional disparities are even more worrying. For employment and welfare, the inflation targeting regime was also better than the monetary targeting regime, although less stable in welfare measures in particular.

On the policy front, the Bank of Ghana and the fiscal authorities must reconsider the medium inflation target to safeguard the credibility of the former since the target is jointly determined. Although inflation has been brought within the targeted limits on some occasions, breaching the target has been a routine, endangering the foundation of the inflation-targeting framework. Moreover, over the inflation-targeting period, the average inflation rate speaks volumes of the level of prices that the country's economic fundamentals can support. Therefore, the forecasting framework of the Central Bank also requires a complete overhaul to one that provides reasonable accuracy to inform monetary policy stance.

References

Abango, M. A., Yusif, H., & Issifu, A. (2019). Monetary aggregates targeting, inflation targeting, and inflation stabilization in Ghana. *African Development Review, 31*(4), 448–461.

Addison, E. (2001). Monetary management in Ghana. In *International Conference on Monetary Policy Framework in Africa, 17–19 September 2001, Pretoria, South Africa*.

Adu, G., & Marbuah, G. (2011). Determinants of inflation in Ghana: An empirical investigation. *South African Journal of Economics, 79*(3), 251–269.

Alagidede, P., Simeon, C., & Adu, G. (2014). *A regional analysis of inflation dynamics in Ghana* (Working paper, International Growth Centre, pp. 1–32).

Anwar, S., & Islam, I. (2013). Should developing countries target low, single-digit inflation to promote growth and employment? In *Beyond macroeconomic stability* (pp. 98–130). Palgrave Macmillan.

Bank of Ghana. (n.d.). *Monetary policy framework*. https://www.bog.gov.gh/monetary-policy/our-monetary-policy-framework/. Accessed 11 Mar 2020.

Bawumia, M., Amoah, B., & Mumuni, Z. (2008). *Choice of monetary policy regime in Ghana* (Bank of Ghana working paper, WP/BOG-2008/07).

Dabalen, A., Gaddis, I., & Nguyen, N. T. V. (2016, March 21). Do changes in the CPI provide a reliable yardstick to measure changes in the cost of living? World Bank. Available at https://blogs.worldbank.org/africacan/do-changes-in-the-cpi-provide-a-reliable-yardstick-to-measure-changes-in-the-cost-of-living (2 July 2020).

Ghana Statistical Service. (2018). *Ghana living standards survey round 7: Poverty trends in Ghana 2005–2017*. Ghana Statistical Service.

Kyereboah-Coleman, A. (2012). Inflation targeting and inflation management in Ghana. *Journal of Financial Economic Policy, 4*(1), 25–40.

Marbuah, G. (2011). On the inflation-growth nexus: Testing for optimal inflation for Ghana. *Journal of Monetary and Economic Integration, 11*(2), 54–82.

Mishkin, F. S. (1996). *The channels of monetary transmission: Lessons for monetary policy* (NBER working paper series, working paper 5464).

Quartey, P., Owusu-Brown, B., & Turkson, F. E. (2017). Monetary policy and inflation management in Ghana: Inflation targeting and outcomes.

Macroeconomy and finance. In E. Aryeetey & R. Kanbur (Eds.), *The economy of Ghana sixty years after independence* (pp. 88–102). Oxford University Press.

UNDP. (2019). *Human development report 2019: Beyond income, beyond averages, beyond today: Inequalities in human development in the 21st century. Technical notes* (pp. 1–16). UNDP.

CHAPTER 3

Monetary Policy Impact on Macroeconomic Performance in Tanzania: Empirical Approach

Jehovaness Aikaeli

INTRODUCTION

The history of central banking in East Africa dates back to 1903, with the establishment of the East African Currency Board (EACB) by the British colonial government. Although few commercial banks have operated since the establishment of EACB, implementation of orthodox monetary policy was not done in the region and Tanzania in particular. The EACB functioned as a "money changer," i.e., only to ensure stable convertibility of East African shilling and British Pound Sterling. East African Currency Board did not implement most conventional instruments of monetary control, notably; open market operations (OMO), discount rate, and reserve requirement, among others (Kasekende & Atingi-Ego, 2008). The nationalist movements since the 1950s ostensibly provoked some artificial change in the monetary framework of the East African Currency

J. Aikaeli (✉)
School of Economics, University of Dar es Salaam, Dar es Salaam, Tanzania
e-mail: jaikaeli@udsm.ac.tz

© The Author(s), under exclusive license to Springer Nature Switzerland AG 2022
A. A. Amin et al. (eds.), *Monetary and Financial Systems in Africa*, https://doi.org/10.1007/978-3-030-96225-8_3

Board. The EACB began to lend to the governments in East Africa in 1955, which loosened the tight link between changes in money supply and the balance of payments outcomes in the region. After attaining political independence in the early1960s, the role of the EACB was irreconcilable with the development vigor of the post-colonial nationalistic governments in the region. The desire for the rapid economic development of the young post-colonial East African countries necessitated the establishment of better monetary authorities than EACB. Thus the EACB was replaced by the independent central banks concurrently established and operational in Tanzania, Uganda, and Kenya in 1966.

The charters of the three central banks were based on conventional central bank roles, such as applying the traditional indirect instruments of monetary policy to achieve price stability. Nevertheless, the operationalization of monetary policy changed in each country. In Tanzania, the *Ujamaa*[1] *Self-Reliance Policy* of the Arusha Declaration of 1967 required the country's central bank, namely the *Bank of Tanzania* (BoT), to regulate and promote economic growth. In this regard, the conduct of monetary policy drifted away from the indirect to direct instruments that included the setting of interest rate caps and exchange rates control, credit rationing to dictated credit allocations in favor of key designated financial institutions, and sectors of the economy.

The application of direct monetary policy instruments to achieve the typically conflicting multiple objectives of the central bank largely undermined the effectiveness and transmission of monetary policy (Ndung'u, 2008). The corrective actions to restore effective monetary policy were put in the economic reform programs, specifically, the liberalization of the financial sector from the mid-1980s. In Tanzania, the Banking and Financial Institution Act (1991) was, in particular, focused on the financial sector liberalization to end interest rates repressions and foreign exchange controls, among other things. In addition, the foreign exchange market was liberalized by the enactment of the Foreign Exchange Act (1992); and there was the initiative to establish and develop the Dar es Salaam Stock Exchange Market.

In areas of monetary policy, the country embarked on secondary financial reforms for the legal and regulatory framework of the banking system.

---

[1] Ujamaa means 'family hood in the Kiswahili language, and this concept formed the basis of Tanzania's social and economic development policies right after Arusha Declaration with socialist ideology.

Also, it enacted the Bank of Tanzania Act of 1995, which had major amendments to the Bank's Act of 1965 and declared attainment of "price stability" as the prime objective of monetary policy. In practice, drive to price stability rested on reserve money programming for which broad monetary aggregate has been used as the intermediate target of monetary policy, seemingly the open market operations and foreign exchange operations (FEO).[2] The other instruments that have been used are; change in reserve requirement, moral suasion, and gentlemen's agreements.

The transition of monetary policy regimes in Tanzania from direct to indirect policy instruments to achieve price stability has been challenging since the early 1990s. Growth rates of money supply remained higher than planned, and inflation was double digits throughout the 1990s (Chart 1). Before 2012 the East African Community (EAC) countries had set an inflation target of 5 percent. However, the inflation rate remained volatile in all EAC countries and above the target. Therefore, the inflation target was adjusted upward to 8 percent in 2012, which was generally achievable. For over two decades, from the mid-1970s to the late 1990s, Tanzania experienced double-digit inflation, and its GDP growth was mostly less than 5 percent and occasionally negative (Fig. 3.1).

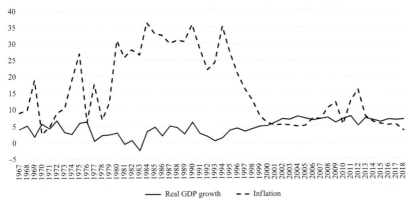

Fig. 3.1 Inflation and GDP growth rates, 1980–2019. (Source: Bank of Tanzania annual reports, 2017/18 & 2018/19)

[2] The Bank of Tanzania occasionally intervenes in the foreign exchange market to smooth excessive volatility in the exchange rate.

During the double-digit inflation period, the average growth rate of the money supply (M2) was 23 percent. Inflation has remained single digit in the country during the 2000s as the growth rate of the money supply declined to an average of 16.9 percent. Monetary policy was targeted to reduce inflation to a single-digit to enhance economic growth and development, and the growth objective seems to be obtained as inflation decreases.

Different policies can influence macroeconomic variables and their evolution results from several factors. Except empirical work is done, it is hard to tell precisely the specific influence of monetary policy on real variables in the economy. In Tanzania, real output, inflation, interest rates, trade variables, exchange rate, among others, have had patterns that can be associated with the implemented monetary policies; however, the extent to which their interaction with monetary policy affect the noticeable outcomes and policy transmission mechanisms should be ascertained. This chapter explicitly focuses on the empirical investigation of the impact of monetary policy shock on some key macroeconomic variables in Tanzania under the monetary programming framework that the country uses to make its monetary policy responses. The key question is whether the monetary policy shock on real variables leads to the theoretically expected outcomes. The second question is whether monetary policy is effective and through which mechanism its impact is transmitted to the real variables.

Monetary Policy Transmission to Real Variables: Insights from the Literature

The theory on monetary transmission mechanism (MTM) is characterized by four main strands of monetary policy transmission to inflation and real economic activity: (i) interest rates channel, which shares both Keynesian and Monetarist schools of thought (Taylor, 1995; Mishkin, 2007; Meltzer, 1995). The adequacy of the interest rate channel of monetary policy transmission is questionable. The monetary policy effect on interest rate is susceptible to external finance premium; that is, the spread between the cost of retained earnings and external finance is affected by the market imperfections. (ii) balance sheet channel, which is argued from the viewpoint of the effect of external finance premium on the cost of funds that affects the asset value and, therefore, the net worth of the potential borrowers. In turn, affecting creditworthiness and consequently investment and output;

(iii) credit or bank lending channel, it is argued that monetary policy influence on interest rate raises or reduces the cost of searching for non- bank alternative sources of loans. As a result of the increase or decrease in external finance premium, a change in the volume of loans and finally economic activity occurs; (iv) the exchange rate channel, this means in the flexible exchange rate, and some degree of price stickiness with perfect capital mobility in a small open economy, monetary policy actions on interest rate affect the net capital inflows through the influence on deposits denominated in domestic currency. The appreciation or the depreciation of the exchange rate causes changes in the net exports, exports-oriented investment, and finally, the output (Mangani, 2012).

There are empirical studies on the channels of the transmission mechanism of monetary policy in different countries. For example, in sub-Saharan Africa (SSA) countries, most studies have applied Recursive Vector Autoregressive (VAR) models using high-frequency data and varying order of lag structure. They test for Granger causality, impulse responses, and variance decomposition. The empirical results suggest that the effective monetary policy transmission channels are variable across the SSA countries. There are studies, for example, Al-Mashat and Billmeir (2007), which found the interest rate to be a weak channel of monetary transmission in Egypt.

Nevertheless, a study on Malawi by Mangani (2012) revealed that the exchange rate was the only effective channel of monetary policy impulses transmission to prices. The key message from the findings was that imported inflation was the main cause of demand pull-inflation, which made the exchange rate policy more relevant in controlling inflation in Malawi than conventional monetary policy. Except the country-specific studies are done, it is difficult to establish the effective channel of the monetary policy transmission mechanism for a specific country. Some studies have found interest rates to be the most effective channel of monetary policy transmission (Cheng, 2007). However, many other studies have found the interest rate channel ineffective; notably, Al-Mashat and Billmeir (2007) for Egypt and Kovanen (2011) for Ghana but prior to establishing an interest rate corridor in the country in 2005.

In the East Africa region, some studies have found the credit or bank lending as the most effective channel of monetary policy transmission. An example of such studies is Buigut's (2009) study in Kenya. In contrast, Nannyonjo (2001) found the credit channel to be ineffective in Uganda;

another study on Uganda by Mugume (2011) revealed that all the three (*interest rate, exchange rate, and credit*) channels of the monetary policy transmission were ineffective. Similarly, Montiel et al.'s (2012) study of financial architecture and the monetary transmission in Tanzania concluded that exchange rate and bank lending channels were weak. However, that monetary policy effect on the real output was neither statistically significant nor economically meaningful. The finding is sensitive for the country because it implies no rationale for monetary policy implementation in Tanzania. However, before making an implication that the country may not need to implement monetary policy at all, it needs to be rigorously reconfirmed.

For Tanzania in particular, some other available empirical evidence is inconclusive about the effective channels of the monetary policy transmission mechanisms. Minja and Magian (2009) utilized quarterly time series data for 1995–2007 to investigate the link between monetary policy and bank lending in Tanzania. The study concludes that Treasury bills had a fairly significant crowding-out effect on bank lending in both volume and yield. In addition, the findings show that the level of financial development was explained by development in banks competition that seemed to lower the lending rate, but a decline in inflation to a single-digit did not seem to play a significant role in the bank lending rate as it failed to make loans cheaper. Mbowe (2008) applied the VAR method to time series data and shows that positive shocks on reserve money and broad money accelerated inflation and output growth, while shocks to interest rates as indicated by the Treasury bill rate decelerated inflation as well as output.

Moreover, a study by Aikaeli (2007), which applied Generalized Auto Regression Conditional Heteroscedastic (GARCH), indicates that the current changes in the money supply would affect inflation significantly starting in the seventh month ahead, and the impact of money supply on inflation was not a sort of one time-strike on inflation but a persistent shock. Thus, both studies of Mbowe and Aikaeli show that there is policy transmission, but they do not establish the specific transmission mechanisms. Therefore, this empirical work seeks to bridge this gap, among other things.

Monetary Policy and Economic Performance in Tanzania

Methodology

The Bank of Tanzania (BOT) uses indirect monetary policy instruments to stabilize the price level and guide effective economic growth. The bank applies monetary programming framework to control reserve money, and the narrowly defined money supply (M1) is reckoned as the key target policy variable that reflects movements of the reserve money.

Macroeconomic variables are usually interdependent and interactive, which means their developments have joint dynamic behavior. Therefore, we use models that have been widely used in monetary policy analyses to underscore the policy impacts on the real variables. Among the most popular models used in analyses of the impact of monetary policy are the vector autoregressive (VAR) and structural vector autoregressive (SVAR) models. The structural vector error correction (SVEC) model has been used widely because SVAR studies have some weaknesses, such as being nonstationary and using short sample spans. These problems may generate unreliable results and economic puzzles. Thus, the SVEC model has emerged as a new analytic tool for analyzing the effects of macroeconomic shocks, notably the monetary policy effects on the economy, and this study adopts SVEC.

The SVEC model requires both contemporaneous and long-run restrictions (Faust & Leeper, 1997; Fung & Kasumovich, 1998). Therefore, using both short-run and long-run restrictions in SVEC is recommended to improve estimations. It is also possible to impose identification schemes on the cointegration matrix of a VECM. Jang and Ogaki (2004) noted that SVEC has some advantages over SVAR models since the SVEC estimators are more precise than the SVAR model. The advantages of SVEC are that:

(i) it allows the use of cointegration restrictions, and that is possible to impose long-run restrictions to identify shocks, which are attractive as they are more directly related to the macroeconomic model;
(ii) it allows incorporation of both the mixed I(1) and I(0) data and supports cointegrating relationships in the same modeling framework. This means that an SVEC model needs fewer restrictions than an SVAR model (Fisher & Huh, 2014; Pagan & Pesaran, 2008); and

(iii) restrictions about the economy's underlying structure can be imposed may provide a better fit to the data. Thus, it can investigate how the economy responds to monetary policy and other shocks.

Some studies have used VAR to analyses monetary policy responses in Tanzania (Mbowe, 2008; Mkai and Aikaeli 2020). It will be interesting to use the SVEC model to investigate monetary policy responses in Tanzania. Our objective is to run an SVEC model to produce key macroeconomic variables' practical and consistent impulse responses to monetary policy shocks. The reasonable restrictions based on economic theory will be imposed on the identification scheme in the short and long run.

We use the SVEC modeling approach to investigate the monetary transmission mechanism and mechanics of the economy under the monetary programming framework in Tanzania. The real and monetary variables included are; real GDP (Y), consumer price index (P), monetary policy variable.[3] (M0) which is high powered money whose effect on interest rate is anchored by the discount rates[4] (DR), real effective exchange rates (REER) and the trade balance (TB). Long data series of these variables available since the establishment of the BOT in 1966 to 2018, have been sourced from the Bank of Tanzania and the National Bureau of Statistics, are used in the analyses. The transmission of monetary policy actions from M0 to real output is illustrated in Fig. 3.2, which hypothesizes the impact of monetary policy from the domestic variables/factors and the exogenous shocks of oil price and food price that are key

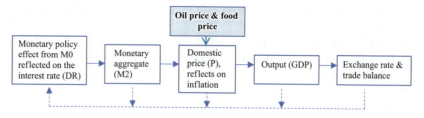

Fig. 3.2 Interactions between monetary variables and real output

[3] M0 is reserve money, which comprises currency in circulation outside the banking system, cash held in banks' vaults, and banks' deposits kept with the Bank of Tanzania in local currency.

[4] The Bank of Tanzania interest rate at which it lends to banks, and an anchor of interest rates in the economy.

to non- core inflation (inflation that includes food and energy prices) in the country.

Starting from the vector error correction VAR model, its basic form consists of a set of K endogenous variables,

$$y_y = A_1 y_{t-1} + \ldots + A_p y_{t-p} + u_t \qquad (3.1)$$

A_i is ($K \times K$) coefficient matrices of $i = 1, \ldots, p$ and UI is a K-dimension error process system with expected value $E(u_t) = 0$ and time-invariant positive definite covariance matrix $E\left(u_t u_t^T\right) = \Sigma_u$, which is white noise. Thus, a VAR system contains a set of m variables, each expressed as a linear function of p lags of itself and the other $m - 1$ variable, plus an error term, which can be comprehensively written as specified in Eq. (3.2).

$$y_t = \beta_{y0} + \beta_{yy1} y_{t-1} + \ldots + \beta_{yyp} y_{t-p} + \beta_{yx1} x_{t-1} + \ldots$$
$$+ \beta_{yxp} x_{t-p} + \ldots + \beta_{yz1} z_{t-1} + \ldots + \beta_{yzp} z_{t-p} + v_t^y$$
$$x_t = \beta_{x0} + \beta_{xy1} y_{t-1} + \ldots + \beta_{xyp} y_{t-p} + \beta_{xx1} x_{t-1} + \ldots$$
$$+ \beta_{xxp} x_{t-p} + \ldots + \beta_{xz1} z_{t-1} + \ldots + \beta_{xzp} z_{t-p} + v_t^x$$
$$z_t = \beta_{z0} + \beta_{zy1} y_{t-1} + \ldots + \beta_{zyp} y_{t-p} + \beta_{zx1} x_{t-1} + \ldots \qquad (3.2)$$
$$+ \beta_{zxp} x_{t-p} + \ldots + \beta_{zz1} z_{t-1} + \ldots + \beta_{zzp} z_{t-p} + v_t^z$$

This system has no variables that uniquely appear on the right-hand side, it crudely means regressors are weakly exogenous, and given time, if the variables are stationary, the ordinary least squares (OLS) can produce asymptotically desirable estimators. According to Pfaff (2008), the following vector error correction specifications do exist from the simple Eq. (3.1), which can be written as,

$$\Delta y_t = \alpha \beta^T y_{t-p} + \Gamma_1 \Delta y_{t-1} + \ldots + \Gamma_{p-1} y_{t-p+1} + u_t, \qquad (3.3)$$

with

$$\Gamma_i = -\left(I - A_1 - \ldots - A_i\right), \quad i = 1, \ldots, p-1, \qquad (3.4)$$

and

$$\Pi = \alpha\beta^T = -\left(I - A_1 - \ldots - A_p\right) \qquad (3.5)$$

The Γ_i matrices contain the cumulative long-run impacts; thus this VECM implies long-run form, while the other common specification is,

$$\Delta y_t = \propto \beta^T y_{t-1} + \Gamma_1 \Delta y_{t-1} + \ldots + \Gamma_{p-1} y_{t-p+1} + u_t \qquad (3.6)$$

with

$$\Gamma_i = -\left(A_{i+1} + \ldots + A_p\right), \quad i = 1,\ldots, p-1. \qquad (3.7)$$

Reviewing the VECM from Eq. (3.6), we can apply the logic of SVAR models to SVEC models, especially when the equivalent level-VAR of the VECM is applied. Nevertheless, the cointegration properties of the variables contain information that is not used for identifying restrictions on the structural shocks. Therefore, it is typical to use a contemporaneous matrix, B, and hence SVEC model for estimation can be written as,

$$\Delta y_t = \propto \beta^T y_{t-1} + \Gamma_1 \Delta y_{t-1} + \ldots + \Gamma_{p-1} y_{t-p+1} + B\varepsilon_t, \qquad (3.8)$$

Where $u_t = B\varepsilon_t$ and $\varepsilon_t \sim N(0, I_K)$. To harness this information, the Beveridge-Nelson moving average of variables y_t is,

$$y_t = \Xi \sum_{i=1}^{t} u_i + \sum_{j=0}^{\infty} u_i \Xi_j^* u_{t-j} + y_0^*, \qquad (3.9)$$

and is considered as consistent with the VECM represented by Eq. (3.6). The variables contained in y_t can be decomposed into a part integrated of I(1) and the other part integrated of I(0). The last term on the right-hand side of Eq. (3.9) refers to the *system's common trend*, and this term drives the system y_t. The middle term is integrated of I(0), and it is assumed that the infinite sum is bounded; that is, Ξ_j^* approaches zero as $j \to \infty$, whereas the initial value is y_0^*. For the SVEC modeling, the interest is on the common trends in which the long-run effects of shocks are captured. The matrix Ξ is of reduced rank $K - r$, whereby r is the count of stationary cointegration relationships. Thus, the matrix is defined as:

3 MONETARY POLICY IMPACT ON MACROECONOMIC PERFORMANCE... 73

$$\Xi = \beta_\perp \left[\alpha_\perp^T \left(I_K - \sum_{i=1}^{p-1} \Gamma_i \right) \beta_\perp \right]^{-1} \alpha_\perp^T. \qquad (3.10)$$

Since its reduced rank can only be $K - r$ and the common trends drive the system, knowing about the rank of Π, we can conclude that most r of the structural errors can have a transitory effect. Therefore, at most r columns of Ξ can be set to zero, and combining the Beveridge-Nelson decomposition with the relationship between the VECM error terms and the structural innovations, the common trends term is then $\Xi B \sum \varepsilon_t$, while the matrix ΞB captures the long-run effects of the structural innovations. The cointegration structure of the model makes $r(K - r)$ restrictions on the long-run matrix. The other restrictions are placed on either matrix, whereby at least $r(r - 1)/2$ should be imposed directly on the contemporaneous matrix B.

From the approach proposed in Pfaff (2008) and Ltkepohl (2005), our 6 variables locally just-identified SVEC require a total of $(n(n - 1)/2)$ restrictions, which are 15. Assuming 1 monetary policy transitory shock, there should be 5 restrictions $r(n - r)=5$ on the long-run matrix as the permanent shocks. The monetary policy variable influence is assumed to be transitory, and variable monetary adjustment is required for the cointegrating relationship to hold. If we assume that a cointegrating rank (r) is equal to 1, there is 1 transitory shock and 4 permanent shocks. The transitory shock is identified without the additional restrictions ($r(r-1)/2=0$). Nonetheless, the permanent shocks are identified and require at least (($n - r)(n - r - 1)/2$) = 10 further restrictions, which can be imposed on contemporaneous restrictions of matrix B.

The Bank of Tanzania sets the policy variable ($M0$) in response to the current price level (p) and two exogenous variables (oil and food prices). Changes in $M0$ affect the process of money creation through changes in interest rate anchored by the discount rate (dr) in this case of Tanzania. Further, is assumed that the reaction of real output (y) to changes in money supply comes with lags. The second variable in the rows of the matrix stands for the conventional money demand (m). Money demand responds contemporaneously to the monetary policy variable, price level (p), and real output (y). The third row of the matrix is for the price level, which is contemporaneously affected by the policy rate (dr) and m. The fourth row stands for the real output, which is contemporaneously influenced by the policy rate (dr), money (m), and price level (p). The fifth row of the matrix is for the real effective exchange rate ($reer$), which is contemporaneously affected by all variables save for the trade balance (tb). Finally, the last row represents the trade balance (tb) that is contemporaneously affected by all variables of this system.

Data and Empirical Results

Data Source and Definitions

The analyses use secondary data collected from the National Bureau of Statistics (*output and price/inflation*), Bank of Tanzania, and IMF International Financial Statistics (*monetary statistics*). In addition, long annual time series, 1966 to 2019, were collected for all variables.

Definition of the variables used in the estimation are as follows: The policy rate is determined by the Bank of Tanzania, and we take discount rate (dr) as its proxy since it is reflected from the Treasury bills and bonds rates weekly, and it also anchors the level of interest rate in the country. The monetary aggregate.

(m) is measured by the log of narrow monetary aggregate ($M2$), which does not include foreign exchange deposits. The price level (p) is measured by the log of consumer price index (2015=100). The real output.

(y) is measured by the log of Gross Domestic Product. The real effective exchange rate ($reer$) is measured by the log of the real effective exchange rate. Finally, the trade balance (tb) is measured as the logarithm of the ratio of exports to imports.

Empirical Results

The time-series properties of the data are tested, and we find that most of the variables have unit roots at their levels, and a few are stationary. In view of this, we resort to using the SVEC model, which allows incorporation of both the mixed I(1) and I(0) data and supports cointegrating relationships in the modeling framework. First, we do the lag-order selection, which is estimated, and the four information criteria; final prediction error (FPE), Akaike's information criterion (AIC), Schwarz's Bayesian information criterion (SBIC), and the Hannan and Quinn information criterion (HQIC) are produced, of which two of these; FPE and HQIC indicate 3 optimal lag length. Then, cointegration analysis is performed using the Johansen test, which produces the maximum eigenvalue and trace statistic that indicates three cointegrating relationships/vectors. With this result, we assume one cointegrating relationship (r = 1) in our estimation for simplicity and focus on the impulses from the respective policy rate to the response variables.

Long-Run Relationship
Pursuing price stability is the main goal of monetary policy. The long-run relationship in the cointegrating vector has an error correction term that is negative and significant at the 1 percent level. The restricted long-run SVEC results are in Table 3.1 indicates that the error correction terms – ec1 of consumer price index (CPI) convergence is significantly determined by all variables included in the model.

Impulse Response Functions
We have estimated the fully identified model, and the impulse responses of the key variables are reported. Our focus is on the impulse responses of the identified macroeconomic variables to the two monetary policy shocks in the country. The policy (discount) rate is used by the Bank of Tanzania to anchor interest rates in the economy and hence the money creation process, and eventually the price response. Though with lag, there should be a possibility to see price response to a shock on the policy rate, i.e., to assess the monetary policy effectiveness in the country (see Fig. 3.3). The figure has four columns; the first and second show responses of the policy variable/rate to the shocks in macroeconomic variables (that is likely from policy actions to address the challenges as they arise). The next two columns show the ultimate variable (price) responses to the impulse in the policy rate and other intermediate variables. This reflects on price/inflation as the single ultimate objective of the monetary policy.

Table 3.1 Long-run parameters identification by Johansen normalized restriction

Beta	Coef.	Std. Err.	z	P>z	[95% Conf. Interval]	
_ce1						
CPI	1	.	.	.	.	.
Discount rate	-0.5648875	0.2859664	-1.98	0.048	-1.125371	-0.0044037
Money supply	26.50105	6.402797	4.14	0.000	13.9518	39.05031
GDP	-196.3223	30.95636	-6.34	0.000	-256.9956	-135.6489
Real effective exchange rate	-31.46114	16.84192	-1.87	0.062	-64.4707	1.548425
Trade balance	38.23859	11.32824	3.38	0.001	16.03565	60.44153
_constant	1279.609	.	.	.	.	.

Source: Author estimation

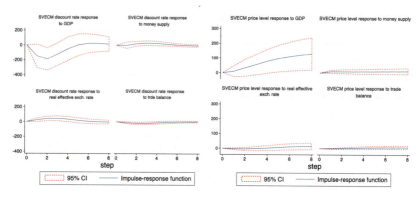

Fig. 3.3 Monetary policy impulse response functions from SVEC model

A rise in GDP initially leads to a fall in the discount rate, likely owing to expansionary policy decisions, and then reverts to the equilibrium from the fourth to sixth month. Depreciation in the real effective exchange rate is followed by some increase in policy rate mostly due to stabilization option of the monetary authority in pursuit of the smooth exchange rate. During the fifth and sixth months, the policy rate stabilizes. A slight increase follows an increase in money supply in the discount rate, which reverts to its stable trend in the next five to six months. This happens since the central bank is likely to reduce the money creation process when there is a rise in the money supply since it can lead to instability. As a result, the discount rate and trade balance are relatively stable.

The response of the ultimate monetary policy variable, price, rises with GDP. The theoretical point of price-incentive underpins this to output (non-zero optimal inflation). Once the price is triggered to the higher side, it is sticky downward, implying a big need for monetary policy to contain it from overstretching to the high side. Generally, there is some rise in price owing to expansionary monetary policy, but it dissipates right from the second month, and this casts doubt as to whether inflation is largely a monetary phenomenon in the country. The real effective exchange rate increase seems to have a smooth upward effect on the price level. This means slight export competitiveness arises from depreciation as this begins sometime later, after at least four months.

Forecast Error Variance Decomposition

Table 3.2 presents SVECM error variance decomposition results. The table has three parts; first are the responses of the policy rate to shocks in

Table 3.2 Forecast error variance decomposition of the policy variable and price level

Decomposed variance of discount rate responses to shocks in macroeconomic variables

Period	GDP shock	Money supply shock	Real effective exch. Change shock	Trade balance shock	Price level shock
0	0.000	0.000	0.000	0.000	0.000
1	0.000	0.000	0.000	0.000	0.000
2	0.029	0.007	0.027	0.032	0.000
3	0.055	0.056	0.085	0.087	0.002
4	0.056	0.109	0.127	0.113	0.003
5	0.052	0.138	0.145	0.132	0.004
6	0.051	0.148	0.149	0.133	0.005
7	0.051	0.148	0.148	0.131	0.011
8	0.050	0.146	0.145	0.129	0.024

Decomposed variance of money supply responses to shocks in macroeconomic variables

Period	GDP shock	Price level	Real effective exch. Change shock	Trade balance shock	Discount rate shock
0	0.000	0.000	0.000	0.000	0.000
1	0.000	0.000	0.000	0.000	0.119
2	0.030	0.005	0.029	0.062	0.123
3	0.026	0.018	0.084	0.047	0.093
4	0.038	0.035	0.101	0.041	0.065
5	0.051	0.061	0.109	0.036	0.049
6	0.065	0.093	0.107	0.029	0.041
7	0.077	0.132	0.099	0.025	0.037
8	0.086	0.173	0.091	0.022	0.038

Decomposed variance of price level responses to shocks in macroeconomic variables

Period	GDP shock	Money supply shock	Real effective exch. Change shock	Trade balance shock	Discount rate shock
0	0.000	0.000	0.000	0.000	0.000
1	0.000	0.000	0.000	0.000	0.071
2	0.000	0.003	0.007	0.000	0.094
3	0.007	0.004	0.008	0.002	0.117
4	0.020	0.008	0.006	0.012	0.131
5	0.014	0.177	0.005	0.026	0.134
6	0.064	0.034	0.007	0.039	0.131
7	0.088	0.054	0.133	0.051	0.125
8	0.109	0.073	0.025	0.060	0.119

macroeconomic variables, second are responses of the money supply to the policy rate and macroeconomic variables, and third is the responses of the ultimate objective variable (price/inflation) to the policy rate and macroeconomic variables. Generally, responses or impacts are observed during the medium and long-term periods.

Looking at the error variance decomposition for the policy rate, money supply and real effective exchange rate have relatively higher and more or less the same weight in terms of sources of variation in discount rate in the country, meaning that the policy rate responds mainly to developments in money supply and exchange rate. Next to exchange rate and money supply are GDP and price level; these two come as ultimate monetary policy targets.

The second panel of variance decomposition shows responses of the intermediate variable (money supply), of which the policy rate largely causes variations in the short run. However, the medium and long- term variations are mainly attributed to the real effective exchange rate and the price level. Therefore, it implies that the policy rate effectively affects the money supply. Eventually, exchange rate and price signals have an important bearing on the country's determination of the level of the money supply.

Regarding inflation anchored by the price index, its variations owe mainly to the policy rate implying that the discount rate anchor is critical to the money creation process and ultimately influences the price/inflation level. However, the impact of other variables on price is much lower than that of the policy rate and is passively observed in the long term.

CONCLUSION

This chapter sought to establish monetary policy's impact on macroeconomic performance in Tanzania, particularly through its influence on price stability. Structural vector error correction model is applied to Tanzania's data of 1966 to 2019. The results show that monetary policy in the country is effective in terms of its single objective of price stability since both the impulse responses and error variance decomposition reveal that most of the variations in the price level resulted from the policy rate. If price responds significantly to the monetary policy rate, inflation is a monetary phenomenon. Thus, the Bank of Tanzania has a role in influencing macroeconomic performance by setting and monitoring the execution of monetary policy in the country.

A key policy implication established from these findings is that monetary policy can be implemented through inflation targeting once the policy rate effectively alters the price level. The Bank of Tanzania currently does monetary targeting in its policy framework; however, in our estimations, variations in price level were less responsive to money supply than the policy rate. To ensure a more effective impact of monetary policy, it would be much better to do inflation targeting pursued by an appropriate policy rate.

REFERENCES

Aikaeli, J. (2007). Money and inflation dynamics: A lag between change in money supply and corresponding inflation response in Tanzania. *NBAA Journal.*
Al-Mashat, R., & Billmeir, A. (2007). *The monetary transmission mechanisms in Egypt.* IMF Working Paper, No. o7/285.
Buigut, S. (2009). *Monetary policy transmission mechanism: Implication for the proposed East African Community Monetary Union.* http://www.csae.ox.ac. uk/conferences/2009-edia/papers/300-buigut.pdf 4-01-2016
Cheng, K. C. (2007). *A VAR analysis of Kenya's monetary transmission mechanism: How Does the Central Bank REPO rate affect the economy?* IMF Working Paper, No. 06/300.
Faust, J., & Leeper, E. M. (1997). When do long-run identifying restrictions give reliable results? *Journal of Business and Economic Statistics.* https://doi.org/10.2307/1392338
Fisher, L. A., & Huh, H. S. (2014). Identification methods in vector-error correction models: Equivalence results. *Journal of Economic Surveys, 28*(1), 1–16.
Fung, B. S., & Kasumovich, M. (1998). Monetary shocks in the G-6 countries: Is there a puzzle? *Journal of Monetary Economics, 42*(3), 575–592.
Jang, K., & Ogaki, M. (2004). The effects of monetary policy shocks on exchange rates: Structural vector error correction model approach. *Journal of the Japanese and International Economies, 18*(1), 99–114.
Kasekende, L., & Atingi-Ego, M. (2008). Financial system and monetary policy in Uganda. In M. Nkube (Ed.), *Financial system and monetary policy in Africa.* African Economic Research Consortium, Mills Litho.
Kovanen, A. (2011). *Monetary policy transmission in Ghana: Does interest rate channel work?* IMF Working Paper, WP/11/275.
Ltkepohl, H. (2005). *New introduction to multiple time series analysis.* Springer.
Mangani, R. (2012). *The Effect of Monetary Policy on Price in Malawi.* African Economic Research Consortium (AERC) Research Paper, No. 252.

Mbowe, W. (2008). *Monetary policy implementation and its effect on inflation: An empirical investigation on Tanzania*, PhD thesis, University of Dar Es Salaam, Tanzania, Unpublished.

Meltzer, A. H. (1995). Monetary, credit and (other) transmission processes: A monetarist perspective. *Journal of Economic Perspectives, 9*(4), 49–72.

Minja, E. J., & Magian, N. G. (2009). An assessment of the bank lending channel of monetary policy transmission in Tanzania. *Tanzania Economic Trend, 20*(2), 101–117.

Mishkin, F. (2007). *The economics of money, banking and financial markets*. Creg Tobin.

Mkai, H. A., & Aikaeli, J. (2020). Monetary policy transmission mechanism in East Africa: A comparative study of Tanzania, Kenya and Uganda. *Tanzanian Economic Review, 10*(1).

Montiel, P., Adam, C., Mbowe, W., & O'Connel, S. (2012). *Financial architecture and the monetary policy transmission mechanisms in Tanzania*. CSAE Working Paper, WPS/2012-03.

Mugume, A. (2011). *Monetary transmission mechanism in Uganda*. Bank of Uganda Working Paper, No. 01/2011.

Nannyonjo, J. (2001). *Monetary policy and credit under market imperfections*. Ph.D. thesis, University of Gothenburg, Gothenburg.

Ndung'u, N. S. (2008). Financial system and monetary policy in Kenya. In M. Nkube (Ed.), *Financial system and monetary policy in Africa*. African Economic Research Consortium, Mills Litho.

Pagan, A. R., & Pesaran, M. H. (2008). Econometric analysis of structural systems with permanent and transitory shocks. *Journal of Economic Dynamics and Control, 32*(10), 3376–3395.

Pfaff, B. (2008). VAR, SVAR and SVEC models: Implementation within R package vars. *Journal of Statistical Software, 27*(4), 1–32.

Taylor, J. B. (1995). The monetary transmission mechanisms: An empirical framework. *Journal of Economic Perspectives, 9*(4), 11–26.

CHAPTER 4

Effects of Monetary Policy Transmission on Economic Growth in Sierra Leone

Elkanah Faux

INTRODUCTION

Like several countries once colonized by European powers, Sierra Leone became a traditional source of unprocessed raw materials and consumers of manufactured imports. Since gaining independence in the 1960s, Sierra Leone has neither freed itself from its colonial heritage nor evolved into a vibrant modern economy that leverages technological innovation. Investment in human capital has been low and is accompanied by corruption and episodic intermittent warfare over natural resources curse (Jackson, 2016; Krishnankutty, 2011). The horrendous political and economic deterioration spectacle has portended unsavory prospects for the macro-economy. In the steady-state of an agricultural economy and bourgeoning political democracy, belatedly encouraged by external intervention, the economy can best be characterized as a small open economy that cannot successfully withstand overpowering external global shocks. Accordingly, the external economic circumstances generate

E. Faux (✉)
Bowie State University, Bowie, MD, USA
e-mail: efaux@bowiestate.edu

macroeconomic consequences that challenge routine (conventional) macroeconomic policies designed to attain stabilization objectives.

In Sierra Leone, the primary macroeconomic policy tools available to achieve sustained growth, price stability, and increased employment are fiscal and monetary policies. (Tarawalie & Kargbo, 2020 concluded that monetary policy is more effective than fiscal policy in promoting economic growth in Sierra Leone. In Sierra Leone, the monetary policy ensures adequate growth rates of selected monetary aggregates.

In Sierra Leone, Monetary policy is conducted within an operational target to link the Central Bank's ultimate policy goals and operating target on reserve money used for day-to-day policy operations. Targets on reserve money are set quarterly by the guidelines of the international monetary Fund- supported and monitored programs, consistent with program targets on inflation and economic growth. With an expansionary monetary policy, M1 ("narrow money") increased from 20.6% to 41.37% between 1976 and 1979 and 1980 and 1985, respectively (Numerates LTD, Bank of Sierra Leone). M2 (broad money) increased from 23.7% to 35.3% between 1976–1979 and 1980–1985. It also decreased from 24.0% to 19.60% between 2001 and 2009 and between 2011 and 2014 (Numerates LTD, Bank of Sierra Leone).

Before the 2008–2009 global economic crisis, the economy was relatively stable, with GDP growth rates stabilizing at around 4% and even doubling in 2007 (Table 4.1). A steep decline followed this in 2008, which continued until 2009 because of the slowdown in the world economy. The government's expansionary policy, evidenced by the growth in M2, led to some significant improvements that continued till 2013. Then in 2014, the Ebola crisis hit, which devastated the economy. There were some uneven improvements between 2016 and 2019, only to have the net gains reversed with the COVID-19 crisis in 2020.

In Fig. 4.1, M2 as a percentage of real GDP has been relatively stable for the most part. In addition, credit to the private sector has also been the most durable and consistent monetary policy variable even when the economy is experiencing significant downturns. The sharp decline in real output growth in 2015 and 2020 is due to the Ebola that affected all fabric of life, including the Sierra Leonean economy and the outbreak of the COVID-19 pandemic that is ravaging economies, especially vulnerable ones like that of Sierra Leone. However, one of the main transmission mechanisms (monetary sector credit to the private sector) has been stable but hardly attained 10% of GDP in the last decade.

Table 4.1 Monetary aggregates in Sierra Leone

Year	MSCPS (% GDP)	M2%	Broad money (% of GDP)	GDP growth %
2005	3.345696	31.14543	14.86024	4.505096
2006	3.383748	21.66055	15.44246	4.223914
2007	4.327044	17.10933	15.67091	8.058145
2008	5.574822	26.539	17.10477	5.398285
2009	8.224497	34.52963	20.68999	3.188051
2010	7.823819	24.15489	20.80949	5.346466
2011	7.666651	29.62799	21.61688	6.315045
2012	6.219049	21.98469	20.43324	15.18177
2013	4.769306	10.67632	17.52056	20.71577
2014	4.889161	23.91545	20.39788	4.556772
2015	5.386254	11.75665	24.15339	−20.5988
2016	5.824829	17.8619	26.37392	6.055474
2017	5.144321	6.990975	23.74734	4.19261
2018	5.695147	14.45112	23.03852	3.464602
2019	6.176436	14.30926	23.23119	5.254241
2020	5.959022	38.17994	29.52301	−1.96895

Source: World Development Indicators 2021

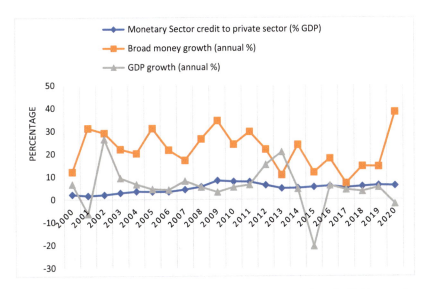

Fig. 4.1 Relationship between monetary aggregates and real GDP growth. (Source: Created by author from World Development Indicators, 2021)

In 2006, a joint mission team of the IMF and World Bank team undertook an extensive analysis of the financial sector in Sierra Leone under the Financial Sector Assessment Program (FSAP). The review identified several weaknesses in the financial system, including institutional, administrative, legal, and physical impediments. As a result, the Sierra Leone authorities developed and implemented the Financial Sector Development Plan (FSDP) to address these weaknesses and reform the financial sector, based on the recommendations from the FSAP.

As a result, these reforms led to consider institutional reforms, which amongst other things, included the promulgation of new laws and regulations to regulate the financial sector and oversee the reorganization, and restructuring, including privatization of commercial banks. As a result, these reforms in the financial sector have engendered substantial growth, with total assets increasing to Le 10.7 trillion in December 2018 compared to Le 5.9 trillion as of December 31, 2014, leading to a growth rate of about 80% between 2015 and 2018 (Bank of Sierra Leone, 2018).

Notwithstanding these significant growths, the financial system remains shallow when measured in assets as a percentage of gross domestic product and an array of instruments available, albeit limited, in the financial markets. Commercial banks continue to hold sway over the financial system in Sierra Leone, with total assets amounting to Le8.5 trillion, which is about 80 percent of the total assets of the financial system. Next is the state-run National Social Security and Insurance Trust (NASSIT), about 17 percent. Other Financial Institutions, including discount houses, financial services association (FSAs), and Apex bank) account for about 3 percent and community banks for less than 1 percent (Bank of Sierra Leone, 2018).

This depiction of the financial sector indicates the likelihood of banks dominating the funding sources for the private sector, thereby strengthening the case for the bank lending channel. Furthermore, the banking industry in Sierra Leone remains relatively concentrated, with big banks dominating assets and deposits in the Industry (Bank of Sierra Leone, 2018). This, depending on the type of banks, has implications for competitiveness in the industry as the banks with a high asset value share may be less sensitive to monetary policy shocks than the small banks that highly depend on borrowing from the central bank. Under this scenario, small businesses will be disadvantaged, and the banking system will not adequately respond to their needs.

The big banks would prefer to make larger loans to businesses and earn more in interest (Bank of Sierra Leone, 2018). That means, from an operational perspective, a more prominent is less inclined to make smaller loans that benefit small businesses compared to smaller banks. Given that banks dominate the financial sector in Sierra Leone, the role of banks in the propagation of monetary policy shocks merits more profound research. Therefore, this paper seeks to address questions about the integrity and strength of the bank lending channel as a tool of monetary policy transmission in Sierra Leone.

Following this introduction, the paper will look at the theoretical foundations of transmission mechanisms as monetary policy tools and some empirical evidence from Sierra Leone to present its financial sector and monetary policy framework to better understand and analyze the monetary policy transmission in Sierra Leone. Section "Methodology" describes the methodology and data used in this paper. Section "Regression Results" discusses the empirical results. The conclusions, along with some and policy implications, are presented in section "Conclusion and Recommendations".

Review of Previous Studies

There is a consensus among academics and policy makers about the important contribution of monetary policy to economic stability and growth, but less agreement on how precisely monetary policy exerts its influence on the economy. The literature review shows various channels through which monetary policy actions are transmitted to output and inflation in the economy. Figure 4.1 depicts an eclectic view of monetary policy transmission schematically, identifying the major channels that have been distinguished in the literature and which have been fashioned after Mishkin (1995).

The channels are mainly through asset price, interest rate, exchange rate, credit, and expectations. In most conventional macroeconomic models, the interest rate channel is the primary mechanism in the process. With some price rigidities, increases in interest rates could trigger increases in real interest rates and the user cost of capital, which would invariably lead to a reduction in consumption and investment expenditures (Bernanke & Gertler, 1990). The linkage between interest rates and asset prices, whereby interest-rate reductions occasioned policy changes, causes a reduction in the value of long-lived financial assets (stocks, bonds), and invariably a reduction in household resources and hence a reduction in consumption. The interest rate channel might be restrictive in the context of Sierra Leone because of the underdeveloped nature of its financial markets.

Most authors agree that the exchange rate channel affects economic growth, save for a few who concluded that the exchange rate channel does significantly affect economic growth. Most of the literature on credit channels indicates that an increase in credit is directly related to an increase in economic growth. However, there are those who argue against a linear relationship between credit and economic growth. Krishnakutty (2011) for example, states that because of default in payments and lack of monitoring by authorities, credit does not impact economic growth in a positive way.

With respect to the interest rate channel, most studies indicate that no significant relationship exists between investment expenditure and the market interest rate, thus suggesting the existence of impediments of monetary policy on economic growth via the interest rate channel. On the asset price channel, the literature indicates that the existence of this channel is mixed in various countries. While it reveals that different policy instruments affect output and inflation, most contradict expectations derived from theory. There is no consensus on why some monetary policy actions do not affect economic growth through some channels.

However, a consensus in the literature supports the view that a change in monetary policy stance somehow translates into aggregate demand growth, leading to a rise in output; since the monetary expansion induces more lavish spending on goods and services (Mankiw, 2019). However, the internal process of this transformation is a bit complex. Therefore, it has led economists to search out specific channels of monetary policy mechanism that explain how the process works in stimulating growth in real GDP (aggregate demand, and therefore real output).

Some studies have analyzed the importance of monetary policy by employing the VAR model. Azali and Matthews (1999) emphasized the importance of money as an essential determinant of output during the post-liberalization period. Fung (2002) concluded that almost all impulse responses to interest rate shocks were insignificant post-crisis. Furthermore, some "logical impossibilities" found in the VAR analysis (such as output problems), which reduced the accuracy of the results. Meanwhile, Cheng, 2006 found that a contractionary monetary policy led to an initial increase in output which eventually fell. In a study of monetary policy in Pakistan, Akhtar (2006) suggested that monetary policy concluded that the monetary policy of Pakistan promoted price stability and economic growth.

How policy achieves its goal here is intuitively linked to how it targets monetary aggregates, including growth in broad money supply as an intermediate target and reserve money as an operational target following real GDP growth and inflation targets set by the government. Kuttner and Mosser (2002) indicated that monetary policy affects the economy through several transmission mechanisms, including the interest rate channel, the exchange rate channel, Tobin's q theory, the wealth effect, the monetarist channel, and the credit channels, including the bank lending channel and the balance-sheet channel.

Evidence from Sierra Leone

Tarawalie and Kargbo, 2020, show that money supply, real exchange rate, and inflation are the significant variables that influence economic growth in Sierra Leone in the long run. The results show a positive relationship between money supply and economic growth. In addition, the result shows a direct relationship between money supply and economic growth. The results suggest, in the long run a one percentage increase in the money supply will lead to a 2.001% increase in real GDP. This is however inconsistent with the findings of Goher Fatima et al. (2011), Okorie et al. (2017), Adegoriola (2018).

The results also reveal that the real exchange rate and inflation have adverse effects on real GDP. Thus, real exchange rate improvements cause decreases in real GDP growth. As for example, a 1% appreciation of the real exchange rate will decrease real GDP growth by 1.48%. These results are typical for an import-driven economy like Sierra Leone, with inelastic demand for imports and exports.

Furthermore, high rates of inflation thwart real GDP growth in the long run, a finding that is consistent with inflation-prone economies, like Sierra Leone.

Other studies have examined the importance of different monetary policy transmission channels in Sierra Leone, including smaller banks (Tucker, 2005; Kadima, 2008; Olawale Ogunkula & Tarawalie, 2008; Lavally & Nyambe, 2019). They have utilized aggregated data within the vector autoregression framework. To date, there is little evidence of studies investigating the transmission mechanism of monetary policy in Sierra Leone using secondary data from the central bank of Sierra Leone using bank-level data. Against this backdrop, this study will fill the knowledge gap by investigating the effectiveness of each of the variables. It is unquestionable that these channels are not mutually exclusive and that an economy's response to monetary policy actions will incorporate the impact of a combination of them.

To determine the potency of transmission mechanisms of monetary policy in Sierra Leone, as in most developing countries where stock exchange rates are not fully established or non-existent, interest rate, exchange rate, and credit are the main channels. (Lavally & Nyambe, 2019) made use of the following variables: consumer price index (CPI), real interest rate (RIR), the exchange rate (ER), private domestic credit (PDC),, gross capital formation (GCF), and gross domestic product per capita (GDPPC) to assess the transmission mechanism in Sierra Leone and concluded that, even though the results show that the channels are ineffective, Private domestic credit (PDC) which represents the credit channel can transmit the biggest shocks to output as compared to the interest rate and exchange rate channels despite its transmission being insignificant.

In general, changes in the structure of the economy tend to alter the effects of a given monetary policy measure, thus requiring central banks to continuously reinterpret monetary transmission channels, the mechanism via which monetary expansion induces more lavish spending on goods and services (Kamin et al., 1998). The effectiveness of a monetary policy transmission channel depends on whether the economy would achieve macroeconomic stability as set by the central bank. For large developed economies, interest rates play a leading role. In order to identify the most effective channel(s) in Sierra Leone, it is necessary to determine the policy instruments, the timing of policy changes, and the central bank's restrictions.

For the interest rate channel to work effectively and efficiently, changes in the short-term policy rate should feed into the economy's bank and other market rates. The critical issue in Sierra Leone is how monetary transmission operates through credit to the private sector, interest rate and real exchange rates to the economy. The exchange rate channel depends on arbitrage between long-term bonds on the one hand and equities and tangible assets, affecting stock market values and real estate prices.

These impact household wealth and consumer spending, which are essential components of the asset channel.

The real exchange rate is affected by arbitrage between assets denominated in domestic and foreign currencies, which alters consumption and investment spending between domestic and foreign goods. Wang (2018) argued in a survey paper that reviewed the theoretical development of monetary policy transmission mechanism that monetary policy adjustment cannot be effective only through one channel but through many channels at the same time on the overall economy. Sourcing data from the IMF Excel Database and various publications of the World Bank regarding monetary aggregates and real GDP, we postulated a relationship between Real GDP and the monetary aggregates to investigate the transmission channels of monetary policy in Sierra Leone.

Methodology

A simple model relating real gross domestic product to domestic credit to the private sector (CRDT), inflation (INF), the real exchange rate (REER), and interest rate (INTR) on the real gross domestic product (RGDP) can be specified as:

$$RGDP = f(CRDT, INF, REER, INTR) \quad (4.1)$$

Where RGDP is the dependent variable that measures the state of the economy, INF is the inflation rate, REER is the real exchange rate, and INTR is the inflation rate. The function represented in (1), which also shows a monetary transmission mechanism from especially credit to the private sector and monetary policy tools, can be written as an estimable log-log transformation as follows:

$$\ln RGDP_t = \beta_0 + \beta_1 \ln CRDT_t + \beta_2 \ln INF_t + \beta_3 \ln REER_t + \beta_4 \ln INTR_t \in +_t \quad (4.2)$$

RGDP is the real gross domestic product, CREDIT is private domestic credit representing the credit channel that can transmit the biggest shocks to output, INF is the inflation rate, REER is the real exchange rate, and INTR is the real exchange rate interest rate, and ϵ is the random error. The log-log transformation captures the elasticities while correcting any skewness in the data. The estimation of Eq. (4.2) requires that the series are stationary. However, most macroeconomic data are non- stationary, and OLS estimations using non-stationary data would lead to spurious estimates. Thus, the Augmented Dickey-Fuller (ADF) test was conducted to test for the presence of unit roots in data. The results of the ADF estimates are presented below in Table 4.2.

Table 4.2 ADF unit test results

Variable	Intercept		Intercepts & Trends	
	Level	First difference	Level	First difference
RGDP	0.3268	-5.6662**	-1.1064	-5.9740*
CREDIT	-2.0866	-7.0409*	-2.2784	-7.2730*
INF	-2.6578	-8.3542*	-3.3209	-8.2367*
REER	-1.4242	-4.8720**	-1.5864	-4.8536*
INTRATE	-2.5956	-2.1466	-5.3446*	-2.3750

*,**represents significant at 1% and 5% respectively

The results show that all variables except interest rate are stationary after the first difference and are likely to have a long-run relationship. The FMOLS has an advantage over OLS. It provides optimal estimates of cointegrating regression by modifying ordinary least squares to account for serial correlation effects and the endogeneity problem in the regressors resulting from a cointegrating relationship (Phillips & Hansen, 1990).

REGRESSION RESULTS

Table 4.3 reports the estimated results from the FMOLS regression. The results reveal a significant positive effect of private domestic credit on the real gross domestic product, implying that a 1% increase in credit by the monetary sector to the private sector will result in a 0.66% increase in RGDP. The results also reveal that both the real exchange rate and inflation with estimated coefficients of -0.034 and -0.893 respectively have adverse effects on real GDP and will cause the latter to fall by 0.034% and 0.893%. Consequently, if the real exchange rate appreciates, real GDP would decrease. This finding is typical for a small developing economy like Sierra Leone, which manages its currency, conducts an independent monetary policy, and frequently uses seigniorage to increase the money supply. As is typically the case in inflation-prone economies, real GDP growth will slow down in the long run. Curiously, interest rates have the expected negative sign but do not significantly affect real GDP in Sierra Leone.

R-squared adjusted shows that the regressors explain about 48% of the variability in the real GDP. The Hansen test is significant and shows that the variables included in the estimation have a long-run cointegrating

Table 4.3 Relationship between RGDP and monetary aggregates, 1981–2019

Variable	Coefficient	Std. Error	t-Statistic	Prob.
lnCREDIT	0.6627	0.1589	4.1707	0.0002
lnINF	−0.0340	0.0574	−05922	0.5576
lnREER	−0.8933	0.3978	−2.2457	0.0313
lnINRATE	−0.4080	0.6285	−0.6491	0.5206
Constant	30.9690	1.5812	19.5857	0.0000
R-squared=0.5363		Adjusted R squared=0.4818		
Cointegration Test-Hansen Parameter Instability		Lc statistic = 0.4610 (Prob >0.2)		

relationship. Thus, discipline in the conduct of monetary policy will likely lead to better economic performance.

Conclusion and Recommendations

In investigating the effectiveness of monetary transmission mechanism in Sierra Leone, the study examined credit to the private sector, the real exchange rate, inflation, and interest rates channels suitable to Sierra Leone. The FOMLS model was used, and the analysis of the results reveal the importance of the credit channel in capturing the dual effects that changes in the supply of banking system reserves exert on aggregate demand. This is done via changes in the terms on which bank customers access loans via the bank lending channel and through changes in the external finance premium. **However, the financial system of Sierra Leone continues to be inefficient and shallow and is dominated by commercial banks in terms of assets.**

Financial markets are in their infancy and Inter-bank market activity is minimal. To increase interbank market activities, the central bank should promote interbank activity. The size of the financial sector relative to the country's GDP is small and so limits the central bank's ability to influence aggregate demand. In this regard, the BSL should address the structural challenges of monetary policy and require sequenced institutional and operational reforms, and this should be done through effective communication and implementation strategy. The BSL should develop a transparent monetary policy that allows for comprehensive assessments of the transmission mechanism. The policy should affect critical economic variables. The BSL should make the economic environment more predictable for effective monetary policy by enhancing its communication strategy, particularly concerning discussing and explaining adjustments to forecast and targets.

The BSL should also strengthen the exchange rate targeting framework by setting limits for exchange rate fluctuations. However, the combined effect of money supply and bank lending channels must be considered while crafting policy, and such policy should allow for better bank supervision by the BSL. The outcome should culminate in enhancing fiscal-monetary-led economic growth, job creation, and low inflation. Also, efforts must be made towards achieving financial sector development and deepening, improving currency management by way of optimal monetary aggregate growth consistent with economic growth. These policy considerations will go a long way in strengthening the transmission channels in Sierra Leone.

References

Adegoriola, A. E. (2018). An empirical analysis of effectiveness of monetary and fiscal policy instruments in stabilizing economy: Evidence from Nigeria. *Social Sciences, 7*(3), 133–140.

Akhtar, S. (2006). Perspectives on Pakistan's Monetary Policy Developments, at the Woodrow Wilson Center, Washington, DC. Address as Chief Guest at the Woodrow Wilson Centre, Washington DC, USA on April 24, 2006.

Azali, M., & Matthews, K. G. P. (1999). Money-income and credit-income relationships during the pre- and the post-liberalization periods: Evidence from Malaysia. *Applied Economics, 31*(10), 1161–1170.

Bank of Sierra Leone, Financial Stability Report 2018.

Bernanke, B., & Gertler, M. (1990). "Financial fragility and economic performance." *The Quarterly Journal of Economics, 105*(1), 87–114.

Cheng, C. K. (2006). *Var analysis of Kenya's monetary policy transmission mechanism: How does the Central Bank's repo rate affect the economy?* International Monetary Fund Working paper 06/300.

Fatima, G., Ahmed, A. M., & Rehman, W. U. (2011). Foreign aid and recipient government behavior in Nicaragua. *International Journal of Trade, Economics and Finance, 2*(6), 501–504.

Fung, B. S. C. (2002). *A VAR analysis of the effects of monetary policy in East Asia.* BISS Working Paper No. 119.

Jackson, E.A. (2016). Phronesis and Resource Curse hypothesis in Post-independent Sierra Leone. Ilorin Journal of Economic Policy. Vol. 3: 1–11

James, Y. M. (2014). *Debt overhang and natural resources: Revisiting the resources curse hypothesis.* Unpublished Ph.D., Birkbeck College, University of London.

Kadima, K. (2008). *The monetary transmission mechanism in Sierra Leone.* IMF, Sierra Leone Selected Issues.

Kamin S. B, Turner, P., & Van 't Dack, J. (1998). *The transmission of monetary policy in emerging market economies: An overview.* Bank for International Settlements Policy Paper, (3).

Krishnankutty, R. (2011). Role of banks credit in economic growth: A study with special reference to North-East India. *The Economic Research Guardian, 1*(2), 60–71.

Kuttner & Mosser. (2002). The monetary transmission mechanism: Some answers & further questions, Federal Reserve Bank of New York. *Economic Policy Review,* 15–26.

Lavally, M., & Nyambe, J. M. (2019). The effectiveness of transmission mechanisms of monetary policy in Sierra Leone. *Journal of Economics Management and Trade, 23,* 1–13.

Mankiw, N. G. (2019). *Macroeconomics* (10th ed.). Worth Publishers.

Mishkin, F. S. (1995). Symposium on the monetary transmission mechanism. *Journal of Economic Perspectives, 9*(4 Fall), 3–10.

Okorie, D. I., Sylvester, M. A., & Simon-Peter, D.-A. C. (2017). Relative effectiveness of fiscal and monetary policies in Nigeria. *Asian Journal of Social Science Studies, 2*(1).

Olawale Ogunkula, E., & Tarawalie, A. B. (2008). Monetary policy transmission mechanism in Sierra Leone: A Vector Error Correction (VEC) approach. *Journal of Political Economy,* 207–237.

Phillips, P. C. B., & Hansen, B. (1990). Statistical inference in instrumental variables regression with I(1) processes. *The Review of Economic Studies, 57,* 99–125.

Tarawalie and Kargbo. (2020). Efficacy of fiscal and monetary policy in Sierra Leone: An Ardl bound testing approach. *International Journal of Economics and Financial Issues, 10*(3).

Tucker. (2005). An analysis of the channels of monetary policy transmission in Sierra Leone: A vector auto regression approach. *West African Journal of Monetary and Economic Integration, 5,* 227–256.

Wang, O. (2018). *Banks, low interest rates, and monetary policy transmission.* NYU Stern School of Business, presented at the 1st International Conference on Economic Management and Green Development (ICEMGD), 2018, July 30th, Beijing, China.

PART III

Regional Financial Sector Issues

CHAPTER 5

The Monetary Union and Economic Integration: Challenges of the Creation of the West African Single Currency, Eco

Mohamed Ben Omar Ndiaye

INTRODUCTION

Since the creation of the Economic Community of West African States (ECOWAS) in 1975, the main objective pursued by the union has been to strengthen cooperation between its member States, to create an economic and monetary union that can help raise the standard of living of its population through increased development of trade and integration into global value chains. To achieve these ambitious objectives, concrete actions have been initiated, including harmonizing monetary, financial, and commercial policies. In this regard, it is important to stress that a consensus is beginning to emerge on the virtues of regional monetary integration, which is now considered an effective buffer against the possible systemic effects of financial globalization. This means that, in the case of ECOWAS, effective monetary integration, is an unconditional requirement that

M. B. O. Ndiaye (✉)
Institut des Politiques Publiques, Universite Cheikh Anta Diop, Dakar, Senegal
e-mail: mohamedbenomar.ndiaye@ucad.edu.sn

© The Author(s), under exclusive license to Springer Nature Switzerland AG 2022
A. A. Amin et al. (eds.), *Monetary and Financial Systems in Africa*, https://doi.org/10.1007/978-3-030-96225-8_5

would likely promote an acceleration of the process of integration of the economies of member countries.

Since then, ECOWAS has encountered difficulties in achieving economic integration, and especially monetary integration, despite the adoption over thirty years ago of the ECOWAS Monetary Cooperation Program (EMCP), and despite a desire to speed the creation of the single currency, regularly renewed by the political leaders of the region. As a result, the economic situation and, by extension, the profile of ECOWAS convergence are also very mixed.

Although good performance has been recorded for specific macroeconomic indicators, particularly certain economic convergence criteria, disparities seem to persist between the different economies of the member states. The delay in creating the ECOWAS Monetary Union is mainly linked to the fact that the leaders of the region were keen to ensure that all the economic and financial conditions were met before the launch of the single currency to guarantee the viability and stability of the future currency.

The renewed desire of the Heads of State and Government of the ECOWAS to make the single currency project a reality in 2020 has also led to an evolution of the agreement between France and the WAEMU countries; while the ECOWAS countries had already endorsed the decision to create a single currency that would operate under a flexible exchange rate regime and a monetary policy framework based on inflation targeting.

The launch of the single currency of ECOWAS was thus postponed several times (2003, 2005, 2009, 2015, and 2020) for several reasons, mainly the insufficient level of preparation and economic convergence between the member states. There is also the issue of convergence criteria not met by a large number of ECOWAS countries, the pooling of foreign exchange reserves, the future headquarters of the Central [federal] Bank of West Africa (CBWA), necessary administrative and information technology procedures related to a change of currency and the production of coins and banknotes, the economic impact of the Covid-19 health crisis. As a result, the convergence criteria have been temporarily suspended, the foreign exchange reserves of central banks have been severely tested, and several questions still need to be resolved before the practical implementation of the single currency within the ECOWAS countries.

The rest of the chapter discusses the current economic situation of ECOWAS, presents a summary of the evolution of the EMCP, presents the overall situation and performance in the economic policy harmonization and macroeconomic convergence in the ECOWAS zone, discusses the cost-benefit analysis of participating in a monetary union, and concludes with suggestions for reforms and economic policies.

RECENT ECONOMIC SITUATION OF ECOWAS

This section analyzes the current economic conditions in ECOWAS and gives some stylized facts on the performance in terms of macroeconomic convergence and harmonization of economic policies (Table 5.1).

Declining Economic Growth Is Dependent on Fluctuations in the Global Economic Environment and Socio-Political Instability: Therefore Is Exposed to External Shocks

West Africa has recorded one of the highest growth rates in Africa or even the world in recent years (United Nations, 2015). The real growth of the ECOWAS zone has been steadily above 5% from the early 2000s until 2014. However, the performance of its economies remains dependent on fluctuations in agricultural production in almost all countries of the union, to the resumption of activity in the manufacturing sector and buildings and public works, especially in the WAEMU zone. The region recorded a drop in growth to 0.5% in 2016, before rebounding to 2.7% and then to 3.2% respectively in 2017 and 2018 (IMF, 2018). Overall, real GDP growth has continued, despite global turmoil. As a result, the community's economic activity rebounded to 3.3% in 2019. This growth dynamic was sustained in most member states, which recorded growth rates above 5.0%, due to the

Table 5.1 ECOWAS macroeconomic indicators

	2016	2017	2018	2019
Real GDP growth (%)	0.2	2.3	3.0	3.3
Inflation (%)	15.3	12.9	9.7	9.8
Budget deficit (excluding grants)/GDP (%)	2.9	2.5	1.8	1.4
Public debt/GDP (%)	25.7	25.1	23.4	24.1
Current account/GDP (%)	-1.0	0.9	-0.3	-4.0
Gross foreign exchange reserves (in months of import)	4.1	4.8	4.9	4.3
Growth in money supply (%)	26.7	4.0	13.6	8.5

Source: Author's calculation based on statistics from WAMA, ECOWAS

excellent performance of the mining, construction, agriculture, and services sectors, particularly communications, information technology, and financial services. However, following the emergence of the COVID-19 pandemic, ECOWAS's real GDP contracted in 2020 by about 2.1%.[1]

An Economic Environment Under Heavy Inflationary Pressures

The community's economic activity has taken place against slightly increasing inflationary pressures. Indeed, the ECOWAS average inflation rate stood at 8.4% and 13.5%, respectively, in 2015 and 2016, against 7.4% in 2014. Moreover, inflation increased in 2015 in all ECOWAS member countries, except Guinea and Liberia. The upward trend in the general price level is attributable to several factors, including rising food prices, depreciation of some currencies, constraints on energy supply, and upward adjustments in public service prices and oil prices.

Globally, average annual inflation increased slightly, from 9.7% in 2018 to 9.8% in 2019, reflecting, in particular, the increase in inflationary pressures, particularly in Nigeria. However, most economies recorded a decline in their inflation rates during the review period.

A Slight Recovery in Public Finances Is Tempered by a Continuous Increase in Debt, a Persistent Deficit in the Balance of Payments, and Significant Depreciation of National Currencies

Consequently, the **public finance** situation in ECOWAS further deteriorated slightly in 2015 and 2016, with a budget deficit that fell from 2.9% to 3.5% respectively, against 2.2% in 2014.

The community's economic performance has recently improved, narrowing the overall budget deficit (excluding grants), which fell from 1.8% of GDP in 2018 to 1.4% of GDP in 2019. Including grants, this budget deficit fell to 1.0% of GDP in 2019, compared to 1.5% of GDP the previous year. This increase is mainly due to increased budgetary revenues and the moderation of capital expenditure in some regional countries.

In addition, the total outstanding debt of ECOWAS stood at 25.70% of GDP in 2016, an increase relatively to 2014 (19.1%) and 2015 (22.8%), respectively. Overall, the region's public debt stock is trending upward,

---

[1] ECOWAS Macroeconomic Convergence Report, WAMA, 2019/20.

from 23.4% of GDP in 2018 to 24.1% in 2019, mainly concerning the increase in domestic borrowing during the reporting period. In recent years, the ECOWAS balance of payments and trade deficit improved slightly in 2016, with a deficit falling to 0.4% of GDP, against 1.1% and 1.3% in 2015 and 2014, respectively.

Generally, over the recent period, the performance of the region's external sector has been mixed, although the overall deficit of the community's current account has widened considerably to stand at 4.0% of GDP in 2019. Indeed, trade has been less dynamic in some Member States, still exposed to variations in the prices of raw materials and climatic hazards that cause agricultural production to fluctuate.

Moreover, most of the national currencies have experienced significant depreciation. Nonetheless, the community's money supply grew steadily between 2013 and 2015, going from 4.3% to 18.9%, respectively, thus causing a substantial liquidity increase in most ECOWAS countries. Money creation is believed to be the primary source of the expansion of net credit to the government, net domestic credit (especially credit to the private sector), and net foreign assets.

Given the COVID-19 pandemic, the region could face the significant challenge of controlling the budget deficit. The latest projections show a decline in income and a sharp increase in extra-budgetary spending to mitigate the pandemic's adverse effects. Hence, the region's budget deficit (excluding grants) is expected to increase from 1.4% of GDP in 2019 to 6.7% in 2020.

This mixed and uncertain economic situation will inevitably impact the implementation of the ECOWAS monetary cooperation program. In addition, the uncertainty of the economic situation will negatively affect the countries' performance in meeting the macroeconomic convergence criteria and harmonizing economic policies.

The West African Monetary Cooperation Program (ECOWAS)

ECOWAS Heads of States and Governments of ECOWAS launched, in May 1983 in Conakry, Guinea, the idea of creating a single currency and decided to devote all the necessary attention as an essential step in the integration. Thus, a Monetary Cooperation Program was instituted in July 1987 with the ultimate objective of creating one central bank with a single currency.

Context and History of Monetary Cooperation in West Africa: Colonial Monetary Arrangements and the West African Clearing House (WACH)

Historically, West Africa's economic and monetary integration dates back to colonial times. Before independence, colonial territories (Anglophone and Francophone) were linked to their respective metropolises by monetary arrangements that allowed them to use the same currency in the colonies. Thus, in the English-speaking area, The Gambia, Ghana, Nigeria, and Sierra Leone were governed by an arrangement concluded with the West African Currency Board, which was managed by Great Britain and was in charge of issuing and redemption of the British Pound in banknotes and coins in these four countries. As for the French-speaking countries of the sub-region, in this case, Benin (former Dahomey), Burkina Faso (former Haute-Volta), Côte d'Ivoire, Guinea, Mali, Niger, Senegal, and Togo, they had a similar arrangement with France which was based on the use of the CFA franc as the common currency. However, the arrangement of the English-speaking countries was abolished in the early 1960s following independence, while that of the French-speaking countries was consolidated and even transformed into a monetary union in 1962. Guinea withdrew from the system in 1960 to create its currency. Mali returned to the CFA zone in 1984 after its exit in 1962. Nonetheless, Guinea Bissau, a Portuguese-speaking country, has adhered to it since 1997.

The ECOWAS Monetary Cooperation Program (EMCP)

The EMCP has as its ultimate objective the creation of a monetary zone using a single currency managed by a common central bank. More specifically, it aims to set up common management institutions and a harmonized monetary system and achieve the convertibility of national currencies in commercial transactions within the region. In May 2009, a roadmap for creating the single ECOWAS currency was adopted by the ECOWAS Convergence Council.[2] This roadmap emphasized the key role of macroeconomic convergence and the alignment across countries. The roadmap will guide structural policy changes to ensure macroeconomic stability before the launch of the single West African currency set for 2020.

[2] The Convergence Council comprises the Ministers of Finance and the Governors of the Central Banks of the ECOWAS Member States.

The Issues and Challenges of the ECOWAS Monetary Cooperation Program (EMCP)

The issues and the main challenges of the EMCP can be analyzed through the different components of monetary cooperation, namely the conditions for macroeconomic convergence, the ECOWAS multilateral surveillance mechanism, the ECOWAS exchange rate mechanism, and the integration of systems of payment within ECOWAS.

Macroeconomic Convergence

Macroeconomic convergence is an essential component of the EMCP. Accordingly, members adopted measures to ensure the convergence of national economic policies, facilitating a harmonized monetary and financial system and common management institutions. As such, member countries must i) respect the established macroeconomic convergence criteria; ii) harmonize their budgetary, monetary, and financial policies; iii) harmonize their exchange rate regulations and adopt a market-determined exchange rate regime; iv) create an efficient community market through trade liberalization, removing both tariff and non-tariff barriers; and v) liberalize their money and capital markets, and facilitate the creation of regional stock exchanges to stimulate savings and growth.

In order to achieve the objective of monetary integration, a multilateral surveillance mechanism has been set up to ensure very close coordination of the economic policies of the Member States and the convergence of national economies (Decision A / DEC.17/12/01 of December 21, 2001, of the Conference of Heads of State and Government of ECOWAS member countries).

Compliance with the criteria allows progress to be assessed towards achieving macroeconomic convergence. The convergence criteria adopted by ECOWAS are classified into primary and secondary criteria[3] (Table 5.2). These criteria have evolved over time both in number and at the level of required thresholds.

It is important to stress that the macroeconomic convergence assessment mechanism was revised in June 2012 before being rationalized in May 2015 by the Conference of Heads of State and the Governments of

---

[3] The primary criteria are the variables considered essential for the achievement of convergence. The secondary criteria are the intervention tools that contribute to achieving the primary criteria.

Table 5.2 The situation of the ECOWAS convergence criteria

Convergence criteria	Thresholds	
	Old	New[a]
Primary		
1. Ratio of budget deficit (commitment basis)/GDP	≤4% (excluding grants) or ≤3% (including grants)	≤3% (including grants)
2. Average inflation rate	≤ 5%	≤10%
3. Financing of the budget deficit by the Central Bank	≤10% of tax revenue from the previous year	≤10% of tax revenue from the previous year
4. Gross foreign reserves	≥6 months import coverage	≥3 months import coverage
Secondary		
1. Nominal exchange rate stability	±10% (or the real exchange rate)	±10%
2. Public debt/GDP ratio	≤70%	≤70%
3. Tax revenue/GDP ratio	≥20%	Abandoned
4. Ratio of payroll/total tax revenue	≤35%	Abandoned
5. Ratio of public investment financed by internal resources/tax revenue	≥20%	Abandoned
6. Positive real interest rate	–	Abandoned
7. Ban on the accumulation of new arrears and clearance of all existing arrears	–	Abandoned

[a]Following the rationalization of the convergence criteria in 2015, involving the abandonment of five secondary criteria, the total number of convergence criteria has been reduced from eleven to six.

ECOWAS. Thus, since May 2015, the total number of convergence criteria has changed and has been set at six (6) against eleven (11) previously (Table 5.3). This rationalization was also accompanied by modifying the target (threshold) for specific criteria.

The Intensification of the Process of Macroeconomic Convergence and the Adoption of a So-Called Fast-Track Approach for the Implementation of the EMCP

The assessment of the implementation of the EMCP carried out in 1999 revealed that progress has undoubtedly been made in terms of

5 THE MONETARY UNION AND ECONOMIC INTEGRATION: CHALLENGES... 105

Table 5.3 Total number of convergence criteria (primary and secondary) fulfilled per country in ECOWAS

	2014		2015		2016		2017		2018		2019	
	Primary	Secondary	Primary	Secondary	Primary	Secondary	Primary	Secondary	Primary	Secondary	Primary	Secondary
Benin	4	2	3	2	3	2	3	2	4	2	4	2
Burkina	4	2	4	2	3	2	3	2	3	2	4	2
Cap-Vert	3	1	3	1	3	1	3	1	4	1	4	1
C. d'Ivoire	4	2	4	2	3	2	3	2	3	2	4	2
Gambia	2	0	1	1	1	1	1	1	3	1	3	2
Ghana	1	1	2	0	1	1	2	2	2	2	3	2
Guinea	3	2	1	0	3	1	3	2	2	2	3	2
G. Bissau	4	2	3	2	3	2	4	2	3	2	3	2
Liberia	3	2	3	2	3	2	4	2	1	1	1	1
Mali	4	2	4	2	3	2	3	2	3	2	4	2
Niger	3	2	3	2	3	2	3	2	4	2	4	2
Nigeria	4	2	4	1	3	1	3	1	2	2	2	2
Senegal	3	2	3	2	3	2	3	2	3	2	3	2
S. Leone	3	2	3	2	1	1	2	2	1	2	3	2
Togo	3	2	3	2	4	1	4	1	4	1	4	2

Source: Author's calculation based on statistics from WAMA, ECOWAS

macroeconomic convergence but that it was insufficient to ensure the launch of monetary union in 2000. Other than the problem of macroeconomic instability and the impact of external shocks, political instability, in some countries, was among the factors behind these modest results.

Consequently, during its session held in Lomé in December 1999, the Assembly of Heads of State and Government decided to postpone the ECOWAS currency from 2000 to 2004. On this same occasion, the Conference adopted several measures aimed at speeding up the integration process, particularly the intensification of the process of macroeconomic convergence and the adoption of a so-called accelerated approach for the rapid implementation of the integration process. They also adopted the creation of a second monetary union, the West African Monetary Zone (WAMZ).[4] The monetary zone will be transitional and will eventually merge with WAEMU to form a larger monetary union, large grouping together all fifteen ECOWAS countries.[5]

The Challenges of the ECOWAS Monetary Cooperation Program
The persistence of fiscal problems and political instability have been identified as significant obstacles to achieving convergence. Despite the need for macroeconomic convergence and policy harmonization, significant challenges remain to be overcome in the desired direction. Several sets of challenges can be identified. The first series concerns the non-ratification of protocols or the low level of implementation of those ratified; weak statistical capacity to generate high frequency/high quality harmonized data to inform the development of good quality policies and plans; insufficient awareness to ensure ownership of the program. The second set of challenges relates to external shocks; political instability due to poor governance; the weakness of democratic institutions; failure to take Community criteria into account in national policies and programs; the persistence of the existence of non-tariff barriers; the existence of two major exchange rate regimes; and, among other things, insufficient funding for the various activities of the EMCP.

The third set of challenges relates to the predominance of budgetary problems, which plagues the macroeconomic environment, thus causing

---

[4] The member countries of the WAMZ are The Gambia, Ghana, Guinea, Nigeria, and Sierra Leone. Recently, in 2010, Liberia joined the WAMZ.
[5] The new deadline for the launch of the ECOWAS single currency was to be operational in 2020.

the inability of member states to meet the agreed convergence criteria sustainably. Finally, the fourth set of challenges relates to civil strife and political instability; the decline in economic activity resulting in unemployment, social tensions, and a low degree of democratization. In addition, there have been changes in political regimes through coups d'état over the past decades, and almost all countries in the sub-region have experienced political changes. Such an unstable environment is likely to engender macroeconomic instability. However, whatever the quality of the policies formulated, their implementation will be doomed to failure if the necessary climate of peace and stability is not assured. This problem has significantly affected the pace and direction of regional cooperation and the ECOWAS integration agenda over the years.

Perspectives and New Developments of the ECOWAS Monetary Cooperation Program
The most salient facts in the recent orientations of the EMCP are, essentially, first the adoption since 2009 of a roadmap based on a strategic plan to accelerate the process of creation of the single currency of ECOWAS, and then the establishment since 2013 of the Presidential Working Group to oversee the process.

Adoption of the Roadmap for the Creation of the Single Currency of ECOWAS

The interinstitutional meeting, organized from February 16 to 18, 2009, in Abuja, resulted in developing a roadmap for creating the single currency of ECOWAS by 2020. This underlined the need for macroeconomic convergence, necessary harmonization of policies, the gradual strengthening of institutional and legal frameworks, and the completion of the common market as the building blocks of a viable monetary union.

The Establishment of the Presidential Task-Force

The voluntarism of the leaders of ECOWAS for the creation of the single currency is increasingly marked. Thus, because of the slow progress made towards achieving the single currency of ECOWAS, the Conference of Heads of State and Government of ECOWAS considered that it was imperative to take measures to speed up the process. It is in this context that four (4)[6] Heads of State: from Côte d'Ivoire, Ghana, Niger, and Nigeria, were appointed by their peers to supervise and accelerate the creation of the common currency of the ECOWAS. On this occasion, a Working Group was set up whose mission is to assess the progress made towards creating the single currency while examining the constraints inherent in the project and making concrete proposals to speed up ongoing processes. However, during the 57th ordinary session of the Conference of Heads of State and Government of the ECOWAS, held in Niamey on September 7, 2020, the launch of the currency initially scheduled for July 2020 has been postponed to a later date. In addition, the development of a "new road map" was also announced, without however determining a new timetable.

OVERALL SITUATION AND PERFORMANCE IN TERMS OF ECONOMIC POLICY HARMONIZATION AND MACROECONOMIC CONVERGENCE IN ECOWAS

Performance in Harmonizing Economic Policies and Institutional Arrangements

The harmonization of policies is an integral part of the economic and monetary integration of ECOWAS. As such, member states are required to comply with several common principles in terms of, among other things, exchange rate policies, monetary policies, capital account liberalization, the functioning of financial markets and payment systems, banking supervision and regulation, trade liberalization, and statistical.

Significant progress has been made in harmonizing the balance of payments (BOP) statistics with adopting the methodological guide for compiling the BOP and international investment position (IIP) statistics in ECOWAS member states. However, modest progress has been made in harmonizing monetary policy frameworks, banking, and financial

---

[6] First, the heads of state of Niger and Ghana were appointed in October 2013, during the Extraordinary Summit of Heads of State and Government of ECOWAS. Second, they were joined in 2015 by the heads of state of Côte d'Ivoire and Nigeria (given the economic weight of their respective countries in the community) together to supervise and accelerate the creation of the common currency of ECOWAS. harmonization. They should also strive to apply and adopt adequate institutional arrangements to achieve the objectives advocated by various legal, technical, and administrative instruments of ECOWAS.

legislation and supervision, developing payment systems, harmonizing exchange rate regimes, and establishing an exchange rate mechanism. Thus, most harmonization projects are embryonic, and there are delays in their implementation. Nevertheless, the deadlines set for their execution have been met or even exceeded for the most part. Moreover, certain structural or cyclical constraints (such as the Ebola virus epidemic, the COVID-19 pandemic) have slowed down the harmonization process.

In summary, the economic situation and, by extension, the profile of ECOWAS convergence are very mixed, and this is at the deadline of 2020, previously announced by the political authorities for the launch of the single currency of ECOWAS. Thus, the current level of implementation of the main components of the EMCP through macroeconomic convergence and the harmonization of economic policies raises questions, even concerns about the expected efficiencies of regional economic integration, as a prelude to the creation of monetary union and a single currency for ECOWAS. Therefore, the performances in terms of macroeconomic convergence and the level of implementation of the EMCP, which will be analyzed in the next section, will give more insights on the new orientations and the level of achievement of the process of creation of this regional currency.

Performance in Terms of Macroeconomic Convergence in ECOWAS

A Deterioration in the Macroeconomic Convergence Profile of ECOWAS with a Downward Trend in the Number of Countries That Meet All the Criteria

The profile of macroeconomic convergence within ECOWAS has deteriorated slightly on average in recent years. For all the primary and secondary criteria, the number of countries that have reached the required threshold has decreased, at least until 2016, except for the criterion relating to gross foreign exchange reserves. Performance on macroeconomic convergence improved relatively to the criteria for the budget deficit and central bank financing of the deficit but remained unchanged for standards for inflation and gross reserves of change in 2019. Only six of the fifteen ECOWAS countries met all the first-rank criteria in 2019, compared to two in 2018 and three in 2017. In 2016, no country had succeeded in meeting all six convergence criteria. In addition, only Togo has satisfactorily satisfied all of the first-rank criteria over the 2017–2019 period.

However, with the outbreak of the coronavirus pandemic on a global scale, the progress made over the years in macroeconomic stability and convergence for the creation of a single currency is threatened. Furthermore, growth is expected to decline in 2020 due to the adverse effects of the Covid-19 pandemic. As a result, performance under the macroeconomic convergence criteria is expected to deteriorate considerably in 2020, especially concerning the criteria relating to the budget deficit and the financing of the deficit by the central bank. However, the number of countries that would meet all of the first-rank criteria in 2020 would be much lower than in 2019.

Forecasts for 2020 point to a significant worsening of the budget deficit at the regional level, driven by increased spending on health and social programs, as well as lower revenues, in a context of considerable deterioration in the current account. The analysis of convergence performance shows that the number of countries meeting the convergence criteria varies depending on the year and the criterion selected. The ECOWAS countries do not respect the convergence criteria in a sustainable manner, which is a necessary condition, but not sufficient, before the launch of the single currency. In addition, it appears that a significant challenge for the countries concerns above all the respect of the primary criterion relating to the budget deficit, even if 11 countries succeeded in respecting this criterion in 2019. The 3% threshold in terms of the budget deficit continues to be a problem for most member states due to low fiscal pressure and high spending. Likewise, countries in the region, particularly some members of the WAMZ, have yet to make efforts to contain inflation. On the other hand, the stability of exchange rates and the financing of the deficit by the Central Bank is experiencing fairly sustained changes, reflecting the performance of ECOWAS countries in compliance with these convergence criteria. Also, despite the accentuation of external constraints, significant performance was recorded for gross foreign exchange reserves in 2019, with thirteen (13) countries having reached the required target of at least three months of import coverage.

Regarding the secondary criteria, the outstanding public debt requires special monitoring attention given the continued increase in recent years of this aggregate in almost all ECOWAS countries. On the nominal exchange rate stability benchmark, countries' performance was also encouraging. In general, except for the budget deficit (including grants), performance against the recently adopted convergence criteria has generally improved. For the past five years, at least eleven (11) countries have managed to meet the first and secondary criteria, notwithstanding the consistency of the countries in respecting any criterion.

However, these modest performances hide some important realities to highlight. First, the tendency for countries to meet all the convergence criteria is a roller coaster and often declining. Second, no country has continuously met all the convergence criteria over several years. Finally, the number of countries fulfilling all the convergence criteria (7 countries out of 15 in 2019) still seems low to constitute the desired critical mass for the feasibility of launching the single ECOWAS currency, the deadline set to 2020. Ultimately, the overall profile of convergence, like the economic situation in ECOWAS, is currently very mixed. What about performance in terms of harmonization of economic policies and institutional arrangements? The developments in the following section will give more elements of an answer to this question.

Convergence Tests: An Analysis of Cyclical Convergence (or Convergence of Economic Policies) and Structural Convergence (or Convergence of Economic Structures) in ECOWAS

Presentation of the Model

The economic stability of the zone in terms of the convergence of cyclical variables (of economic policies) and the convergence of structural variables (of economic structures), both real and nominal, are tested using cross-sectional data on the retained criteria. Furthermore, the method of variable coefficients based on Recursive Least Squares (RLS) makes it possible to study the changes in the speed of convergence towards the value of the reference criterion (or the leading country of the zone) chosen as reference. In other words, the example of a model that we will study within the framework of the RLS is that of the linear model with time-dependent coefficients. The reason for choosing this model with variable coefficients is that the RLS method is less demanding in terms of statistical data for relatively short time series (as is the case here: 1980–2000), unlike the method based on the Kalman filter, for example, which is applicable for relatively long time series.

Thus, this model lets us know if a country X tends towards the country (reference) I or the country (reference) J, and at what speed. For this, we consider the macroeconomic variable $Z.t$ for country X and the two countries taken as "reference," I and J, through the following regression:

$$Z_{It} - Z_{Xt} = \alpha_{Xt} + \beta_{Xt}(Z_{It} - Z_{Jt}) + \varepsilon_{Xt} \qquad (5.1)$$

Information on convergence can be obtained from the temporal evolution of the parameters α_{xt} and β_{xt}. Thus, we consider that country X has started a process of convergence or quite simply is converging:

- towards the country I, if $E[\lim(\beta_{Xt})] = 0$ and $E[\lim(\alpha_{Xt})] = 0$
- towards the country J, if $E[\lim(\beta_{Xt})] = 1$ and $E[\lim(\alpha_{Xt})] = 0$

However, this exercise does not seek to determine whether the countries have converged but whether they have started a convergence process.

Indeed, a test of convergence from X to I is equivalent to a test based on the regression of Eq. (5.1) where the values of the parameters are not statistically different from:

$$\beta_{Xt} = 0; E(\alpha_{Xt}) = c \text{ and } \mathrm{Var}(\alpha_{Xt}) = \sigma^2 . \alpha_{Xt} < \infty$$

The estimation of Eq. (5.1) using Recursive Least Squares (RLS), when α_{Xt} tends to zero, gives the following events:

(a) $E[\lim(\beta_{Xt})] = 0 \Rightarrow Z_{Xt} = Z_{It}$
(b) $E[\lim(\beta_{Xt})] = 1 \Rightarrow Z_{Xt} = Z_{Jt}$

Thus, several cases may arise depending on whether $Z_{It} > Z_{Jt}$ or $Z_{It} < Z_{Jt}$:

- If $Z_{It} < Z_{Jt}$, three cases can arise:

  (c) $0 < E[\lim(\beta_{Xt})] < 1 \Rightarrow Z_{It} < Z_{Xt} < Z_{Jt}$
  (d) $E[\lim(\beta_{Xt})] > 1 \Rightarrow Z_{It} < Z_{Jt} < Z_{Xt}$
  (e) $E[\lim(\beta_{Xt})] < 0 \Rightarrow Z_{Xt} < Z_{It} < Z_{Jt}$

- If $Z_{It} > Z_{Jt}$, three scenarios can also arise:

  (c') $0 < E[\lim(\beta_{Xt})] < 1 \Rightarrow Z_{Jt} < Z_{Xt} < Z_{It}$

(d') $E[\lim(\beta_{Xt})] > 1 \Rightarrow Z_{Xt} < Z_{Jt} < Z_{It}$
(e') $E[\lim(\beta_{Xt})] < 0 \Rightarrow Z_{Jt} < Z_{It} < Z_{Xt}$

Thus, we will appreciate from the graphical evolution of β_{Xt}, the tendency towards convergence of country X, and at what speed. Indeed, when the coefficients β_{Xt} tend towards zero (or respectively 1), for $\alpha_{Xt} \approx 0$, one will say that the process of convergence towards the reference I (or respectively J) is started.

The interest here is to determine the convergence speed, measured by the rate at which the coefficients β_{Xt} tend towards 0 (or 1). The period considered in this study is 1990–1999, during which the EMCP was operational in all member countries of the community. We then try to see if the implementation of this program has made it possible to achieve the objective of convergence of policies and economic structures concerning a few economic indicators retained within the framework of multilateral surveillance, in the whole of ECOWAS, and empirically analyze the process. The study also analyzes the results of econometric tests in terms of convergence around the criteria retained by the multilateral surveillance of ECOWAS.

The choice of these indicators (and the economic convergence criteria) is thus guided, on the one hand, by objectives of economic growth and sustainability of fiscal deficits and, on the other hand, by compliance with the objectives of price stability, variability of the external position and strengthening of the international competitiveness of the Member States.

This study also allows us to compare relative performance against convergence objectives, in general, to see which macroeconomic indicator is the best performing and to try to find an explanation for this. Finally, we compare the performances achieved in terms of real convergence compared to nominal convergence and the convergence achieved in terms of economic policies (or cyclical convergence) compared to the convergence of economic structures.

The choice of the "reference" country relates to either the country that has achieved the best performance in the region over the period or the reference value (criterion) set within the framework of Multilateral Surveillance. The data used for this study covers 1990–2019 and comes mainly from the World Bank (World Development Indicators).

However, compared to the period studied, the contingencies relating to statistical information for certain countries led us to carry out this study without considering the indicators concerning them. Therefore, in the same logic, only the indicators of the inflation rate, the debt rate, the budget balance, the GDP growth rate, and the investment rate will be considered.

Our analysis distinguishes nominal variables (indicators) and real variables relating to the convergence of economic policies and the convergence of structures. Thus, for nominal convergence, we consider the average annual inflation rate as an indicator of cyclical nominal convergence (or of economic policy) and the debt ratio as an indicator of nominal structural convergence. For real convergence, we consider real GDP growth as an indicator of real cyclical convergence (or economic policy), while the budget balance to GDP and the investment rate are considered indicators of real structural convergence.

Analysis of the Results of Empirical Tests of Economic Convergence in ECOWAS

The tests show that ECOWAS member countries have generally started a relatively slow convergence process of their economic policies and structures. Thus, the strongest convergences have been noted at the level of debt rates and investment rates. In contrast, the most notorious divergences in ECOWAS are noted at the level of budget balances, inflation rates, and to a lesser extent at the level of GDP growth rates.

Indeed, if it exists, convergence is often towards the least performing benchmark, reflecting the relatively slow nature of this process in all the countries of the region. This phenomenon raises the problems of public finance management and tax revenue mobilization, the control of inflation, and the achievement of sustained and sustainable GDP growth rates. Moreover, the best performances in terms of macroeconomic convergence are often influenced by cyclical phenomena, mainly linked to the nature of exports and external shocks.

Overall, performance on nominal convergence indicators, such as real convergence, is mixed. This situation is characteristic of the ECOWAS zone, whose project to build a monetary union is underway with shallow progress in the frameworks for harmonizing national economic policies (monetary policies, budgetary policies, fiscal policies, trade policies, and more).

This problem would arise less concerning nominal convergence for the member countries of the WAEMU area, which have long been linked within the framework of monetary cooperation with France and practice standard economic policies, mainly monetary policy, for example. Since 1994, with the creation of WAEMU, an important objective, among others, has been the harmonization of national economic policies.

Similarly, the performance in terms of convergence of economic structures depends on the installation of economic structures and their levels of harmonization. These, if they exist in ECOWAS, are in an embryonic state both in their design and in their implementation: this is the case, for example, of projects for the harmonization and implementation of payment systems, statistics, legislative and regulatory frameworks, the exchange rate mechanism, the regional central bank, the regional financial market (regional stock exchange), and the TEC.

Ultimately, the efforts in constructing the ECOWAS monetary union should then go toward revitalization and a rapprochement of the structures of harmonization of national economic policies. Likewise, the achievements in the convergence process should be consolidated, but rigor should be more appropriate to ensure the reconciliation and convergence of the economies. This double recommendation aims to achieve stable and lasting economic integration, build a monetary union, and create a credible single currency for ECOWAS.

Thus, the study of the economic policy convergence criteria in ECOWAS shows that opportunities for economic convergence exist. However, the evolution and speed of convergence of a criterion depend on the economies' nature, which is often oil rents or agricultural revenue (MBO NDIAYE, 2007).Thus, regardless of the indicator considered, there are often trends towards divergence or resistance to convergence. As a result, the convergence of economic policies is weak and is not accompanied by a real and effective convergence of economies.

Therefore, a profound restructuring of the economies is necessary to strengthen the already established system of economic convergence and complete economic and monetary integration in the ECOWAS region. The question that remains is what may be the opportunities that the participating countries can expect from the project to create the ECOWAS monetary union? In other words, what can be the gains (advantages) of this participation? The following section will be the subject of a benefit-cost analysis of membership in the ECOWAS monetary union (Eco zone).

The Cost-Benefit Analysis of Joining the ECOWAS Monetary Union (Eco Zone)

This approach to monetary unions was proposed by Bean (1992) subsequently to Ishiyama (1975) and Tower and Willet (1976). It consists of analyzing the costs and benefits that result from a country's entry into a monetary union.

The Advantages of Joining the Monetary Union

In theory, the adoption of a single currency in the ECOWAS region would lead to the disappearance of transaction costs linked to the differences in currencies from one country to another, an expansion of intra-community trade, increased mobility of factors of production, and faster growth in actual activity. The monetary authority responsible for managing the single currency would see its credibility strengthened due to its regional status, which would ultimately translate into greater macroeconomic stability. The opportunity for businesses in a member country to face a more extensive market would generate substantial economies of scale. It would therefore follow an expansion of real economic activity, job creation, improvement of the living conditions of the populations.

According to the United Nations Economic Commission for Africa (UNECA, 2014), the economic and monetary integration of ECOWAS should boost foreign direct investment (FDI) and encourage offshoring. It is expected to improve the efficiency of the private sector as a result of increased competitive pressures. Cooperation and the pooling of resources (rivers, roads, railways, electricity networks) should make it possible to increase the quality and quantity of public goods at the regional level. The report also notes that reducing the risk of conflict and increasing cooperation on security issues would also be essential for economic and monetary integration. In summary, the advantages of joining a monetary union are threefold: improving the liquid value of money, eliminating currency speculation, and eliminating the costs of managing external resources.

The Costs of Joining the Monetary Union

However, a country's entry into a monetary union also entails the abandonment of its monetary sovereignty. This implies the impossibility of resorting to monetary policy to respond to the asymmetric exogenous economic shocks that specifically concern it. Therefore, it is optimal for a country to enter into a monetary union only if the expected gains outweigh the costs resulting from the loss of monetary autonomy.

For the case in West Africa, Masson et al. (2014) have already shown that the enlargement of the WAEMU to other ECOWAS countries would lead to net gains (even if they are reduced) for both current members only for The Gambia, Ghana, and Guinea. On the other hand, the introduction of Nigeria would not be beneficial for the current members, although it could improve the prosperity of Nigeria, which would then benefit from a more stable currency. Table 5.4 presents the net gains or losses in terms of prosperity resulting from adding countries one by one, as a percentage of GDP as shown by Masson, Debrun, and Patillo (2014).

In summary, the costs attached to a monetary union are: there is a loss of implications for national fiscal policy and worsening of the inflation-unemployment relationship; we have a supranational central bank; we move away from the manipulation of the exchange rate, an essential instrument of monetary policy; high growth regions will attract capital from the union to the detriment of low growth regions.

The cost-benefit analysis poses the problem of joining a monetary union regarding a country's sacrifices when it renounces its currency. Thus, the costs of a monetary union result from the country's inability to resort to an independent monetary policy at the very moment when it loses the instrument of the exchange rate as a variable of adjustment to an external shock. Thus, projected in the long term, the dynamic

Table 5.4 Net gains or losses in terms of prosperity resulting from the addition of countries one by one to the West African Economic and Monetary Union (percentage of GDP)

For new members	Net gain or net loss in prosperity	For current members						
		Benin	Burkina Faso	Côte d'Ivoire	Mali	Niger	Senegal	Togo
The Gambia	-0.0015	0.0006	0.0006	0.0005	0.0005	0.0006	0.0006	0.0006
Ghana	0.0129	0.0037	0.0038	0.0043	0.004	0.0038	0.0037	0.004
Guinea	0.0024	0.0009	0.0008	0.0005	0.0007	0.001	0.0009	0.0006
Nigeria	0.0229	-0.0128	-0.0134	-0.0175	-0.016	-0.0133	-0.0114	-0.017

Source: Masson, Debrun and Patillo (2014)

gains of a union outweigh the costs, which, by nature, are transitory (Fratianni et al., 1992).

Conclusion and Recommendations of Economic Policies

In West Africa, ECOWAS is still experiencing difficulties in achieving economic integration, especially monetary integration, despite the adoption over thirty years ago of the ECOWAS Monetary Cooperation Program (EMCP). Although good performances were recorded for specific macroeconomic indicators, especially some economic convergence criteria, disparities seem to exist and persist between the different countries. This raises many questions about the expected efficiencies of economic integration and raises concerns about the future of the ECOWAS monetary union. The convergence of economic policies is weak and is not accompanied by a real and effective convergence of economies.

Therefore, a profound restructuring of the economies is necessary to strengthen the already established system of economic convergence and complete economic and monetary integration in the ECOWAS region. Indeed, if it exists, convergence is often towards the least performing benchmark, reflecting the relatively slow nature of this process in all the countries of the region. This phenomenon raises the problems of public finance management and tax revenue mobilization, the control of inflation, and the achievement of sustained and sustainable GDP growth rates. Moreover, the best performances in terms of macroeconomic convergence are often influenced by cyclical phenomena, mainly linked to the nature of exports and external shocks.

Overall, performance on nominal convergence indicators, such as real convergence, is mixed. This situation is characteristic of the ECOWAS zone, whose project to build a monetary union is underway with deficient progress in the frameworks for harmonizing national economic policies (monetary policies, budgetary policies, fiscal policies, trade policies). A cost-benefit analysis indicates that participation in a monetary union is better than not participating or adopting independent policies (and separate currencies) for all ECOWAS member countries except Nigeria.

Finally, the establishment of the ECOWAS Monetary Union also leads to integrating other aspects of economic and financial integration necessary to guarantee the stability and credibility of the single currency.

Therefore, an essential aspect of monetary integration is pursuing and consolidating macroeconomic convergence and harmonization of economic policies.

A critical reform concerns establishing the Fiscal Union through the harmonization of tax policies (or even a standard tax policy), the unification of the banking system, and solid institutional frameworks. Thus, the observation of the multifaceted difficulties and the desire to succeed in the construction of a monetary union in West Africa of ECOWAS inspire us to formulate a certain number of economic policy recommendations to help a better orientation for the creation of a single stable, credible and competitive currency, respond to the development needs of trade and economies in West Africa. Therefore, it is essential to adopt a shared community vision, more precisely, on the orientation of monetary integration in ECOWAS while keeping in mind the will of the leaders of ECOWAS to surround themselves with all necessary precautions before the creation of the single currency. Thus, for the establishment of the common currency in West Africa, three sets of recommendations can be formulated:

(a) *Growth and stability policies of macroeconomic convergence*

These are structural transformation policies aimed at promoting production, value creation, and trade development by improving the business environment to increase the attractiveness of direct investment and ensure the diversification of the economy and exports. The first step here will be to promote investments in productive capital. This is to promote the emergence of a modern and dynamic industrial fabric to transform primary products into finished or semi-finished products and facilitate the regional market penetration for small and medium-sized enterprises. This is not only the basis of the creation of added value and currencies (foreign exchange reserves), the diversification of products as well as of trade partners, both at the regional level (intra-community trade) and at the continental level and the world level (globalization), but also guarantees inclusive and structurally sustainable growth. Furthermore, the increase in revenue and the tax base that could result from this would make it possible to contain budget deficits, resulting from the modernization of the tax administration, the reinforced control of exemptions, and the control of operating expenses, in particular the wage bill as well as transfers and subsidies. Consequently, this can have good repercussions on controlling the budget deficit, and thus avoid the recourse for its financing of the Central

Bank and the indebtedness and thus cause less pressure on the other criteria of convergence, namely, inflation and the exchange rate.

(b) *Policies for consolidating harmonization programs and other institutional arrangements*

It is imperative to harmonize or merge the payment systems of different countries or economic zones in the ECOWAS region in the medium or long term. Therefore, the following actions should be taken to harmonize the payment systems of the participating countries:

- The modernization of telecommunications systems through cutting-edge technology allowing the promotion of cashless payments, the incentive for the increase and easy use of the banking system by economic operators and the general public;
- The development of transport infrastructure and electricity production without which the promotion of payment systems would be uncertain;
- The interconnection of the region's banking network in order to facilitate cross-border payments;
- Strengthening the fight against poverty in our countries and the education and training of the populations in the use of the banking and financial system. This will be to the development of the financial sector and financial inclusion, strategies sectoral and liberalization policies that reduce unemployment.
- Sensitization and encouragement of informal sector operators to use the banking sector through, among other things, streamlining of procedures, reduction of costs, training, ratification of protocols, and their effective implementation.

Other measures such as the liberalization of capital accounts in the area can help increase cross- border investments and stimulate production. To this must be added the need to promote the development of the regional financial market and the regional stock exchange of ECOWAS. Furthermore, it would be helpful to review some considerations on the basic principles of the current monetary integration process in West Africa and work on a common and precise strategy for monetary cooperation in Africa. These basic principles can be found in:

- The assessment of the regional integration model's relevance, or even the opportunities, is based on the development of trade (currently the preferred model) compared to the model based on the development of the financial sector and services. This second option would make it possible to stimulate production from the development of finance (liberalization of capital).
- Avoid creating a sub-regional currency and transitional institutions of short duration and cost as much as possible.

(c) *Policies for consolidating socio-political stability and good governance*

Failures in socio-political stability and good governance adversely affect the effectiveness of all policy and economic integration initiatives. Therefore, it is crucial to consolidate the actions underway to resolve socio-political and security crises in the region. In addition, the fight against corruption, money laundering, cybercrime, fraud, tax evasion, and embezzlement of public funds is an exercise to which special attention should be paid. Therefore, it is vital to improve the quality of institutions and the business environment and promote peace and social cohesion.

Ultimately, a structural transformation is required for the economies of West African countries, ECOWAS and Africa in general, following the example of the lessons learned from the so-called emerging countries today, which should constitute references in the conduct of economic and social policies, for a good dynamic performance and emergence of African economies.

Finally, we must maintain measures to prevent and fight against epidemics such as the Ebola virus epidemic, Covid-19.

References

Bean, C. R. (1992). Economic and monetary union in Europe. *Journal of Economic Perspectives, 6*(4), 31–52. https://doi.org/10.1257/jep.6.4.31

Fratianni, M., von Hagen, J., & Waller, C. (1992). German dominance in the EMS: The empirical evidence. *Open Economic Review, 3*(1), 127–128.

International Monetary Fund (IMF). (2018). *Worl Economic Outlook: Challenges to Steady Growth*. Washington DC: IMF.

Ishiyama, Y. (1975). The theory of optimum currency areas: A survey (La théorie des zones monétaires optimales : étude de la théorie des zones monétaires optimales: Un examen). *IMF Staff Papers, 22*(2), 344–383.

Masson, P., C. Pattillo, & Debrun, X. (2014). The future of African monetary geography. In C. Monga & J. Y. Lin (Eds.), *The Oxford handbook of Africa and economics, Volume 2: Policies and practices*. Presses universitaires d'Oxford.

Ndiaye, M. B. O. (2007). Respect des critères de convergence versus harmonisation des critères de convergence économique: une étude comparative des performances des indicateurs de convergence économique dans la Zone Franc en Afrique *(UEMOA et CEMAC)*. *Revue Africaine de l'Intégration et du Développement*, 1(2).

Tower and Willet. (1976). *The theory of optimum currency areas and exchange-rate flexibility*. International Finance Section, Department of Economics, Princeton University. Special papers in international economics, no. 11.

United Nations (UN). (2015). *World Economic Situation and Prospects*. New York: United Nations DESA.

United Nations Economic Commission for Africa (UNECA). (2014). *Economic report on Africa 2014*. Addis Ababa, Ethiopia: Dynamic Industrial policy in Africa.

CHAPTER 6

The Political Economy of a Monetary Union in ECOWAS: The Case of the ECO Currency

Rachael Ntongho

INTRODUCTION

There is much literature on economic, social, institutional, and mainly monetary integration of Eco, a single currency of ECOWAS intended to be launched in January 2020 (Mati et al., 2019; Miles, 2017). In addition, the authors wrote convergence reports each year, identifying and addressing economic drawbacks (Mati et al., 2019).

They considered currency synchronization and Optimal Currency Area (OCA) issues. In the end, the failure of eco to become fruition was not the absence of socio-cultural or economic factors nor imperfect synchronization among member states or weaknesses in the OCA. Politics, or lack of it, ended up being the Achilles heel to the demise of a single currency union in West Africa. The conflict between Francophone member states and the rest of the member states proved to be the barrier to a single currency union in ECOWAS. Former French colonies still tied economically, politically, culturally, socially, and institutionally to France were unable to

R. Ntongho (✉)
University of Manchester, Manchester, UK
e-mail: rachael.ntongho@manchester.ac.uk

© The Author(s), under exclusive license to Springer Nature Switzerland AG 2022
A. A. Amin et al. (eds.), *Monetary and Financial Systems in Africa*, https://doi.org/10.1007/978-3-030-96225-8_6

disentangle themselves from monetary agreements signed with their colonial master after independence.

The French stronghold of Africa can be traced back to the colonial era, and paragraph 119 of the Treaty of Versailles, which handed some German colonies such as Cameroon, Benin, and Togo to France after the allies defeated Germany in World War one (Von Epp, 1937). Despite independence, liberalization, and globalization, French influence has shifted from direct to indirect control (Marchesin, 1998). Globalization, which has introduced new economic powers such as China and India in Africa, was expected to lessen the grip of France and other European countries in the continent. However, this has not been the case, and French presence is still felt in many areas. Moreover, it may remain so for a few more decades (Utley, 2002) since France benefits enormously from its former Africa colonies and is unlikely to leave without bloodshed (Vetlesen, 2000) or clever diplomacy (Uchehara, 2014).

France is the only G8 country still dependent on African resources to stay as the 7th economic power of the World (Willsher, 2019). Meanwhile, former French colonies are some of the poorest countries in the World. Most of these countries in central and west Africa still use CFA (Communauté Financiere Africaine or African Financial Community changed from French Colonies of Africa) Franc (CFAF), a colonial currency.

Any attempts by these former French colonies to relinquish themselves from any area of French stronghold in their countries are met with strong economic and military sanctions by France (Utley, 2002). Even regulatory changes are all influenced by France. A case in point is the OHADA (Organisation for the Harmonisation of Business Law in Africa) legislation agreed by mostly French-speaking African countries which govern business law in member states (Ntongho, 2012).

However, two areas of French domination of Africa are glaring and cause numerous debates among scholars: military presence and currency control.[1] There are merits and demerits of the continuous use of the franc CFA in Africa (Wilson, 2020; Koddenbrock & Sylla, 2019; Taylor, 2019).

---

[1] For more on French control of Francophone Africa, see Gregory, S., 2000. The French military in Africa: Past and present. *African Affairs*, 99(396), pp.435-448; Yates, D.A., 2018. French military interventions in Africa. *The Palgrave Handbook of Peacebuilding in Africa* (pp. 391-408). Palgrave Macmillan, Cham; Legum, C., 2020. Foreign intervention in Africa (I). In *The Year Book of World Affairs 1980* (pp. 76-94). Routledge.)

Though some authors have pointed to the benefit of the CFAF as a common currency in former French-speaking colonies, several more perceive the continued use of CFAF by 14 former French colonies as one of the crudest means of control and abuse and exploitation by France (Taylor, 2019).

ECOWAS' attempt to institute a new single Eco currency in the region would have given the eight French-speaking ECOWAS countries monetary independence from France and the freedom to decide monetary policies without the intervention of their former colonial master. However, as articulated below, these French African countries were bound to face resistance from France, as history has indicated.

ECOWAS member states fail to fully understand the history of monetary conflicts in French Africa and address French influence on Francophone member states. This failure has proved to be the most significant demise of a West African Currency Union and the reason why this chapter focuses on the political economy of monetary Union in ECOWAS. It examines the Francophone and non-Francophone monetary dichotomy in the region and the best mechanism to address this divide by analyzing the France-Afrique relationship and French influence on monetary policy in Africa and Eco currency.

Thus, this chapter analyses the unsuccessful attempt of ECOWAS to introduce a common Eco currency acceptable by all member states as expected in 2020. It argues that ECOWAS member states underestimated the influence of France in Africa and appeared immature in overlooking French monetary dominance in the region and, in particular, the history of the struggle for currency independence by French African countries. Finally, it proposes alternative routes to advance monetary unity and autonomy in the region and rebuild trust between Francophone and the ECOWAS member states.

We divide the chapter into five sections. The first section is the theory of interest group influence. The second section provides a brief history of the Eco currency. The third section analyses France-Afrique monetary relations and the struggles for currency independence in Francophone Africa. The fourth section examines the dichotomy between Francophone and other ECOWAS member states resulting from the Macron-Ouattara announcement. Finally, the fifth section advances recommendations to rebuild trust between French and non-French-speaking ECOWAS countries before concluding.

Politics and Interest Group Influence

Organisational politics defines politics in relation to specific issues. Firstly, in their treatment of organisations and change, Harvey and Mills (1970) view political behaviour as actions that lay claims on the resource-sharing system of the organisation. The idea is that any adaptation changes will disrupt the distribution of resources, which will cause conflict between interest groups. Such conflicts are resolved through bargaining between interest groups and coalition formation (Mayes & Allen, 1977).

Politics is also viewed in relation to power, control, and influence. That is the ability of groups to use their power and authority to influence policies (Martin & Sims, 1974). For instance, in analysing the allocation of budget and policy consideration, Wildavsky (1968) defines politics as the bargain for whose preferences should prevail over the preferences of others (Cyert & March, 1963). Politics in several respects determines how power within the state affects policies (Gourevitch & Shine, 2005; Roe, 2003).

The political argument holds that whether the monetary policy would reflect economic or socio-cultural aspects depends on the political forces behind those propagating the monetary policy. This paper supports this argument by demonstrating that monetary policies in ECOWAS depend on political influence. Moreover, politics deserves more consideration because it sets the stage on which the other determinants evolve.

Political channels can either be the ballot in democratic states, interest groups as foreign interest, or lobbyists (Olson, 2012; Samuel, 1997). Studies on interest group pressure have focused on lobbyist influence on the legislative, executive, and judiciary (Epstein & Rowland, 1991). This chapter deals with influence on the executive, but we shall allude to influence on the legislature if necessary. The chapter illustrates the influence of France as an interest group in the creation of Eco currency. The aim of influence by France is personal gain (Harvey & Mills, 1970).

BRIEF HISTORY OF ECO CURRENCY

Currently, there are eight different currencies in use in the ECOWAS region.[2] Eight Francophone countries use the CFAF while the other member states use their respective national currencies. Francophone CFAF countries set up the West African Economic Monetary Union (WAEMU) to establish the new Eco currency. In contrast, the non-Francophone countries set up the West African Monetary Zone (WAMZ) in 2000.

Eco, the new currency intended for circulation and use in ECOWAS states, was Ghana and Nigeria's initiative and vastly prepared in Ghana's West African Monetary Institute. Launched in Guinea Conakry in 1983, the task of creating the single Eco currency was entrusted to West African Monetary Agency (WAMA) with its creation in 1996. The common West African Central Bank also plays a crucial role in minimizing asymmetric shocks and ensuring compliance with qualitative and quantitative benchmarks.

As per the June 29, 2019, announcement in Abuja at the 55th Ordinary session of ECOWAS head of states and government, a single Eco currency was to be introduced in January 2020 after almost three decades in preparation (Amato & Nubukpo, 2020). The Eco currency replaces the eight currencies in the region, which the ECOWAS central bank would manage.

However, while ECOWAS leaders were preparing to launch the single currency in January 2020 as agreed, Alassane Ouattara, the Ivorian president, and Emmanuel Macron, the French president, on December 21, 2019, announced that the CFAF in WAEMU states would be reformed and renamed as Eco currency. The terms of the Eco agreed by WAEMU states and France or what shall hereafter be referred to as French Eco differed considerably from those discussed by ECOWAS member states for the currency to be introduced in January 2020. The announcement was perfectly timed to be on the same day ECOWAS members were having a meeting to discuss the final adoption of the Eco.

As expected, the non-CFAF ECOWAS member states rejected the French Eco as the terms differed from those discussed by the member states. On January 16, 2020, in Abuja, Nigeria, the convergence Council of WAMZ distanced itself from the Ouattara-Macron announcement and

---

[2] Benin, Burkina Faso, Cote d'Ivoire, Guinea Bissau, Mali, Niger, Senegal, Togo use the CFA franc. At the same time, the other countries each have their currency. Cape Verdean escudo (Cape Verde), Guinean franc (Guinea), Dalasi (Gambia), Cedi (Ghana), Dollars (Liberia), Naira (Nigeria), Leone (Sierra Leone).

expressed concern about the announcement (Udo, 2020). However, they equally reiterated their intention to continue creating the single Eco currency on the terms agreed by all the members.

The fact that the currency would be pegged to the Euro and controlled by the French treasury was perceived as a French attempt to control the Eco currency as it did with the CFAF and, by implication, exert economic control over the whole region. Apart from a few amendments to the original monetary pact between CFAF countries and France, the French Eco ratified by the eight francophone states is all but in name a continuation of the CFAF. The French-backed Eco is still pegged to the Euro and controlled by the French treasury instead of a flexible exchange rate and control of the currency being vested to ECOWAS central bank as was initially agreed by the members.

Thus, instead of a currency Union in ECOWAS as intended, the region currently has an Eco currency ratified by Francophone member states and rejected by non-Francophone member states.

In September 2020, Ouattara announced the use of Eco in Ivory Coast within three to five years after France adopted a bill to amend the French monetary Union in WEAMU states by replacing CFAF with Eco (Smith, 2020).

France-Afrique Relationship

To analyze the monetary conflict between the Francophone ECOWAS countries and its non-Francophone counterpart, which failed to establish a single currency, one must comprehend the historical gulf between the two sets of member states.

After independence, the British and Portuguese allowed their colonies to rebuild and thus had minimal control over their former colonies. On the other hand, the French never left. They are accused time and again of exploiting African countries, especially with the continued use of CFAF. A good example is the 2019 vociferation between Italy and France over African immigrants. The then Italian deputy prime minister, Luigi Di Maio, regarded the migrant crisis in Europe as caused by France's exploitation of the economies of African countries for its economic benefit. The exploitation has thereby stifled African economies and forced Africans to seek a better life elsewhere. That results in the mass migration of Africans to Europe (Jon Nazca, 2019). Presumable, France would be the 15th economic power, not the 7th, without exploiting Africa (Jon Nazca, 2019).

France retained control over their former colonies' economic, social, and political development through several agreements. Monetary independence, as mentioned above, is one area where French dominance is hugely felt. While English-speaking and other ECOWAS countries each have their monetary policy controlled by their respective central banks, French-speaking ECOWAS countries and seven other French-speaking African countries are still using the French-controlled CFAF.

The CFAF is a currency introduced in 1939 and instituted by France for its colonies on December 26, 1945 (Amin, 2000). Most African countries were members of the union, but some countries dissociated themselves after independence and established their currency. North African countries were the first to leave. Tunisia left the union in 1958, Morocco in 1960, and Algeria in 1964, respectively. Madagascar and Mauritania left in 1973. In Sub-Sahara Africa (SSA), the story has been different. Many CFAF countries found it difficult to dissociate themselves from the Union as France perceives it as seeking to reject its control and influence over the region.

The two main monetary Unions making up the fourteen CFAF countries are the Central Africa Economic and Monetary Union (CEMAC) and the West African Economic and Monetary Union (WAEMU).[3] Each region has its central bank. CEMAC central bank, based in Yaoundé Cameroon, is known as the BEAC, and WAEMU is BCEAO. Before introducing the current French-backed Eco in 2020, the French representative had seats on the board of both banks for oversight. France continues to have seats on the BEAC board but ceased to sit on the WAEMU board as part of the terms of the new Eco currency.

The CFAF used by these two blocks are pegged to the Euro (formerly pegged to the French Franc). Between 1945–1973, 100 percent of the foreign currency reserve was deposited in the French treasury and controlled by France. It was reduced to 65 percent between 1973–2005 and then to 50 percent from 2005 (Agbohou, 2008). However, WAEMU states would no longer maintain a currency reserve in France as one of the conditions of introducing Eco is to move their foreign reserve to Senegal (Amato & Nubukpo, 2020). The CFAF countries have no access to this reserve though it can be loaned with interest. In addition, France has veto

---

[3] CEMAC has six member states: Cameroon, Chad, Gabon, Central African Republic, and Equatorial Guinea, while WAEMU consists of the eight ECOWAS CFA countries made up of Benin, Burkina Faso, Cote D'Ivoire, Guinea Bissau, Mali, Niger, Senegal, and Togo.

power on the monetary policies of the two unions (Amin, 2000). There are also legal, institutional, and policy requirements that must be met. Estimates from the Institute of International and European affairs show that the French treasury receives nearly $500 billion from FCFA countries every year and would do everything to keep it (Spagnol, 2019).

Some authors argue that the rationale for the currency is to protect these countries from economic crisis, monetary instability, and war (Vinay, 1988; Giorgione, 2001). However, others, especially Africans, perceive the continued use of the currency as a continuation of colonization (Pigeaud & Sylla, 2018). Many Africans would agree with Di Maio, who stated that "there are dozens of African states in which France prints its currency, the franc of the colonies, and with that, it finances the French public debt." He called on the EU and UN to sanction France for impoverishing these states and inciting its people (Jon Nazca, 2019).

By ECOWAS seeking to establish a single currency, it is competing with France for the purse of fourteen CFAF African countries, mindful that ECOWAS aims to first and foremost establish a single currency with WAEMU expecting that CEMAC states would become part of the union in the future.

Eight of the twelve CFAF countries are members of ECOWAS. If they achieve monetary independence, France will only have control of the remaining six CEMAC states. France is aware that if most CFAF countries depart from the CFAF zone, the rest of the countries will follow. France is currently lobbying CEMAC countries to become members of Eco and form a single block instead of the current two blocks. As a prominent French historian puts it, "the French governments viewed the whole world as a cultural, political and economic battlefield between France and the Anglo-Saxons..." (Prunier, 1995).

There is ample evidence that France would utilize all its might to ensure that the above fourteen CFAF countries do not leave the Monetary Union. Historic cases abound of instances in which France had overthrown Francophone leaders when they attempted to discontinue the use of the CFA France in favor of an independent currency.

A case in point is the 1958 incident in Sekou Toure's Guinea. Toure's slogans against French domination were "we prefer freedom in poverty to opulence in slavery" (Camara, 2000). Toure decided to establish an independent currency for Guinea and leave the CFAF currency union in keeping with the slogans. To dissuade other African countries from similar dreams, France destroyed infrastructures in Guinea in an attempt to cripple the economy before their departure. But Guinea kept its monetary independence and is the only French ECOWAS country that is not a member of the CFAF zone.

Thus far, only Guinea succeeded in escaping the French's snare and establishing its own currency. Mali and Togo, the other two ECOWAS nations that attempted to choose an independent currency, were quickly interrupted by France. In June 1962, the then president of Mali, Modiba Keita, decided to establish a separate currency from the CFAF but was met with resistance from the French. He was eventually overthrown by a former French legionnaire Lieutenant Moussa Traore on November 19, 1968 (Martin, 1986). However, Traore reverted to the Franc zone and re-introduced the CFAF in 1984.

In the same vein, President Sylvanus Olympio, the first post-independent president of Togo, was met with the same fate when he attempted to withdraw from the CFAF and institute an independent currency. Three days after the first currency was printed, Olympio was overthrown by Etienne Gnassingbe, another former French foreign Legionnaire, on January 13, 1963.

Similarly, it is stated that France pushed heavily for the overthrown of Muammar Gaddafi to prevent the former Libyan leader from creating a gold-backed African currency to supplant France's domination of Francophone African countries (Spagnol, 2019).

Thus, France's intervention before the launch of Eco in coercing its protégé Alassane Ouattara, to propose terms that were contrary to those agreed by ECOWAS member states is déjà vu (Wyss, 2014).

Based on the history of monetary independence in French African states, one can conclude that ECOWAS states were immature in overlooking French diplomacy and dominance in Francophone ECOWAS countries when negotiating the introduction of the Eco. This lack of foresight has divided the two monetary unions in ECOWAS and led to a lack of trust between Francophone ECOWAS states and other ECOWAS member states.

Division and Distrust Amongst the ECOWAS Member States

ECOWAS member states were preparing for the grand launch of the Eco currency in January 2020. But they were astounded on December 21, 2019, when WAEMU, spearheaded by Ivory Coast President Alassane Ouattara and Emmanuel Macron, the French president, announced that the CFAF in the WAEMU zone would rename the CFAF as Eco.

A meeting held on Thursday, December 26, 2019 immediately followed this announcement, by the non-CFAF ECOWAS member states, primarily anglophone countries (Ghana, Nigeria, Gambia, Liberia, Sierra Leone, and Guinea). They to denounced the pronouncement of WAEMU member states of replacing the CFAF with Eco and the involvement of France in the announcement. Furthermore, the non-CFAF states objected to the terms of the French Eco and their knowledge of the pronouncement or French participation in establishing a new single ECO currency (Udo, 2020).

This division between Francophone ECOWAS member states and the rest of the ECOWAS members states was reiterated by Muhammadu Buhari, the Nigerian president, in June 2020 in an extraordinary meeting of the Heads of States and Governments of the WAMZ (Daka, 2020). He expressed "an uneasy feeling" over the precarious nature of the Eco currency after the Macron-Ouattara announcement and the fact that WAEMU states intend to replace the CFAF with Eco ahead of the rest of the member states in violation of the Community Act (Daka, 2020).

In the words of Buhari, "It is a matter of concern that a people with whom we wish to go into a union are taking these major steps without trusting us for discussion" (Daka, 2020).

It is also argued that France is seeking to isolate Nigeria from Eco as the economic giant of ECOWAS. France perceives Nigeria's influence in ECOWAS as a threat to her interest in Africa. Nigeria accounts for half of the ECOWAS population (Maduk, 2020) and is the regional leader of ECOWAS in terms of financial contribution and policy influence (Ibrahim & Ahmad, 2020).

Wilson argues that the concessions made by France to CFAF ECOWAS member states can be perceived as the first step towards the monetary independence of these states (Wilson, 2020). Still, one can also argue that Alassane Ouattara and the other CFAF states betrayed the non-CFA ECOWAS members states by utilizing Eco as a bargaining chip for a better deal with France. By unilaterally accepting the terms of the Eco as suggested by France, the CFAF member states demonstrated that there were working with both parties at the same time and by so doing negotiating on two fronts. Thus, while the other member states were putting all the efforts towards ensuring the success of monetary unity of the Region, Francophone countries were negotiating on two fronts for a better deal for themselves to the detriment of the other ECOWAS states. Thus, Francophone states had little regard for the effort made by the zone for a single currency acceptable by all.

Non-CFAF states felt the currency had been appropriated by the French as there is no convincing explanation as to why the CFAF should be renamed as Eco, if not to thwart the plans of the other ECOWAS member states and force them to accept the terms of the French Eco (Oxford Analytical).

Currently, instead of ECOWAS working towards a common Eco currency, it is evident that the dichotomy between the two vying fractions is likely to give rise to two different Eco currencies: French Eco used by Francophone ECOWAS member states and African Eco utilized by non-Francophone ECOWAS countries. As the political theory denotes, each group is seeking its own interest.

France was not directly involved in the preparation and design of the Eco from its inception. At least not visibly. As it stands, ECOWAS can no longer ignore French influence or diplomacy in seeking to alter the direction of the Eco currency. France is vying to be involved in the Eco through the CFAF countries. However, the non-Francophone African states are unwilling to involve France in the new currency or, worst still accept her terms and must now seek a new route to creating the Eco currency in the non-Francophone member states.

While some have argued that the Ouattara-Macron announcement of CFAF reform may be the start of liberation from the use of the CFAF by Francophone Africa, it would be a step back for the non-francophone member states (Wilson, 2020). After independence, non-Francophone ECOWAS countries created their independent currencies and, through several hardships, have come to establish separate reliable currencies. The Nigerian naira and Ghanian cedi are all testaments to African countries' ability to manage their currencies without the assistance of their colonial masters. Africans would perceive acceptance of France's management and control of the Eco currency as regressing to the colonial era. Therefore, it is implausible that non-francophone ECOWAS member states would accept French Eco.

Drawing reference from elsewhere, the OHADA Uniform Act on business law in African was intended to harmonize business law in Africa. However, because it is based mainly on French law, it was rejected by Anglophone countries, despite efforts by Francophone countries to lobby for these countries to join the OHADA treaty (Ntongho, 2012).

Nonetheless, it would benefit both fractions if ECOWAS could agree on a common currency. However, considering the current division in ECOWAS, is there a way forward to establishing a single currency? How can currency unity be achieved in ECOWAS?

Way Forward for ECOWAS Monetary Integration

After more than two decades of preparation for integrating monetary policy in ECOWAS, discussions on creating a single Eco for all its members has reached a stalemate. It shall be a lost opportunity and a huge waste of resources if, after several decades of planning, the creation of a single Eco currency is thwarted by colonial division.

While trust has been lost, the stakes are still high, and there is much to be gained or lost if ECOWAS states do not realize their aspiration of a single currency in the region. It will be a travesty if all their hard work for the past three decades does not come to fruition.

Besides macroeconomic factors (including convertibility between currencies, weak financial system and payment channels, ineffective monetary policies, and imbalance between exchange rates of different currencies), the most worrying barrier to a single currency in the ECOWAS region is the inability of Francophone member states to dissociate themselves from the use of CFAF. How then can ECOWAS navigate French might if they choose to do so? Is it their place to interfere, or should it be left to its Francophone brothers? Does ECOWAS as a region have any interest in working with France? This section attempts to answer these questions by discussing three possibilities of how ECOWAS member states, especially non-CFAF member states, can avert French influence and complete the establishment of a single Eco currency and monetary integration in the region.

Francophone CFAF ECOWAS Member States Negotiate an Exit Agreements from the CFAF with France

Successive French presidents and ministers have alluded on numerous occasions that it is up to African CFAF countries to determine when to sever ties from the CFAF colonial currency (Wilson, 2020). Based on this rhetoric by French officials, Wilson (2020) states that it would be up to CFAF African states to decide when to halt the use of CFAF unilaterally. However, this is a very simplistic view as history has shown that France benefits enormously from the CFAF and would not easily relinquish control of the currency. Though foreign reserve requirement which stipulated that CFAF countries deposit their reserve into the French treasury has been abolished by the new terms of the Eco, which accounted for roughly 440 euros into the French treasury yearly and was a major point of discontent by CFAF states, the French still possess enormous benefit in the continuous use of CFAF by Francophone African countries (How Africa, 2018). The Eco is still pegged to the Euro and backed by the French treasury. The convertibility and stability of the Eco is also guaranteed by the Euro (Cook, 2020).

Though it may seem that France would not have direct control of the new French Eco in WAEMU states as France ceases to have seats on the BCEAO board, she is still the guarantor of the new French Eco, which gives her the right to influence the currency. Coupled with its military presence and support it provides to several Francophone presidents to keep them in power, few if any Francophone presidents would dare to sever the use of CFAF unilaterally. They will not attempt because they are worried the repercussions would be substantial.

Thus, a more realistic approach is for CFAF countries to negotiate an exit arrangement as a block. Any unilateral withdrawal from the CFAF by a single country would likely be met with economic and military sanctions by France. While France can impose economic sanctions on eight countries, military intervention would be unlikely.

ECOWAS Negotiate an Exit Agreement with France on Behave of the Whole Region

This suggestion may seem farfetched considering non-Francophone ECOWAS states are still nursing the soft blow they received from their Francophone counterpart and France with the 19th December announcement of replacing CFAF with Eco without their knowledge.

However, mindful of where we are now with the possibility of two Ecos and the realization that France is much a part of the Eco as the rest of ECOWAS member states, it is not conceivable to propose that the region seek to negotiate directly with France. Before the Ouattara-Macron announcement, France was lurking in the shadows and waiting for the right moment to strike, which it did successfully. Now that France has come out of the shadows and is a visible member of the Eco process, the region can directly involve France in the withdrawal process.

This approach can be beneficial in several ways. Firstly, the region can move forward as a block and agree on a road map together without the uncertainty of CFAF states destabilizing the region without their knowledge or an unexpected unilateral announcement, as was the case on December 19, 2019. Secondly, it will dispel doubts from CFAF countries that France may cause economic and political havoc as they did in the past if they withdraw from the CFAF zone. Thirdly, a plan agreed by all parties with their input will have a better chance of success. Fourthly, if ECOWAS succeeds in persuading France to agree on a withdrawal agreement, these countries can benefit from France's superior knowledge and technical assistance. Fifthly, it would reflect good faith from France to truly assist its former colonies and appease Francophone Africa, where France general has a poor reputation for exploitation.

The drawback of this approach is the already existing distrust between Francophone and Anglophone ECOWAS member states. More so, some may argue that there is no benefit for the non-CFAF countries in negotiating with France as this should be left to the CFAF countries to decide if they intend to sever the use of CFAF. Furthermore, France has no direct interest in the Eco and should not be involved in the first place. Negotiating with France may also give the impression that ECOWAS countries are reaching out to France or establishing a monetary union without France is impossible; that may put France in a superior position to make demands and benefit from the monetary union. Worst still, France may perceive this as non-Francophone ECOWAS states seeking to join the French Eco.

However, having a foreign country like France, which is already loathed by Africans involved in the Eco, would be met with suspicion by African citizens (McKesson, 1993). Also, Nigeria, as the dominant nation of the region comprising one-third of ECOWAS economy and seeking to establish itself as the giant of Africa, is unlikely to consider any French involvement in Eco as this would reduce her influence in the region.

Furthermore, Anglophones and other ECOWAS countries have successfully managed their currencies for many years. They would thus be unwilling to cede any monetary independence to a superpower whose continuous presence in Africa is viewed negatively even by western powers.

This approach, while not impossible, would require gigantic planning and negotiation and a complete derailment of course of the Eco. Moreover, it would also be a lengthy process involving economic consideration and equally direct political and socio-cultural issues.

A Piecemeal Approach

The fastest and most likely approach to establish the Eco currency in West Africa, mindful of the current division between French African countries and the rest of ECOWAS states, is to proceed with a piecemeal approach as was the case with the euro currency. Members states that meet the minimum criteria can introduce the currency, and the other member states can join the monetary union when they fulfill the requirements. It is paramount that Nigeria and Ghana, as the largest economies in ECOWAS and the ardent advocates of the Eco, ensure they meet the criteria as it is unlikely for the African Eco to be successful without them (Amato & Nubukpo, 2020; Amaefule & Ibekwe, 2021).

Thus, the probable scenario to establish a unified Eco currency in ECOWAS is for the non-CFAF countries with monetary independence and experience in currency management to create an Eco based on the original vision. As the region's powerhouse, Ghana and Nigeria would need to show leadership and meet the criteria for the new currency and encourage the other non-CFAF countries to do the same. Once the threshold for creating the new currency has been achieved, they can launch the new currency controlled by the ECOWAS central bank. Other ECOWAS states would slowly join the Monetary Union when they meet the minimum criteria. For the single currency to succeed, member states need to meet four essential convergence criteria to avoid shock to the monetary zone. The requirements are: price stability through a single-digit inflation rate, sustainable fiscal balance, government budget limiting central bank finance, and adequate external reserve (Nnanna, 2004).

This approach will also allow non-ECOWAS neighboring states, including CFAF states such as Cameroon and Chad, to join the Eco in the future if they decide to exit the CFAF zone.

This piecemeal approach is advantageous for the following reasons. Firstly, it is less litigious and would avoid any conflict between CFAF and non-CFAF countries as members are not forced to join the single Eco currency. Secondly, it provides CFAF member states the discretion of joining the French Eco or the African Eco. Thirdly, countries that do not meet the minimum criteria cannot join the African Eco, reducing the monetary risk associated with a common currency. Fourthly, it does not penalize countries that meet the minimum standards and work hard to establish the Eco, such as Nigeria and Ghana. Instead, these countries can use the currency, and countries that meet the minimum criteria follow suit.

The drawback of this approach is that it derails the original plan for establishing the Eco as the plan was for a unitary Eco and not two Eco currencies. Secondly, it maintains the current status quo of distrust between the Francophone and non-francophone ECOWAS states. Thirdly, having two Eco currencies would slow the monetary union and economic integration in the region and demotivate monetary integration in Africa.

However, considering the fact that there are currently eight currencies in ECOWAS, having two Eco currencies in the region is better than the current eight currencies. As for the name, there is no reason why after toiling for several decades, the non-Francophone ECOWAS states should not also use the name Eco. Moreover, several countries use the dollar as distinct currencies. Therefore, there can be an African Eco and French Eco coexisting as two separate currencies.

Conclusion

Most of the arguments advanced by scholars against the possibilities of an Eco currency in 2020 are based on economic and monetary factors such as non-convertibility between currencies, weak financial system and payment channels, ineffective monetary policies, and imbalance between exchange rates of different currencies (Senzu, 2020).

This chapter illustrates that for monetary unity in ECOWAS to be successful, the region must find a way to resolve the political dichotomy between the Francophone and the rest of the ECOWAS states. Economic and monetary considerations alone may not suffice as Francophone ECOWAS member states do not possess similar monetary sovereignty as their non-Francophone counterpart in deciding their monetary future.

The failure thus far to agree on a single Eco currency is a lost opportunity for accelerated economic integration and dissociation from the cultural division that has plagued the continent since colonization. As the region prepares to launch the African Eco in 2027, it would greatly benefit the Region and Africa if both fractions could come to a consensus for one Eco currency accepted by all member states without western intervention (France 24, 2021). They can take comfort in that several attempts to launch the Euro failed, but today, it is one of the most solid economic and monetary unions in the World (Dedman, 1998).

References

Agbohou, N. (2008). *Le Franc CFA et L'Euro Contre L'Afrique*. Solidarite Mondiale.

Amaefule, C., & Ibekwe, M. A. (2021). The implication of financial derivable from abroad on West African Monetary Zone's Eco Currency. *European Journal of Sustainable Development Research, 5*(1).

Amato, M., & Nubukpo, K. (2020). A new currency for West African states: The theoretical and political conditions of its feasibility. *PSL Quarterly Review, 73*(292), 3.

Amin, A. (2000). *Long term economic growth of CFA franc zone countries*. United Nations/WIDER.

Buhari urges caution on ECOWAS common currency (premiumtimesng.com).

Buhari urges caution on ECOWAS common currency | The Guardian Nigeria News.

Camara, M. S. (2000). From military politicization to militarization of power in Guinea-Conakry. *Journal of Political & Military Sociology*, 311–326.

Cook, C. (2020, May 30). 8 Francophone countries get new currency (aa.com.tr).

Cyert, R. M., & March, J. G. (1963). *A behavioural theory of the firm*. Prentice-Hall.

Daka, T. (2020, June 23). Buhari urges caution on ECOWAS common currency. *The Guardian Nigeria News*; Buhari urges caution on ECOWAS common currency (premiumtimesng.com)

Dedman, M. (1998). EMU: The first time around. *History Today, 48*(1), 5–7.

Epstein, L., & Rowland, C. K. (1991). Interest groups in the courts: Do groups fare better? In A. J. Cigler & B. A. Loomis (Eds.), *Interest groups politics*. University of Kansas, A Divisional of Congress Quarterly Inc, N.W.

France 24. (2021, June 19). West African regional bloc adopts new plan to launch Eco single currency in 2027 (france24.com)

Giorgione, G. (2001). New evidence on the output-inflation trade-off from developing economies: The case of the CFA Franc Zone. *Applied Economics, 33*(8), 1077–1082.

Gourevitch, P., & Shine, J. (2005). *Political power and corporate control: The new global politics of corporate governance*. Princeton University Press.

Harvey, E., & Mills, R. (1970). Patterns of organizational adaptation: A political perspective. *Power in organizations*, 181–213.

How Africa. (2018). Scandal: According to a German Newspaper, Africa Pays Approximately 400 Billion Euros Annually to France. *How Africa News*.

Ibrahim, Y. K., & Ahmad, A. A. (2020). The role of Nigeria in the ECOWAS and its support towards the common proposed currency ECO. *Asian People Journal (APJ), 3*(2), 86–95.

Jon Nazca, RT. (2019, January 22). *Italian deputy MP calls on EU to Sanction France for its "continued colonisation" of Africa.* Accessed on July 26 2020 at https://www.rt.com/news/449303-france-africa-sanctions-colonializm/

Koddenbrock, K., & Sylla, N. S. (2019). *Towards a political economy of monetary dependency: The case of the CFA franc in West Africa* (No. 19/2).

Maduk, E. A. (2020). Appraising the legal issues with the 'concurrency'. *Nnamdi Azikiwe University Journal of International Law and Jurisprudence, 11*(2), 12–19.

Marchesin, P. (1998). La politique africaine de la France en transition. *Politique africaine, 71,* 91–106.

Martin, G. (1986). The Franc Zone, underdevelopment and dependency in francophone Africa. *Third World Quarterly, 8*(1), 205–235.

Martin, N. H., & Sims, J. H. (1974). Power and tactics. In D. A. Kolb, I. M. Rubin, & J. M. McIntyre (Eds.), *Organisational psychology: A book of readings* (pp. 177–183). Prentice-Hall.

Mati, S., Civcir, I., & Ozdeser, H. (2019). ECOWAS common currency: How prepared are its members? *Investigación económica, 78*(308), 89–119.

Maxpo Discussion paper, & Taylor, I. (2019). France à fric: The CFA zone in Africa and neocolonialism. *Third World Quarterly, 40*(6), 1064–1088.

Mayes, B. T., & Allen, R. W. (1977). Towards a definition of Fred I. Greenstein (1967), 'Personality and politics: Problems of evidence, inference and conceptualization'. *The American Behavioral Scientist, 11,* 38–53. at p. 39.

McKesson, J. A. (1993). France and Africa: The evolving saga. *French Politics and Society,* 55–69.

Miles, W. (2017). How feasible is the West African eco currency union? An investigation using synchronicity and similarity measures. *Journal of Economic Studies, 44*(4), 650–664.

Nnanna, O. J. (2004). The eco currency, expectations and business growth in West Africa. *Economic and Financial Review, 42*(1), 2.

Ntongho, R. A. (2012). Political economy of the harmonisation of business law in Africa. *Journal of Politics and Law, 5,* 58.

Olson, M. (2012). The logic of collective action [1965]. *Contemporary Sociological Theory, 124.*

Pigeaud, F., & Sylla, N. S. (2018). *L'arme invisible de la Francafrique: Une histoire du Franc CFA.* La Découverte.

Prunier, G. (1995). *The Rwanda crisis (1959-1994) history of a genocide* (p. 326). New York/Columbia University Press.

Roe, M. J. (2003). *Political determinants of corporate governance.* Oxford University Press.

Samuel, F. (1997). *The history of government* (pp. 1–111). Cambridge University Press.
Senzu, E. T. (2020). The advanced proposed architecture of eco-currency: Technical analysis of West Africa single currency program. *Journal of Advanced Studies in Finance (JASF), 11*(22), 81–95.
Smith, E. (2020, January 17). West African 'Eco' currency sparks division over timetable and euro peg (cnbc.com).
Spagnol, G. (2019). *Is France still exploiting Africa?* Institut Europeen des Relations Internationales at http://www.ieri.be/en/publications/wp/2019/f-vrier/france-still-exploiting-africa. Accessed on 29 Oct 2020.
Uchehara, K. (2014). France-Afrique model: A declining relationship. *Journal of Administrative Sciences/Yönetim Bilimleri Dergisi, 12*(23), 36–37.
Udo, B. (2020, January 16). ECO crisis deepens as Nigeria, other English-speaking countries condemn French-speaking counterparts. *Premium Times* at (premiumtimesng.com) *Premium Times*. Accessed on 13 Jul 2021.
Utley, R. (2002). 'Not to do less but to do better...': French military policy in Africa. *International Affairs, 78*(1), 129–146.
Vetlesen, A. J. (2000). Genocide: A case for the responsibility of the bystander. *Journal of Peace Research, 37*(4), 519–532.
Vinay, B. (1988). *Zone Franc et Cooperation Monetaire*. Ministere de la Cooperation et du Developpement Paris.
Von Epp, R. (1937). The question of colonies: The German standpoint. *Journal of the Royal African Society, 36*(142), 3–9. Retrieved July 9, 2021, from http://www.jstor.org/stable/717226
Wildavsky, A. (1968). Budgeting as a political process. In D. L. Sills (Ed.), *The international encyclopaedia of the social sciences*. Macmillan Co.
Willsher, K. (2019, January 27). Italy and France Dispute awakens a dark Colonial legacy. *The Guardian*.
Wilson, J. (2020). Losing currency? The shifting landscape of the CFA franc zones. *Third World Quarterly, 42*(4), 736–754.
Wyss, M. (2014). Primus inter pares?: France and multi-actor peacekeeping in Côte d'Ivoire. In *Peacekeeping in Africa* (pp. 152–168). Routledge.

CHAPTER 7

The Effects of Minimum Bank Capital and Governance on the Financing of the EMCCA Economies

Issidor Noumba and André Arnaud Enguene

INTRODUCTION

Research on the regulation of the level of bank capital has evolved, particularly since the Bales agreements. Bales I is a ground element of international banking regulation based on the principle that each risk must be covered by a certain amount of capital to ensure the overall security of the market and minimize risks of a systemic nature. Bales II aims at harmonizing the rules on bank capital requirements. Accordingly, Pillar 2 of this regulation deals with a minimum capital requirement. Additionally, in response to the financial crisis of 2007/2008 and even 2010 with the sovereign debt crisis, the international regulatory authorities enacted Bales

---

The economic and Monetary Community of Central Africa (EMCCA) comprises six countries: Cameroon, Congo Republic, Central African Republic, Gabon, Equatorial Guinea, and Chad.

I. Noumba (✉) • A. A. Enguene
University of Yaounde II, Yaounde (Centre), Cameroon
e-mail: tonfeu_yombi2009@yahoo.com; engueneandre@yahoo.com

© The Author(s), under exclusive license to Springer Nature Switzerland AG 2022
A. A. Amin et al. (eds.), *Monetary and Financial Systems in Africa*,
https://doi.org/10.1007/978-3-030-96225-8_7

III. This latest international banking regulation aims to strengthen capital requirements, particularly with regard to the requirement of bank capital. It equally puts the issue of bank capital back on the agenda.

Bank capital stems from the two complementary notions of "economic capital" and "regulatory capital." Regulatory capital aims at ensuring the soundness and stability of individual banks and the banking system as a whole (Tiesset and Troussard, 2005). It is a collective measure that applies to all market actors, while economic capital is an individual measure that aims at accounting for risks. On the one hand, it is defined by each credit institution, and on the other hand, it makes it possible to measure each type of risk (Tiesset & Troussard, 2005). These two ratios are part of the financial governance that aims to protect customer deposits while improving banking intermediation activity.

Bank capital represents the resources generated by the bank itself, which makes it possible to finance what it has not borrowed. According to Mishkin (2010), "Banks are required to make decisions about the amount of bank capital they should hold for three reasons. Firstly, bank capital is used to avoid bank failures. Secondly, bank capital affects the bank's shareholder return. Thirdly, a minimum amount of capital (minimum regulatory capital) is required by the supervisory authorities". According to the bank lobbying defenders, the bank capital requirement reduces the resources that banks can lend. They hold that ceteris paribus, one "franc" less bank capital is one "franc" less to financing the economy.

In the same vein, Osborne, Fuertes, and Milne (2017), resting on Holmstrom and Tirole (1997), contend that "higher bank capital is associated with higher lending volume and lower lending rates". These three authors also state that "Capital is a source of financing" and ceteris paribus, "a financial institution with more bank capital has more financial resources to lend to economic agents in need of financing."

In this study, we establish a link between the level of minimum bank capital and the financing of economies in EMCCA countries. Compared with the best-capitalized banking systems on the continent (Tunisia, Nigeria, Algeria, Ghana, and South Africa), EMCCA remains undercapitalized. However, the situation has changed with implementing the COBAC Regulation R-2009, fixing and harmonizing the capital.[1] The expectation is that an increase in minimum bank capital may increase the capacity of credit institutions to ensure optimal financing of economies.

---

[1] COBAC Regulation R-2009/01/, fixing the Minimum Bank Capital of the Credit Establishments.

The economy's financing refers to "all the mechanisms by which economic agents (households, companies, and governments) meet their financing needs. Financing can be achieved by mobilizing existing savings (non-monetary financing) or by monetary creation (monetary financing)". Economic agents in need of financing can obtain financing directly from the financial markets (selling bonds or equities). This method of financing requires the intervention of a financial intermediary. Economic agents in need of financing can obtain the resources needed from a financial intermediary.

Governance is an idea descriptive of reality and a normative ideal associated with transparency, ethics, and the effectiveness of public action (Pitseys, 2010). Governance covers both political ethics (absence of corruption), the control of political representatives, the reform of international institutions, the absence of violence in a country, and respect for the laws and regulations in force. As a result, the bank capital held by credit institutions and the level of governance within them or at the global level, i.e., the country, affect how credit institutions provide the economy with the financial resources necessary for its development. Therefore, it is a question of carrying out a non-exhaustive review of previous work on this issue, which seems important to us.

The access to bank credit in EMCCA is one of the lowest in sub-Saharan Africa (Périou, 2014). Indeed, the penetration rate remains low (around 3 percent of the total population), and credit to the private sector is below the average for sub-Saharan Africa (Hugon, 2007). Furthermore, in terms of credit distribution, credit to public administrations amounted to 585 billion francs CFA in 2015, compared with 120 and 84 billion CFA francs respectively in 2009 and 2003. Credits to public enterprises amounted to 394, 178, and 149 billion CFA francs in 2015, 2009, and 2003 respectively. Those granted to the private sectors amounted to 6026, 2455 and 1335 billion CFA francs in 2015, 2009 and 2003 respectively (COBAC, 2003; 2009; 2015). In addition, the analysis by term of the outstanding loans granted in recent years shows a renewed interest in financing investments in EMCCA compared to the period before 2009 (Appendix 7.2).

However, despite the sharp increase in both the level of bank capital and the level of loans distributed by credit institutions over the past few years, the governance indices defined by the WGI are hardly shining. Indeed, EMCCA countries face significant governance challenges. The challenge stems from the political instability in countries like the Central African Republic, Chad, and Cameroon. Political instability and corruption in these countries make it difficult for credit institutions to operate in this environment and encourage others to invest in this market segment. As a result, credit institutions need an optimal framework to play their role in an economy fully.

On the one hand, it is about complying with regulatory requirements. On the other hand, it is about evolving in an environment with optimal governance.

In short, the essence of a banking system is its role in financial intermediation, a role that should be oriented towards the financing of economic agents in need of financing. In this respect, EMCCA banks must transform resources to solve the thorny problem of over liquidity of EMCCA credit institutions. However, the institutions must respect specific prudential requirements, such as holding a minimum level of bank capital. The latter must satisfy the traditional objectives of stability, solidity, and liquidity of the banking system. It must also enable banks to be profitable and provide funds for economic agents in need of financing as shaping governance to address corruption and political instability on the economy's financing. Thus, the chapter raises the problem of the weak bank financing for the EMCCA economy. Therefore the study finds out if bank capital and governance have anything to do with the financing of the countries studied.

This study aims to assess the effect of minimum bank capital and governance on the financing of the EMCCA economies. The main objective is divided into three sub-objectives: to assess the effect of minimum bank capital on the triple dimension of financing of the economy, accounting for some socio-political environment of the sub-region. The remainder of the chapter articulates around three sections. The section "Literature Review" presents the theoretical and empirical foundations of the analysis. "Empirical Strategy and Data" presents the methodological approach adopted, and the section "Results" presents an analysis of the results, while section "Concluding Remarks" concludes.

Literature Review

Nowadays, prudential regulation is at the heart of financial institutions, and it is essentially based on the definition of prudential ratios, with the flagship element being the solvency ratio (Cooke ratio in 1988). However, the first theoretical contributions to the analysis of prudential regulation have difficulty integrating the specificities of banks in relation to the financial market (theory of preference overstatements) and other financial intermediaries (theory of portfolio choices). Recent approaches, known as "optimal regulation", are beginning to incorporate the contributions of the information economy and, more specifically, certain information asymmetries that are essential to understanding banking economics (Miles et al., 2013). However, there is still room for the evolution of the debate by focusing on optimizing the theory of bank financing to the minimum capital requirement of banks.

Regulation of the minimum bank capital requirements for credit institutions and the socio-political environment influence the level and quality of bank credits needed to finance an economy (Conseil d'Analyse Economique, 2012). Indeed, these regulations modify the volume of loans or bank borrowing. However, the impact is more or less moderate depending on the importance of the banking system, the level of corruption, and the level of stability in the economy's financing. Credit institutions react indifferently to the volume of minimum bank capital required to satisfy economic agents' demand and the importance of the country's risk. The purpose of this section is to critically review the theoretical and empirical literature on the effect of credit institutions' capital on the financing of economic activities. Two main theories meet face to face on the subject: the portfolio choice theory and the "credit crunch hypothesis'" or the state preference theory.

The first category of the literature contends that bank capital positively affects the country's economy. The level of bank capital requirements determines the bank lending decisions. We must notice that the evolution of the banking systems through regulatory change has strengthened the role of bank capital in financing the business. The effect of bank capital on lending is a determining factor in the link between "financial conditions and real activity" (Levieuge, 2005). Bank capital plays a vital role in transmitting monetary policy through bank lending because of the portfolio choice theory. The transmission through credits will depend upon the state preference theory. These theories have laid the foundations for existing empirical studies.

Empirically, the bank-lending channel supposes the existence of bank credit as the only means of financing economic agents in need of financing. Consequently, credit institutions are obliged to raise capital only by collecting bank deposits. However, the bank capital channel's functioning depends on two factors: (i) enterprises whose sole source of financing is bank credit. (ii) Credit institutions experience difficulties in granting funds due to information asymmetries.

For example, Van Den Heuvel and Skander (2008) analyze the role of bank lending in the transmission of monetary policy by taking into account the regulation of the level of bank capital. They develop a dynamic methodology for managing assets and liabilities. This model integrates bank capital requirements based on uncertainty and an imperfect credit institutions' regulatory capital market. The authors take into account "a maturity mismatch in the balance sheet of credit institutions". They propose a bank capital channel through which monetary policy affects bank lending by affecting credit institutions' capital. On the other hand, this mechanism is not based on a particular role of bank reserves linked to the bank-lending channel.

Meanwhile, a study conducted by Van Den Heuvel (2002) suggests that a channel independent of monetary policy gives the bank capital channel a vital role in the financing of economic agents. According to this author, a shock on the bank capital channel affects the real economy through the bank-lending channel. Thus, this author considers that bank capital plays a role in transmitting shocks from the financial sector to the real economy. Similarly, Wood (2003) tests the hypothesis of the low level of bank capital on the activity of credit institutions in Japan. Indeed, the low level of bank capital reduced bank-lending activity to the Japanese economy in the 1990s. For this purpose, it uses a sample of credit institutions representing about 90 percent of the assets of this banking system. His analyses focus on the dynamics between the evolution of bank balance sheet items and bank capital. The results of this study corroborate the hypothesis of credit rationing. This credit rationing is mainly due to deterioration in the bank capital of credit institutions. There is thus a positive and statistically significant correlation between the bank capital ratio and the growth in the level of bank loans.

Furthermore, a study by Bernanke and Lown (1991) in the USA coincides with strengthening bank capital regulation.[2] Indeed, the regulatory requirement for bank capital is based on the level of risk incurred by credit institutions. Since the implementation of the Cooke ratio in 1988, several regulatory authorities have implemented it. This requirement is characterized by tightening the criteria for the provisioning of probable losses on bank loans. In the United States, the law on early enforcement actions for

---

[2] Implementation of Cooke ratio from Basel I.

defaulting institutions has been introduced. From there, the adoption of a risk-based regulatory capital requirement has increased the number of credit institutions with capital below the minimum required. The findings of this study support the hypothesis of credit rationing. According to the authors, "it is indeed the pressure on bank capital levels that induces a significant shift to the left of the bank loan supply curve."

In addition, Altunbas et al. (2007) use bank balance sheet data to assess the level of bank lending following the change in bank capital ratios between 1991 and 1999. These authors classify credit institutions according to their size in bank capital. The objective of their study is to find out whether the level of bank capital has a significant impact on the bank-lending channel. The authors use a panel methodology for empirical analyses and find that in European Union banking systems, "banks with low levels of bank capital tend to reduce the level of bank lending." However, these findings differ from country to country. For instance, in France, Germany, Italy, and Spain, there is evidence of a bank-lending channel. In other words, the level of bank capital affects bank lending.

Gambacorta and Mistulli (2004), for their part, examine possible cross-sectional differences in the response of bank lending to the bank capital shock and the GDP shock according to the capital levels of European banks. Their findings highlight that "well-capitalized banks provide adequate financing to firms." Their study confirms that "the hypothesis of the bank lending channel is a function of the capital endowment of credit institutions." Moreover, their study shows that bank lending reacts differently to the monetary policy shock. According to them, this shock is a function of credit institutions' maturity transformation cost levels.

Similarly, Liu and Wilson (2010) analyze the impact between bank capital and monetary policy transmission in Japan. For this study, the analysis of the bank capital channel requires an analysis of its impact on the economy's financing. Thus, they use the empirical model developed by Kashyap et al. (2010) in their study. For these authors, and as predicted by the hypothesis of the bank capital channel, a tightening of monetary policy affects less heavily capitalized credit institutions. Similarly, as predicted by the bank-capital channel hypothesis, credit institutions with higher maturity transformation costs take out bank loans because of a tightening of monetary policy. Thus, the credit supply of highly capitalized financial institutions is less dependent on the business cycle. The findings indicate that it is "important that monetary policy considers the regulation of bank capital and its effect on the economy. Second, credit institutions must be well-capitalized to reduce the pro-cyclicality effect".

Finally, Levieuge (2005), in his article, focuses on the study of the core of the bank capital channel, in this case, the development of the link between "capital and credit supply". This author stresses the importance of the financial health of credit institutions on their lending behavior. For him, Scandinavian and Japanese banking institutions offer convincing clues to this analysis, as institutions close to (or already below) the required capitalization thresholds either tend to ration bank credit or impose stricter bank lending conditions. These same credit institutions are responsible for the weakening of the supply of bank credit.

Let us come now to the studies that conclude on a negative effect of the bank capital on the financing of the economy. Brun, Fraisse, and Thesmar (2013) analyze the real effects of capital requirements on the distribution of credit in France. The authors use the transition from Basel I to Basel II. Their empirical analyses exploit the double variation of bank capital to empirically estimate the semi-elasticity of credit to bank capital requirements. They use a methodology that allows them to correct for credit demand effects at the firm level and credit supply effects at the level of the credit institution. Finally, the authors arrived the conclusion that an additional requirement of one percentage point of bank capital reduces credit distribution by 10 percent.

Likewise, Dietsch and al. (2016) analyze the effects of capital requirements on the distribution of credit to SMEs in France. These authors highlight an underestimation of credit risk in the use of formulas to calculate regulatory bank capital. They assess the impact of regulatory capital requirements on the corporate loan portfolios of the six largest banking groups operating in France. They compare the economic capital requirements measured by a multi-factor model with a portfolio credit risk model. This model considers the heterogeneity of companies requesting funds from credit institutions by differentiating them according to their size. It leads to two types of conclusions. The first is that the formulas used to calculate regulatory capital do not underestimate bank portfolio credit risk since regulatory bank capital requirements are often higher than economic bank capital requirements by a large majority. The second conclusion is that regulatory bank capital models overestimate the sensitivity of borrowers to the business cycle. Thus, economic capital requirements are driven down by diversification effects induced by borrower heterogeneity.

The above analyses clarify any ambiguity about the impact of bank capitalization on the supply of bank loans or the economy's financing. If there is a broad consensus to accept the influence of bank capital on the volume of financing granted, the cost and conditions of the credit are also covered, or the socio-political environment may also provide additional explanation. In the light of these various empirical studies, it is possible to affirm that the bank capital of credit institutions influences the volume and conditions offered and the cost of credit. It should also be noted that, generally speaking, the relationship between bank capital and the supply of credit resides in consideration of regulatory requirements in this area (preservation of regulatory capital). The reviewed studies allow us to verify the working hypothesis set out above empirically.

Corruption is the main obstacle to economic and social development in the world (International Chamber of Commerce, 2008). As a result, corruption affects all of us and can affect the financing of economic agents in need of financing. It is about: (i) Less prosperity. Corruption slows down economic growth, harms the rule of law, and wastes skills and precious resources. When corruption is pervasive, banks hesitate to invest in the face of the markedly high cost of economic activity. Less respect for rights: corruption endangers financial democracy and financial governance by weakening the financial institutions capable of providing the funds necessary to finance the economy. (ii) Less service since corruption robs funds intended to finance essential services, particularly in financing health, education, or even access to drinking water…

Eradicating corruption is critical to achieving the Sustainable Development Goals. Nevertheless, on the other hand, corruption develops moral hazards and adverse selection in financing the economy. Therefore, one would expect a negative relationship between corruption and the economy's financing.

Empirical Strategy and Data

The analysis presented in the previous section allowed us to highlight the link between the level of bank capital and the economy's financing. In other words, the financing of economies could be influenced by the level of bank capital. To deepen the existing studies, we will first present the empirical model, and secondly, we will present the variables and the estimation method.

For Collard and Feve (2008), "the VAR approach allows a modeling of the dynamics of the different exogenous variables using a small number of restrictions." Furthermore, Gossé and Guillaumin (2013) consider that the VAR model, in general, has "thus allowed many authors to quantify the instantaneous and dynamic multiplier effects of economic policies (monetary, fiscal and tax) on economic activity." The above reason explains the reason for using the VAR methodology to assess the impact of minimum banks on the different levels of financing of EMCCA economies. Following Abrigo and Love (2016), we consider a panel VAR model with p-order and k-variables. This model captures a specific fixed-effects panel specified as follows. Model (7.1) below is a vector model.

$$Y_{\cdot it} = Y_{\cdot it-1} A_1 + Y_{\cdot it-2} A_2 + \cdots + Y_{\cdot it-p+1} A_{\cdot p-1} + Y_{\cdot it-p} A_{\cdot p}$$
$$+ X_{\cdot it} B_{\cdot} + \mu_{it} + \xi_{it} \quad i \varepsilon \{1, 2, \cdots, N\}, t \varepsilon \{1, 2, \cdots, Ti\} \quad (7.1)$$

where $Y_{\cdot it}$ is a vector (1*k) of dependent variables; $X_{\cdot it}$ is a vector (1*l) of exogenous variables; μ_{it} et ξ_{it} are respectively the vectors (1*k) of dependent variables for fixed and specific effects and idiosyncratic errors. With μ_{ji}, ϑ_{jt} et ξ_{jit} representing country-specific effects, time-specific effects, and idiosyncratic error, respectively. The (k*k) matrix $A_{\cdot 1}$, $A_{\cdot 2}$,..., $A_{\cdot p}$, and the (1*k) matrix B. are parameters to be estimated. Abrigo and Love (2015) estimate that innovations have the following characteristics: $[\xi_{it}] = 0$, $[\xi'_{it}\xi_{it}] = \Sigma$., and $[\xi'_{it}\xi_{it}] = 0$ for all $t > s$.

Specifically, the notion of financing the economy is a broad term. The economy's financing can be subdivided into three dimensions: cost, structure, and agent. In this study, we seek to see the effect of bank capital and governance on the different EMCCA economy financing layers. Thus, within the framework of this study, we have broken down financing into three dimensions, namely, the cost dimension represented by the overall effective rate (TEG), the structure dimension through the level of short-term (CCT), medium-term (CMT), and long-term (CLT) credits and the agent dimension through the level of credits granted to the economy (CE), public enterprises (CEPU), the private sector (CSP) and non-residents (CNR).

We also highlight the socio-political environment of EMCCA in the analysis of the studied phenomenon. The World Bank chooses six governance indicators. Indeed, the level of corruption (CC) and political instability (IP) can also impact how EMCCA economies access financial resources, particularly the financing of the economy. EMCCA countries are experiencing political tensions through multiple political and security crises in Cameroon, the Central African Republic, and Chad. In addition, the level of corruption is also pervasive in the sub-region. EMCCA scores in this area are the world's lowest according to the World Bank's WGI reports, and some countries have even been ranked first in the world in terms of the most corrupt countries. The above models integrate this dynamic because the socio-political framework seems to influence the financing of the EMCCA economy. Specifically, the PVAR model of Eq. (7.1) above can be rewritten in a form allowing the analysis of the effects of shocks on endogenous variables. It looks like this.

Model 1: Effect of CBM on the Real Cost of Credit (TEG)

$$TEG_{it} = \gamma_{10} + \gamma_{11} TEG_{t-1} + \gamma_{12} CBM_{it-1} + \gamma_{13} CC_{1t-1}$$
$$+ \gamma_{14} IP_{it?1} + \mu_{1i} + \vartheta_{1t} + \xi_{1it} \qquad (7.2)$$

Model 2: Effect of CBM on the Term Structure of Loans

$$CCT_{it} = \alpha_{10} + \alpha_{11} CCT_{it-1} + \alpha_{12} CBM_{it-1} + \alpha_{13} CMT_{it-1}$$
$$+ \alpha_{14} CLT_{it-1} + \alpha_{15} CC_{1t-1} + \alpha_{16} IP_{it-1} + \mu_{1i} + \vartheta_{1t} + \xi_{1it} \qquad (7.3)$$

$$CMT_{it} = \alpha_{20} + \alpha_{21} CCT_{it-1} + \alpha_{22} CBM_{it-1} + \alpha_{23} CMT_{it-1}$$
$$+ \alpha_{24} CLT_{it-1} + \alpha_{25} CC_{1t-1} + \alpha_{26} IP_{it-1} + \mu_{2i} + \vartheta_{2t} + \xi_{2it} \qquad (7.4)$$

$$CLT_{it} = \alpha_{30} + \alpha_{31} CCT_{it-1} + \alpha_{32} CBM_{it-1} + \alpha_{33} CMT_{it-1}$$
$$+ \alpha_{34} CLT_{it-1} + \alpha_{35} CC_{1t-1} + \alpha_{36} IP_{it-1} + \mu_{3i} + \vartheta_{3t} + \xi_{3it} \qquad (7.5)$$

Model 3: Effect of CBM on Economic Agents in Need of Finances

$$CE_{it} = \beta_{10} + \beta_{11} CE_{it-1} + \beta_{12} CBM_{it-1} + \beta_{13} CEPU_{it-1} + \beta_{14} CSP_{it-1}$$
$$+ \beta_{15} CNR_{it-1} + \beta_{16} CC_{1t-1} + \beta_{17} IP_{it-1} + \mu_{1i} + \vartheta_{1t} + \xi_{1it} \qquad (7.6)$$

$$CEPU_{it} = \beta_{30} + \beta_{31} CE_{it-1} + \beta_{32} CBM_{it-1} + \beta_{33} CEPU_{it-1} + \beta_{34} CSP_{it-1}$$
$$+ \beta_{35} CNR_{it-1} + \beta_{36} CC_{1t-1} + \beta_{37} IP_{it-1} + \mu_{3i} + \vartheta_{3t} + \xi_{3it} \qquad (7.7)$$

$$CSP_{it} = \beta_{40} + \beta_{41} CE_{it-1} + \beta_{42} CBM_{it-1} + \beta_{43} CEPU_{it-1} + \beta_{44} CSP_{it-1}$$
$$+ \beta_{45} CNR_{it-1} + \beta_{46} CC_{1t-1} + \beta_{47} IP_{it-1} + \mu_{4i} + \vartheta_{4t} + \xi_{4it} \qquad (7.8)$$

$$CNR_{it} = \beta_{50} + \beta_{51}CE_{it-1} + \beta_{52}CBM_{it-1} + \beta_{53}CEPU_{it-1} + \beta_{54}CSP_{it-1}$$
$$+ \beta_{55}CNR_{it-1} + \beta_{56}CC_{1t-1} + \beta_{57}IP_{it-1} + \mu_{5i} + \vartheta_{5t} + \xi_{5it} \quad (7.9)$$

With i = 1… 6; t represents the time horizon (1998–2016). With μ_{ji}, $\_\vartheta_{jt}$ and ξ_{jit} represent the country-specific effects, time, and idiosyncratic error, respectively. In addition, CBM, TEG, CC, IP, CEPU, CSP, CNR, CCT, CMT, and CLT represent respectively: minimum bank capital, overall effective rate, corruption control, political instability, credit to public enterprises, credit to the private sector, credit to non-residents, short-term credit, medium-term credit, and long-term credit (Table 7.1).

Moreover, the estimation method chosen is the GMM method because of the delayed endogenous variable in the different equations. Thus, several estimators based on the GMM method have been proposed to calculate the estimates in Eq. (7.1) above, particularly when T is fixed and N is large (Canova & Ciccarelli, 2013). Assuming that the errors are uncorrelated, the estimation of Eq. (7.1) from its transformation to first difference can be made by instrumenting the variables in level and difference and level from previous periods (Anderson & Hsiao, 1982). However, this estimator poses a problem because the transformation of the equation into the first difference increases the gap in an unbalanced panel (Abrigo & Love, 2015). For example, if some Y_{it-1} are unavailable, the first difference equation for the period t and t-1 will have missing data. Blundell and Bond (1998) propose orthogonal deviation as an alternative to transforming the first difference equation. Potentially, only recent observations are not used during the Estimation because past observations are not included in this transformation; they remain valid instruments.

Subsequently, a complementary analysis will be developed through the analysis of the variance breakdown of the forecast error. Indeed, the forecast error aims to calculate, for each innovation, its contribution to the variance of the error. Thus, contrary to impulse response functions, the variance breakdown explains the contribution of the innovation of one variable to the fluctuations of another.

Results

In this section, we present the results of descriptive statistics. Then, we, later on, present the results of the GMM estimation in PVAR, and finally, we analyze the variance decomposition of the forecast error.

Table 7.1 Definitions of variables at stake and data sources

Variable	Definitions	Source
CBM (minimum bank capital) (10^6)	Minimum bank capital is the capital required to open a credit institution.	COBAC
CCT (short-term credit) (10^6)	Short-term loans are loans whose duration does not exceed two years.	COBAC
CMT (medium-term loans) 10^6	Medium-term loans are loans with a term between 2 and 7 years.	COBAC
CLT (long-term credit) (10^6)	Long-term loans are loans with a term of more than seven years.	COBAC
CSP (credit to the private sector), 10^6	Loans to the private sector are loans granted to private companies.	COBAC
CEPU (credit to public enterprises) (10^6)	Credits to public enterprises are credits granted to public enterprises.	COBAC
CNR (credit to non-residents) (10^6)	Credits to non-residents are credits granted to economic agents outside the EMCCA zone.	COBAC
CE (credit to the economy) (10^6)	Credits to the economy represent all the means of payment in circulation in an economy for a year.	COBAC
TEG (total effective rate) (%)	The overall effective rate represents the actual interest cost borne by the borrower.	BEAC
CC (level of corruption)	The control of corruption reflects perceptions of the extent to which public power is exercised for private purposes, including petty and grand forms of corruption and state capture by elites and private interests. The estimate of this measure ranges from -2.5 (weak/poor) to +2.5 (strong or better).	WGI
IP (political instability/absence of violence)	Political stability and the absence of terrorism or violence measure the perceived likelihood of political instability and politically motivated violence. The estimate of this measure ranges from -2.5 (weak/poor) to +2.5 (strong or better).	WGI

Source: Authors conception

Data Description

Table 7.2 below presents descriptive statistics for the different variables. The average level of minimum bank capital in EMCCA countries is around 53,006.32 million CFA francs. Also, the level of minimum bank capital of

Table 7.2 Descriptive statistics

Variables	Observations	Mean	Standard deviation	Minimum	Maximum
CBM (10^6 FCFA)	114	53,006.32	49,708.6	4500	176,520
CLT (10^6 FCFA)	114	18,866.66	38,883.8	0	233,554
CMT (10^6 FCFA)	114	252,242.2	406,436.9	0	2430.232
CCT (10^6 FCFA)	114	154,458.9	261,514.5	0	1678.449
CE (10^6 FCFA)	114	38,118.73	99,930.26	1.045	681,209
CEPU (10^6 FCFA)	114	28,720.72	35,496.19	950	146,346
CSP (10^6 FCFA)	114	4410.83	52,054.74	37,643	2276.497
CNR (10^6 FCFA)	114	36,166.47	56,601.63	124	345,289
TEG (%)	114	9.476404	3.654649	1.07	16.46
CC	114	-0,051	1.063	-2,5	1,27
IP	114	0.03	1.58	-2.5	0.79

Source: Author, under Stata v 14

credit institutions in EMCCA varies between 4500 million and 176,520 million CFA francs.

Furthermore, concerning the level of credits by term, it is noted that the average level of long-term credits granted within EMCCA is 18,866.66 million francs CFA; the average level of short-term credits is 154,458.9 CFA francs and for medium-term credits is 252,242.2 CFA francs. In addition, the average level of credits to economic agents in need of financing is 38,118.73 for credits to the economy, 28,720.72 for credits to public enterprises, 4410.83 for the private sector and 36,166.47 for non-residents.

In addition, the average level of the overall effective rate of EMCCA is 9.476 percent during the study period. This rate varies between 1.07 percent and 16.46 percent. In most cases, credit institutions in EMCCA practice a policy of high rates on their credit offer operations. This result shows us that bank credit is costly for these economies.

Likewise, Table 7.3 displays the different correlation coefficients between the variables and their significance level at the 5 percent threshold. There is a positive correlation between the minimum bank capital and variables such as short, medium, and long-term credits; between the minimum bank capital and credits to the economy, public enterprises, private enterprises, and non-residents. Also, a negative correlation exists between the minimum bank capital and the GER.

Furthermore, the relationship between the socio-political framework and the different strata of financing of the economy allows us to draw out

Table 7.3 Matrix of correlation coefficients

	CBM	CLT	CMT	CCT	CE	CEPU	CSP	CNR	TEG	CC	IP
CBM	1.000										
CLT	0.428*	1.000									
CMT	0.593*	0.889*	1.000								
CCT	0.534*	0.360*	0.586*	1.000							
CE	0.617*	0.344*	0.406*	0.152	1.000						
CEPU	0.422*	0.220*	0.423*	0.773*	0.141	1.000					
CSP	0.811*	0.339*	0.575*	0.748*	0.382*	0.498*	1.000				
CNR	0.555*	0.207*	0.470*	0.870*	0.923	0.770*	0.843*	1.000			
TEG	−0.22*	−0.11	−0.14*	−.024*	−0.19*	−0.28*	−0.22*	−0.24*	1.000		
CC	0.133*	0.026*	0.328*	0.008*	0.016*	0.042*	0.009*	0.029*	0.236*	1.000	
IP	0.001*	0.08*	0.10*	0.95*	0.12*	0.06*	0.27*	0.70*	0.39*	0.95*	1.000

Source: Authors, under Stata v 14. *$p < 0.005$

the following analyses: firstly, there is a significant negative correlation between the actual cost of credit (ACC) and both the level of corruption and political instability in EMCCA. Secondly, there is also a negative and significant correlation between the term structure of credit with the level of corruption and political instability. Thirdly, there is a significant negative correlation between corruption and the level of credit extended to the private sector, non-residents, and the economy. However, the correlation is positive with the level of credit extended to public sector enterprises. On the other hand, there is a significant negative correlation between political instability and the level of credits granted to the different economic agents in need of financing.

Results of Econometric Estimations

We carried out Levin – Lin – Chu (LLC) and Im – Pesaran – Shin (IPS) stationarity tests. The results indicate that it is impossible to reject the null hypothesis of the non-stationarity of the variables. It implies that some series contain unit roots (the following series are assumed to be non-stationary in level: CLT, CMT, CCT, CE, CEPU, CSP, CNR, CC, and IP).

As far as the analysis of the findings is concerned, the Estimation of the PVAR in GMM allows us to obtain three results according to the models presented above. Firstly, Table 7.5 presents the results of the impact of the CBM on the TEG.

The results in Table 7.5 show that the level of MBC has a significant negative effect at the 1 percent threshold on the actual cost of credit borne by the borrower. The level of minimum bank capital has a downward influence on the level of the overall effective rate (the same result was found in the analysis of the correlation between the CBM and the TEG). In other words, an increase in the level of minimum bank capital will reduce the actual cost of credit borne by the borrower.

Secondly, Table 7.6 below presents the results of the impact of the minimum bank capital on the term structure of loans. This table successively analyses the impact of the CBM on the levels of short-term, medium-term, and long-term loans. Firstly, the minimum bank capital has a positive and significant impact at the 1 percent threshold on the level of long-term loans. Secondly, the minimum bank capital has a negative and significant influence on the level of medium-term loans. Thirdly, the minimum bank capital has a negative and significant effect at the 1 percent threshold on the level of short-term loans.

In conclusion, the low level of the minimum bank capital leads credit institutions not to grant credits. Conversely, an increase in the level of the minimum bank capital would favor the financing of investments. In other words, holding a high level of minimum bank capital by a banking institution makes it possible for banks to grant more long-term credits necessary for entrepreneurs' financing of productive investments.

Thirdly, Table 7.7 presents the results of the effect of the minimum bank capital on the credits granted to economic agents in need of financing. Four types of effects can be observed. Firstly, the minimum bank capital negatively and significantly affects the level of credits granted to the economy. Secondly, the minimum bank capital has a positive and significant effect at the 1 percent threshold on the level of credits granted to public enterprises. Thirdly, the minimum bank capital has a negative and significant effect on the level of bank credits granted to private sector enterprises. Finally, the minimum bank capital has a negative and significant effect on the level of credits granted to non-resident economic agents. Thus, a 1 percent drop in the level of minimum bank capital reduces the level of credits granted to non-resident economic agents in the EMCCA zone.

On reading these results, everything suggests that the minimum bank capital influences the financing of the economy. For some aspects, the CBM has a positive impact (TEG, CMT, CCT, and CLT). For others, the MBC has a negative effect on the different economic agents in need of financing (except for credits granted to the economy). In addition, some empirical studies have come to this type of result. An increase in the minimum bank capital has a negative effect on the supply of credit to economic agents in need of financing. These results contradict those found by Francis and Osborne (2009). For these authors, the bank capital requirement is positively associated with the supply of credit. Bank capital affects the level of credit granted to loss-making economic agents upwards. However, this increase is a function of the level of minimum bank capital.

On the other hand, our findings partially confirm the results found by Brun, Fraisse, and Thesmar (2013), because according to these authors, a decrease of one percent (1%) in the minimum bank capital reduces the distribution of credits by 10 percent, especially for loss-making economic agents. However, this result is different from the level of the term structure of credits. On the other hand, the minimum bank capital tends to influence the level of the actual cost of credit borne by the borrower. In other words, when a bank has sufficient capital, it tends to lower the cost of borrowing.

Furthermore, the analysis of the effect of the socio-political environment on the financing of the economy allows us to see on the one hand that the level of corruption in the sub-region is not favorable both on the actual cost of credit borne by the borrower (TEG) and on the term structure of credits or for credits granted to the different economic agents in need of financing. This leads to a negative and significant relationship (see Tables 7.3, 7.4, and 7.5 above). On the other hand, the unrest linked to political instability is also not conducive to adequate financing of the EMCCA economy. A negative and significant relationship between the variable political instability and the different strata of financing of the economy in the sub-region.

Table 7.4 Stationarity tests

Variables	Tests Levin-Lin-Chu (LLC tests)		Tests Im-Pesaran-Shin (IPS tests)	
	In level	Difference first	In level	First difference
	P-value	P-value	P-value	P-value
CBM*	0.08	0.028	0.166	0.00
CLT**	0.00	0.00	0.707	0.00
CMT**	0.10	0.00	0.27	0.00
CCT**	1.00	0,00	0,49	0,00
CE**	0.95	0.00	0.89	0.00
CEPU**	0.12	0.00	0.40	0.00
CSP**	0.39	0.00	0.92	0.00
CNR**	0.10	0.00	0.06	0.00
TEG*	0.00	0.00	0.00	0.00
CC**	0.10	0.00	0.04	0.00
IP**	0.27	0.00	0.95	0.00

Source: Authors, under Stata v 14. * Stationary level; ** Stationary in first difference

Table 7.5 Effect of CBM on the actual cost of credit

Equation 7.2/TEG

Variables	Coefficient	Standard deviation	$p > |z|$
CBM (L1)	−0.233	0.164	0.155***
TEG (L1)	−1.042	0.507	0.000***
CC (L1)	0.042	0.555	0.000***
IP (L1)	0.503	0.088	0.000***

Source: Authors, under Stata v 14. ***$p < 0.001$; **$p < 0.005$; *$p < 0.1$; (L1) lagged one period

7 THE EFFECTS OF MINIMUM BANK CAPITAL AND GOVERNANCE... 161

Table 7.6 Effect of CBM on the term structure of loans

Variables	Equation 7.3/CCT			Equation 7.4/CMT			Equation 7.5/CLT		
	Coef.	S.d	$p > |z|$	Coef.	S.d	$p > |z|$	Coef.	S.d	$p > |z|$
CBM (L1)	-0.555	0.416	0.000***	42.845	4.659	0.000***	2.556	0.378	0.000***
CLT (L1)	2.622	0.100	0.000***	40.076	0.835	0.000***	3.892	0.078	0.000***
CMT (L1)	-0.417	0.013	0.016***	-4.370	0.138	0.016***	-0.423	0.126	0.016***
CCT (L1)	0.099	0.022	0.000***	3.813	0.203	0.000***	0.337	0.0183	0.000***
CC (L1)	0.575	3.414	0.000***	0.339	1.814	0.000***	0.141	0.026	0.000***
IP (L1)	0.748	2.820	0.000***	0.575	4.046	0.000***	0.811	3.298	0.000***

Source: Author, under Stata v 14. *** $p < 0.001$; ** $p < 0.005$; * $p < 0.1$; Coef.: Coefficient; S.d: Standard deviation

Table 7.7 Effect of CBM on economic agents in need of finance

Variables	Equation 7.6/CE			Equation 7.7/CEPU			Equation 7.8/CSP			Equation 7.9/CNR		
	Coef.	S.d	$p > |z|$	Coef.	S.d	$p > |z|$	Coef.	S.d	$p > |z|$	Coef.	S.d	$p > |z|$
CBM (L1)	3.07	0.18	0.0**	3.91	0.048	0.0**	-2,54	0,30	0.0**	-4,99	0,053	0.0**
CE (L1)	0.35	0.00	0.0**	0.016	0.004	0.0**	1,53	0,03	0.0**	-0,13	0,003	0.0**
CEPU (L1)	1.75	0.01	0.0**	1.466	0.013	0.0**	1,25	0,08	0.0**	1,12	0,019	0.0**
CSP (L1)	0.04	0.00	0.0**	-0,01	0,000	0.0**	0,23	0,00	0.0**	-0,31	0,000	0.0**
CNR (L1)	0.63	0.00	0.0**	1,00	0,009	0.0**	4,89	0,07	0.0**	-1,06	0,013	0.0**
CC (L1)	-0.11	1.72	0.0**	-0,04	0,021	0.0**	-4,01	3,82	0.00**	-0,02	0,017	0.00**
IP (L1)	0.10	0.65	0.0**	-0,16	0,155	0.0**	0,00	0,02	0.00**	-0,02	0,017	0.00**

Source: Author, under Stata V14. *** $p < 0.001$; ** $p < 0.005$; * $p < 0.1$; Coef.: Coefficient; S.d: Standard deviation; L1 lagged one period

Finally, the analysis of the variance breakdown allows us to draw out heterogeneous conclusions. Based on the analyses' estimates on the forecast error's variance breakdown (Appendix 7.1, 7.2, and 7.3), a double analysis can be made according to the banking and socio-political data.

Concerning the analysis of banking data, i.e., the forecast analysis of the effect of the minimum bank capital on the financing of the economy, a triple analysis can be made at this level. Firstly, two types of effects can be observed concerning the impact of the minimum bank capital on the AER (Appendix 7.1). Firstly, we see that almost 25 percent of the future variation of the AER is explained by the level of the minimum bank capital. Secondly, the AER explains 32 percent of the level of the CBM.

Secondly, concerning the analysis of the impact of the minimum bank capital on the term structure of loans (Appendix 7.2), three effects can be observed. Firstly, the minimum bank capital explains, on average, 13 percent of the level of long-term loans. Secondly, the minimum bank capital explains almost 12 percent of the level of medium-term loans. Thirdly, the minimum bank capital explains almost 7 percent of the level of short-term loans. Based on these results, it can be seen that if a bank increases its minimum bank capital level, it will tend to grant long-term loans to economic agents in need of financing compared to short- and medium-term loans.

Finally, four effects can be identified concerning the impact of bank capital on the types of economic agents to be financed (Appendix 7.3). The first effect concerns the impact of bank capital on the level of credits granted to the economy. It emerges that the minimum bank capital explains almost 24 percent of the level of credit granted to the economy. The CBM explains nearly 22 percent of the loans granted to public enterprises regarding the second effect. The third effect concerns the impact of the CBM on loans to the private sector. Our analyses show that the minimum bank capital influences the level of credits granted to private sector companies by 6 percent. Finally, the fourth effect concerns the impact of the minimum bank capital on loans to non-residents. Our calculations show that the minimum bank capital explains almost 7.5 percent of the credits granted to this category.

However, concerning the effect of the socio-political environment on the financing of the economy in EMCCA, a double analysis can be made at this level. By taking the level of corruption, we can see that it tends to reduce the level of financing of the economy. Thus, a small contribution can be noted, particularly in reducing the actual cost of credit borne by the borrower. In other words, corruption tends to increase the levels of interest rates charged by EMCCA credit institutions. This situation is undoubtedly the cause of credit rationing in this sub-region and one of the explanations for the excess liquidity of credit institutions. This analysis can also be carried out on the term structure of loans and the loans granted to the various economic agents in need of financing. We note a small contribution of corruption to the improvement of the levels of credit distributed. This same result was found in a study before this one. Using the same study framework, Noumba and Enguene (2019) have shown that bank capital has a positive and significant effect on the economy's financing. In this study, there is evidence of the existence of a bank capital channel in EMCCA.

Considering the political instability in the sub-region, economic agents with financing capacity, namely credit institutions, are more inclined to provide the resources that economies need. The contributions of political instability to the different strata of financing of the economy are even lower than those of corruption. Bank credit is almost non-existent in these economies, and the financing of economic activities becomes difficult.

In a nutshell, the analysis of the above findings allows us to draw two main conclusions. The first is persistent instability in the effects of minimum bank capital on the different variables. This instability has its origin in the disparate levels of minimum bank capital of credit institutions in the EMCCA zone. Secondly, the level of minimum bank capital positively affects the term structure of loans in the long term, except for short-term loans. Moreover, the MBC positively impacts the credits granted to the different economic agents in need of financing in the long run. It should also be noted that the CBM tends to lower the actual cost of credit borne by the borrower. Therefore, the minimum bank capital has a positive long-term effect on the financing of the economy, as it makes bank credit available and less expensive. Thus, an increase in the minimum bank capital leads "ipso facto" to decrease the actual cost of credit. The interpretation of impulse response functions shows us that the minimum bank capital has a positive and significant effect on the financing of the economy. These findings allow us to verify our research hypothesis. On the other hand, the socio-political environment in some EMCCA countries tends to limit the economy's financing.

Concluding Remarks

This chapter seeks to show the effect of the level of minimum bank capital of credit institutions on their ability to contribute to the financing of the economy in the EMCCA zone. The analysis of theoretical and empirical studies backs the idea that the minimum bank capital of credit institutions has a positive and significant effect on the financing needs of economies. To this end, the empirical analysis has enabled us to arrive at certain results. We have reached three types of conclusions. First, minimum bank capital has a positive effect on our variables, i.e., an increase in the level of minimum bank capital increases, all other things being equal, the levels of lending discussed in this study.

Furthermore, an increase in the level of minimum bank capital reduces the actual cost of credit borne by the borrower (total effective rate). Second, a positive and significant effect exists on the term structure of credit, although it is negative for the level of short-term credit. This result has been interpreted as reflecting the low level of minimum bank capital in the EMCCA zone. Thirdly, the analysis of impulse response functions allows us to observe instability in the minimum bank capital shock on the different variables. This instability has been interpreted as reflecting the strong disparity in the level of minimum bank capital among institutions in the zone. However, in the long term, the desired effect is positive.

Ultimately, the Banking Commission of Central African States must increase the level and encourage credit institutions in the EMCCA zone to increase minimum bank capital. Likewise, COBAC should ensure strict compliance with this rule, as it ensures the internal stability of credit institutions (stability, liquidity, and soundness) and external stability (provision of resources to economic agents in need of financing). Thus, one franc more in minimum bank capital would be one franc more to keep the economy going. In addition, it is also important to improve the business environment in the sub-region mainly by fighting against the prevailing corruption in these economies and promoting political stability in these countries on the other.

APPENDIXES

Appendix 7.1: Variance Breakdown on TEG

Variable of interest and projection horizon		Impulsion variables			
		CBM	TEG	CC	IP
CBM	0	0	0	0	0
	1	1	0	0.079	0.000
	2	0.7756	0.2243	0.079	0.020
	3	0.7489	0.2510	0.072	0.182
	4	0.7536	0.2463	0.076	0.245
	5	0.7475	0.2524	0.092	0.214
	6	0.7471	0.2528	0.088	0.228
	7	0.7472	0.2527	0.086	0.250
	8	0.7470	0.2529	0.943	0.234
	9	0.7470	0.2529	0.092	0.241
	10	0.7470	0.2529	0.092	0.252

Source: Author, under Stata v 14

Appendix 7.2: Breakdown of the Structure with Regard to Credits

Variable of the interest projection horizon		Impulsion variables					
		CBM	CLT	CMT	CCT	CC	IP
CBM	0	0	0	0	0	0	0
	1	1	0	0	0	0	0
	2	0.885	0.035	0.001	0.077	0.010	0.045
	3	0.796	0.135	0.001	0.666	0.007	0.108
	4	0.713	0.128	0.980	0.061	0.005	0.097
	5	0.713	0.121	0.096	0.068	0.006	0.074
	6	0.695	0.133	0.101	0.074	0.007	0.098
	7	0.670	0.141	0.118	0.069	0.006	0.110
	8	0.665	0.136	0.123	0.0743	0.005	0.090
	9	0.656	0.114	0.124	0.0746	0.006	0.899
	10	0.642	0.147	0.135	0.073	0.006	0.109

Source: Author, under Stata v 14

Appendix 7.3: Breakdown of the CMB Variance on Credits Given to Economic Agents in Need of Financing

Variable of the interest projection horizon	Impulsion Variables						
	CBM	CE	CEPU	CSP	CNR	CC	IP
CBM 0	0	0	0	0	0	0	0
1	1	0	0	0	0	-0.341	0.006
2	0.748	0.161	0.028	0.003	0.057	-0.158	0.001
3	0.461	0.278	0.210	0.012	0.037	0.101	0.004
4	0.419	0.224	0.240	0.008	0.106	-0.006	0.000
5	0.401	0.218	0.271	0.008	0.100	-0.111	0.002
6	0.352	0.320	0.240	0.009	0.076	0.092	0.005
7	0.272	0.334	0.287	0.008	0.097	-0.007	3.111
8	0.274	0.269	0.340	0.008	0.108	3.075	0.183
9	0.298	0.313	0.286	0.007	0.094	0.353	0.005
10	0.225	0.388	0.289	0.007	0.089	-1.753	0.014

Source: Author, under Stata v 14

References

Abrigo, M. R., & Love I. (2015, February). *Estimation of panel vector auto-regression in Stata: A package of programs*, manuscript. Available on http://paneldataconference2015.ceu.hu/Program/Michael-Abrigo.Pdf

Abrigo, M. R., & Love, I. (2016). Estimation of panel vector auto-regression in Stata. *The Stata Journal, 16*(3), 778–804.

Altunbas, et al. (2007). Examining the relationships between capital, risk and efficiency in European banking. *European Financial Management, 13*(1), 49–70.

Anderson, T. W., & Hsiao, C. (1982). Formulation and estimation of dynamic models using panel data. *Journal of Econometrics, 18*(3), 47–82.

Bernanke, B. S., & Lown, C. S. (1991). The credit crunch. *Brookings Papers on Economic Activity, 2*, 204–239.

Blundell, R., & Bond, S. (1998). Initial conditions and moment restrictions in dynamic panel data models. *Journal of Econometrics, 87*(1), 115–143.

Brun, M., Fraisse, H., & Thesmar, D. (2013). Les effets réels des exigences en fonds propres. *Débats économiques et financiers, Autorité de Contrôle Prudentiel, Banque de France, 8*, 1–55.

Canova, F., & Ciccarelli, M. (2013). Panel vector autoregressive model: A survey. *Advances in Econometrics, 32*(4), 34–76.

Collard, F., & Feve, P. (2008). Modèle VAR ou DSGE: que choisir ? *Economie et prévision, 2*(183–184), 153–174.

Commission Bancaire de l'Afrique Centrale. *Rapport annuel*, 2003, 2009, 2015, 2016.
Conseil d'Analyse Economique (2012), *Le financement de l'économie dans le nouveau contexte réglementaire*, Conseil d'Analyse Economique, Paris, 104, 1–228.
Dietsch, M., Dullmann, K., Koziol, P., & Ott, C. (2016). En faveur d'un facteur de soutien aux PME: résultats empiriques au niveau international sur les exigences en capital des prêts aux PME. *Revue Banque de France*, Débats économiques et financiers, Autorité de Contrôle Prudentiel (No. 10, pp. 1–35).
Gambacorta, L., & Mistulli, P. E. (2004). Does bank capital affect lending behavior? *Journal of Financial Intermediation, 13*(13), 436–457.
Gosse, J. B., & Guillaumin, C. (2013). L'apport de la représentation VAR de Christopher A. Sims à la science économique. *L'Actualité économique, 89*(1834), 305–319.
Holmstrom, B., & Tirole, J. (1997). Financial intermediation, loanable funds, the real sector. *The Quarterly Journal of Economics, 12*(3), 663–691.
Hugon, P. (2007). Rentabilité du secteur bancaire et défaillance du financement du développement: le cas de la EMCCA. *Revue Tiers Monde, 192*(3), 771–788.
International Chamber of Commerce. (2008). No abatement of corruption and economic fraud. *The World Business Organization* (pp. 1–7).
Kashyap, K., Stein, J., & Hanson, S. (2010). *An analysis of the impact of substantially heightened capital requirements on large financial institutions*. University of Chicago and Harvard, Working Paper.
Levieuge, G. (2005). Les banques comme vecteurs et amplificateurs des chocs financiers: le canal du capital bancaire. *Economie internationale, 4,* 65–95.
Liu, H., & Wilson, J. O. S. (2010). The profitability of bank in Japan. *Applied Financial Economics, 20*(24), 1851–1866.
Miles, D., Yang, J., & Marcheggiano, G. (2013). Optimal bank capital. *The Economic Journal, 123*(567), 1–37.
Mishkin, F. S. (2010). *Monnaie, banque et marchés financiers*. Pearson Education France.
Noumba, I., & Enguene, A. A. (2019). Capital bancaire minimum et financement de l'économie en zone EMCCA. *Revue Internationale de Gestion et d'Economie (RIGE)*, Série B, Economie, 2 (7), 4–32.
Osborne, M., Fuertes, A. M., & Milne, A. (2017). In good times and in bad: Bank capital ratios and lending rates. *International Review of Financial Analysis, 51,* 102–112.
Périou, C. (2014). Evolutions du secteur bancaire africain: nouveaux acteurs, nouveaux modèles? *HPS Financial Review, Banque & Finance, 1*(1), 71.
Pitseys, J. (2010). Le concept de gouvernance. *Revue interdisciplinaire d'études juridiques, 65*(2), 207–228.
Tiesset, M., & Troussard, P. (2005). Capital réglementaire et capital économique. *Revue de la stabilité financière, Banque de France, 17*(11), 1–32.

Van Den Heuvel, S. J. (2002). *The bank capital channel of monetary policy.* The Wharton School, University of Pennsylvania, mimeo.

Van Den Heuvel, S. J., & Skander, J. (2008). The welfare cost of bank capital requirement. *Journal of Monetary Economics, 55*(3), 298–320.

Wood, D. (2003). In search of capital crunch: Supply factors behind the credit slowdown in Japan. *Journal of Money, Credit, and Banking, 36*(6), 1019–1038.

CHAPTER 8

Facts and Prospects of Monetary Union in East Africa

John Sseruyange

INTRODUCTION

There are six countries in the East African Community (EAC). They gained independence at different times—Burundi (1962), Kenya (1963), Rwanda (1962), Tanzania (1961), Uganda (1962), and of recent, South Sudan (2011). There is a consensus among them that fighting the problem of poverty requires rapid economic growth and development. As such, many EAC member states, have implemented economic reforms, e.g., trade reforms aimed at addressing the external trade imbalances, fiscal reforms aimed at addressing their internal imbalances—mainly through enhancing domestic resource mobilization and monitoring their resource allocations and monetary policy reforms for inflation and exchange rate stability (UNCTAD, 2007).

While the East African countries continue to pursue economic growth and development, they suffered from many years of shocks that have caused macroeconomic instabilities such as high inflation and exchange

J. Sseruyange (✉)
School of Economics, Makerere University, Kampala, Uganda
e-mail: John.sseruyange@mak.ac.ug

© The Author(s), under exclusive license to Springer Nature Switzerland AG 2022
A. A. Amin et al. (eds.), *Monetary and Financial Systems in Africa*,
https://doi.org/10.1007/978-3-030-96225-8_8

rate volatilities, high-interest rates in some member countries. These shocks have constrained the regional investment potentials. In addition, their fiscal indisciplines have led to persistent budget deficits, structural distortions, infrastructural bottlenecks. Furthermore, the undemocratic political systems in the region have partly led to civil wars and ethnic conflicts. Moreover, such shocks have failed some East African countries to fully gain from external trade (AfDB, 2019), triggering regional cooperation policies.

This chapter provides some insights into the origin of East African cooperation and shows how the East African Community has evolved. Moreover, we provide some evidence relating to the use of a common currency in East Africa, which shows that such currencies date to historical times. Finally, we discuss some facts about the structural attributes of the EAC member countries and present some insights relating to the potential success of the East African Monetary Union.

The Evolution of the East African Cooperation

Although establishing the railway line between 1897 and 1901 across Uganda, Kenya, and Tanganyika (which became Tanzania after a political merger with Zanzibar) aimed to ease the administrative activities of the colonial masters, it provided a foundation for the cooperation of East African countries. The completion of the railway line increased the flow of goods to the interior while agricultural products and mineral resources were moved to the ocean shores, especially Mombasa port, for export. In 1905, a Postal union was established, and it was followed by the formation of the court of Appeal for East Africa in 1909 for hearing appeals in civil and criminal cases in British territories and their neighbors.

The East African Currency Board (EACB) was formed in 1919 to supply and oversee the currency of British colonies. In the same year, Kenya and Uganda integrated into a customs Union to simplify the flow of goods between Mombasa port and Uganda's destinations. The union gained momentum in 1927 when Tanganyika became a member. To bring the governors in the British territories of Kenya, Uganda, Tanzania, Northern Rhodesia, and Nyasaland, the British convened the East African Governor's Conference in 1926. At the same conference, the governors also shared advice on strengthening the cooperation between their territories. In 1940, the British established the East African Income Tax Board and the

Joint Economic Council to serve all East African countries—Kenya, Tanganyika, and Uganda.

Between 1947 and 1961, the East African High Commission (EAHC) came into existence to form a federation of the three East African British territories (Kenya, Tanganyika, and Uganda). Precisely, the EACH was to coordinate the activities of the customs union, oversee the development of a standard external tariff, and observe the flow of shared services like transport and communication. The East African Common Services Organisation (EACSO) created between 1961 and 1966 showed progress toward building East African cooperation. Many political analysts observed EACSO as a step toward the political federation of Kenya, Uganda, and Tanzania.

In 1967, the East African Community (EAC) came into existence following the Treaty of East African Cooperation. At its establishment, EAC was intended to have a common market, a customs union, and a public service to achieve balanced economic growth within the region. Moreover, community citizens were allowed to move freely across member states, showing strong cooperation. However, due to lack of political will, disagreements between Ugandan president of the time Idd Amin and Tanzanian president Julius Nyerere, differences in development and trade flows resulted into disproportionate sharing of benefits by the member states, and the EAC was dissolved in 1977.

However, after the collapse of the community, member states negotiated and signed a conciliation agreement in 1984. This agreement was intended to guide each member's responsibility for assets and liabilities left at the time of dissolving of the community. Kenya, Uganda, and Tanzania decided to explore future cooperation in the same deal. Thus, in 1999, the treaty for establishing the East African Community was signed, and the current East African Community came into existence in 2000. Box 8.1

Box 8.1 The Principles to Enhance Policy Harmonization and EAC Integration

- The attainment of sustainable growth and development of the partner states by promoting a more balanced and harmonious development of the partner states.
- The strengthening and consolidation of the cooperation in agreed fields that would lead to equitable economic development within the partner states and which would in turn, raise the standards of living and improve the quality of life of their populations.

(continued)

> **Box 8.1** (continued)
> - The promotion of sustainable utilization of natural resources and taking of measures that would effectively protect the natural environment of the partner states.
> - The strengthening and consolidation of the long-standing political, economic, social, cultural, and traditional ties and associations between the people of the partner states to promote a people-centered mutual development of these ties and associations.
> - The mainstreaming of gender in all its endeavours and the enhancement of the role of women in cultural, social, political, economic and technological development.
> - The promotion of peace, security and stability within and good neighbourliness among the partner states.
> - The enhancement and strengthening of the partnerships with the private sector and civil society in order to achieve sustainable socioeconomic and political development.
> - The undertaking of such other activities calculated to further the objectives of the community, as the partner states may from time to time decide to undertake in common.
>
> Source: Regional Economic Communities. A publication on East African Community by United Nations Economic Commission for Africa (2018).

summarizes the principles stipulated in the treaty to enhance policy harmonization and strengthen cooperation in the region.

The EAC was re-established by three member states, Kenya, Uganda, and Tanzania, with Burundi and Rwanda becoming members in 2007 and South Sudan in 2016.

The Genesis of a Common Currency in East Africa

Although the East African coastal areas had access to some currencies like the Indian rupee, silver rupee minted between 1600–1858 by the British East India Company, and Pice, such currencies started moving inland with the construction of the railway. The Pice, which was legalized to bear the name East African Protectorate, became the most used currency in the region, though other currencies remained in use. When the Pice reached inland as a unit of exchange, the Swahili-speaking people, mainly from Kenya, termed it "Pesa". Later on, different language-speaking people gave it other names translated from Pesa.

Although a great deal of trade was generally through barter system, many East Africans yearned to have those currencies which provided a strong foundation for their widespread acceptance. Thus, in 1906, the Indian rupee was stopped and replaced by the East African rupee (commonly known as rupee). This served as a currency for the British East African colonies and protectorate. The rupee served up to 1920, and it was substituted with the East African florin and then immediately changed to shillings.

The British established East African Currency Board in 1919. The Board controlled the supply and stability of the common currency within the British colonies. The African Currency Board replaced the Board of Commissioners of Currency formed in 1905 (Mwangi, 2001). According to Mwangi, EACB was mandated to produce and oversee a currency for East Africa and implement actions to exclude other currencies from the region. However, following the establishment of independent central banks in the three East African countries (Central Bank of Kenya, Bank of Uganda, and Bank of Tanzania) in 1965, EACB stopped its operations in 1966 (its insolvency mainly drove this), and adoption of each country's currency took the space.

THE RENAISSANCE OF THE EAST AFRICAN MONETARY UNION

Although the issues relating to the formation of monetary unions in Africa have been of great interest to policymakers, key questions have been on whether to adopt an Optimal Currency Area (OCA) or peg the exchange rate to a given foreign currency like the case of West African Economic Monetary Union (WAEMU). WAEMU member countries decided to peg their currencies to the Euro, with the French treasury providing an unlimited convertibility guarantee (Edwards, 2006). This far, well knowing that the rebirth of the EAC in 2000 provoked the formation of a common currency zone in East Africa, a protocol for establishing the East African Community Monetary Union (EAMU) was signed in 2013. This protocol stipulated the need for promoting and maintaining monetary and financial stability among the EAC member states to strengthen the economic cooperation and attainment of sustainable growth and development within the community. Monetary unionization aimed to attain convergence in the stipulated principles of the union.

THE CONVERGENCE CRITERIA AND THE SUCCESS OF MONETARY UNIONS

The convergence criteria assert that for integrated countries to benefit from a monetary union, they need to be similar in structures (UNECA, 2018). The harmonization of the systems, such as policies, institutions, and regional infrastructures, helps the member countries use integrated instruments for absorbing the shocks. Moreover, the convergence criteria have been observed as obligatory for all countries seeking to join a monetary union (UNECA, 2018). Convergence stresses synchronizing monetary and fiscal policies and joint macroeconomic stability to strengthen the monetary union. Drummond et al. (2014) maintain that convergence helps strengthen economic integration through trade, investment, and factor mobility and can lead to a strong economic performance that necessitates adopting a single currency. However, in Africa, the high expectations, especially from its leaders, about the future benefits of monetary union (e.g., lower financial transaction costs resulting from the integration of the monetary and financial market, stability in monetary conditions, exchange rates, and prices together with the anticipation of increased solidarity), some existing and planned monetary unions are driven without meeting the required convergence criteria.

THE STRUCTURAL ATTRIBUTES IN EAST AFRICAN COMMUNITY AND THE SUCCESS OF A MONETARY UNION

This section discusses the structural attributes that explain the EAC member countries' convergence possibility. We derive our discussion from the arguments presented in Drummond et al. (2014) and UNECA (2018) that convergence in structures by integrating countries strengthens the cooperation and enhances the regional economic performance—thereby necessitating the adoption of a common currency. Our discussion focuses on exchange rates, interest rates, inflation, fiscal deficit, public debts, trade, monetary institutions' concentration, and spread. We end this section by discussing trade flows within the EAC and also provide a brief hint on how political differentials affect regional integration prospects.

CAN OPTIMAL CURRENCY AREA BE FEASIBLE FOR THE EAST AFRICAN COMMUNITY?

The resolution for the formation of an Optimal Currency Area (OCA) requires a comprehensive examination of the economic characteristics of the interested countries (Ogrodnick, 1990). Therefore, we base this resolution on the fact that countries interested in the OCA must choose to follow a flexible exchange rate or fixed exchange rate system to ease trade flow.

Although EAC member states mainly follow flexible exchange rate systems, the synchronization of benefits from the integration and the success of a monetary union requires exchange rate convergence. The convergence can help absorb irregular shocks in cases where an individual country's exchange rates have failed. Devaluation in the real exchange rates improves trade balance, and a glance at the exchange rates in EAC member states becomes vital. Over the years, exchange rates in East Africa have been volatile. Uganda exhibits the highest variation, followed by Tanzania, Burundi, and Rwanda. Kenya portrays the least exchange rate variations (Fig. 8.1).

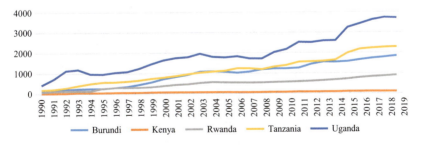

Fig. 8.1 Official exchange rate (LCU per US$, period average) except South Sudan. (Source: World Development Indicators, 2020)

Although the EAC is steadily growing in trade and investments, the need to use exchange rates as a tool for external adjustment and smoothening economic shocks is essential. For example, suppose the nominal exchange rates are allowed to fluctuate in some trading partners continuously. That case reflects inconsistencies in the overall economic variables like interest rates, the balance of payments, and government expenditure, possibly prompting government borrowing. Moreover, if the fluctuations occur in real exchange rates, the relative prices with trading partners are also changing (Ajevskis et al., 2014), and trade flows are changing.

INTEREST RATES, INFLATION, AND INVESTMENT IN EAST AFRICA

Interest rates and inflation are real influencers of a country's investment capacity. High-interest rates increase the cost of borrowing, causing two implications on investment. First, the profitability of investment ventures that seek loans targeting business expansion must have a higher rate of returns. Second, the use of loans for business establishments requires a higher expected rate of returns. With the dominance of small and medium-sized enterprises in East African countries, whose survival greatly depends on credit, any imposition of high-interest rates constrains their growth.

Similarly, inflation affects the investment sector by discouraging demand or altering the real interest rates (inflation in the EAC is discussed in later paragraphs). Higher prices cause a fall in real interest rates. For the lending institution to avoid losses, they are forced to raise the nominal interest rates, and as a result, loans become expensive. This has a direct effect on the profitability of investment options. Although Kenya has tried to keep the interest rates lower and manageable—to the extent of even imposing an interest rate cap, interest rates are still high in other countries like Uganda and Burundi. This demonstrates a prevailing failure in realizing interest rate convergence within the region. To better understand the volatility of exchange rates in EAC member countries, we look at the interest rate spread between EAC member states and West African Economic and Monetary Union (WAEMU) member states (Fig. 8.2).

Interest rate spread measures the gap between the lending and deposit rates. In the right panel, most WAEMU member states have relatively homogeneous trends in the interest rate spread. However, around 2017, the trends exhibited convergence because they pegged their respective

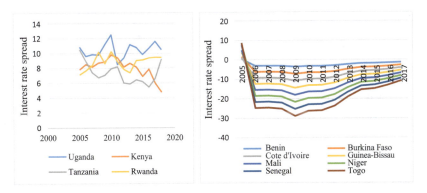

Fig. 8.2 Interest rate spread (%) in EAC and WAEMU countries. Notes: The left panel shows interest rate spread in the EAC countries excluding Burundi and South Sudan, while the right panel shows interest rate spread in WAEMU member countries. (Source: World Development Indicators, 2020)

currencies to the Euro. On the other hand, there are wider variations in the interest rate spread between the EAC member countries in the left panel. Uganda has the highest spread, followed by Rwanda and then Tanzania and Kenya. From the two panels, we make two key conclusions: First, the fluctuations in the interest rate spread among the EAC member states show no sign of convergence which can affect the success of the regional monetary union. Second, the interest rate spread in Kenya is declining. According to information provided by World Bank, lending rates in Kenya started falling in 1994 with only a tiny spike between 2004 and 2012. Since then, the rates have continued to decline. This continuous decline in the interest rates partly explains the persistent dominance of Kenya's investment sector in the region—investors in Kenya have access to cheaper loans and, thus, an advantage to exploit the regional market.

We now turn our discussion to inflation. Inflation convergence is an essential requirement for the success of a monetary union. According to Dridi and Nguyen (2019), once member countries are experiencing asymmetric inflation rates, the regional central bank aims at stabilizing inflation within the region may find it hard to apply a single nominal interest rate. Ever since the establishment of the EAC, inflation has tended to converge. Using data on Burundi, Kenya, Rwanda, Tanzania, and Uganda, Dridi and Nguyen (2019) show that inflation differentials in those are not persistent, indicating that inflation has been converging (Table 8.1).

Table 8.1 Average inflation (%) in East African community excluding South Sudan

	Burundi	Kenya	Rwanda	Tanzania	Uganda	Average	Dispersion
Pre-2000	31.44	15.23	13.49	19.96	8.38	14.10	3.72
Post-2000	9.00	7.85	6.45	7.43	6.87	7.52	0.88

Source: Extracted from Dridi & Nguyen (2019). Assessing inflation convergence in the East African Community. Journal of International Development, 31(2), 119–136

In their discussion, Dridi and Nguyen (2019) attributed the convergence in inflation to the homogeneity of shocks and foreign factors that affect inflation in the region. For example, almost all EAC member states have continuously been affected by droughts, causing uniform food prices. Similarly, they faced unvarying foreign inflation.

Fiscal Deficits, Debt, and Exchange Rate Volatility

Achieving economic growth in many developing countries has forced many governments to increase their public expenditure. As a result, fiscal discrepancies have also been rising, and borrowing from either internal or external sources has proved to be a short–term solution for addressing their budget deficits. However, the causative relationship between fiscal deficit and public debt has great implications for exchange rate stability. Our discussion starts by exploring the interaction between fiscal deficit and public debt. The government's excessive spending (whether actual or planned) on non-investment options can cause fiscal deficits (see Mawejje & Odhiambo, 2020), which are sometimes inevitable, especially during a recession. In addition, many developing countries governments are stressed with population demands.

Nevertheless, their domestic revenue mobilization potentials are constrained. As a result, governments are forced to take loans to finance public provisions. Conversely, public debts are repayable except for Islamic banking and sometimes with attached interest. Countries that are already constrained by their domestic revenues continue to borrow to finance the deficits and interest.

External borrowing is in foreign currencies, and similarly, their repayments are also made in foreign currencies. Therefore, depending on the volume of foreign exchange inflows or outflows, exchange rates can become volatile, affecting their convergence among the trading partners.

The East African Monetary Union's success requires member states to harmonize their fiscal policies—if they are to use fiscal policy as a tool for stimulating regional output. It also requires a proper debt management approach. Based on the information provided in 2019 by the African Development Bank Group, the fiscal balance excluding grants (as a percentage to GDP) for all EAC countries stood at a deficit. Burundi had the highest debt of 11.3 percent, followed by Kenya with 8.9 percent. Rwanda's fiscal deficit was at 6.4 percent, and countries with the least fiscal deficit were Tanzania at 3.1 percent and Uganda at 4.8 percent. The disproportionate fiscal deficits in individual countries can partly explain the differences in public debts among the EAC member states. Except for Burundi and South Sudan, whose data were missing, the external debt in the EAC member states has been on the rise over the last decade (Table 8.2). Kenya, Uganda, and Rwanda's external debt nearly halve the respective country's GDP.

While the EAMU member states fixed the public debt-to-GDP ratio at a threshold of 50 percent, by the year 2018, some countries' debt sizes were nearing the set threshold. For example, Burundi's debt-to-GDP ratio stood at 14.9 percent, while Kenya's debt-to-GDP was 47.6 percent. In addition, Rwanda and Tanzania had accumulated a debt-to-GDP ratio of 41.4 percent and 34.6 percent, respectively, while Uganda's debt-to-GDP ratio had risen to 45.0 percent (AfDB, 2019). The enormous public debts in each country have resulted in different macroeconomic disturbances, calling for different policy responses, including

Table 8.2 External debt accumulation in EAC countries excluding South Sudan (% of GDP)

Country	2008	2009	2010	2011	2012	2013	2014	2015	2016	2017	2018
Burundi	94.2	21.2	22.4	24.0	22.6	21.0	18.9	18.2	16.7	15.3	14.9
Kenya	19.9	28.8	29.9	31.1	30.2	29.3	35.9	40.4	43.4	46.3	47.6
Rwanda	13.7	15.6	17.6	20.2	20.3	25.2	26.8	29.3	36.7	40.0	41.4
Tanzania	18.2	21.0	23.1	24.9	25.3	26.1	27.3	32.9	34.7	34.0	34.6
Uganda	18.1	21.3	25.3	27.4	28.2	30.8	31.2	39.0	39.7	42.7	45.0

Source: Annex 2 of the East Africa Economic Outlook, 2019 published by African Development Bank Group

exchange rate policy reforms—this can potentially affect exchange rate convergence.

Monetary Institutions in East Africa

Monetary institutions such as the central bank, commercial banks, cooperative banks, currency boards, and development banks are important in promoting economic growth and development. Unlike the central bank responsible for the country's financial stability, commercial banks receive deposits and lend money to potential borrowers mainly to finance trade and investments. Cooperative banks are commonly known for extending credit to agriculturalists, while development banks promote economic development. Although forming the common currency zone requires convergence in the monetary and financial systems, EAC member states own individual central banks and no uniformity in the number of commercial banks; commercial banks are key in facilitating investments in the region. According to information provided by the EAC secretariat, in 2019, Kenya commercial banking industry had 43 commercial banks and two mortgage financial institutions; Tanzania had 26 commercial banks while Uganda had 21 commercial banks. Rwanda had eight commercial banks, one development, and one mortgage bank, while Burundi had seven commercial banks, one development bank, and one housing fund. South Sudan had about 23 commercial banks.

The EAC bloc has four operational stock exchange markets: NSE in Kenya, RSE in Rwanda, DSE in Tanzania, and USE in Uganda. The regional stock exchange has 110 companies, with over 56 percent of the companies owned by Kenya. NSE accounts for about 55 percent of the regional total equity market capitalization of US dollars 22 Billion. Following the integration of the East African countries, cross-border expansion in the banking business has also expanded. However, Kenya still stands out as the biggest beneficiary in the regional banking service provisions (Table 8.3).

Kenya dominates the commercial banking services in the region. It owns Bank of Africa, Commercial bank of Africa, Cooperative Bank of Kenya, Diamond Trust Bank, Equity bank, Fina Bank, I&M Bank, Imperial Bank, KCB, and NIC bank. Although the establishment of the EAC led to the expansion of trade and investments in the region, many domestic, commercial banks from Burundi, Rwanda, South Sudan,

Table 8.3 Banks with cross-border operations in the EAC

Banks	Regional countries in which banks have operations					
	Burundi	Kenya	Rwanda	South Sudan	Tanzania	Uganda
ABC Bank		✓				✓
Bank of Africa	✓	✓			✓	✓
Commercial Bank of Africa	✓	✓			✓	✓
Cooperative Bank		✓		✓		
Diamond Trust Bank	✓	✓			✓	✓
Equity Bank		✓	✓	✓	✓	✓
Fina Bank		✓	✓			✓
I&M Bank		✓	✓		✓	
Imperial Bank		✓				✓
KCB Bank	✓	✓	✓	✓	✓	✓
NIC Bank		✓			✓	✓
Bank of Kigali		✓	✓			
CRDB Bank	✓				✓	

Source: Recent Trends in Banking in Sub-Saharan Africa from Financing to Investment. Published by European Investment Bank (2015). Notes: Bank of Kigali owns a representative office in Kenya, and it is the first foreign bank from within the region to establish a representative office in Kenya

Tanzania, and Uganda are still constrained by a lack of sufficient capital to allow for expansion of their banking services across borders. Nevertheless, the rise in the flow of trade forced many Kenyan commercial banks to follow their customers who have expanded or moved to other member states—a reason for the expansion of Kenyan commercial banks in the region.

INTERREGIONAL TRADE IN EAST AFRICA

Countries previously trading together forms monetary unions. The purpose of the monetary union is to soften the transaction costs among the trading partners. However, the disproportionality in the gains from trade (in many developing countries, the gains from trade greatly depend on quantities of the goods and services exchanged) can affect the success of the monetary union (see Faruqee, 2004). This can occur when some member countries disrespect some contents in the monetary union pact. Nevertheless, trade among the EAC member states has prevailed for a long. Historically, most

Table 8.4 Interregional trade in East Africa excluding South Sudan and Tanzania (% of total exports)

Country	2012	2013	2014	2015	2016	2017
Burundi	8.9	8.3	9.5	10.2	9.8	6.6
Kenya	33.9	25.8	27.1	28.6	29.9	25.1
Rwanda	36.8	41.3	29.3	13.8	15.2	14.3
Uganda	41.0	42.2	45.9	47.4	37.1	40.2

Source: Extracted from East Africa Economic Outlook (2019). Macroeconomic developments and prospects, UNCTADstat.8

trade deals mainly were in agricultural products, but the trend has steadily changed to manufactured products and services (Table 8.4).

Some shocks still constrain the flow of interregional trade in East Africa. The region has been susceptible to natural disasters, including droughts, low rainfall totals, and sometimes excessive rain affecting agricultural production. The effects of such shocks are worsened by the poor state of infrastructure in some EAC member states and the rampant conflicts between some member states. The conflict between Rwanda and Burundi, which has persisted for a long, manifests political disagreements between the two countries. Uganda and Rwanda have also continuously conflicted, though their conflict became evident in early 2019 when Rwanda closed its border from Ugandans and Uganda's exports. The most recent trade conflict occurred in 2020 when Kenya blocked some exports from Uganda, including milk, sugar, and sugar cane. Tanzania also blocked Ugandan sugar exports in the same year. Combining such trade challenges demonstrates a need for a firm commitment to harmonizing trade policies and political ideologies among EAC member states.

CONCLUSION

This chapter has provided some facts about the structural attributes of the EAC member countries and has also presented some insights relating to the success of the East African Monetary Union. A monetary union eliminates the transaction costs of exchanging currencies and exchange rate volatilities. As a result, the flow of trade among trade partners gets smoothened. But the success of any monetary union also depends on some conditions. First, the member countries' monetary authorities must accept country-specific monetary policies and exchange rate policies as instruments for responding to shocks. Second, the convergence of the structural characteristics of the concerned states.

Our discussions showed how the East African Community has evolved to its present state. At first, the community started with cooperation triggered by establishing the first railway line that joined Kenya, Tanganyika, and Uganda between 1897 and 1901. Then, the cooperation became more robust when the member states continued enjoying joint services provided through the Postal union, East African Currency Board, East African High Commission, and East African Common Services Organization. As a result of the cooperation, the first East African community came into existence in 1967. Still, it collapsed in 1977 due to deterioration in political will, disagreements between the presidents of Uganda and Tanzania, and the disproportionate sharing of benefits by the member states. Finally, in 2000, the East African countries established the present East African Community.

We further presented the origin of a common currency in the East African region—we showed that using a common currency by East African countries was also rooted in establishing the railway line that opened up the interlard to the coastal areas. Remember, the coastal areas were already using currencies like the Indian rupee, Silver rupee, and Pice. Finally, to better understand the East African Monetary Union and also be able to predict its success, we discussed the structural attributes of the EAC member states that can potentially affect the progress of the monetary union. Although we observed some similarities in the structural characteristics of the EAC member countries, some country-specific shocks still exist, limiting the attainment of the convergence requirement for the success of any monetary union. So far, the success of the EAMU requires increased harmonization of monetary and fiscal policies and increased collaboration in other macroeconomic indicators like trade and debt management. In addition,stability in exchange rates is a fundamental requirement for the success of any monetary union.

References

African Development Bank. (2019). Uganda Economic Outlook. https://www.afdb.org/en/countries/east-africa/uganda/uganda-economic-outlook

Ajevskis, V., Rimgailaite, R., Rutkaste, U., & Tkačevs, O. (2014). The equilibrium real exchange rate: pros and cons of different approaches with application to Latvia. *Baltic Journal of Economics, 14*(1–2), 101–123.

Dridi, J., & Nguyen, A. D. (2019). Assessing inflation convergence in the East African Community. *Journal of International Development*, *31*(2), 119–136.

Drummond, P. F. N., Wajid, S. K. S., & Williams, O. (Eds.). (2014). *The quest for regional integration in the East African Community*. International Monetary Fund.

East Africa Economic Outlook. (2019). *Macroeconomic developments and prospects*. Published by African Development Bank Group.

Edwards, S. (2006). Monetary unions, external shocks and economic performance: A Latin American perspective. *International Economics and Economic Policy*, *3*(3–4), 225–247.

European Investment Bank. (2015). *Recent trends in banking in Sub-Saharan Africa from financing to investment*.

Faruqee, M. H. (2004). *Measuring the trade effects of EMU* (No. 4–154). International Monetary Fund.

Mawejje, J., & Odhiambo, N. M. (2020). The determinants of fiscal deficits: a survey of literature. *International Review of Economics*, *67*(3), 403–417.

Mwangi, W. (2001). Of coins and conquest: The East African currency board, the rupee crisis, and the problem of colonialism in the East African protectorate. *Comparative Studies in Society and History*, *43*(4), 763–787.

Ogrodnick, R. A. (1990). Optimum currency areas and the international monetary system. *Journal of International Affairs*, 241–261.

UNCTAD. (2007). *Reclaiming policy space. Domestic resource mobilization and developmental states*. UN Conference on Trade and Development.

United Nations Economic Commission for Africa. (2018). *The East African monetary union: Ready or not?* ISBN: 978-99977-775-1-5.

World Bank. (2020). World Development Indicators.

CHAPTER 9

The Development Cost of Maintaining Price and Economic Stability in Central and West African CFA Franc Zone

Aloysius Ajab Amin

INTRODUCTION

The financial system is critical in promoting private business activities, economic growth, and development. However, monetary arrangements in the CFA franc (CFAF) zone countries have encouraged the outflow of valuable resources (and promoted the non-valued supply chain) from the zone. This chapter examines how the CFAF zone economy has been inhibited by the financial system firmly anchored by the monetary arrangement put in place by France even before 1945 and strengthened after that. As a result, the financial sector has not grown to perform the development role. The CFAF countries have a monetary union with a convertible currency and a fixed exchange rate. However, they also operate within other reinforcing mechanisms imposed by France under the colonial pacts (Agbohou, 1999, 2012; Koutonin, 2014).

A. A. Amin (✉)
Clayton State University, Morrow, GA, USA
e-mail: AloysiusAmin@clayton.edu

© The Author(s), under exclusive license to Springer Nature Switzerland AG 2022
A. A. Amin et al. (eds.), *Monetary and Financial Systems in Africa*,
https://doi.org/10.1007/978-3-030-96225-8_9

The CFAF zone countries differ in cultural, social, economic fundamentals, legal, administrative, governance, and colonial legacies. However, their resemblance is in producing similar primary exports. They face asymmetric shocks. Under the CFAF monetary union, these countries were bound together in one financial and monetary system to direct their raw materials towards France and Europe (Tchundjang, 2000). The primary goods or commodities, including fruits, oils and oilseeds, rubber, cotton, cocoa, timber, and minerals, were exported to France before 1919 (Keltie & Epstein, 1921). As of 2020, these same raw materials remain the main exports of these African countries.

The chapter's objective is to analyze the impact of the special arrangements of the CFAF on financial development and the impact on socio-economic development of the countries. We address these issues to gain better insight into the performance of the CFAF economies as influenced by the monetary arrangements. We address the following questions: Why have the advantages of low inflation, greater stability, and discipline from this particular arrangement not generated better outcomes in these economies? How have these arrangements affected these countries' financial development and economic growth and development? These have far-reaching implications for the development of the CFAF region and the continuation of CFAF arrangements with France/Europe.

There is considerable interest in the long-term growth of CFAF zone economies which have been somewhat tied to the French economy through the CFAF arrangements and even after the 1960s independence. However, the CFAF economies have performed very poorly since the mid-1980s, despite their high growth and development potentials. The domestic policy failures coupled with severe external shocks resulted in the sharp decline of these African economies in the 1970s and 1980s. This scenario negated the positive discussions on the CFAF zone countries' benefits derived from the monetary union (Van de Walle, 1991; Allechi & Niamkey, 1994, 1997; Elu & Price, 2010).

France and Francophone Africa

The CFAF zone consists of 15 countries: (i) eight in West African countries (Benin, Burkina Faso, Guinea Bissau, Ivory Coast, Mali, Niger, Senegal, and Togo) forming the West African Economic and Monetary Union (UEMOA); (ii) six in Central African countries (Cameroon, Central African Republic, Chad, Congo Republic, Equatorial Guinea, and

Gabon) forming the Central African Economic and Monetary Union (CEMAC); and (iii) Comoros in the East coast of Africa. These countries inherited different colonial legacies, producing different outcomes and facing other challenges. Therefore, we focus on the 14 CFAF zone countries of West and Central Africa.

The French language is the only official language used in the CFAF zone. However, there are three other linguistic groups within the two CFA franc regions. After the United Nations referendum of February 11, 1961, the British Southern Cameroons and the Republic of Cameroon joined and formed the Federal Republic of Cameroon on October 1, 1961. Since 2016, the union has been in a severe crisis. Equatorial Guinea (a former Spanish colony) became a member of the CFAF zone in 1983. Guinea Bissau, the former Portuguese colony, joined the monetary union on May 2, 1997, adopting the CFA franc with 1 CFAF equivalent to 65 Guinea Bissau pesos.

These countries grouped under the CFAF have had many arrangements with France. Other European colonial powers have had similar agreements, such as monetary cooperation with their former colonies. Nevertheless, that of France and former colonies went much further and deeply intertwined with much economic, cultural, military, social, and political accords and administrative and legal legacies that reinforced the monetary union arrangements (Koutonin, 2014; Nubukpo et al., 2016). France has used these colonial pacts to have a stronghold on the former colonies. According to many, these countries have not been an integrated economic body for the regions; instead, the treaties have grouped them for the benefit of France (Agbohou, 1999, 2012; Nubukpo et al., 2016).

The rest of the chapter continues by tracing the origin of the CFA franc with its peg to French Franc and the introduction of commercial banks with the Central Banks. Next, it discusses the implications of the four main principles of the CFA francs, with stress on operation accounts and the production of raw materials. The chapter continues by analyzing the economic cost of the monetary arrangement as embedded in the monetary policy and credit facilities. It further examines the CFA franc (CFAF) zone as primary product producers despite the weak business environment. Finally, the chapter concludes with a summary and policy implications.

EVOLUTION OF CFA FRANC: THE BEAC AND BCEAO

April 1959 marked the establishment of the Banque Centrale des Etats de l'Afrique de l'Ouest (BCEAO) and the Banque Centrale des Etats de l'Afrique Equatoriale et du Cameroun (BCEAC), with each central bank having an operation account in the French treasury. On November 23, 1972, BCEAC became BEAC. In May, 121,962 l'Union Monétaire Ouest-Africaine (UMOA) was created. The two central banks were established as the Central Banks for the Central and West African countries. Still, the governance of these Central Banks was initially entirely French- even when some authority was delegated to the Africans, the Africans were still supervised by the French authorities. Before these changes, the Headquarters of the CFAF was in Paris, under the complete control of the French authorities, and the French continued to make critical decisions. For instance, in June 2017, the Statutes of the Banks of Central African States (CEMAC) with Article 29 were revised but still maintain French control. According to Article 29, the Board of Directors has fourteen members with two directors for each member State, including France. Consequently, France still has veto powers in the governance of the Central Bank (BEAC). As a result, the governance of the African CFA central banks includes the French authorities with a decisive voice on the two regional central banks (Koddenbrock, 2020; Koddenbrock & Sylla, 2019; Taylor, 2019). This type of hold, coupled with the sovereignty loss of the Central Banks with the foreign reserve holdings, has caused much tension in the regions (Pigeaud & Sylla, 2018).

For the period 1945–1958, CFA stood for "colonies francaises d'Afrique (French colonies of Africa); for the period 1958–1959, CFA stood for Communaute francaise d' Afrique (French community of Africa); in 1960s years of independence, CFA stood for Communaute financiere Africaine (African financial community). There are really two names: (i) For West Africa the CFA stands for communaute financiere d'Afrique (financial community of Africa)—Banque Centrale des Etats de l'Afrique de l'Ouest (BCEAO). The Head Office of the Central Bank is based in Dakar, Senegal. The region consists of eight countries of West African Economic and Monetary Union – Union economique et monetaire oust africaine (UEMOA). (ii) For the Central Africa, the CFA stands for cooperation financiere en Afrique central, and its regional central bank is known as the Banque des etats de l'Afrique central (BEAC). The Head Office of the Bank is based in Yaoundé. The region consists of six countries of the Economic and monetary community of Central Africa. Six Central African

Countries of CFA monetary Community (CEMAC). The currency is printed by the Banque de France in Chamalieres, Auvergne-Rhone-Alpes and distributed by the two regional central banks. The two CFA francs are fixed at the same parity to the euro; it was originally fixed to the French Franc prior to 1999. But the CFA franc monies are two separate currencies. One CFA franc of the BEAC sub zone does not have the same value of exchange rate as one CFA franc of the BCEAO sub zone both in principle and in practice.

The Central Africa CFA franc is not interchangeable with the West Africa CFA franc. It has been suggested that the central Africa bank authorities dictated this difference. They thought they had a better natural resource base, including oil, than the West African franc zone. Nevertheless, it hindered trade between the two similar monetary zones. Furthermore, the West African CFA franc has been overvalued over many periods relative to the Central African CFA franc. The differences have created black markets for the two regions – creating an arbitrage. However, the African CFA franc Central banks and the French authorities could always decide the exchange rate between these two CFA francs. Although the exchange rates are the same as all other currencies, they cannot control the arbitrage, generating much rent and increasing transaction costs without additional production (Baye & Khan, 2008).

Changes in CFA Franc Exchange Rates and Devaluation

There have been significant changes in the fixed exchange rate and value of the CFA franc relative to the French Franc and Euro. Between 1945 and 2000, France made these changes in the currency value, with the value of the CFA franc relative to the French franc, especially the changes in 1945, 1948, 1994, and 2000 (BCEAO, 2000).

The parity of the CFAF was fixed at 0.5 CFAF to 1FF in 1948 to meet the Bretton Woods requirements. However, there was a change in its nominal parity following the French currency reform in 1960. This parity, however, remained unchanged until 1994, although announced in Dakar, France, and the Bretton Woods institutions decided in Paris to devalue the franc CFA.

From 1949 to 1994 the rate stood at 1FF = 50 CFAF. Still, it was the French decision with little African countries' input. In January 1999, the Euro replaced the French franc as a currency in the Eurozone, where France is a member with 1 euro = 655.957 CFAF resulting in a devaluation of the CFAF (Table 9.1). In all, France decided on every step of

Table 9.1 The CFA franc (CFAF): Creation and changes

CFA franc creation/changes	Date	Rate of Exchange	Comment
Creation of the CFA franc	December 26, 1945	1 CFAF = 1.70 FF	French decision
Devaluation of the French franc	October 17, 1948	1 CFAF = 2.00 FF	French decision
A new French franc	January 1, 1960	1 CFAF = 0.02 FF	French decision
Devaluation of CFA	January 12, 1994	1 CFAF = 0.01 FF	French with IMF decision
Pegging the CFA to euro	January 1, 1999	655.957 CFAF = 1 euro	French decision

Source: BCEAO (2017)

changes in the parity without inputs or consent of the African regional authorities, which underscored the question of loss of central bank sovereignty.

Although the major devaluations were in 1948 and 1994, whenever the French franc or the Euro depreciated or appreciated their currencies, the CFA franc was affected immediately and greatly impacted the CFA franc zone economies. Therefore, the purpose of the devaluations in the 1990s was to promote the exports of the franc zone countries. However, the policy seems ineffective because of the low supply elasticity of primary products (main exports). Instead, because of low demand elasticity, it was harder to import necessary capital imports and cheaper to export the zone's primary goods, including minerals, to Europe at higher volume for lesser value (Amin, 2000).

There is also the possibility of frequent modifications of the exchange rate of the CFAF, depending on European Union economic policy and the strength of the Euro vis-à-vis other major currencies, especially the US dollar (Yasser & Tsangarides, 2010). An increase in interest rate, for example, may affect the exports and debts of the CFA countries negatively. Nevertheless, an important issue here is that the CFAF zone countries are also severely restricted in using their fiscal policy tool. Therefore, the convergence criteria impose on the franc zone countries that their adherence to these criteria restricts their proper economic management. Although, some (Elu & Price, 2010; Guillaumont & Guillaumont, 1984; Mvondo, 2019) argued that the criteria should significantly reduce perceived risk to investors, among other things.

Origin of the Banking System, Operation Account, and Trade

By the nineteenth century, the French had established an African financial community, and on June 15, 1825, the French issued an ordinance prohibiting the circulation of African currencies in Senegal. With the ordinance, the French authorities introduced a unified financial system about 1840. Before 1850 private French banks were issuing banknotes. The first commercial bank started in French-speaking Africa with the April 27, 1848 decree that compensated former slave owners. A portion of the compensation was used in founding loans and discount banks in the colonies. However, the French denied compensation to the victims of inhuman activities (slave trade). With the law of July 11, 1851, the French started to establish a series of loans and credits banks in Senegal, Algeria, Martinique, Guadeloupe, Reunion, Guyana, New Caledonia, Indochina, and Madagascar. The Bank of Senegal was replaced by the Bank of West Africa (BAO) in 1901, with its activities extended to Equatorial Africa (Monga, 1997, Semedo & Villieu, 1997).

BAO, the only bank, purchased and sold local currencies, granted agricultural and mining activities credit, discounted commercial bills, and transferred funds to France. With the First World War over, the French expanded the activities of the banks in Cameroon and Senegal that deliberately managed French investments with little or no investment in the economies of the regions. Across the colonies, the banks targeted only the French businesses and created business relationships directly with clients in Paris and large French companies in Cameroon and Senegal. Gradually, France granted certain business autonomy to its colonies, and at the same time, the French authorities opened operation accounts that started with Morocco (1922) and Madagascar (1925). The French began to establish a well-unified financial colonial empire with these accounts. The central role of the (CFA) franc currency was to facilitate the exploitation of raw materials, including minerals, perennial crops, for inputs into the manufacture of goods in European (French) factories (Semedo & Villieu, 1997; Tchundjang, 2000).

The CFA Franc Introduction

After World War II, France had to ratify the Bretton Woods Agreement. The French franc was very weak as a result of the disastrous war. Under the Marshall Plan, the USA gave France a substantial grant that was a nonrepayable and small amount of credit. Estimates put the total amount at about $5.1 billion (US Bureau of Census, 1954/55). The size of the relief amount showed the extent to which the French economy was devastated and the French franc weakened. The French ratification of the Bretton Woods agreement meant the French franc had to be devalued to set an appropriate exchange rate with the US dollar, then the world's reserve currency. Before devaluing one French Franc (FF) was equal to one local (African) franc, the French officially created a new currency in French colonies- the CFAF was fixed to the devalued French franc at 1.70FF = 1CFA franc in 1945.

The creation of the CFA franc in 1945 in the French colonies was because of the devastating French economy and extremely weak French Franc (FF). It was essential to make the CFAF much higher value than the depreciated French franc. This arrangement was a sound economic rationale, beneficial to the French economy. It protected French trade with its colonies against other countries. The French easily obtained raw materials and other resources from colonies and exported manufactured goods produced from the raw materials to the African colonies. It was like a type of reserve money put away by the French to cushion any French leaving the gold standard and adopting the dollar as the leading international currency.

Furthermore, the exports from the colonies became more expensive to other countries giving France a trade advantage to import goods from its colonies and export goods to its colonies. However, the goods exported were mainly to the French in their colonies. Hence, the French benefited enormously in exports and imports (Tchundjang, 2000). The CFA franc zone became closely connected with the French franc and economy. After all, the accounts of the colonies were managed by the French in Paris. The French created the CFA franc to facilitate transactions with their colonies. The French managed the accounts of the colonies in Paris, and the colonies had no say in the creation. History shows that it was not for the interest of the African countries (Koddenbrock & Sylla, 2019; Nubukpo et al., 2016).

The Operating Principles of CFA Franc

The functioning of the franc zone is built on four main operating principles, which clearly distinguish CFAF zone countries from any other developing countries' monetary arrangements:

First, the guarantee of **unlimited convertibility** of the CFAF was supposedly "issued" by the different African Central Banks and supported by the French Treasury. The CFAF is not traded on the foreign exchange market but was fully convertible into the French franc. Today, it is fully convertible into the Euro under convertibility guaranteed by the French Treasury through its operation accounts. The operation accounts opened for the two central banks at the French Treasury can be credited up to the stated limit but debited without limits.

Second, there is a **fixed parity** of the unlimited convertibility of the currency within the zone. For example, the currency union maintains a fixed parity between the French franc before 1999 (and then the Euro) and the CFA franc. Any policy change on these issues, such as parity change, must be in total agreement between France and the two central banks. Given this arrangement, member countries individually operate under fixed exchange rate regimes with no monetary policies since the central banks are independent of the national authorities of the two zones. Accordingly, this minimizes inflationary tendencies and consequently should offer these countries higher purchasing power. However, economists are unanimous that a country's overall low price level or inflation rate results from the monetary policy.

Consequently, countries with loose monetary policy may be exposed to inflation risk. On the other hand, the CFAF countries have managed to maintain stable prices due to the strict respect of the clauses of the membership in this union which restrict them from printing and issuing their own money (Tables 9.2 and 9.3). But at what cost? These countries anchored their national price levels to the main currency (French franc or Euro) by adopting a fixed exchange rate. They thereby maintain the price levels similar to the rate experienced in France or the European Union. However, European Union with France has economic structures utterly different from those of the CFA franc zone economies.

Third, there is a **free transfer** within the zone and France/Eurozone. Until 1992, there was supposed to be unlimited transferability and free mobility of money and capital within the zone and between France/Europe in principle, but in practice, the free transfer is mainly between the CFA franc zone (individually or collectively) France or the Eurozone. Instead, in 1993 some restrictions were imposed on currency convertibility between the two CFA franc regions (Tables 9.2 and 9.3). As a result, the central banks suspended the repurchase of their exported notes outside their respective zones of "issue" (BEAC and BCEAO). The

Table 9.2 CEMAC: Selected economic and financial indicators, 2012–2020

Year	Real GDP growth	Inflation	Exchange US $	Naira (% change)	REER
2012	7.3	3.8	510.56	6.3	0.0
2013	1.3	2.0	493.90	-3.6	1.5
2014	4.0	3.2	493.76	-3.5	-5.5
2015	1.6	2.5	591.21	-0.2	-38.5
2016	-1.4	1.1	592.61	-19.6	7.3
2017	0.7	0.9	580.66	-18.2	12.6
2018	1.8	2.3	555.45	-21.4	9.1
2019	2.0	2.0	585.91	5.5	-5.8
2020					

Source: Banque des États de L'Afrique Centrale. Rapport Annuel 2020

Table 9.3 UEMO: Selected economic and financial indicators, 2012–2020

Year	Real GDP growth	Inflation	Exchange US $	Naira	Interest rate
2012	6.94	2.40	510.23	3.29	7.99
2013	6.00	1.50	493.89	3.12	7.56
2014	6.71	-0.13	493.63	3.03	7.26
2015	6.42	1.00	591.45	3.05	7.01
2016	6.19	0.35	593.00	2.47	6.93
2017	6.48	1.10	582.02	1.91	6.92
2018	6.39	1.20	555.58	1.82	6.79
2019	5.70	-0.74	585.67	1.90	6.68
2020	1.51	2.10	575.59	1.74	6.59

Source: Banque des États de L'Afrique Centrale. Rapport Annuel 2020; Banque Centrale des Etats de l'Afrique de l'Ouest – www.bceao.int

suspension has tended to create informal markets with significant changes in parity between the two CFAF areas and even with Non-CFAF franc zones. Sometimes, the CFAF of a central bank in the zone is over-valued relative to other central banks because of the volume of trade and the strength of the respective economies. Also, the CFA franc's convertibility against the unconvertible currencies such as the Naira (Nigeria currency) or Cedi (Ghanaian currency) plays a vital role in cross-border trade.

Fourth, there is **centralization of foreign exchange reserves** in the French Treasury. With the operation, account opened in the French Treasury, the CFA Franc's full convertibility into the French franc and later into the Euro following the adoption of a single monetary unit of

European countries, including France, guaranteed with the special operation account, not by the French Central Bank. France opened these operation accounts in the name of the central banks- the Bank of Central African States (BEAC), the Central Bank of West African States (BCEAO), and the Central Bank of Comoros (BCC). The foreign exchange reserves centralization enables France to exercise its unlimited guarantee and control of the CFA franc, including the foreign exchange reserves of each country. Just imagine another country controlling the reserves of another country. The operation accounts can have a positive balance or can run into deficits. In the case of a positive balance, the account bears interest. The French Treasury invests the foreign reserves of the CFA franc zone. In the case of a deficit, interest is paid under certain conditions to French Treasury. The deficit country may also be offered unlimited overdraft facilities, thus allowing the CFA countries to avoid short-run balance of payment constraints. While France benefits, deficit countries tend to incur huge debts, and surplus countries tend to finance the deficit countries (Pigeaud & Sylla, 2018).

CFA Franc Zone Foreign Exchange Reserves in French Operation Account

In exchange for the guarantee, each of the two regional central banks is required to deposit a large percent of the region's foreign exchange reserves into the operating account. The period 1945–1973 was 100 percent; the percentage was reduced to 65 percent for 1973–2005 and then reduced to 50 percent from 2005 to the present. The French Treasury maintains at least 20 percent of these countries' foreign exchange reserves to cover their sight liabilities. Furthermore, the French Treasury limits the CFA franc zone countries' credit to a ceiling of 20 percent of the country's tax revenue of the preceding year. The 20% ceiling on expenditure while not fully relaxed as from 2001, countries are allowed to seek additional funding from financial markets through bonds, a severe implication to the commercial banks. Initially, with a 100% foreign exchange deposit into the French Treasury, the Franc zone countries had no access to their own money for their national development. The CFA franc countries often do not know how much foreign reserves they have in the French Treasury. Even when these countries borrow, they tend to borrow their own money, and the French Treasury offers the loans at commercial rates. Nevertheless, the loans must not exceed 20% of their previous year's revenue. Their money is invested in the Paris Bourse in the name of the French Treasury. Furthermore, these countries have to stick to these stringent monetary and fiscal rules (Hadjimichael & Galy, 1997; Nubukpo et al., 2016).

The Euro and CFA Franc Process

Comparing the European Union with the CFA franc zone African countries, one can observe a fundamental similarity of regional integration being that of progressive deepening and widening of their respective integration more so within the European Union. However, there are significant differences in substance and intent. An important distinction is the process of integration and union. Member countries have been fully involved in promoting the European agenda and their respective interests and ensuring the European objectives coincide with their own countries' interests (Banque de France, 2005).

In contrast, the Franc CFA zone started as an economical raw materials supplier to France. The natural resources were exploited from the colonial territories with the labor of the indigenous peoples. The CFA franc was created to facilitate the transfer of resources. The franc CFA zone members had no say in creating the monetary union. Thus, the history of the CFA franc zone cannot be seen as an "integrated" monetary and economic union, even today. The African countries have not benefitted from the union. With still a narrow industrial base, the economic structure of the zone's economies has hardly changed since the inception of the CFA franc in 1945 (Irving, 1999; Tchatchouang, 2015; Kamga, 2020). Since the First World War, these countries are still producing and exporting the same primary goods (Table 9.4).

European Union (EU) and European Central Bank: No Obligation!

France joined the Eurozone and carried along with the CFA franc countries. The European Union Council discussed the monetary arrangement between France and the CFA franc zone countries without directly including the CFA franc zone countries themselves. As a result, the European Union reached an agreement with the French Treasury that guaranteed the full and free convertibility at a fixed rate between the Euro and the CFA franc with no obligation of the European Central Bank to support

Table 9.4 CEMAC and UEMOA: Production and trade structure: Primary and commodity exports 2020

Country: CEMAC	Exports	Oil exports percentage of total exports	Country: UEMOA	Exports; (percent of total exports in (%))
Cameroon	Crude oil, petroleum products gas, forest product, cocoa, banana, aluminum, coffee, cotton, palm oil, rubber, gold	53.60	Benin	Cotton (54.9%), Fruits & Nuts, oilseeds, gold, copper, coconut, Brazil nuts, cashew, animal/vegetable fats, oils & waxes, wood products, salt, sulfur, stone, meat, iron
Chad	Cotton, crude oil, petroleum, livestock, gold, textiles	93.31	Burkina Faso	Gold, gems & precious metals (69.6%), cotton. Zinc ore, oilseeds, fruits and nuts, mineral fuels
Central African Rep	Diamonds, gold, tin ore, precious stones, forest product & timber, cotton, cocoa, coffee, tobacco, fruits	0.43 (53.83% of minerals in total exports)	Ivory Coast	Cocoa (53.6%), mineral fuels, rubber, gems & precious metals, fruits & nuts, Ores, cotton, wool, meat & fish, animal/vegetables fats oil waxes
Congo	Oil, forest product & timber, sugar, cocoa, coffee, diamonds, copper, cobalt	90.26	Guinea Bissau	Coconuts, Brazil nuts &, cashews, (51.8%) gold, fish, wood, aluminum
Equatorial Guinea	Crude oil, petroleum & natural gas, forest product, cocoa, coffee, fish	94.20	Mali	Cotton (25.26%), oilseeds & oleaginous fruits, wood, dates, animal products, vegetables
Gabon	Crude oil, forest product, cocoa, coffee, manganese, uranium	76.24	Niger	Oilseed (51.9%), mineral fuels, gems, and precious metals, rawhides, and skins, leather, vegetables, uranium
			Senegal	Gold, gems &precious metals (18.9%), mineral fuels, fish, groundnut, ores, slag ash, oilseeds, salt, sulfur, stone, vegetables
			Togo	Mineral fuels (49.4%), oilseeds, salt, sulfur, stone, cotton, iron, fruits and nuts, animal/vegetable fats, oil, and waxes, copper

Sources: Author's compilation from COBAC, WTO, World Bank, CEMAC, UEMOA, OEC

the convertibility of the CFA franc. Furthermore, the French guaranteed the European Union no likely effects of the agreement between the CFA franc and the Euro on the Eurozone. Accordingly, any changes in the CFA franc agreement must be approved by the Council of the European Union. In short, the Eurozone or the European Central Bank (ECB) has no obligation in any aspect. The ECB may not consider the financial and economic conditions of the CFA franc zone in conducting the ECB monetary policy. Hence, the decision to peg the CFA franc to the Euro at a fixed exchange rate supported by the French Treasury creates no obligation whatsoever on the ECB towards the CFA franc countries. If there is any responsibility at all, that is the responsibility of France (the French Treasury). Such arrangement has severe implications for the CFA franc when any change in the Euro, the ECB, and the EU benefits with no responsibility.

The critical point here is that the CFA franc zone has no central bank in the real sense. The two CFA Franc regional central banks have no authority or power to perform the functions of a central bank. The regional CFA franc central banks do not fulfill the central bank's role, such as the primary function of printing and issuing the currency. At best, the two regional CFA franc central banks distributed the money printed in Paris by France and sent to the CFA franc central banks in Central (BEAC) and West Africa (BCEAO) for distribution, with severe implications for monetary policy in the CFA franc zone.

Economic Costs to CFA Franc Countries

The central bank of a country holds its foreign reserves. These assets could include foreign currencies, bonds, treasury bills. Most of the foreign reserves are usually held in US dollars because the currency is the most traded in the world. A country uses its foreign reserves to maintain a stable value of its currency, maintain the price of its exports competitively, maintain liquidity during a crisis, confidence for investors. Notably, a country needs foreign exchange to pay its external debts, finance or fund its economic development such as education, health, and infrastructural development, and diversify its portfolios. Furthermore, the country uses the reserves to influence its monetary policy and back its obligations. None of these functions is performed by the two central banks or the CFA franc zone countries (Tchatchouang, 2015; Tchundjang, 2000).

Countries create their central banks to print, issue, and control their currencies. The central bank derives earnings by printing and issuing currency notes and selling them to the public. The central bank's core responsibilities are formulating and implementing the country's monetary authorities to ensure economic and financial stability with both internal and external currency/price stability. Internal stability maintains price stability with stable purchasing power and prevents it from deteriorating. External stability deals with exchange rates volatility. Since the last global financial crisis and today with the COVID-19 crisis, the central banks have expanded their tools in dealing with risks related to financial stability, exchange rates volatility, and macroeconomic stability. Thus, the central bank has multiple goals and tools to deal with the economy's problems. The central bank's responsibility covers many issues, including environmental risks (Dikau & Volz, 2018; Benlialper & Comer, 2016; Archer & Moser-Boehm, (2013).

In contrast, the CFA franc is backed by another country- France. Unlike the Euro that is supported by the European Union's member states and not by the government of another country (Eichengreen, 2011). This type of support has far-reaching implications. With these restrictions, the CFA franc central banks can hardly provide any channel for development. The CFA franc monetary arrangements were designed to serve French interests in the (ex-)colonies. Pegging reduces transaction costs relative to France with the franc zone- easy and at no cost of money transfer and capital, movement mean resources and economic surplus are transferred easily from the CFA franc zone to France. The currency union should promote growth and intra-trade among its members that does not happen in the CFA franc zone. Yet, there is little trade creation, no stable trade, no improvement of price co-movements among the members; despite the long existence of the currency union since 1945 (Tsangarides et al., 2008; Kamga, 2020).

A sound financial system is important (Herring & Santomero, 1991) and tend to have many components: (i) Central bank stabilizes domestic finances, administers or manages international financial matters, ensures monetary stability, and oversees public finances and public debt management. (ii) Variety of banks including domestic and foreign banks, internet banking, credit unions, savings and loans associations, investment banks and investment companies, brokerage firms. Banks in essence offer credit, and pool risk among consumers, promote economic activities and manage markets, (iii) Mortgage companies and health insurance institutions that manage risk, invest their financial resources, and provide financial resources to other financial institutions; (iv) Well performing capital markets including securities markets (Singh et al., 2009; World Bank, 2020). However, much is still needed to have such a functioning system in the CFA franc countries where the financial sector is still shallow (Paudyn, 2014; Alter & Yontcheva, 2015).

Monetary Policy in the CFA Franc Zone Countries

An effective monetary policy is more than an instrument for controlling inflation (Hasan & Mester, 2008). It is an instrument of stabilizing the real exchange real rate and impacting the country's socio-economic development. Notably, a channel for monetary policy implementation is influencing credit creation through tools such as (1) open market operations; (2) affecting private-sector borrowing rates through the interest rate; (3) commercial banks borrowing from the Central banks at which rates reflect the situation of the economy; (4) having a reserve requirement that is conducive to the proper functioning of the banks and the economy; (5) regulating and promoting financial system- financial markets, capital/securities markets and as the banks' bankers; and (6) equally carrying out social functions primarily through financial institutions like the commercial banks and development banks.

Central Banks engage in credit allocation and the management of international capital flows. We know that high inflation rates tend to hinder macroeconomic stability. Inflation targeting is only an aspect of the monetary policy and cannot be the sole role of monetary policy. It is counterproductive by stressing very narrowly on maintaining a low inflation rate to neglect other important variables such as real variables that significantly impact the economy. These real variables include poverty reduction, job (creation), employment, and growth with economic transformation. Inflation targeting may lead to credit restriction and reduction of opportunities for a trade-off between the inflation level and these real variables, particularly (un)employment. The CFA franc zone economies have low inflation rates (levels), yet their growth rates are relatively low and unemployment rates relatively high. There should be a balance between unemployment and inflation and not too much stress on low inflation to neglect unemployment (Amin, 2000; Amin & Dubois, 2009; IMF, 2015; Kamga, 2020).

The Central Bank should generate and promote employment, economic growth with development, and credit allocation and management of capital flows. Monetary policy should not be limited to inflation rate targeting but should also involve real economic variables that promote economic growth and development. On inflation targeting, the role of the Central Bank, studies (UNCTAD, 2009) has shown that the adverse effects of inflation occurred when inflation rates are more significant than 4–6 percent.

However, the rates pursued by BEAC and BCEAO are much below these. In addition, extensive literature (Alter & Yontcheva, 2015; Singh et al., 2009; Allen et al., 2014, 2016; Abdullah & Inaba, 2020) has shown that financial development significantly impacts economic growth and development with a critical role in reducing inequality and poverty. These studies go further to show that the financial sector of the CFA franc zone countries lags far behind other Sub-Sahara African countries in financial inclusion and development.

The African CFAF countries are less developed and less inclusive financial sectors than other regions with similar structural characteristics. They have shallow financial sectors which remain relatively less inclusive. Allen et al. (2014) constructed the development gap by measuring the gap between the actual level of development and the expected financial development level from a sample of Sub Sahara African countries, with the CFAF countries showing the most significant gap. The CFAF countries come out with the least developed financial sector in Africa. The factors hampering financial deepening and inclusion are institutional factors established by the CFAF pact linked to macroeconomic and governance factors in the regional economies. Countries with a large proportion of natural resources to GDP, as in African CFAF zone countries, have Africa's least developed financial sector.

Natural resources revenues boost the GDP much more than the other sectors of the economy. Foreign conglomerates invest in the oil and mining industries. The foreign companies bring financial resources from abroad with better and well-developed financial sectors. Most of the financial transactions are therefore performed in developed economies. Little or no financial transactions are carried in the host countries (Allen et al., 2016, 2014). There are limited financial institutions in natural resource-rich countries. The crucial factors for financial development are the number of banks and branches, availability of quality credit information, registry coverage, operation costs (likely transferred to customers), and financial sector governance. In addition, institutional factors like the rule of law positively affect financial development.

These factors are extremely weak in CFAF countries, making the region not conducive to financial development (Ahokpossi et al., 2013; World Bank, 2020). Improved credit information coupled with the rule of law positively impacts financial development. Countries with strong institutions and government effective tend to have good and well development inclusive financial systems (Ahokpossi et al., 2013; Singh et al., 2009; Adrian & Yontcheva, 2015; Devarajan & de Melo, 1991).

Credit Facilities for Investment and Business Growth with Entrepreneurship

The CFA franc zone has small financial markets; the capital markets are thin. The commercial banks were initially French and Western, and today the dominant banks are still foreign banks. Transferring money even within the zone is more expensive than moving money from the zone to France and other western countries. The stock exchange markets are still in the embryonic stage. There is about three nascent stock exchange in the CFA franc zone countries: the (i) Douala Stock Exchange (DSX) based in Douala. (ii) Bourse des Valeurs Mobiliers de lAfrique Centrale (BVMAC) based in Libreville. (iii) Bourse Régionale des Valeurs Mobilières SA(BRVM) serving all the eight West African CFA franc countries with market offices located in each country.

These stock markets are still embryonic; the stock market has been in the early stage of development for a long time and still performing very poorly due to the strict monetary regulations of the CFA franc. According to Weeks, "the effectiveness of monetary policy relies on a viable domestic market for trading public securities and commercial banking sector willing and able to lend to the private sector" (Weeks, 2010, p. 1). However, the sounder commercial banks in the CFA franc countries are mainly foreign banks with high liquidity and a solid capital base. Therefore, they are unwilling to lend to the private sector (Nubukpo et al., 2016). Moreover, even if they lend, they do so to the foreign entities, which in turn hardly invest in the country's long-term projects (Table 9.5). This pattern partly explains why the domestic private sector is poorly developed, despite the CFA franc Central Banks (Singh et al., 2009; Sy, 2006; IMF, 2014; World Bank, 2020).

A developed and well-operating financial market facilitates savings and investment flow and capital accumulation and contributes to goods and services, thus generating economic expansion (Lall et al., 2006). Hence, a properly functioning financial system performs many services and has many purposes, emphasizing mobilizing financial resources domestically, promoting the country's growth and economic development. Moreover, a good financial system also directly offers facilities and indirectly strengthens growth by creating a suitable environment for investment and attracting investors (Rousseau & Sylla, 2001). Thus, to the extent that the financial system performs these functions well, economies tend to grow faster. However, the economy is constrained when banks do not adequately perform these functions, as seen in Gabon (Table 9.5).

Table 9.5 Banking sector and MFIs in Gabon 2000–2020

Year	No. banks	Deposits with commercial banks – Billion FCFA	Credit from commercial banks – Billion FCFA	Net banking income – Billion FCFA	Deposits with microfinance institution – Billion FCFA	Credit from microfinance institution – Billion FCFA
2000	6	1130.8	705.6	58347.0	10.8	8.3
2001	6	1347.3	431.5	78.2	12.0	8.2
2002	6	1436.1	352.7	78.2	12.4	8.2
2003	6	1179.9	446.3	88.6	11.9	8.5
2004	6	1103.6	405.9	76.0	14.5	10.1
2005	6	1034.0	418.8	82.0	15.4	14.1
2006	7	842.9	505.3	91.3	14.0	13.7
2007	7	1284.8	611.0	117.9	15.4	12.5
2008	7	986.0	644.2	139.0	18.3	17.3
2009	9	1034.0	681.4	118.7	17.3	16.7
2010	9	1258.4	818.4	92.1	17.8	16.2
2011	9	1645.3	1161.1	134.8	19.1	19.0
2012	10	1927.7	1462.8	163.4	20.7	24.4
2013	10	2055.6	1740.1	188.2	32.6	24.5
2014	10	2107.7	1760.2	194.4	31.7	31.8
2015	10	2103.6	1681.4	178.6	36.9	28.5
2016	10	2073.8	1792.6	208.7	39.2	30.8
2017	10	1857.9	1633.2	240.1	43.4	34.6
2018	10	2071.9	1695.4	220.5	57.9	45.0
2019	10	2478.9	2328.3	304.0	42.2	40.0
2020	10	2466.6	2025.4	391.1	41.5	40.0

Source: COBAC, CIMA

The CFA franc zones lack long-term and short-term investment funds from the financial sector. The CFAF zone economies are still dominated by foreign commercial banks that hardly provide resources for long- term investments. Allen et al. (2018) study the link between the real economic structure and the country's financial system to determine if the real economic structure affects the financial system. Applying dynamic panel techniques, they observed that physical-asset-intensive economies seem to be bank-based financial systems. In contrast, knowledge-based and intangible- asset–intensive economies tend to be market- based financial systems. They are implying that the financial needs of firms tend to influence the development of financial institutions and markets, and consequently, the characteristics of the real economy.

Market discipline needs three interrelated factors – "information, sound incentives, effective corporate governance mechanism' (Levine, 2011). Using macro-level data, Pelgrin et al. (2002) and Leahy et al. (2001) demonstrated the importance of financial development in the economy. Their estimates of the ratios of the size of financial intermediation and external finance to the GDP had a " significant positive impact on growth." The impact was either directly through productivity or indirectly through the effect of knowledge and physical capital accumulation. When the financial system functions well, it positively affects economic growth, income distribution, and poverty reduction. This finding was quite robust both for developing and developed economies. The CFAF countries were slow in adjusting to the financial liberalization, not able to adjust due to the rigidity in the system and the poor functioning of the financial institutions (Singh et al., 2009; Tchatchouang, 2015).

In CFAF countries, the financial sector crises are partly the result of the banking sector's insolvency, where public enterprises are usually financed by bank loans or governments subsidies drawn from the banking sector. As has been seen, a prolonged recession and loss of competitiveness can complicate the reform process. The recession is mainly due to the rigid institutional arrangements. Even after the 1994 devaluation, the CFAF zone's problems were not entirely resolved (Elbadawi & Majd, 1992; Elbadawi & Soto, 1997). The financial liberalization process did not take into consideration the macroeconomic environment. Economic restructuring meant that the governments could not pay their debts to the banks. The insolvent banks, the issue of bad loans and debts was poorly resolved. They could not ascertain which banks were to be recapitalized. Foreign banks dominate the banking sector; besides the French banks, the region has Moroccan and Pan-African banks. Gradually the region's commercial banks like ECOBANK are increasing their presence in the regions. The ECOBANK has branches in over thirteen African countries with the "largest trans-national bank operating in the CFA franc zone," In terms of GDP trade volume, Senegal and Cote d'Ivoire have more than fifty percent of the bank's assets (Sy, 2006; Diop, 2015). Still, the limited bank lending to businesses restricts private sector development and consequently limits economic expansion.

Trade-in Manufactured and Agricultural Goods

It is important to stress that the CFA franc countries are all primary goods and commodities producing countries or exporters of natural resources (Table 9.4). The production of these goods depends on many factors out of the control of the producers or countries concerned. The most significant proportion of the goods exported takes quite a long time to produce – many exogenous factors, including weather conditions, global conditions, and world prices. Hence the changes in the price of the outputs do not always immediately affect the output nor bring forth the necessary price responses as in manufactured goods and services. Across–the–board devaluation, such as in the 1994 devaluation, increased capacity utilization rather than capacity expansion in almost all the franc zone countries (Amin, 1997; Amin & Dubois, 2009).

Even on the theoretical foundation basis of elasticity of supply and demand of the goods, devaluation does not work well in terms of primary goods, given their low elasticities of demand and supply. Generally, the high value of the CFAF favors imports and disfavors exports as imports tend to be cheaper. Since the creation of the CFAF, the CFAF has frequently fluctuated due to the changes in the French currency and today the European currencies (See Samuel and Heckscher-Ohlin trade theory, as analyzed by Yoshihara and Kurose (2016). The CFAF system is said to promote the CFAF economies, and it is claimed that any member country that exits has not been able to do well out of the zone. History shows that France created and instituted the CFA franc covering many areas in the world. Nevertheless, many countries left the zone and issued their currencies. Countries like Vietnam, Tunisia, Morocco, and Djibouti perform much better socioeconomically than the existing CFAF zone countries (BCEAO, 2000; Tchatchouang, 2015; Taylor, 2019; Britannica, 2018).

Optimum Currency Area (OCA)

Much has been written on optimum currency area (OCA). Theoretically, OCA should have large intra- regional trade with free mobility of factors of production in diversified economies. However, the CFAF zone has extremely thin trade with little factor mobility. The economies are not diversified; there is no price and wage flexibility, there is a low level of infrastructural development. The zone is exposed to asymmetrical external shocks and different terms of trade for agricultural and oil exports. The countries produce and export similar goods (raw materials). However, there is a large trade volume between the zone and France/Europe, generating much disequilibrium to the CFAF zone. French imports have been overpriced partly because of protection, including tied aid and non-tariff barriers (Kohnert, 2005; Coulibaly & Gnimassoun, 2012; Zinsou, 2014; Tchatchouang, 2015; Taylor, 2019).

The zone has existed for so long that some authors have instead used sustainability to explain its benefits to the zone (Couharde et al., 2012). The sustainability hypothesis is tested using exchange rate dynamics since the real exchange rate is generally affected by other policies. Accordingly, they conclude that the real exchange rate may not converge to equilibrium faster in the CFAF zone than in other non-CFAF SSA countries. Because the economic fundamentals play a crucial role in the convergence process of the CFAF countries, but in the other countries, the exchange rate policy significantly impacts the adjustment process.

Using a structural VAR method, Zhao and Kim (2009) compare the CFAF zone economies to the European Economic and Monetary Union by applying the optimum currency area criteria on output shocks. They find that regional shocks are significantly crucial in the European countries while country-specific shocks (on output) are pretty significant in the CFAF countries. They conclude that because the CFAF countries are structurally different, they are more likely vulnerable to asymmetric shocks and do not seem to consist of an optimum currency area. Hence the CFAF union has been quite costly for the zone—individually and collectively.

ADJUSTMENT: THE CFA FRANC AND ECONOMIC PERFORMANCE OF THE ZONE

The CFAF fixed to French franc or Euro is less appropriate to adapt to the African changing socio-economic environment. The CFAF institutional arrangements have distinguishing features that impose serious policy restrictions on the CFAF zone countries. The nominal exchange rate, for example, is not a policy variable because it is predetermined. These countries individually or collectively cannot use the nominal exchange rate as a policy without France or the European Union's agreement. The regional central banks and France/EU ensure the monetary and exchange rate policies and a solid commitment to the fixed exchange rate regime. This put pressure on other macroeconomic policies.

Before the 1980s, the CFAF zone countries showed satisfactory economic performance and even outperformed Sub-Saharan Africa in real growth rates and controlling inflation. The satisfactory performance was attributed to the high competitiveness of exports from the region and also to the pegging of the CFAF to a weak French Franc that had depreciated against the US dollar in 1958 and 1969. During this period, the zone countries benefited from the export of primary goods prices of these exports enabled these countries to generate large export earnings. But the increase of the commodity prices did not affect the productive capacity of these economies, nor did they facilitate the diversification of the economies (Amin, 2000; Amin & Dubois, 2009).

This situation changed in the mid-1980s when CFAF countries recorded very poor performances. This period also coincided with the recession that was aggravated by many factors, including declining terms of trade which led to a sharp fall in commodity and oil price shocks, the French policy of a strong franc which saw an appreciation of the French franc against the US dollar and the competitive devaluations by neighboring countries notably Nigeria (Naira) and Ghana (Cedi). The deterioration in the CFAF zone's growth performance resulted from the changes in the international economic environment (Allechi & Niamkey, 1994). Some authors have attributed the poor performance to the unique arrangement with France, which reduces the need for these countries to carry out timely adjustments (Devarajan & De Melo, 1991; Amin, 1997). The sharp decline in the CFA countries came as a surprise because of earlier views by Guillaumont and Guillaumont (1984) and Devarajan and de Melo (1987) was that membership in the CFAF zone guarantees growth and economic stability (Mvondo, 2019). However, this was growth without development. There has been no structural transformation; the production structure in the zones has not changed, despite the longevity of the agreement.

The consequences of these two situations were that the collapse in dollar-denominated primary export prices resulted in a fall in export revenue. At the same time, the appreciation of the French franc to which the

CFAF was pegged relative to the dollar led to a loss in the competitiveness of products from the zone. The combined effect was a significant worsening of the current account deficits. The French government's decision to appreciate its currency was triggered by its desire to converge with the German Deutschmark under the single currency program (Agbohou, 2012). However, there was a suggestion that the same institutional arrangements that contributed to their good economic performance before the 1980s have also hindered them from adjusting timely to both internal and external shocks (Devarajan & De Melo, 1991). The treaties established by the monetary arrangements included strict fiscal and monetary rules, which provided financial and monetary or price stability while limiting economic growth.

The strict monetary and fiscal rules restrain the CFAF zone countries from using the fiscal and monetary policy tools efficiently to effect any changes in their economic structure. The CFA franc agreements are designed such that the countries continue to largely remain primary commodity producers and exporters, with the main aim of continuously supplying European economies with key economic and industrial inputs. So far, no country has ever developed without being industrialized and at the same time putting in place a robust system of protection of its infant industries and economy (Chang, 2009; Sylla & Leye, 2014).

Primary Producers and Trade

Trade offers countries the opportunity to produce and export goods and import those they do not create, reinforcing interdependence. Trading within these regions is supposed to spur intense economic and financial integration. Instead, the regions export mainly commodities with crude oil in CEMAC. The two regions produce and export similar commodities and are poorly linked physically (Table 9.4). The intraregional trade was as low as 1% in 2005. It rose to 3% in 2009 and declined to 2% in 2013. In 2018 it was around 3 percent. The lowest relative to other African regions (Byiers, 2017; Kangami, 2019; Ngepah & Udeagha, 2018).

The economies of CFAF countries depend on varying degrees on agriculture, where development has been quite slow. The CFAF zone economy is based on limited regional intra-trade, reliance on exporting primary commodities, small industrial base, vulnerable to both internal and external shocks. In WAEMU, intra- regional trade is 11 percent of total external trade, while in CEMAC, it is 9 percent. All result from limited industrialization and export diversification in the two regions (Amin,

2000; Tchatchouang, 2015; Pigeaud et al., 2020). Most agricultural exports had preferential treatment from France much more than other former African colonized countries had from their former colonial European countries. The preferential treatment had strongly promoted and encouraged raw materials, agricultural commodities, minerals, and oil to neglect manufactured goods for export. Recently, Africa has become the fastest-growing region globally. There is growth, but the growth is based mainly on the export of raw materials combined with increases in world commodity prices, with no profound structural transformation of the economies and no increase in labour productivity. The developed countries put escalating tariffs for African exports- taxing heavily manufactured goods with no tax on primary goods to discourage African economies from manufacturing goods (Taylor, 2019; IMF, 2015; Chang, 2009).

Business and Investment Environment

In 1990, the World Bank classified Benin; Burkina Faso; Central African Republic; Chad; Equatorial Guinea; Guinea-Bissau; Mali; Niger; Togo, which are CFAF zone countries, as Low-income countries, and after so many years in 2020, these countries remain classified as low-income countries despite their natural resources and economic growth potentials (World Bank, 2021). The various indexes/indicators such as (a) UNDP-DI, PI, (b) the World Bank indicators including the classification on Doing business (based on the business environment), the non-CFA franc countries tend to do much better than the CFAF countries: In non-CFAF countries, it is much easier to do business; they have ease customs clearance for exports and imports; they have cheaper and better internet and telephone communication, etc. (UNDP, 2020; World Bank, 2013, 2021).

Furthermore, the World Bank's Doing Business yearly publication ranks countries according to ease of doing business. There has been little change in the economic performance of the CFAF zone countries between 2013 and 2020. These countries remain at the bottom of the ranking of conduciveness to doing business index. In 2013 there were 185 countries, and in 2020, there were 190 countries. There has not been much improvement since 2013 when the ranking was as follows: Mali 153, Burkina Faso 151, Togo 156, Comoros 158, Cameroon 161, Equatorial Guinea 162, Senegal 166, Gabon 170, Benin 175, Niger 176, Côte d'Ivoire 177, Guinea-Bissau 179, Congo Rep183, Chad184, and the Central African Republic 185- the last out of 185 countries. In 2020, sorting 190 countries according to the ease of doing business in their economies relative to their most efficient regulatory performance, the World Bank had the following ranking: Côte d'Ivoire 110, Senegal 123, Niger 132, Mali 148, Benin 149, Burkina Faso 151, Comoros 160, Cameroon 167, Gabon 69, Guinea-Bissau 174, Equatorial Guinea 178, Congo Republic 180, Chad 182, and the Central African Republic 184. One thing stands out; nearly all the CFA franc zone countries perform very poorly through these periods (World Bank, 2013, 2020).

Infrastructural Development

Infrastructure is a prerequisite for economic development. It consists of many components: i) transportation include rails, roads, bridges, seaports, airports, telecommunications; ii) energy production and distribution, maintenance of electrical networks (grids); iii) social infrastructure as well as portable water production, management, and distribution, sanitation and sewage; iv) health, education, and training (Rao & Srinivasu, 2013; Timilsina et al., 2020). Transportation costs and regulations are major weaknesses of the CFAF economies. The transportation systems in these countries are poorly developed. The transportation system is still based on colonial infrastructure and communication systems.

The colonial communication and transport system – mailing, telephone, telecommunication, railways, motorized roads, air, and water transport-including seaports were linked directly to France and other European countries to facilitate the transfer of primary goods. There were no viable communication and transportation networks within the colonized countries. Even after independence, it has not been much improvement in the domestic transport and communication network despite decades of independence (Taylor, 2019).

CONCLUSION

In theory, membership in the monetary union strengthens the economic integration and interdependence among member states- since they share a single monetary system with a common currency. The single currency and monetary policy promote trade and strengthen financial ties, increase economic integration, promote economic coordination of economic policies. However, the CFAF arrangement has not done all these for its African members. The lack of flexibility in adjusting exchange rates to external shocks demonstrated the weakness of the CFAF zone arrangements

(Devarajan & Rodrik, 1991; Amin & Dubois, 2009). More so, the poor performance of the CFAF zone countries is attributed to the rigid institutional rules governing the functioning of the zone, which reduced the need for the necessary adjustment.

Moreover, the CFAF became overvalued following the competitive devaluation of its neighbors and competitors in the world market because of the agreements. More importantly, the system highly promotes primary goods production for the European economy without any diversification of the economic structure of the zone. As a result, despite its longevity, the CFA franc has had no positive socio- economic impact on the countries' economies. The system has not stimulated trade among its members; instead, it has deprived its members of valuable resources for development, leaving the regions less developed (Pigeaud et al., 2020a).

Until recently, the CFAF zone countries traded mainly with France. Their trade with France has been more important than with any other country. The arrangements have enabled France and its companies to enjoy a vast market for its products with a stable supply of cheap raw materials, all facilitated by the monetary system put in place by France. France's political, military, and economic dividends from such a relationship have been the incentive for maintaining the monetary union.

However, these French benefits have been and continue to be at enormous cost to the CFA franc economies and countries. The special arrangements and policies have constrained and impeded the development of these Central and West African countries. The monetary arrangements have crowded out, stifled, and repressed the growth of sound financial and capital markets in the CFAF zone countries. There are no well-functioning capital markets to mobilize resources for private sector development. As designed, the CFAF has not connected and integrated the region's economies. The CFAF was and is still ill-adapted to the domestic conditions. A monetary development disconnected from the domestic context for such a long time is costly to the development of these economies.

The African decision-makers must think seriously about a good method of developing their economies by completely removing the impediments of the CFA franc to their country's development. The CFA franc countries can create their independent central bank(s), print, and issue their domestic currency backed by their economies. The central bank(s) performs all the duties and responsibilities of modern central banks that maintain internal with external stability. The main obstacles are the accompanied colonial pacts, including the military advisers and military bases, which prevent member states from leaving the CFAF monetary union. Nevertheless, the region has to find ways of carrying out structural transformation with changes in the production structure of these economies, diversify the economies and promote regional trade. Without a change in product structure and diversification in production, intraregional trade would remain thin, and the region would remain less developed.

References

Abdullah, O. M., & Inaba, K. (2020). Does financial inclusion reduce poverty and income inequality in developing countries? *A Panel Data Analysis Economic Structures, 9*(37), 1–25.

Adrian, A., & Yontcheva, B. (2015). *Financial inclusion and development in the CEMAC.* (IMF Working Paper WP/15/235). https://doi.org/10.5089/9781484317556.001

Agbohou, N. (1999). *Le Franc CFA et L' Euro Contre L'Afrique.* Solidarite Mondiale.

Agbohou, N. (2012). *Le Franc CFA EST Une Propriété De La France.* Paper presented at an educational conference in France on The Future of the CFA franc zone.

Ahokpossi, C., Ismail, K., Karmakar, S., & Koulet-Vickot, M. (2013). *Financial depth in the WAEMU: Benchmarking against frontier SSA countries* (IMF Working Paper WP/13/161).

Allechi M'Bet, & Niamkey, M. (1994). Evaluating the net gains from the CFA franc zone membership: A different perspective. *World Development, 22*(8), 1147–1160.

Allechi M'Bet, & Niamkey, M. (1997). *European economic integration and the Franc zone: The future of the CFA franc after 1999 par II.* (AERC Research Paper Series No. 53).

Allen, F., Carletti, E., Cull, R., Qian, J., Senbet, L., & Valenzuela, P. (2014). The African financial development and financial inclusion gaps. *Journal of African Economies*, 1–29.

Allen, F., Carletti, E., Cull, R., Qian, J., Senbet, L., & Valenzuela, P. (2016). Resolving the African Financial development gap: Cross-country comparisons and a within-country study of Kenya. In S. Edwards, S. Johnson, & D. N. Weil (Eds.), *African successes, Volume III: Modernization and development* (Chapter One, pp. 13–62). Chicago: University of Chicago Press.

Allen, F., Laura, B., Xian, G., & Oskar, K. (2018). Does economic structure determine financial structure? *Journal of International Economics, 114*, 389–409.

Alter, A., & Yontcheva, B. (2015). *Financial inclusion and development in the CEMAC IMF working paper WP/15/235*, Washington, DC.

Amin, A. (1997). *Fiscal policy: Wider macroeconomic and financing links-Francophone experience*. AERC African Senior Policy Seminar presentation October 3 Accra, Ghana.

Amin, A. (2000). *Long-term growth in the CFA franc zone countries*. UNU World Institute for Development Economic Research, UNU/WIDER, RP 25.

Amin, A., & Dubois, J.-L. (Eds.). (2009). *Croissance et Développement au Cameroun: D'une croissance équilibrée à un développement équitable*. Langaa Research Publishing & Michigan State University Press.

Archer, D., & Moser-Boehm, P. (2013). *Central bank finances* (Bank for International Settlements (BIS) Paper No 71).

Banque de France. (2005). *Annual Report Banque De France*, Eurosystem, Paris.

Baye, & Khan. (2008). Real exchange rate misalignment in Cameroon, 1970-1996. In A. Amin (Ed.), *Developing a sustainable economy in Cameroon*. CODESRIA.

BCEAO. (2000). https://www.bceao.int/en/content/presentation-bceao

BCEAO. (2017). *Histoire du Franc CFA*. http://www.bceao.int/Histoire-du-FrancCFA,55.html

Benlialper, A., & Comer, H. (2016). Central banking in developing countries after the crisis: What has changed? In H. Comert & R. Mckenzie (Eds.), *Growth, inequality, and development in the aftermath of the great recession* (pp. 84–122). Edward Elgar Publishing.

Britannica, T. Editors of Encyclopaedia. (2018). *Franc. Encyclopedia Britannica*. https://www.britannica.com/topic/franc

Byiers, B. (2017). *Understanding regional economic policies in Central Africa: Struggling to integrate in an intertwined region European Centre for Development Policy Management (ECDPM)*. www.ecdpm.org/pedro.

Chang, H-J. (2009). Bad Samaritans: The myth of free trade and the secret history of capitalism Bloomsbury, .

Couharde, C., Issiaka, C., David, G., & Valérie, M. (2012). Revisiting the theory of optimum currency areas: is the CFA franc zone sustainable? *Journal of Macroeconomics, 38*(2), 428–441.

Coulibaly I., & Gnimassoun, B. (2012). *Optimality of a monetary union: New evidence from exchange rate misalignments in West Africa* (Working Paper, Economix UMR 7235 2012–37).

Devarajan, S., & Rodrik, D. (1991). *Do the benefits of fixed exchange rates outweigh their cost? The franc zone in Africa* (CEPR Discussion Paper, No. 561).

Devarajan, S., & de Melo, J. (1987). Adjustment with fixed exchange rate: Cameroon, Côte d'Ivoire and Senegal. *The World Bank Economic Review, 1*(3), 447–487.

Devarajan, S., & de Melo, J. (1991). Membership in the CFA Zone: Odyssean Journey or Trojan Horse? In A. Chibber & S. Fisher (Eds.), *Economic Reforms in Sub-Saharan Africa*. A World Bank Symposium, Washington D.C.

Dikau, S., & Volz, U. 2018. *Central banking, climate change, and green finance* (ADBI Working Paper 867). Asian Development Bank Institute.

Diop, S. (2015). L'évolution du système bancaire en zone franc. *Techniques financières et développement,* 4(121), 59–69.

Eichengreen, B. (2011). *Review of exorbitant privilege: The rise and fall of the Dollar and the future of the international monetary system.* Oxford University Press.

Elbadawi, I., & Majd, N. (1992). *Fixed parity of the exchange rates and economic performance in the CFA zone: A comparative study* (Working Paper Series No. 830). Country Economic Department, World Bank.

Elbadawi, I., & Soto, R. (1997). Real exchange rates and macroeconomic adjustment in sub-Saharan Africa and other developing countries. *Journal of African Economic,* 6(3), 74–120.

Elu, J. U., & Price, G. N. (2010). *The impact of the Euro-CFA Franc zone on economic growth in Sub-Saharan Africa.* Proceedings of the African Economic Conference 2008.

Guillaumont, Patrick, and Sylviane Guillaumont (1984). Zone Franc et Developpement Africain (Economica, Paris, pp. 337).

Hadjimichael, M. T., & Galy, M. (1997). *The CFA franc zone and EMU* (IMF Working paper).

Hasan, I., & Mester, L. (2008). Central Bank institutional structure and effective central banking: Cross-country empirical evidence. *Comparative Economic Studies,* 50, 620–645. https://doi.org/10.1057/ces.2008.36

Herring, R., & Santomero, A. (1991). *The role of the financial sector in economic performance* (Working Paper 95–08). Wharton School Center for Financial Institutions, University of Pennsylvania.

IMF. (2014, February). *Issuing international Sovereign bonds-opportunities and challenges for Sub Saharan Africa.* IMF.

IMF. (2015). Regional economic outlook: Sub-Saharan Africa-navigating headwinds, .

Irving, J. (1999). For better or for worse: The Euro and the CFA Franc. *Africa Recovery,* 12(4) 1, 25.

Kamga, G. E. K. (2020). Empty currency and the mechanics of underdevelopment within the franc zone. *Journal for Juridical Science,* 45(1), 120–140

Kangami, D. N. (2019). *Common currency intra-regional trade flows and economic growth: Evidence from CEMAC customs union thesis.* University of The Witwatersrand.

Keltie, J. S., & Epstein, M. (1921). *The statesman's yearbook: statistical and historical annual of the states of the world for the year 1921.* Macmillan and Co. Limited, London.

Koddenbrock K., & Sylla, N. S. (2019). *Towards a political economy of monetary dependency: The case of the CFA franc in West Africa* (MaxPo Discussion Paper, No. 19/2, Paris).

Koddenbrock, K. (2020). Hierarchical multiplicity in the international monetary system: From the slave trade to the franc CFA in West Africa. *Globalizations,* 17(3), 516–531.

Kohnert, D. (2005). The WEAMU and the franc CFA-zone: A new culture of co-operation within francophone Africa? *Schriften des Deutschen Übersee-Instituts, Hamburg Nr., 65*(2005), 115–136.

Koutonin, M. (2014). *14 African countries forced by France to pay colonial tax for the benefits of slavery and colonization.* https://siliconafrica.com/france-colonial-tax/

Lall, S., Cardarelli, R., & Tytell, I. (2006). Chapter 4: How do financial systems affect economic cycles? In *World economic outlook.* IMF.

Leahy, M., Schich, S., Wehinger, G., Pelgrin, F., & Thorgeirsson, T. (2001). *Contributions of financial systems to growth in OECD countries* (OECD Economics Department Working Papers, No. 280).

Levine, R. (2011, August 25–27). *Regulating finance and regulators to promote growth.* Brown University, the National Bureau of Economic Research, and the Council on Foreign Relations. Hole Symposium, "Achieving Maximum Long-Run Growth."

Monga, C. (1997). *L'argent des autres.* Banques et petites entreprises en Afrique: Le cas du Cameroun Paris, L.G.D.J.

Mvondo, T. (2019). Oil shocks and macroeconomic effects of occasionally binding constraint on external reserves of CEMAC. *International Journal of Business and Economics Research, 8*(6), 422–438.

Ngepah, N., & Udeagha, M. C. (2018). African regional trade agreements and intra-African trade. *Journal of Economic Integration, 33*(1), 1176–1199.

Nubukpo, K., Belinga, M. Z., Dembele, D. N., & Tinel, B. (2016). *Getting Africa out of monetary bondage. Who benefits from the CFA franc?* La Dispute Edition, Paris.

Paudyn, B. (2014). *Credit rating and sovereign debt- the Political Economy of Creditworthiness through Risk and Uncertainty.* Palgrave Macmillan.

Pelgrin, F., Schich, S., & de Serres, A. (2002). *Increases in business investment rates in OECD countries in the 1990s: How much can be explained by fundamentals?* (OECD Economics Department Working Papers, No. 327).

Pigeaud, F., Sylla, N., & Fazi, T. (2020). At the Service of the Françafrique. In *Africa's last colonial currency: The CFA franc story* (pp. 86–102). Pluto Press.

Pigeaud, F., Sylla, N., & Fazi, T. (2020a). An obstacle to development. In *Africa's last colonial currency: The CFA franc story* (pp. 103–119). Pluto Press.

Pigeaud, F., & Sylla, N. S. (2018). *The invisible weapon of Françafrique. A history of the CFA franc.* La Découverte.

Rao, P. S., & Srinivasu, B. (2013). Infrastructure development and economic growth: Prospects and perspective. *Journal of Business Management & Social Sciences Research, 2,* 81–91.

Rousseau P. L., & Sylla, R. (2001). *Financial systems, economic growth, and globalization-NBER Working Paper 6323*

Semedo, G., & Villieu, P. (1997). *La zone franc mécanismes et perspectives macroéconomiques.* Ellipses.

Singh, R. J., Kpodar, K., & Ghura, D. (2009). *Financial deepening in the CFA Franc zone: The role of institutions* (IMF Working Paper WP/09/113).

Sy, A. (2006, September). *Financial integration in the West African economic and monetary union* (Working Paper, No. 07/214). Washington, DC, International Monetary Fund.

Sylla, N., & Leye, D. (2014). Redeeming the free market as a solution to poverty: The limitations of the FT economic model. In *The fair trade scandal: Marketing poverty to benefit the rich* (pp. 85–119). Pluto Press.

Taylor, I. C. (2019). *France à fric: the CFA Zone in Africa and neocolonialism*. Third World Quarterly, Latest Articles.

Tchatchouang, J.-C. (2015). The CFA franc zone: A biography in *Célestin Monga and Justin Yifu Lin ed.* In *The Oxford Handbook of Africa and Economics: Volume 2: Policies and Practices*. Oxford University Press.

Tchundjang, P. J. (2000). *Monnaie, Servitude et Liberté: la Répression Monétaire de l'Afrique*. 2eme trimestre MENAIBUC, Yaoundé.

Timilsina, G., Hochman, G., & Song, Z. (2020). *Infrastructure, economic growth, and poverty: A review* (World Bank Policy Research Working Paper Series).

Tsangarides, C. G., Ewenczyk, P., & Michal Hulej (2008). *Stylized facts on bilateral trade and currency unions: Implications for Africa* (IMF Working Paper/06/31 IMF).

UNCTAD. (2009). *Enhancing the role of domestic financial resources in Africa's development: A policy handbook,* .

UNDP. (2020). *Human Development Index 2019*.

US Bureau of the Census. (1954). *Statistical abstract of the United States: 1954* (1955) table 1075 p 899 online edition file 1954–08.pdf

Van de Walle, N. (1991). The decline of the franc zone: Monetary politics in francophone Africa. *African Affairs, 90*, 383–405.

Weeks, J. (2010). *Development viewpoint #53 of CDPR*.

World Bank. (2013, 2020). *Doing business: Comparing business regulation in economies*. World Bank.

World Bank. (2020). *Housing finance in the CEMAC region: Current status, opportunities, and a way forward for affordable housing world bank group P167882*. World Bank.

World Bank. (2021). *Global waves of debt causes and consequences*. World Bank.

Yasser, A., & Tsangarides, C. (2010). FEER for the CFA franc. *Applied Economics, 42*(16), 2009–2029.

Yoshihara, N., & Kurose, K. (2016). *The Heckscher-Ohlin-Samuelson model and the Cambridge capital controversies* (Economics Department Working Paper Series. 204). http://scholarworks.umass.edu/econ_workingpaper/204

Zhao, X., & Kim, Y. (2009). Is the CFA franc zone an optimum currency area? *World Development, 37*(12), 1877–1886.

Zinsou, L. (2014). *Le Compte des Operations du Franc CFA au Ttrésor Français Est UN Fantasme*. Gabon Review.

CHAPTER 10

Banking Development in West Africa

Regina Nsang Tawah

INTRODUCTION

The financial system is comprised of financial institutions, assets, and markets and plays a unique and critical role in every economy. Financial institutions serve as intermediaries between lenders and borrowers, and between savers and investors. As intermediaries, the financial institutions help to mitigate transaction costs and risks and ensure a more efficient allocation of resources. Levine (2005) suggests that effective financial intermediation could positively affect economic development. All economic sectors require an effective and efficient financial sector to survive and progress, and businesses need financing to start, expand or innovate. Households need it to bridge gaps in their needs, and the public sector needs it to function. The pioneer banks in West Africa were established to fulfill the functions highlighted above, supporting foreign trade and the other activities of the colonialists. The minimum is that the financial sector should develop to accommodate economic growth and development.

The relationship between the financial sector and growth has been through various phases. Gurley and Shaw (1955) take the view expressed

R. N. Tawah (✉)
Bowie State University, Bowie, MD, USA
e-mail: RTawah@bowiestate.edu

by Schumpeter (1911) on the critical role of credit markets in development. The financial sector enhances capital accumulation and growth by mobilizing savings from surplus entities and efficiently allocating them to deficit entities (investors). Gurley and Shaw (1960) classify a financial system as undeveloped when money is its sole financial asset.

They note that such a system would limit saving, capital accumulation, and allocation of savings to investments and thus would weaken economic growth.

McKinnon (1973) suggests that the way for developing countries to finance investment beyond self-financing is to save and grow bank deposits that could be used to finance investment projects. Meanwhile, Shaw (1973) also indicates the importance of financial intermediation in promoting investment and economic growth. In a study of 50 African countries, Musamali, Nyamongo, and Moyi (2014) found a positive and a two directional relationship between financial development and economic growth. This finding is even more significant between credit to the private sector and economic growth than the broad money to GDP ratio.

Commercial banks are the most common financial intermediaries compared to credit unions, savings banks, investment banks, and mortgage banks. Vitenu-Sackey and Hongli (2019) utilize banking sector development indicators in an empirical study of the role of commercial banks in West Africa in effecting financial inclusion, which in turn should promote economic growth. Long-run estimates show that the number of bank branches per 1000 square kilometers, the number of automatic teller machines, and the total amount of loans granted directly impact economic growth.

Despite its limitations, a large proportion of private sector financing in sub-Saharan Africa is self-financing, which could be overcome through financial intermediation. The most basic of them is matching financing amounts and terms with a financing need and enabling investments beyond the investor's self-financing abilities. Societies that are better off are characterized, among other things, by the ability of households and businesses to have access to external finance for meeting household needs and investment, respectively.

The performance of the financial sector, in general, would have important implications for the countries' economic performance and development. African financial systems are less developed when compared to those of other developing economies, and the West African sub-region is at the low end compared with the rest of Africa, as data from the World Development Indicators, 2019 shows.

This chapter examines the determinants of banking sector development in West Africa. It begins with an introduction and the rest of the chapter continues with an overview of banking evolution in West Africa, a review of selected literature, and a discussion of the methodology used in the study. Finally, the chapter presents the empirical results, followed by a discussion of the results and the conclusion.

An Overview of Banking Evolution in West Africa

The West African sub-region is comprised of fifteen countries, nine of which are low-income with a national income per capita of less than $1026, and the remaining six are lower-middle-income with an average income of between $1026 and $4035 according to the 2020 World Bank classification. The low-income countries are Burkina Faso, Gambia, Guinea, Guinea Bissau, Liberia, Mali, Niger, Sierra Leone, and Togo, while the lower-middle-income countries include Benin, Cape Verde, Cote d'Ivoire, Ghana, Nigeria, and Senegal.

The countries listed above are members of the Economic Community of West African States (ECOWAS) with a sub-group belonging to the West African Economic and Monetary Union (WAEMU). Eight countries are resource-intensive, including Nigeria, the only one with substantial oil reserves, while some have experienced conflict. The WAEMU countries have a banking system rooted in the French system, while the other countries, despite their ties to Britain at the beginning, have shaped their banking systems their way.

Commercial Banking in West Africa

Commercial banking began in West Africa in 1855 when the French established the Banque du Senegal in Dakar, Senegal. The British followed with the Bank of British West Africa (BBWA) in Lagos, Nigeria, in 1894 (Buckle et al., 1999). The BBWA extended to Accra, Ghana, in 1896, while the Banque d'Afrique Occidentale (BAO), a replacement for the Banque du Senegal, started in 1901 and served all French colonies in West Africa (Bain, 2018). Colonial Bank was the next to start operations in Ghana in 1918. It later merged with other banks to become the Barclays Bank, while the BBWA became Standard (Chartered) Bank across the countries (Adeoye, 2019). These examples of British and French colonial banks, today's foreign banks, existed before the emergence of indigenous banking systems.

Formal financial systems in West Africa, as in Sub-Saharan Africa in general, proceeded to another phase as countries gained independence. The new governments took significant ownership control of the financial sector through nationalizing existing banks or creating state-owned banks. The ownership structure changed again in the 1980s and 1990s due to privatization that was part of the structural adjustment programs. While state ownership decreased, foreign bank ownership bloomed with cross-border African banks' entrance in multiple countries throughout the sub-region.

Nigeria is the only country in the economic region with a predominantly indigenous banking landscape. In 2014 out of 23 banks, only five were foreign (Alade, 2014). While hardly has any foreign bank established in the country in the past ten years, Nigerian banks have expanded across the sub-region and beyond, establishing subsidiaries in South Africa, London, New York, Paris, and Hong Kong (Alade, 2014). Senegal's banks are over 50% foreign-owned, and Ghana's are about 45% foreign-owned.

While there have been changes over time, the financial sectors in West African countries are still relatively underdeveloped. Figure 10.1 depicts the amount of domestic credit that went to the private sector relative to

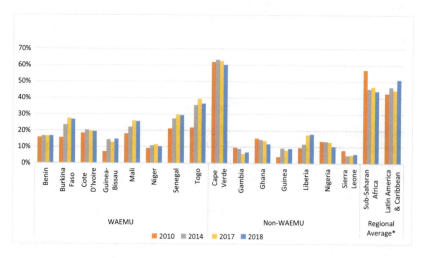

Fig. 10.1 Domestic credit to private sector as percentage of GDP. (Source: Based on data from IMF International Financial Statistics *, Regional averages exclude high-income countries)

the GDP by country with available regional information for comparison. All the countries except Cape Verde fall below the ratios for sub-Saharan Africa (excluding high-income countries). The low-income countries in West Africa underperform, while the middle-income West African countries do not match the ratios for lower-middle-income countries overall. The WAEMU countries have done slightly better than the non-members in lending to the private sector.

Domestic credit to the private sector is part of financial intermediation, an essential function of banking institutions. A low ratio of domestic private credit to GDP indicates a lack of financial depth, which is characteristic of a low level of financial development. Except for Cape Verde, all the other West African countries fall below the average for Latin America and the Caribbean countries. The sub-Saharan Africa (SSA) ratios are comparable to Latin America and the Caribbean (LAC). SSA ratios tip downward from 57% to 44% between 2010 and 2017, while for LAC, the ratios increase by about 8.4 points from 42.7% to 51.1% within the same period.

Another financial development indicator used to evaluate the West African banking sector is the liquid bank reserves to total assets ratio. This liquid bank reserves to total assets ratio represents the ratio of currency banks hold, deposits at other banks, and deposits at the central bank to all claims on the rest of the economy, including government, nonfinancial public establishments, and the private sector, and other banking institutions. The central bank usually mandates commercial banks to meet given reserve requirements specified as a percentage of all deposits the bank receives. In principle, these serve as a cushion for banks to draw from to meet their liabilities at critical times.

Liquid reserves also serve as a monetary policy tool through which the monetary authorities influence the availability of funds for lending, raising the ratio to restrict lending or lowering it to release funds. Moreover, banks choose whether or not to have excess reserves by placing more than the required in the reserve account. Thus, adequate reserves can indicate the stability of the banking sector.

Figure 10.2 presents the bank liquid reserves to total assets ratio in the West African countries. All the countries hold excess reserves at varying levels. The WAEMU countries have a required reserve ratio of 3% from a previous level of 5%, so the reserve excesses are minimal compared with the other countries. Nigeria's required reserve ratio was raised from 22.5% in 2018 to 27.5% in 2019.

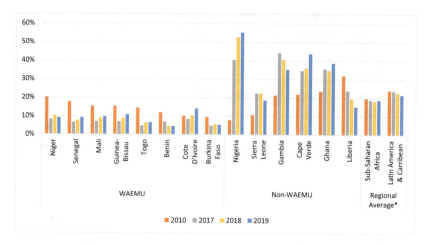

Fig. 10.2 Bank liquid reserves to total assets ratio. (Source: Based on data from IMF International Financial Statistics *, Regional averages exclude high-income countries)

As shown in Fig. 10.2, Nigeria's excess reserves ranged from 17.5 in 2010 to 27.5 percentage points in 2019. Ghana and the Gambia have required reserve ratios of 8% from 10% in 2015 and 13% from 15%, respectively. Ghana's actual reserve ratio is quadruple, and the Gambia's is tripled the required approximately. Although all appear to be cautious and guard against any destabilizing events, the WAEMU countries hold less excess reserves than the rest of the West African countries. The high reserve ratios may also mean that possible loanable funds are made unavailable to the economy.

West Africa has about 268 banking institutions, of which 152 are in the WAEMU countries (BCEAO, 2021). The proximity of banks to clients enhances access to formal financial services. Figure 10.3 presents the distribution of bank branches for every 100,000 adults per country. For example, Cape Verde has over 30 branches per 100,000 adults, which is about six times more than each of the other countries in the sub-region except the Gambia, and for one of the years, Ghana and Nigeria have about four times more.

There are more prospects of providing access to the formal banking sector using mobile phones. Already West Africa has 163 million registered mobile banking accounts, representing 40% of all sub-Saharan

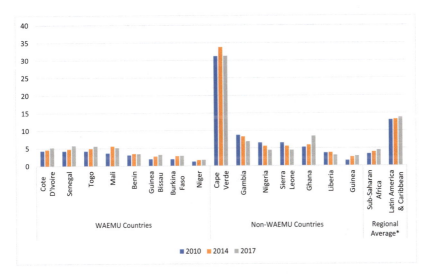

Fig. 10.3 Commercial bank branches per 100,000 Adults. (Source: Based on data from IMF Financial Access Survey. *Regional averages exclude high-income countries)

African subscribers. Of the 163 million registered accounts, 56 million, about 34% are active. This number puts West Africa in second place after East Africa regarding the number of registered and used mobile banking accounts (Loaba, 2021). The banks can leverage such financial technology as mobile banking to extend their services to those who otherwise have not been included.

Commercial banks are critical as conduits of monetary policy and vital financial intermediaries operating alongside savings banks and insurance companies. The central bank policy instruments, reserve requirements, discount rates, or open market operations need the commercial banks to carry them out. The central bank regulates and supervises commercial banks. A broad overview of central banking in West Africa forms an integral part of this section.

Central Banking in West Africa

Central Banks in West Africa are the offshoot of two colonial financial institutions, the West African Currency Board (WACB) and the Bank of West Africa (*Banque d'Afrique Occidentale*) – BAO. The WACB was created in 1912 with headquarters in London and was responsible for controlling the money supply in the then British West Africa consisting of the Gambia, Ghana, Nigeria, and Sierra Leone. As these countries became independent, they started to issue their national currencies, and the WACB facilitated the withdrawal of its West African Currency Notes. The Bank of Ghana was established immediately after independence in 1957 and made the first issue of its currency, the *cedi*, in 1958 (Buckle, 1999). The Central Bank of Nigeria was created in 1958 and went fully operational in 1959, while the Bank of Sierra Leone followed in 1963 and the Bank of Gambia in 1971 (Uche, 1996, 2010).

On the other hand, the French government granted BAO the authority to print currency, which amounted to assuming the role of the central bank for its colonies. An offshoot of BAO, the *Institut d'Emission de l'Afrique Occidentale Francaise et du Togo* took up the administration of the Franc of the French Colonies of Africa (*Franc des colonies francaises d'Afrique*) – FCFA between 1941 and 1958. As a result, BAO continued its operations, branching out to all the major towns in French West Africa.

BAO was re-chartered in 1962 as the Central Bank for Francophone Countries in West Africa (BCEAO) when these countries gained independence. In this process, the West African Economic and Monetary Union (WAEMU) was formed, and the currency became the franc of the African Financial Community *(Franc du Communaute Financiere Africaine)* – FCFA. The member countries remain the same except Mauritania dropped out, and Guinea Bissau joined the union. In addition, Dahomey and Upper Volta took on new names, Benin, and Burkina Faso, respectively. (BCEAO, 2017). The headquarters of the BCEAO remained in Paris until 1973, when it moved to Dakar, Senegal, and the places on the Executive Board occupied by the French went from one-third to one-seventh (Jeanneney, 2006).

Today, one umbrella central bank for the member countries of WAEMU and the central bank for each of the other countries sit on the foundations set decades ago. These are the BCEAO and the Bank of Cape Verde, the central bank of the Gambia, the bank of Ghana, the central bank of Guinea, the central bank of Liberia, the central banks of Nigeria, and Sierra Leone.

The BCEAO regional office is located in Dakar. In addition, there is a National office in each of the member countries, crafting and implementing monetary policy to ensure the banking and financial system stability and the proper functioning and supervision of the payment system, among other functions. Monetary policy and supervision are the responsibility of the regional authorities of BCEAO. However, the distribution of responsibilities with the national authorities can be challenging. For example, the national authorities are in charge of licensing and resolution of banks, but the supervision is done at the regional level (Mecagni et al., 2015). The other central banks also formulate and implement monetary policy, ensure monetary and price stability, issue currency, serve as bankers to commercial banks and the government, and regulate and supervise the banks.

A Review of Previous Studies

Several studies seek possible explanations of the state of financial development in Africa and elsewhere. In a study of over 100 countries selected from every region, Huang (2005) examines over thirty potential determinants of financial development with the parameters broadly grouped under institutions, policy, geography, and others. All three taken as a whole explain different levels of financial development. Under institutions, the usual indicators are considered along with the British (common law) legal origin versus French, Germany, and Scandinavia (civil law) legal origins of the countries in the study. Both legal origins are found to affect financial development.

Aluko and Ajayi (2018) cast a wide net in their exploration of determinants of the depth, efficiency, and stability, all aspects of banking sector development in Sub-Saharan Africa. They investigate, among other factors, population density, ethnic diversity, religion, geography, income level, economic growth, inflation, capital, trade openness, financial liberalization, institutional quality, and law. Their estimation using a two-step system generalized method of moments yields the following results: population density and trade openness interacting with capital enhance the development of the banking sector while financial liberalization constrains it. On the other hand, institutional quality, population density, and trade openness deepen the banking sector. The determinants of bank sector efficiency include law, inflation, and religion, while latitude, trade openness, income level, and ethnic diversity do not.

Ibrahim and Sare (2018), in their study of 46 African countries, find that when trade openness interacts with human capital, they result in a statistically significant relationship with financial development. They also show that openness to trade taken separately has a more substantial effect on private credit than domestic credit. The authors also found that real GDP per capita and government expenditure significantly affect financial development.

In another study based on a panel of 32 countries, Aluko and Ibrahim (2020) analyzed the relationship between macroeconomic factors and the development of financial institutions in SSA from 1985 to 2015. They utilize a two-step system generalized method of moments dynamic panel model in their investigation and find that trade openness, income, inflation, and government expenditure affect overall financial development while inflation is a deterrent to financial development. However, when the measures of financial development are examined individually, financial institutions' depth, efficiency, and access each show a statistically significant relationship with inflation and has the expected negative sign. In addition, income is a statistically significant determinant of financial institution efficiency and access, while financial openness and population density are also statistically significant determinants of access.

Naceur, Cherif, and Kandil (2014) studied the determinants of financial development in the Middle Eastern and North African (MENA) countries. The study found that institutional quality can influence financial development positively and significantly overall, while the effect of some institutional dimensions is more substantial than others. Other impactful factors include investment, inflation, savings, trade openness, and financial liberalization.

Allen et al. (2012) find population density a more vital determinant of banking development using liquid liabilities and private credit as a percent of GDP in Africa compared to other developing countries. Apart from population density, they also note that roads per square kilometer and bank branch dispersion are correlated with liquid liabilities as a percent of GDP. Another finding from the study is that macroeconomic stability and institutional quality determine banking sector development more in other developing countries than in Africa.

One determinant of financial development that runs through almost all the selected literature is institutional quality, and the most used indicator of financial or banking development is credit to the private sector. Institutional development averages six institutional development measures, including government effectiveness and the rule of law (Huang, 2005), and the others keep it limited to two or three measures. This chapter uses the governance indicators regulatory quality, the rule of law, control of corruption, and government effectiveness as separate independent variables. In addition, it uses four different measures of banking development.

Methodology

This section describes the variables, data sources, and empirical models used to estimate the relationship between governance indicators and bank development.

Data

This chapter utilizes data from the World Bank World Development Indicators and the World Bank Worldwide Governance Indicators (WGI) from 2007 to 2017. Table 10.1 contains the parameters used in the chapter, their definitions, and the data sources specifying the known sources even though they were obtained through WDI.

Empirical Model

To investigate the link between governance indicators and bank development in West Africa, the following multiple regression equation is specified:

$$\text{bbranch}_{it} = \beta_0 + \beta_1 \text{rq}_{it} + \beta_2 \text{rol}_{it} + \beta_3 \text{coc}_{it} + \beta_4 \text{govef}_{it}$$
$$+ \beta_5 \text{gdppc}_{it} + \beta_6 \text{gdpr}_{it} + \varepsilon_{it} \quad (10.1)$$

where bbranch is the number of banking institutions branches per 100,000 adults, Rq is regulatory quality, rol, the rule of law, coc, the control of corruption, govef government effectiveness, gdppc, gross domestic product per capita and gdpgr the growth rate of the gross domestic product. At the same time, i represents the country, t the time from 2007 to 2017, β_s are the parameters to be estimated while ε_{it} is the error term.

$$\text{BD}_{it} = \beta_0 + \beta_1 \text{rq}_{it} + \beta_2 \text{rol}_{it} + \beta_3 \text{coc}_{it} + \beta_4 \text{govef}_{it} + \beta_5 \text{lngdppc}_{it}$$
$$+ \beta_6 \text{gdpgr}_{it} + \beta_7 \text{intspred}_{it} + \beta_8 \text{infla}_{it} + \varepsilon_{it} \quad (10.2)$$

where BD represents banking development will be variedly estimated in terms of domestic credit to the private sector by banks (dcreditsps), depositors with commercial banks (dcbks), bank liquid reserves to total assets (blrba), and claims on central government (ccg).

Table 10.1 Variables, definitions, and data sources

Variable	Description	Sources of data
\multicolumn{3}{l}{Dependent variables}		

Dependent variables

Variable	Description	Sources of data
bbranch	Commercial bank branches are defined as the median of retail locations separated from main offices of resident commercial and other resident banks that provide financial services to customers per 100,000 adults.	IMF financial access survey, 2020.
dcreditps	Banks' domestic credit to the private sector is defined as the weighted average of financial resources provided to the private sector by formal deposit-taking financial institutions except central banks expressed as a % of GDP.	IMF international financial statistics and data files, and World Bank and OECD GDP estimate.
blrba	Bank liquid reserves to bank assets, the variable is defined as the median of "the ratio of domestic currency holdings and deposits with the monetary authorities to claims on other governments, nonfinancial public enterprises, the private sector, and other banking institutions".	IMF, international financial statistics, and data files.
ccg	Claims on central government are loans to central government institutions net of deposits expressed as a % of GDP.	IMF, international financial statistics, and data files
Independent variables		
rq	Regulatory quality shows the estimated perceptions of the governments' formulation and implementation of policies and regulations that are conducive to private sector development. The estimate ranges from about −2.5 (weak) to 2.5 (strong) governance performance.	World Bank worldwide governance indicators (WGI), 2020
rol	The rule of law reflects society's perceptions regarding the quality of contract enforcement, property rights, the police, the courts, and the extent of crime and violence. The estimate of the measure ranges from about −2.5 (weak) to 2.5 (strong) governance performance.	World Bank WGI, 2020
coc	The control of corruption reflects perceptions of the extent to which private gain drives public power, including all forms of corruption and "capture" of the state by elites and private interests. The estimate ranges from about −2.5 (weak) to 2.5 (strong) governance performance.	World Bank WGI, 2020

Table 10.1 (continued)

Variable	Description	Sources of data
govef	Government effectiveness is the perceptions of the quality of public services, the civil service and its independence from political pressures, the quality of policy formulation and implementation, and the credibility of the government's commitment to such policies. The estimate ranges from about -2.5 (weak) to 2.5 (strong) governance performance.	World Bank WGI, 2020
gdpgr	The growth rate of the gross domestic product is the annual % growth rate of GDP at constant 2010 US dollars.	World Bank world development indicators
gdppc	Gross domestic product per capita is defined as gross domestic product/population	World Bank world development indicators
infla	The inflation rate is measured by the annual percentage change in the consumer price index.	International Monetary Fund (IMF) international Financial statistics and data files
irspd	Interest rate spread defined as lending rate minus deposit rate %	IMF international finance statistics And data files

EMPIRICAL RESULTS

Empirical estimates, as well as the specification tests, are presented in the following section. First, we discuss tests used in deciding between the fixed and the random-effects models, followed by a presentation of the estimation results of the four equations retained for the study.

Hausman Specification Test

The analysis begins with running the Hausman test to determine the appropriateness of choice between the random-effects and fixed-effects models. It informs of any endogeneity in the regressors present in the model. The null hypothesis is that random effects sufficiently model the individual-level effects, and the model is preferred. The alternative hypothesis is that the fixed effects model is preferred to the random-effects model. Of the four specifications, the random effects were preferred in three equations (see Tables 10.2, 10.3, 10.4, and 10.5).

Table 10.2 Regression results for domestic credit to the private sector

Variable	Robust OLS	Random effects	Fixed effects
rq	-22.740***	-5.752*	-4.281
	(2.503)	(2.956)	(3.038)
rol	26.381***	3.943	0.728
	(4.527)	(3.337)	(3.290)
coc	6.590	5.181*	4.758
	(4.154)	(2.992)	(3.045)
govef	-0.001	-0.002	-0.011*
	(0.001)	(0.002)	(0.005)
lngdppc	3.493*** (0.538)	6.498*** (1.048)	9.506*** (1.854)
gdpgr	-0.259	-0.167*	-0.162*
	(0.235)	(0.098)	(0.093)
intspred	-0.533***	-0.163	-0.115
	(0.104)	(0.134)	(0.134)
infla	-0.735*** (0.217)	-0.580*** (0.168)	-0.492*** (0.163)
const	10.327***	-13.108*	-27.836***
	(3.383)	(6.854)	(9.032)
N	132	Hausman	6.12
			(0.634)

Standard errors are in parenthesis. *p < 0.10, **p < 0.05 and ***p < 0.01

Table 10.3 Regression results for claims on central government

Variable	Robust OLS	Random effects	Fixed effects
rq	-4.815***	-4.678***	-4.710***
	(1.132)	(1.478)	(1.601)
rol	-1.373	2.466	2.590
	(2.046)	(1.665)	(1.734)
coc	6.033*** (1.745)	1.705	1.002
		(1.495)	(1.605)
govef	0.000	0.001	0.002
	(0.001)	(0.001)	(0.003)
lngdppc	2.657***	2.853***	2.343**
	(0.285)	(0.529)	(0.977)
gdpgr	-0.015	-0.058	-0.055
	(0.065)	(0.049)	(0.049)
intspred	0.485***	0.133**	0.080
	(0.054)	(0.067)	(0.070)
infla	0.017	0.003	-0.020
	(0.130)	(0.084)	(0.086)
const	-14.462***	-14.876***	-12.283**
	(1.788)	(3.453)	(4.760)
N	132	Hausman	13.60
			(0.093)

Standard errors are in parenthesis. *p < 0.10, **p < 0.05 and ***p < 0.01

Table 10.4 Regression results for commercial bank branches per 100,000 adults

Variable	Robust OLS	Random effects	Fixed effects
rq	-14.620***	-1.211	-0.468
	(1.331)	(1.241)	(1.154)
rol	9.880*** (2.027)	1.531	0.725
		(1.398)	(1.249)
coc	8.922***	1.810	0.033
	(1.854)	(1.221)	(1.129)
govef	0.001***	0.000	-0.001
	(0.000)	(0.001)	(0.002)
lngdppc	1.524*** (0.197)	2.466*** (0.446)	2.181*** (0.697)
gdpgr	-0.122	-0.085**	-0.071**
	(0.117)	(0.041)	(0.035)
const	-0.191	-6.426**	-5.367
	(1.506)	(3.453)	(3.380)
N	132	Hausman	11.37
			(0.078)

Standard errors are in parenthesis. *p < 0.10, **p < 0.05 and ***p < 0.01

Regression Results

Table 10.2 shows the first set of regression results using the robust least squares, random-effects, and fixed-effects models. Domestic credit to the private sector by banks expressed as a percentage of GDP is a proxy for banking development and is regressed on a host of independent variables.

The random-effects model is preferred over the fixed effects, based on the Hausman test that yielded a p-value greater than 0.05. The results based on the random-effects model in column 3 show a strong positive relationship between domestic credit to the private sector by banks expressed as a percentage of GDP and the natural ln of GDP per capita (lngdppc) and inflation. The natural ln of GDP per capita has a positive sign, and with a coefficient of 6.498, a one percent increase (or decrease) in lngdppc would increase (decrease) the domestic credit to the private sector by banks expressed as a percentage of GDP by about 6.5%. Conversely, an increase in one percent inflation would lead to a decrease of domestic credit to the private sector by 0.58%.

Regulatory quality (rq), control of corruption, and GDP growth rate (gdpgr) are also statistically significant individually at the 0.10 level. An increase by one percent in Regulatory quality and GDP growth rate (gdpgr), both with negative signs, would decrease the domestic credit to the private sector by banks expressed as a percentage of GDP by 5.75% and 0.17%, respectively. The control of corruption is also statistically significant as a determinant of domestic credit to the private sector by banks expressed as a percentage of GDP and would change the credit to the private sector by 5.2% if it changed by 1% in the same direction.

Table 10.3 contains the regression results obtained from robust OLS, random-effects and fixed-effects models. Claims on the central government (ccg) are another indicator for banking development. They consist of loans to the central government institutions minus central government deposits as a percentage of GDP. Again, the random-effects model is preferred, given the Hausman test that yielded a p-value greater than 0.05.

Regulatory quality with a negative sign and lngdppc a positive sign is significant at the one percent level, while interest spread with a positive sign is significant at the 5 percent level. For example, an increase of 1 percent in the regulatory quality would decrease claims on the central government by about 4.7%; meanwhile, an increase of 1 percent in the lngdppc would increase claims on the central government by about 2.9%. Furthermore, if interest spread were to rise by 1 percent, the claims on the central government would rise by 0.13 percent.

The last set of regression results uses bank branches, an indicator of banking development, as the dependent variable and regresses it on a host of independent variables. Table 10.4 summarizes the robust ordinary least squares (OLS) regression results, random-effects, and fixed-effects models. The random-effects model is preferred since the p-value is larger than 0.05 from the Hausman test. The random-effects model shows that only the natural log of GDP per capita (lngdppc) and GDP growth rate (gdpgr) significantly influence the branchification of commercial banks. The natural log of GDP per capita is highly significant and has a positive sign, and if it increased by one percentage point, the number of bank branches would increase by about 2.5%. Meanwhile, the GDP growth rate would account for a change of -0.085% in bank branches per 100,000 adults with a unit increase in either independent variable. According to the estimation results, regulatory quality, government effectiveness, the rule of law, and control of corruption do not affect commercial bank branches per 100,000 adults.

Table 10.5 summarizes estimation results for the ratio of liquid bank reserves to total assets regressed on various governance indicators, gross domestic product per capita, interest spread, and inflation. The Hausman test yielded a p-value less than 0.05; hence the null hypothesis is rejected

Table 10.5 Regression results for bank liquid reserves to bank assets ratio

Variable	Robust OLS	Random effects	Fixed effects
rq	4.320	-1.594	-4.836
	(3.442)	(2.933)	(3.045)
rol	-8.150*	-1.195	-0.044
	(4.324)	(3.333)	(3.297)
coc	11.664***	2.688	0.446
	(3.577)	(2.974)	(3.053)
govef	-0.002*	0.004*	0.015***
	(0.001)	(0.002)	(0.005)
lngdppc	2.647***	5.749***	3.859**
	(0.419)	(1.006)	(1.859)
gdpgr	-0.030	-0.174	-0.045
	(0.132)	(0.098)	(0.093)
intspred	0.493***	-0.051	-0.075
	(0.124)	(0.133)	(0.134)
infla	-0.298	0.297*	0.266
	(0.226)	(0.168)	(0.163)
const	-2.703	-28.041***	-25.776***
	(2.926)	(6.628)	(9.053)
N	132	Hausman	60.21
			(0.000)

Standard errors are in parenthesis. *p < 0.10, **p < 0.05 and ***p < 0.01

in favor of the fixed-effects model. Results from the fixed-effects model show that government effectiveness is statistically significant at 1 percent level. With a positive coefficient of 0.015, enhanced government effectiveness will increase the bank liquid reserves to total assets ratio. The ln of GDP per capita is significant at 5% level. If GDP per capita increased by one percent, liquid reserves to total assets ratio would increase by about 3.9%.

Discussion

As the results show, the amount of credit to the private sector depends on the governance indicators, regulatory quality, and control of corruption. Governance indicators usually range from -2.5 (weak) to + 2.5 (strong). As of 2019, all the West African countries had negative values on both governance indicators. Regulatory quality has a significant but negative effect on domestic credit to the private sector measured as a percentage of GDP and claims on the central government. Credit to the economy, especially the private sector, is an important ingredient in fostering the private sector and small and medium enterprises, the breeding ground and drivers of entrepreneurship that is so much needed to grow and develop the West African region. Good governance is critical to providing an enabling environment (Mbaku, 2020). Fagbemi et al. (2018) provide evidence that the rule of law, corruption control, and the quality of institutions strongly influence the development of the financial sector. There is thus an urgent need to bring corruption under control. This goes along with ensuring the rule of law and high-quality regulation. Institutions should be reinforced to control corruption and ensure accountability in both the public and the private sectors.

An increase in per capita GDP would increase credit to both the private and public sectors (claims on central government). Efforts to support income-generating activities in industry, agriculture, and services sectors and especially small and medium enterprises could benefit banking development in the long run. Inflation adversely affects the amount of credits that go to the private sector. The monetary authorities should continue to take measures as needed to control inflation.

The branch network is a proxy for access to finance which implies that the denser the network, the greater the access to banking institutions. Evidence has shown that proximity to banking offices and hence access afforded through branches could improve the mobilization of savings. In Malaysia, increased bank branches resulted in increased access to financial services (Ang, 2011). However, a similar assumption led the government to legislate branch openings in Nigeria, requiring commercial banks to establish rural areas. As a result, the anticipated improvement in savings mobilization, banking services, and credit to the rural population failed to materialize (Okorie, 1992). The possible lesson from this may be that business decisions should not be legislated. Instead, the government should provide an enabling environment, including communication and road networks that will serve both the financial institutions and the general public.

Conclusion

The chapter examined the determinants of the banking sector development in West Africa. Four banking sector development proxies were used: domestic credit to the private sector relative to GDP, commercial bank branches per 100,000 adults, liquid bank reserves to total assets ratio, and claims on the central government. The key finding is that overall governance significantly affects the development of the banking sector. For example, the control of corruption and regulatory quality influence domestic credit to the private sector relative to GDP, with regulatory quality also important for claims on the central government. In addition, government effectiveness affects bank liquid reserves to bank assets ratio.

Per capita GDP is important for banking development affecting credit to the economy, the number of bank branches, and bank liquid reserves. The study suggests that banking sector development hinges on governance issues, effectively combatting corruption, instituting and implementing the rule of law, improving regulatory and government effectiveness. Government effectiveness entails multiple aspects, and further studies may be done to pinpoint and target priority aspects in each country to employ the resources necessary. For example, the quality of public services, the independence of the civil service, the quality of policies, and the credibility of governments' commitment to the policies are interwoven. When these are given the attention and necessary steps taken to create the enabling environment the comes with good governance, avenues to create opportunities that enhance the development of the financial sector and banking, in particular, banks would be in a better position to intermediate more effectively and possibly extend services beyond their traditional clients and improve opportunities that bring in higher incomes.

References

Adeoye, A. M. A. (2019). *The origin, growth, and development of banking in Nigeria.* http://bowenstaff.bowen.edu.ng/lectureslides/1588157614.pdf

Alade, Sarah O. 2014. *Cross-border expansion of Nigerian banks: has it improved the continent's regulatory and supervisory frameworks?* (Bank of International Settlements papers No 76). www.bis.org/publ/bppdf/bispap76h.pdf

Allen, F., Carletti, E., Cull, R., Qian, J., Senbet, L., & Valenzuela, P. (2012). *Resolving the African financial gap: Cross-country comparisons and a within-country study of Kenya* (Working paper 18013).

Aluko, O. A., & Ajayi, M. A. (2018). Determinants of banking sector development: Evidence from sub-Saharan African countries. *Borsa Instanbul Review, 18-2*, 122–139. www.elsevier.com/journals/borsa-istanbul-review/2214–8450

Aluko, O. A., & Ibrahim, M. (2020). On the macroeconomic determinants of financial institutions development in sub-Saharan Africa. *International Review of Economics, 67*(1), 69–85. https://doi.org/10.1007/s12232-019-00332-x

Ang, J. B. (2011). Savings mobilization, financial development and liberalization: The case of Malaysia. *Review of Income and Wealth, 57*(3), 449–470.

Bain, S. (2018). *A balance sheet analysis of the Banque de l'Afrique Occidentale.* Studies in Applied Economics, No. 100.

BCEAO. (2017). Annual Report, Banque Centrale des Etats de l'Afrique de l'Ouest, Dakar Senegal

Buckle, V. L. & Co. (1999, April 12). Ghana: The history of banking in Ghana, *Mondaq.* https://www.mondaq.com/antitrust-eu-competition-/1300/the-history-of-banking-in-ghana

Fagbemi, F., Abiodun, J. O., & Ige, P. A. (2018). West African financial sector development: Empirical evidence on the role of institutional quality and natural resource rents. *Journal of Economics and Sustainable Development, 9*(6), 157–172.

Gurley, J. G., & Shaw, E. S. (1955). Financial aspects of economic development. *The American Economic Review, 45*(4), 515–538.

Gurley, J. G., & Shaw, E. S. (1960). *Money in theory of finance.* Brookings.

Huang, Yongfu. (2005). What determines financial development? (University of Bristol Discussion Paper No. 05/580).

Ibrahim, M., & Sare, Y. A. (2018). Determinants of financial development in Africa: How robust is the interactive effect of trade openness and human capital? *Economic Analysis and Policy.* https://doi.org/10.1016/j.eap.2018.09.002

Jeanneney, S. G. (2006). Independence of the central Bank of West African States: An expected reform? *Revue d'economie du developpement, 14*, 43–73. www.cairn.info/revue-d-deconomie-du-developpement-2006-5-page-43.htm

Levine, R. (2005). Chapter 12: "Finance and growth: Theory and evidence," handbook of economic growth. In P. Aghion & S. Durlauf (Eds.), *Handbook of economic growth* (Vol. 1, 1st ed., pp. 865–934). Elsevier.

Loaba, S. (2021). The impact of mobile banking services on saving behavior in West Africa. *Global Finance Journal.* https://doi.org/10.1016/j.gfj.2021.100620

Mbaku, J. M. (2020). *Good and inclusive governance is imperative for Africa's future, deepening good governance, foresight Africa* (pp. 21–33). Brookings Institution.

McKinnon, R. (1973). *Money and capital in economic development.* Brookings Institution Press.

Mecagni, M., Marchettini, D., & Maino, R. (2015). *Banking in sub-Saharan Africa: Key features and challenges. On recent trends in banking in sub-Saharan Africa from financing to investment* (pp. 9–38). European Investment Bank.

Musamali, R. A., Nyamongo, E. M., & Moyi, M. D. (2014). The relationship between financial development and economic growth in Africa. *Research in Applied Economics, 6*(2), 190–208.

Naceur, S. B., Cherif, M., & Kandil, M. (2014). What drives the development of the MENA financial sector? *Borsa Istanbul Review.* https://doi.org/10.1016/j.bir.2014.09.002

Okorie, A. (1992). Rural banking in Nigeria: Empirical evidence of indicative policy variables from Anambra state. *Agricultural Economics, 7*(1), 13–23. https://doi.org/10.1016/0169-5150(92)90018-T

Schumpeter, J. A. (1911). The theory of economic development. In Adusei M. (Ed.) (2012). *Financial development and economic growth: Is Schumpeter right? British Journal of Economics, Management, and Trade, 2*(3), 265–278. Harvard University Press.

Shaw, E. (1973). *Financial deepening in economic development.* Oxford University Press.

Uche, C. (1996). From currency board to central banking: The politics of change in Sierra Leone. *African Economic History, 24,* 147–158. https://doi.org/10.2307/3601850

Uche, C. (2010). Indigenous Banks in Colonial Nigeria. *International Journal of African Historical Studies, 43*(3), 467–487. www.jstor.org/stable/230.

Vitenu-Sackey, P. A., & Hongli, J. (2019). Financial inclusion and economic growth: The role of commercial banks in West Africa. *The International Journal of Business and Management Research, 12*(1). https://doi.org/10.32893/IJBMR.2019.12

CHAPTER 11

Capital Markets Development and Economic Growth in North Africa

Augustin Ntembe, Aloysius Ajab Amin, and Regina Nsang Tawah

INTRODUCTION

The chapter examines the correlation between capital markets development and economic performance in Algeria, Egypt, Morocco, and Tunisia. Well-developed capital markets provide savings for capital investments and relevant resources for long-term growth and sustainability of the economy (Soumaré et al., 2021). However, the financial sectors in North Africa are diverse, with Morocco having the most developed and vibrant system dominated by private banks (Kireyev et al., 2019). Although Tunisia has a relatively developed private banking sector, the public bank sector (government-owned banks) is weak, with an enormous burden of nonperforming loans (Kireyev et al., 2019). However, government-owned banks

---

A. Ntembe (✉) • R. N. Tawah
Bowie State University, Bowie, MD, USA
e-mail: nntembe@bowiestate.edu; RTawah@bowiestate.edu

A. A. Amin
Clayton State University, Morrow, GA, USA
e-mail: AloysiusAmin@clayton.edu

© The Author(s), under exclusive license to Springer Nature Switzerland AG 2022
A. A. Amin et al. (eds.), *Monetary and Financial Systems in Africa*, https://doi.org/10.1007/978-3-030-96225-8_11

dominate the financial systems in both Algeria and Egypt. Despite substantial progress in the past decade, access to finance in North African countries is limited, and the problem is more severe for small and medium-sized enterprises (SMEs).

North Africa's capital markets were hit hard by the Arab spring riots that struck the region in 2011, especially Egypt, Morocco, Tunisia, and Libya. The riots disrupted economic activity resulting in a sharp drop in stock market trading (Hancock, 2012; Al-Amine & Al Bashir, 2014). The expectation was that economic liberalization in North Africa would facilitate foreign investments. Instead, the riots culminated with the stagnant global economic challenges that seriously impacted North African economies.

Trade on each exchange market plummeted, with the Egyptian Exchange (EGX) experiencing the worst performance in 2011, falling by about 35%. The Tunisian stock exchange market dipped by 22 percent before 15 percent during the next nine months. The composite Moroccan-All Share Index (MASI), a value-weighted measure comprising all 75 listed companies in the Casablanca Stock. Exchange, fell by 12.86 percent during 2011 (Hancock, 2012). However, lessons from the Arab Spring pushed these countries to initiate and implement reforms as authorities embarked on rebuilding capital markets by introducing financial products such as short sales, derivatives, and exchange-traded funds (ETFs). In addition, the North African market seeks to increase liquidity by promoting the listing of small and medium-sized enterprises (SMEs), and these efforts led to a significant turnaround.

MACROECONOMIC PERFORMANCE OF THE NORTH AFRICAN ECONOMIES

The worldwide crisis from 2007 to 2009 was felt in the four North African countries selected for this study. In particular, the economies of the Arab Republic of Egypt, Morocco, and Tunisia showed strong growth during 2007, with a sharp decline in 2009. The economies of Egypt and Tunisia were hit harder by the political and social unrest during the Arab Spring in 2011. As a result, the decline in GDP growth in these countries was dramatic, with Egypt and Tunisia dipping to 1.8% and -1.7%, respectively. However, the economy of Morocco declined but remained relatively stable than the economies of Algeria, Egypt, and Tunisia (Table 11.1).

Table 11.1 Real GDP (constant 2015 US$) and GDP growth (annual %), 2006–2020

	Algeria		Egypt		Morocco		Tunisia	
Year	$billion	%	$billion	%	$billion	%	$billion	%
2006	126.50	1.7	228.39	6.8	70.09	7.6	35.64	5.2
2007	130.80	3.4	244.58	7.1	72.57	3.5	38.03	6.7
2008	133.94	2.4	262.08	7.2	76.86	5.9	39.64	4.2
2009	136.08	1.6	274.33	4.7	80.13	4.2	40.85	3.0
2010	140.98	3.6	288.45	5.1	83.18	3.8	42.28	3.5
2011	145.07	2.9	293.54	1.8	87.55	5.2	41.58	−1.7
2012	150.00	3.4	300.07	2.2	90.18	3.0	43.21	3.9
2013	154.20	2.8	306.63	2.2	94.27	4.5	44.13	2.1
2014	160.06	3.8	315.57	2.9	96.79	2.7	45.33	2.7
2015	165.98	3.7	329.37	4.4	101.18	4.5	45.78	1.0
2016	171.29	3.2	343.68	4.3	102.25	1.1	46.29	1.1
2017	173.52	1.3	358.05	4.2	106.60	4.3	47.33	2.2
2018	175.43	1.1	377.08	5.3	109.96	3.1	48.52	2.5
2019	177.18	1	398.04	5.6	112.83	2.6	49.20	1.4
2020	168.14	−5.1	412.25	3.6	105.73	−6.3	44.68	−9.2

Data from the database: World Development Indicators, 2021

The global pandemic (COVID-19) that stroked the world towards the end of 2019 had a more devastating effect on the economies of North Africa, just like in other world economies. While the economies of Algeria, Morocco, and Tunisia experienced negative growths in 2020, the Egyptian economy was more resilient and slightly declined from 5.6% percent growth in 2019 to 3.6% in 2020.

The hydrocarbons sector dominates the Algerian economy. The sector has a high production level, generating foreign exchange and revenues. In 2015, the sector contributed a quarter of the country's GDP, 50% of export earnings, and budget revenue of 48% while the non-hydrocarbons sector of about 48% represent industry and services. However, industry and service sectors are funded from revenue generated from the hydrocarbon sector (Mabruka, 2019). In 2020, to contain the COVID-19 pandemic, North African economies like in the rest of the world were locked down. The economic lockdown and the sharp decline in hydrocarbon revenues were a considerable challenge to the Algerian government. Also, the fall in global oil prices and OPEC cut in production quotas led to a sharp decline in Algeria's export and hydrocarbon production. These factors, including a fall in oil and tax revenues, aggravated the external imbalance, fiscal deficit and bank liquidity problems. Depreciating the Dinar did not help as the budget deficit significantly increased in 2020. Estimates show that the Algerian economy will grow by 2.5 percent in 2022 from benefitting from a recovery in oil production in 2021 and gradual recovery of the non- hydrocarbon sector, and the return to the central bank financing the fiscal deficit (World Bank, 2021).

Algerian Financial Development

Algeria had independence in 1962. With its inherited colonial banking system, Algeria went through five critical periods of its development: the colonial period, sovereignty period, nationalization and socialization period, restricting period, and liberalization period (Hacini & Dahou, 2018). During the colonial period, the Bank of Algeria was an extension of the bank of France. The Bank of Algeria's primary objective was to provide financial resources for the colonial economic activities. The banks operating in Algeria were branches or subsidiaries of French banks. After Algerian independence in 1962, the Algerian State developed its economy away from the colonial economy. The authorities adopted a socialist economy where the State played a dominant role in the economy with the main purpose of improving the wellbeing of its citizens. However, financial institutions and activities sharply decreased during this period because the French departed with businesses and transferred all their capital and investment to other countries. The remaining few banks further contracted their activities since they could not comply with the liberal economic doctrine of the government. Hence the Algerian government had to establish a government banking system to finance the state development program called 'Algerianisation'.

By the end of 1967 the government of Algeria had established three state owned commercial banks. In this nationalization period, the authorities expanded the network that resulted from the nationalization of foreign banks. They were: (i) The "Banque Nationale d'Algérie (BNA) succeeded the foreign banks including Le Credit Foncier D'Algerie et de Tunisie, La Banque National pour le Commerce et l'Industrie, La Banque du Paris et des Pays-Bas. (ii) The Crédit Populaire d'Algérie" (CPA) took over Caisse Centrale Algerienne de Credit Populaire, Societe Marseillaise de Credit, Companies Francaise de Credit et de Banque. (iii) The "Banque Extérieure d'Algérie" (BAE) took over the activities of Credit Lyonnais,

Credit du Nord, Societe Generale, Banque Industrielle de l'Algerie et de la Mediterranee. As the Algerian banking sector evolved, the government created additional three specialized banks – (i) La Banque de L'Agriculture et du Developpement Rural (BADR) in 1982, (ii) Caisse nationale d'Epargne et de prevoyance and (iii) La Banque de Development Local (BDL) in 1985. During this period, the government restructured the public enterprises and expanded the banking system to cover all the sectors of the economy. Such that by 2016, there were six public banks, fourteen foreign owned private banks with the exception of one private bank with private nationals control. There are also about eight financial companies including three public companies and two foreign own companies that provide loans for investments. These are mainly leasing companies.

During the liberalization period of the 1970s, the country's macroeconomic indicators were good. But starting in 1980, the country faced severe economic problems. A sharp decline in oil prices generated a reduction in export revenues, a decline in foreign reserves, and growth in external debt with debt servicing with a fall in growth rate. In addition, the failed state-own enterprises worsened the insolvency of the banks. These factors led to economic reforms. The government empowered the state banks with greater autonomy and operated with the profit objective, not solely with the social objective. The central bank had to carry out its traditional role to stabilize the economy.

Bank deposits dropped as oil revenues fell and deepened as retail depositors cut their savings in the Poste d'Algerie leading to a reduction in the liquidity of the State-owned enterprises (SOE) as the Treasury financed the budget deficit from the SOE. To ease the liquidity situation, the central bank cut down the reserve requirement ratio from 10% in March to 6% in April 2020. The central bank again reduced the requirement to 2% in February 2021.

Nevertheless, between May and October 2020, the broad money (M2) remains lower than the May 2020 level as the additional liquidity was converted into circulation, and banking deposits were reduced more. As a result, currency in circulation grew by six percent. Furthermore, the improvement in oil price and dependence on savings from the Treasury to fund budget deficit made it possible for the banking liquidity and broad money and banking to improve in 2020 (World Bank, 2021).

The crisis seriously affected public and private firms. Hence the State with the Banque d'Algier (BdA) eased the prudential constraints by lowering the statutory liquidity coefficient to 60 percent and suspending the mandatory liquidity. In addition, BdA ordered banks to reschedule debts owed by firms due to the COVID-19 pandemic and grant the firms any requests they make for refinancing their debts. Despite all the measures, credit fell in 2020 to 3.1 percent from12.3 percent in 2018.

There are incentive differences between private enterprises and state-owned enterprises (SOEs). While the SOE weighs up political and commercial objectives, the incentive issues of the private sector concern only the shareholders and the management, with profitability being the primary objective. There is a range of instruments to enhance incentives, which the SOEs do not have. However, a faster reform of the private sector to boost its growth will be crucial for its current structural transformation, away from the hydrocarbon industry towards a more diversified and inclusive economy. From the historical experience, Algeria introduced public banking enhanced by its natural resources, particularly hydrocarbon. However, the country's reliance on hydrocarbon limited the development of the financial sector- especially the capital markets.

Financial Market Development in North Africa

Morocco has a thriving private sector and a relatively stable macroeconomic environment. The country also enjoys a stable political system in a volatile region. With its pivotal location between Europe and Sub-Saharan Africa and robust infrastructure, Morocco has a strong position in the African continent. The Kingdom has a relatively deep, liquid, and sophisticated capital market and is one of the best on the continent. The country's sound macroeconomic fundamentals are friendly and attract foreign investments in the export sector. The African Union successfully launched the African Continental Free Trade Area (ACFTA) in January 2021 which will reinforce Morocco's position as the gateway to Africa. Morocco occupied the 53rd position in 2020 in the World Bank's Doing Business Index with its highly developed infrastructure and stability. Moroccan banks are some of the largest in Africa.

Despite the progress made, unemployment in Morocco is high, and the country is weak in protecting intellectual property rights, has a government that is inefficient and bureaucratic with slow progress in regulatory reforms. Moreover, unlike in Algeria, Tunisia, and Egypt, where a significant share of the banks are state-owned, Morocco does not have public banks and thus does not issue nonperforming loans on bank books like in the former (Arezki & Senbet, 2020).

The Casablanca capital market (CSE) dates to 1929 as Office de Compensation des Valeurs Mobilières or Office for Clearing of Transferable Securities. It is the most performing stock exchange market in North Africa and is the third-largest in Africa after the Johannesburg Stock exchange and the Nigerian Stock Exchange based in Lagos. Since its establishment, the CSE has gone through several structural reforms. However, structural shortcomings existed that hindered the attractiveness of the market to investors. In a quest to overcome this limitation, the government initiated reforms in 1967 which culminated in creating a well-organized legal and technical framework.

Tunisia and Egypt registered strong GDP growth up to the revolution in 2011, and even as their growth rates continued to be positive in the aftermath, they were around 2% for Tunisia and 2–3% for Egypt, compared to 4% up to the uprising (World Bank, 2020a, b). The relatively good performance in Tunisia and Egypt shielded some underlying problems, including unemployment, poverty, and inequality, that partly caused the revolution (Boughzala, 2012).

Tunisian financial markets account for a modest 8% of private-sector gross fixed capital formation financing. However, these markets meet international standards and have a relatively advanced technical structure and the required expertise. The Tunis Stock Exchange (BVMT) in operation since 1969, has gradually grown its listings over time even though it remains small compared to Morocco's. The equity market does not adequately finance long-term investments. As in Morocco, Tunisia offered SMEs an alternative market in 2007 even though it faces problems, such as quality information, which deters the proper functioning of the financial market (Oxford Business Review, 2019).

Egypt had known and operated capital markets since 1883 when one of its two stock exchanges, the Alexandria Stock Exchange, opened. The other is the Cairo Stock Exchange. Egypt's Stock Exchange (EGX) has been undergoing some structural reforms since 2016. The expectation is to enhance the EGX, improve communication among the listed companies and other actors, and intermediation by ensuring that technology is up to date and a conducive environment. (Egyptian Exchange, 2019).

Like most African countries, Morocco implemented a structural adjustment program in 1986. The reforms aimed to eliminate structural problems to control its high debt and inflation. Market reforms implemented in 1993 provided measures to modernize the financial market, thus providing the stock exchange market with a modern organizational structure to reinforce its role in financing the economy. The reforms led to the creation of the Société de Bourse des Valeurs de Casablanca or the SBVC. The latter was a private company that managed the Casablanca Stock Exchange, with share capital being owned by authorized brokerage firms. In 2000, the SBVC became known as the Casablanca Stock Exchange, a joint-stock company with a board of directors and a supervisory board.

The key role of the stock exchange market is to provide products and services and develop financial infrastructure to contribute to development. The stock exchange is a regulated market on which financial instruments are publicly traded. The Casablanca Stock Exchange is one of the best performing stock exchanges in Africa, and at the end of September 2021, its capitalization was estimated at 74.71 billion USD, and its volumes are estimated at 5.27 billion USD. The CSE has strengthened its openness to African financial centers. There is a lack of liquidity and few new issuers in the Casablanca Stock Exchange (CSE), particularly large institutional issuers. However, it is also true that a lack of investable deals limits the development of equity investment.

The Algerian capital markets have great potentials because of the enormous size of the Algerian economy. Algeria has tried to boost the Algiers bourse, but it is still minimal with minimal capitalization compared to Tunisia and Morocco. Algeria has three main capital markets: (i) the corporate stock and bond exchange opened in 1998, (ii) the Treasury bill instituted in 2008, and (iii) small and medium-sized enterprise exchanges introduced in 2002. The Société de Gestion de la Bourse des Valeurs (SGBV), is a joint stock company owned by the private bank BNP Paribas and six Algerian public banks.

The capital markets are thin. They have light trading. Because of their shallowness, investors wait for the state-owned enterprises to expand capitalization to make them viable. Market officials and regulators promote trading and listing, but the banking sector with cheap loans does not seem to support bringing new participants in the capital markets. With the decline in oil revenues and liquidity crush, there may be new opportunities to improve the capital markets and enhance their role in financing the economy.

Figure 11.1 shows market capitalization in selected countries. Morocco is the top stock exchange hub in North Africa compared to Egypt and Tunisia. In terms of financial depth measured by market capitalization, Morocco had a market capitalization of 74% in 2010 compared to the other countries and was second only to South Africa, which has the

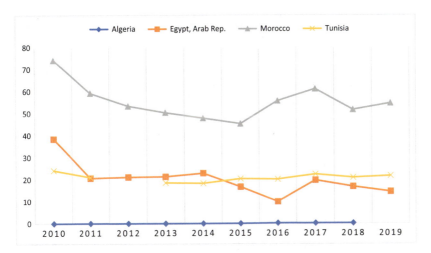

Fig. 11.1 The market capitalization of listed domestic companies (% of GDP). (Source: World Development Indicators, 2021)

highest market capitalization in Africa. Although market capitalization fell to 54% in 2019, the country still maintains its ranking across Africa in terms of performance. Algeria has the lowest market capitalization in the region and hardly reached 1 percent of GDP for the period ranging from 2010 to 2019. Before the great recession of 2007–2009, Egypt was the second most performing country in Africa in terms of financial depth with a market capitalization of 107% of GDP in 2007 before plummeting to 53% in 2008, equivalent to a 50% drop from the previous year (Allen et al., 2011).

In terms of equity market capitalization, Egyptian equity comprises the main market with shares of companies that exceed EGP100 million and the Nile Stock Exchange (NILEX) with shares of small and medium-sized enterprises with capital less than EGP100 million (Raubenheimer, 2019). The Egyptian and the Moroccan stock exchanges are the most developed in North Africa. These markets date back to 1929 but are not as old as the Alexandria and Cairo Exchanges established in 1898 and 1904, respectively (Raubenheimer, 2019). It should be recalled that both the Egyptian and the Moroccan market was adversely affected by the global financial crises of 2008, causing these markets to decline from their 2007 peak. The decline was more accentuated for the Egyptian market than for the Casablanca market, which recovered from its weak performance (Wilson, 2012).

The Egyptian market experienced a dramatic decline from the beginning of 2010 (Table 11.2) and was lowest in 2016 when the market capitalization of listed companies as a percentage of GDP was only 10.02% compared to 38.49 percent in 2010. The market in Egypt suffered further from the political and social tension in North African Arab countries. Also, the nationalization of most of the listed companies under the leadership of President Nasser accounts for the demise of the Egyptian market (Wilson, 2012). Although capital market development in North African countries is low, compared to other African countries, Morocco and Egypt stand out as some of the best in terms of capitalization except for the South African and Nigerian markets.

Market Breadth-Listed Companies

The number of companies listed on the stock market provides a measure of the stock market's breadth (Wilson, 2012). The larger the breadth, the greater the breadth of a stock exchange market and the more diversified the market is. A more extensive and diversified market allows investors with a more diversified portfolio that helps to reduce risk. The Egyptian market imposed more stringent measures that affected the listing of private companies. This policy saw a sharp decline in listed companies from 1075 in 2000 to just 241 in 2021. There were 75 listed companies in the Moroccan market in 2020, which stands at 76 in 2021. The growth in the listed companies was consistent between 2000 and 2010 but stagnated since 2011. The Tunisian capital market has increased the number of listed companies since 2000, from 44 to 79 in 2021 (Table 11.3).

Table 11.2 The market capitalization of listed domestic companies (% of GDP)

Country	2010	2011	2012	2013	2014	2015	2016	2017	2018	2019	2020
Algeria	0.07	0.10	0.08	0.08	0.08	0.09	0.26	0.21	0.21	0.22	0.23
Egypt	38.49	20.70	21.20	21.37	22.93	16.76	10.02	19.75	16.82	14.58	11.39
Morocco	74.18	59.28	53.41	50.39	47.92	45.39	55.73	61.13	51.72	54.65	58.10
Tunisia	24.18	21.09	19.59	18.60	18.36	20.43	20.22	22.42	20.94	21.69	21.85

Data from the database: World Development Indicators, 2021

Table 11.3 Listed domestic companies, total

Year	2000	2005	2006	2007	2008	2009	2010	2011	2012	2013	2014	2015	2020	2021
Morocco	53	54	63	73	77	76	73	75	76	75	74	74	75	76
Tunisia	44	45	48	51	50	52	56	57	59	71	77	78	80	79
Egypt	1075	744	595	435	373	312	227	231	234	235	246	250	240	241

Data from the database: World Development Indicators, 2021

Market Liquidity

The liquidity indicator for all markets (turnover ratio) is shown in Table 11.4. The value for stocks traded and the turnover ratio of domestic shares (%) were 4.98% in Morocco, 5.38% in Tunisia, and 25.26% in Egypt compared to 8.82%, 44.16%, and 17.23% for Morocco, Egypt, and Tunisia in 2010. From Table 11.4, the turnover ratio for Egypt, Morocco, and Tunisia declined to 20.66%, 4.98%, and 5.38% in 2010, 2013, and 2019 respectively. There was also a 26.7% decline for Egypt from 2018 to 2019. However, the Egyptian and Moroccan markets rebound in 2020, with the turnover ratio for Egypt increasing to 38.89% compared to 25.26% in 2019. There was also a slight increase for Morocco during this period (10.6%).

Evolution of Traded Stocks

The value of stocks traded as a percentage of GDP is the total number of shares traded, including domestic and foreign shares multiplied by the matching prices for each market. The data also include companies admitted to listing and admitted to trading. The stocks traded, total value as a percentage of GDP was 17%, 6.5%, and 4.17% respectively in Egypt, Morocco, and Tunisia during 2010. Its highest level was 17% for Egypt in 2010, while its lowest level was 3.03% in 2016. The highest level in the data in Table 11.5 was 6.54% in 2010 for Morocco and 4.17% for Tunisia.

Capital Market and Economic Growth: Empirical Evidence

Deep and resilient capital markets contribute to the financing of governments and businesses and can contribute to a higher rate of economic growth and financial stability. To investigate the contribution of capital market development to economic growth in the selected North African countries, we specify and estimate a relationship that links real GDP growth to employment growth, market capitalization, rear effective exchange rate, and inflation rate.

The relationship allows us to determine the effects of capital market development on real output growth specified as follows:

$$lnRGDP_t = \alpha_0 + \alpha_1 EMPG_t + \alpha_2 MKCAP_t + \alpha_3 REER_t + \alpha_4 INF_t + \varepsilon_t \quad (11.1)$$

Table 11.4 Stocks traded, turnover ratio of domestic shares (%)

Country	2010	2011	2012	2013	2014	2015	2016	2017	2018	2019	2020
Algeria											
Egypt	44.16	32.54	28.88	20.66	37.73	26.74	39.21	30.71	34.47	25.26	38.89
Morocco	8.82	6.81	6.66	6.01	5.76	6.36	6.27	6.30	6.39	4.98	5.50
Tunisia	17.23	10.87								5.38	

Data from the database: World Development Indicators, 2021

Table 11.5 Stocks traded, total value (% of GDP)

Country	2010	2011	2012	2013	2014	2015	2016	2017	2018	2019	2020
Algeria	–	–	–	–	–	–	–	–	–	–	–
Egypt	17.00	6.74	6.12	4.42	8.65	4.48	3.03	6.12	5.80	3.68	4.43
Morocco	6.54	4.04	3.55	3.03	2.76	2.88	3.08	3.85	3.30	2.72	3.20
Tunisia	4.17	2.29	2.78	1.00	1.86						

Data from the database: World Development Indicators, 2021

where, $RGDP_t$ is the yearly gross domestic product at time t, $MKCAP_t$ is the market capitalization as a percentage of GDP, $REER_t$ is the real effective exchange rate, $EMPG_t$ is employment growth, INF_t is the inflation rate, and ε_t is the error term.

Analyzing the effect of capital market development on the growth of real GDP in Morocco requires that we analyze the stationarity properties of the time series using Ng-Peron's (2001) unit root tests.

The Ng-Peron test provides results compared to other conventional unit root tests for small samples. After investigating the stationarity of the series, we study the long-run cointegration between the variables using the bound test approach proposed by Pesaran et al. 2001. Next, the ARDL model is used to analyze the short-term and long-term relationship between real GDP, market capitalization, real GDP, inflation, and employment growth in North Africa using panel data. Finally, the analysis ends with estimating the Markov Switching regression model to investigate the dynamic spillover relationship between capital market development and real GDP growth in the four North African countries.

EMPIRICAL RESULTS

The dependent variable real GDP is hypothesized to be significantly related to capital market development (market capitalization). Therefore, the analyses start by checking the stationarity of the variables by employing the Ng-Peron unit root test (Table 11.6). The results are presented in Table 11.7.

The null hypothesis for MZa and MZt show unit root, and the null hypothesis MSB and MPT test indicate stationarity. The results in Table 11.7 show that RGDP and MKCAP are integrated of order one I(1) while all other variables are integrated of other zero I(0). Next, we investigate the short- run and long-run cointegration using the Bound test approach proposed by Pesaran et al. (2001). The advantage of the Bound test approach over the conventional cointegration approach is that the approach can be used even if the levels of integration of the regressors are not the same, the approach is relatively efficient in the presence of small samples, and the estimates of the long-run relationship provided are unbiased (Harris & Sollis, 2003).

Table 11.6 Ng-Peron unit roots test

Variable	MZa	MZt	MSB	MPT
RGDP	−2.49340	−0.94834	0.38034	8.99428
ΔRGDP*	−20.9838	−3.23583	0.15421	1.17909
MKCAP	−6.47110	−1.79127	0.27681	3.81147
ΔMKCAP*	−19.8098	−3.14720	0.15887	1.23678
EMPG*	−28.3803	−3.76562	0.13268	0.86758
INF**	−20.6785	−3.21182	0.15532	1.19761
REER**	−1408.65	−26.5382	0.01884	0.01786

The Ng-Peron critical values for RGDP, MKCAP, INR, REER: MZa, MZt, MSB, and MPT, respectively, are 1% level of significance -13.80, -2.58, 0.17, and 1.78; for 5% level of significance -8.10, -1.9, 0.23, and 3.17

Table 11.7 Cointegration test results: Dependent variable: Δ$lnRGDP$

K	F_Statistic	Critical value at 1%	Level of significance
4	7.32	Bottom Bound 3.29	Upper Bound 4.37

The equation that is used in exploring the long-run relationship between economic growth and capital development is specified as follows:

$$\Delta lnRGDP_t = \alpha_0 + \sum_m^{i=1} \alpha_{1,i} \Delta lnRGDP_{t-i} + \sum_m^{i=1} \alpha_{2,i} \Delta MKCAP_{t-i} + \alpha_3 \Delta INF_t$$
$$+ \alpha_4 \Delta REER_t + \alpha_5 lnRGDP_{t-1} + \alpha_6 \Delta MKCAP_{t-1} + \varepsilon_t \quad (11.2)$$

where, Δ is the first difference operator, $\Delta lnRGDP$ is the change in the natural logarithm of real GDP and a suitable proxy for economic growth. The terms with a summation sign in Eq. (11.2) represent the error correction dynamics, while those without summation represent a long-term relationship. The ARDL requires the Granger causality test to determine the short-run and the long run relationship between the variables of the model. The test is conducted using the cointegration Bound test shown in Eq. (11.3). The calculated F- statistic (7.32) exceeds the upper bound (4.37) at a 1% significance level, thus providing evidence of a long-run relationship between economic growth and capital market development in the selected North African countries. Having shown that there is a long-run relationship between the variables of the model, we can calculate the static short-term spillover coefficients between MKCAP and economic growth using the ARDL model, which is specified as follows:

$$lnRGDP_t = \alpha_0 + \sum_m^{i=1} \alpha_{1,i} lnRGDP_{t-i} + \sum_n^{i=0} \alpha_{2,i} MKCAP_{t-i} + \alpha_3 \Delta INF_t$$
$$+ \alpha_4 \Delta REER_t + \alpha_6 \Delta MKCAP_{t-1} + \varepsilon_t \quad (11.3)$$

The maximum number of lags was determined automatically using the Schwarz criterion, giving the following selected best-fitted model, ARDL (1, 4,4,4,4). Table 11.8 presents the long-term estimates while the short-term estimates are shown in Table 11.9.

The diagnostic and stability checks confirm that the estimates are reliable and stable. The estimates in Table 11.8 indicate that market capitalization has a positive and significant effect on real output growth in the long term. Also, the short-term dynamics strongly indicate a robust short-term impact of market capitalization on economic growth in the North African countries included in the panel. In addition to the static analysis, a Markov Switching Regression was estimated as a dynamic modeling tool. Table 11.10 Show the estimated output of the Markov Switching regression.

Table 11.8 Estimated long-term spillover coefficient (Dependent variable: $lnRGDP$)

Variables	Coefficients	T-Statistics	Prob.
MKCAP	1.606**	3.927	0.036
EMPG	0.019***	1.749	0.097
REER	0.085*	4.177	0.000
INF	−0.327**	−2.762	0.013
C	18.268*	11.746	0.000

Table 11.9 Estimated short-term spillover coefficients (Dependent variable: $\Delta lnRGDP$)

Variables	Coefficients	T-Statistics	Prob.
DMKCAP	0.015	6.650*	0.000
DMKCAP-1	0.012	6.014*	0.000
DMKCAP-2	0.006	3.943*	0.001
DMKCAP-3	0.003	1.926***	0.070
DEMPG	0.084	0.095	0.925
DEMPG-1	−1.938	−1.517	0.147
DEMPG-2	−4.888	−3.592*	0.002
DEMPG-3	−3.398	−3.445*	0.003
DREER	0.005	3.257*	0.004
DREER-1	−0.016	−7.568*	0.000
DREER-2	−0.012	−6.480*	0.000
DREER-3	−0.010	−5.439*	0.000
DINF	−0.004	−0.007	0.994
DINF-1	0.061	8.127*	0.000
DINF-2	0.055	7.760*	0.000
DINF-3	0.079	9.422*	0.000
ECT	−0.191	−7.493*	0.000
Diagnostic Checks			
Adjusted R square	0.872	Stability checks	
Durbin-Watson	1.899	Cusum	Stable at 5%
Normality Test	2.387(0.303)	Cusum Square Test	Stable at 5%
Serial Corr LM test	6.963(0.061)		
Heteroscedastic test	17.160(0.701)		

Table 11.10 Markov switching regression model

Variable	Coefficient	Prob
Regime 1(high volatility)		
C	21.687*	0.000
MKCAP	0.019*	0.000
Regime 2 (low volatility)		
C	22.890*	0.000
MKCAP	0.005	0.068
Control variables		
REER	−0.026*	0.000
INF	−0.050*	0.000
EMPG	0.005	0.7418

The Markov switching regression is a linear regression characterized by nonlinearities that arise from discrete changes in the regime. The two regimes assumed for the economies are a high volatility regime (regime 1) and a low volatility regime (regime 2). The estimated results from the switching model are consistent with the results from the static model that MKCAP is positively and significantly related to real GDP while REER and INF inf are negative.

Conclusion and Policy Implications

The Capital Markets line assists countries in developing deep and resilient capital markets that contribute to the financing of government and companies, and therefore growth and financial stability (Coşkun et al., 2017). However, there are no well-documented studies on the relationship between capital markets in North African countries and economic growth. This chapter contribute in filling that gap. The results are consistent with those obtained for Turkey (Coşkun et al., 2017) and Nigeria (Ugbogbo & Aisien, 2019). Apart from the Moroccan market, which dates back to 1929, and the Egyptian market that showed substantial progress until the depression in 2007 when its indicators plummeted and were overtaken by the Casablanca exchange, there is hardly adequate data to investigate the impact on growth in these countries.

The current chapter, which uses panel data on, Egypt, Morocco, and Tunisia, attempts to determine the relationship between economic growth and capital market development. The indicator of interest was selected because of its role as the main indicator of capital market development and also due to the availability of data has a robust short-run effect on output growth in the selected countries. The estimation shows solid statistical evidence of a long-term relationship between capital market development and economic growth in North African countries. Therefore, policymakers in North Africa may support policies that improve market capitalization in these countries. Such policies must encourage the development of a robust private sector that attracts investments from domestic investors and the listing of foreign companies that can boost the growth of capital markets.

References

Al-Amine, M. A. B. M., & Al Bashir, M. (2014). *Islamic finance and Africa economic resurgence: Opportunities and challenges*. Islamic Research and Training Institute.

Allen, F., Otchere, I., & Senbet, L. W. (2011). African financial systems: A review. *Review of Development Finance, 1*(2), 79–113.

Arezki, R., & Senbet, L. W. (2020). *Transforming finance in the Middle East and North Africa*. The World Bank.

Boughzala, M. (2012, April 26 & 27). *Economic reforms in Egypt and Tunisia – Revolutionary change and an uncertain transition*. ARD Annual Conference, https://fsi-live.s3.us-west-1.amazonaws.com/s3fs-public/Boughzala%2C_Mongi._Economic_Reforms_in_Egypt_and_Tunisia-_Revolutionary_Change_and_an_Uncertain_Transition.pdf

Coşkun, Y., Seven, Ü., Ertuğrul, H. M., & Ulussever, T. (2017). Capital market and economic growth nexus: Evidence from Turkey. *Central Bank Review, 17*(1), 19–29.

Egyptian Exchange, The. (2019). *Annual report*. Retrieved from https://www.egx.com.eg/en/Services_Reports.aspx

Elhannani, F. E., Boussalem, A. B., & Benbouziane, M. (2016). Financial development and the oil curse: Evidence from Algeria. *Topics in Middle Eastern and African Economies, 18*(1), 112–125.

Hancock, M. (2012). After the Arab spring: The revival of north Africa's capital markets. *The Banker*. https://www.thebanker.com/World/Africa/Tunisia/After-the-Arab-Spring-the-revival-of-north-Africa-s-capital-markets?ct=true

Hacini, I., & Dahou, K. (2018). The evolution of the algerian banking system. *Management Dynamics in the Knowledge Economy, 6*(1), 145–166. 10.25019/MDKE/6.1.09ISSN2392-8042. https://www.zbw.eu/econis-archiv/

Harris, R., & Sollis, R. (2003). *Applied time series modelling and forecasting*. Wiley.

Kireyev, A. et al. (2019). *Economic integration in the Maghreb: An untapped source of growth.* Retrieved from https://policycommons.net/artifacts/441556/economic-integration-in-the-maghreb/1414452/ on 08 Dec 2021. CID: 20.500.12592/9cr0b2.

Mabruka M. (2019). *Monetary policy and financial markets in Algeria And Kuwait.* PhD Thesis, Institute of Social Sciences, Ankara Yıldırım Beyazıt University.

Ng, S., & Perron, P. (2001). Lag Length Selection and the Construction of Unit Root Test with Good Size and Power. *Econometrica, 69,* 1519–54.

Oxford Business Review. (2019). *Regulators deepening Tunisia's Capital Markets.* https://oxfordbusinessgroup.com/overview/expanding-field-regulators-look-deepen-capital-market-offerings

Pesaran, M. H., Shin, Y., & Smith, R. J. (2001). Bounds testing approaches to the analysis of level relationships. *Journal of applied econometrics, 16*(3), 289–326.

Raubenheimer, H. (Ed.). (2019). *African capital markets: Challenges and opportunities.* CFA Institute Research Foundation.

Soumaré, I., Kanga, D., Tyson, J., & Raga, S. (2021). Capital market development in sub-Saharan Africa: Progress, challenges, and innovations. Joint FSD Africa and ODI working paper. London: Overseas Development Institute.

Ugbogbo, S. N., & Aisien, L. N. (2019). Capital market development and economic growth in Nigeria. *International Journal of Development and Management Review, 14*(1), 14–24.

Wilson, R. (2012). Capital market development in North Africa: Current status and future potential. *AfDB Economic Brief.*

World Bank. (2020a). *Reaching new heights: Promoting fair competition in the Middle East and North Africa.* MENA Economic Update October 2019.

World Bank. (2020b). *Tunisia economic monitor – Rebuilding the potential of Tunisian firms world federation of exchanges database,* 2021.

World Bank. (2021). *Algeria economic monitor accelerating reforms to protect the Algerian economy spring 2021 world bank.*

PART IV

Continental Monetary Policy and the Financial Systems

CHAPTER 12

Economic Performance Across Monetary Unions in Africa

Joseph Onjala

INTRODUCTION

The chapter examines the current literature on the economic integration and economic performance nexus and discusses trends in the economic performance of the African regional economies by analyzing the possible financial Integration and economic performance nexus. The final aim of the chapter is to provide lessons for government and policymakers to facilitate better, more accurate, and informed decision-making around their participation in financial and economic Integration. Further to the introduction, the remainder of the paper is divided into three sections. The theoretical and empirical economic Integration and economic performance nexus are explored in section "Theoretical and Empirical Literature on Effect of Monetary Unions on Economies". Section "Empirical Literature", using data from international sources (UNDP, Human Development Indicators, and World Bank's World Development

J. Onjala (✉)
Department of Economics and Development Studies, University of Nairobi, Nairobi, Kenya
e-mail: jonjala@uonbi.ac.ke

© The Author(s), under exclusive license to Springer Nature Switzerland AG 2022
A. A. Amin et al. (eds.), *Monetary and Financial Systems in Africa*, https://doi.org/10.1007/978-3-030-96225-8_12

Indicators), reviews the economic performance within and across the regional economies. Economic growth performance, GDP per capita, Exports and Imports, GDP, Foreign Direct Investment flows, and Human Development performance are the main indicators in examining a nexus with financial Integration. Section "The State of Integration as a Pathway to Monetary Unions in Africa" highlights the main challenges of monetary Integration; the final section will conclude with some policy recommendations.

Theoretical and Empirical Literature on Effect of Monetary Unions on Economies

Theoretical evidence postulates that economic union or Integration can promote economic performance, productivity, and capital accumulation. As the illustration in Fig. 12.1 illustrates the potential channels via which economic Integration influences economic performance and includes the acceleration of international trade, capital accumulation via foreign direct investment, and increased productivity.

Economic theories indicate that economic and monetary Integration lends itself to strong macroeconomic benefits. Such performance benefits

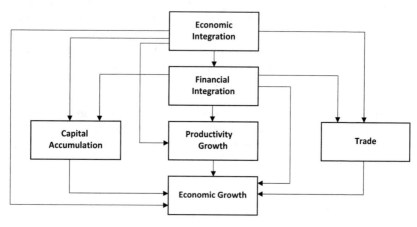

Fig. 12.1 The conceptual framework of potential relationship patterns between financial Integration, economic Integration, capital accumulation, trade, and economic performance. (Source: Kizito Uyi Ehigiamusoe & Hooi Hooi Lean, 2018)

include economic stability, price transparency, sound macroeconomic institutions, consolidation and exploitation of markets, and reduced exchange rates volatility (Conti, 2014). Furthermore, economic Integration can facilitate Research and Development (R&D) by inducing increased foreign direct investment (FDI). Additional benefits of monetary Integration include financial Integration, the import of financial services, and intensifying competition. Integration serves to spur more investment and growth and speed up the operations and development of the domestic financial sector. (Klein & Olivei, 2008; Levine, 2001).

At the regional and country level, integration efforts go beyond trade liberalization ambitions and monetary unity. It requires massive infrastructural investments in both institutional and physical settings. Thus, connectivity infrastructure (roads, railways, airports, telephone) is essential. At the same time, greater labor mobility, the management of shared natural resources, common approaches to macroeconomic policy, and the harmonization of regulations and standards are important preconditions.

Empirical Literature

Empirical studies investigate the benefits of economic and monetary Integration on such outcomes as capital accumulation, productivity growth, financial Integration and development, and international trade. These studies generally seek to establish the interactions between economic growth, welfare, and Economic Integration. In general, the findings vary significantly regarding the nature of their interactions. Thus, the empirical work has less been in convergence with economic theories since they are yet to agree on the postulated economic performance effect of economic Integration.

In Africa, the work by Deme and Ndrianasy (2017) on the estimates of welfare effects of regional Integration indicates that in the Economic Community of West African States (ECOWAS), there are significant benefits around trade creation and, therefore, positive outcomes for welfare within member countries as a group. Equally, a few recent studies report negative or no results on economic growth from economic and monetary Integration. According to Tumwebaze and Ijjo (2015), there is limited empirical evidence to demonstrate that Integration yields positive growth impacts on the region. The study uses an annual panel dataset from the years spanning 1980–2010 to investigate the effect of COMESA integration on regional economic growth. This position is supported by an earlier study by Vamvakidis (1999), indicating that economic and monetary Integration negatively impacts growth. Golit and Adamu (2014) posit that the intra-African trade fostered by regional Integration has not effectively cartel economic growth. The underlying cause of the poor linkage is in the inappropriate policies, an example being preferential trade liberalization schemes, which reinforce diverting trade effects by encouraging African countries to focus on trade among themselves (Ogbuabor et al., 2019).

Dion (2004) determined that regional economic Integration also affects growth performance through technology diffusion within the region, where knowledge spillovers spread to lagging countries from leading partners. This reinforces the need for deep Integration in crucial infrastructures, such as road, rail, and energy, to function effectively. Henrekson et al. (1997), Coulibaly (2004), Amurgo-Pacheo and Pierola (2007), Jong-Wha et al. (2008), and Nwosu et al. (2013) all support the thesis that economic Integration enhances is growth performance. According to Berthelon (2004), the effects of economic Integration in development also depend on the country's size.

The economic performance of economic Integration and cooperation in a country reinforces overall human development. If managed in a manner that safeguards migrants and human rights, specifically as it pertains to women and young workers, greater labor mobility has the potential to contribute to empowerment in addition to incomes. If, due to regional Integration, there is an incentive to improve the management of cross-border natural resources, then there would be a corresponding improvement in the notion of sustainability within the human development paradigm (UNDP, 2011). According to UNDP (2011), factors such as the age and gender of those affected by regional Integration are important considerations in assessing the overall welfare impacts of regional Integration on human development. Many 'hard' and 'soft' contextual factors underpin the varied welfare outcomes within different communities and countries. Complex contextual factors include difficulty or slow change, an example of these being climatic and geographical conditions. On the other hand, soft contextual factors involving policies predicated on their proper design and implementation could potentially shape capacities and institutions towards inclusive growth and human development.

THE STATE OF INTEGRATION AS A PATHWAY TO MONETARY UNIONS IN AFRICA

Boosting regional Integration, specifically intra-regional investments and trade, is one of the primary aims of pursuing monetary unions in Africa. Therefore, the establishment of monetary unions forms part of the broader integration agenda of the Regional Economic Communities in Africa. There is a long history of some countries in Africa sharing common currencies; for instance, many countries use the CFA Franc within the West African Economic and Monetary Union (UEMOA). Initially pegged to the French Franc, this is now based on the Euro. Countries using the CFA franc also include those belonging to the Economic and Monetary Community of Central Africa (CEMAC). In addition, some countries are pegged at par with the South African Rand. This effectively means that they have a common monetary policy. A summary of RECs is provided in Table 12.1. The Common Market for Eastern and Southern Africa – COMESA seems to enjoy the most considerable space in terms of geographical size, followed by SADC and ECCAS. The largest is COMESA, followed by ECOWAS and SADC in terms of population. COMESA maintains the lead in economic size (GDP), followed by ECOWAS and SADC. The GDP per capita for the regional economies is highest in AMU, followed by SADC and COMESA.

COUNTRY COMPARISONS OF INTEGRATION ACROSS AFRICA

The ninth edition of *Assessing Regional Integration in Africa (ARIA IX)*, a publication developed jointly by the African Development Bank (AfDB), African Union Commission (AUC), United Nations Conference on Trade and Development (UNCTAD), and Economic Commission for Africa (ECA) provides an assessment of regional Integration for different African countries (UNECA, AU, UNCTAD and AfDB, 2019). They made appraisals for the trade and investment integration, infrastructure integration; macroeconomic convergence and monetary and financial Integration, governance, peace and security, migration and free movement of persons, macroeconomic convergence in RECs, health integration, and infrastructure integration;

Based on the above assessments, Morocco is the most integrated country in Africa, precisely the macroeconomic dimension. Morocco's score of 0.809 places it far ahead of Mauritius's runner-up, with a score of 0.633.

Table 12.1 A summary of the RECs

Name of the RECs/other regional blocs	Area (km²)	population	GDP (PPP) In billions	($US) per capita	No. of member states
Common Market for Eastern and Southern Africa – COMESA	12,873,957	552,457,938	2211.90	7232.50	21
Economic Community of West African States (ECOWAS)	5,112,903	355,515,321	1500.80	2651.80	15
Southern African Development Community (SADC)	9,882,959	353,936,030	1411.7	7578.10	15
Economic Community of Central African States – ECCAS	6,667,421	198,465,962	480.9	5448.4	11
West African Economic and Monetary Union – UEMOA	3,505,375	103,796,756		1075.20	8
Intergovernmental Authority on Development – IGAD	5233604	279.214,113	635.4	2558.40	7
Economic and Monetary Community of Central Africa – CEMAC	3,020,142	136,887,573		3585.10	6
Arab Maghreb Union – AMU	5,782,140	102,522,690	1133.3	10,924.20	5
East African Community – EAC	1,817,945	190,068,673	442.3	2005.70	5
Greater Arab Free Trade Area (GAFTA)	5,876,960	198,385,067		4728.50	5
Southern African Customs Union – SACU	2,693,418	66,629,895		5481.70	5
Community of Sahel-Saharan States – CEN – SAD					
The Mano River Union – MRU					

Source: World Development Indicators, World Bank Data, 2020

This is followed by Egypt, Rwanda, and Mali, with respective scores of 0.632, 0.570, and 0.542. The top scorers are typically countries with readily convertible currencies to other currencies. South Sudan and Angola are the two least macroeconomically integrated countries in Africa with scores of next to zero, respectively, 0.023 and 0.077. Other lower-ranked countries include Eritrea, Malawi, and Zambia, scoring 0.270, 0.219, and 0.185. Africa's least favorable inflation rate is held by South Sudan, with no bilateral investment treaties (UNECA, AU, UNCTAD and AfDB, 2019).

On **trade integration**, Trade integration is one of the issues outlined within the 2009 Minimum Integration Programme and Agenda 2063 of the African Union. Phase three of the Abuja Treaty tasked RECs with establishing customs unions and free trade areas before consolidating them into a continent-wide customs union in its fourth phase. This has, however, not been actualized since a majority of RECs have not yet advanced to customs unions. Intra-African trade accounts for a small share of Africa's total exports and imports over 2010–2017. The continent engages in more trade with the rest of the world than internally. The largest destination of African exports is the European Union, averaging at least 30 percent. All RECs procure more imports from the EU than from other African countries. In terms of export trade, the leading RECs are EAC (20%), SADC (19%), IGAD (14%), COMESA (9%), and ECOWAS (9%). The CEN-SAD and AMU are lagging in trade integration. For import trade, the leading RECs are EAC (17%), SADC (16%), IGAD (14%), COMESA (9%) and ECOWAS (8%).

There are widespread country variations in terms of trade integration in Africa. Eswatini is the best performer in Africa, scoring 0.730 and engaging in most of its trading within its region. Namibia follows this at 0.715 and Lesotho (0.655), South Africa (0.627), and Zimbabwe (0.550). Four of the top performers are Southern African Customs Union (SACU) member countries. With a complete customs union and strongly interdependent economies, SACU has attained significant levels of trade liberalization. The remaining member of SACU, Botswana, occupies a seventh place on the continent regarding trade integration in Africa. Even though not a SACU member, Zimbabwe benefits from a favorable tariff rate within the region.

Further, the country has ratified the AfCFTA agreement. Most top-performing countries, including Eswatini, South Africa, Namibia, and Côte d'Ivoire, have also approved the AfCFTA agreement. With a score of 0.111, Somalia has the most negligible integrated trade in the region. Somalia is preceded by Sudan (0.178), Tunisia (0.189), Comoros (0.200), and Algeria (0.226). The import tariffs for Comoros, Sudan, Somalia, and Tunisia, are the highest. Algeria's low score is attributable to the region's low import and export volume (UNECA, AU, and AfDB, 2019).

Comoros, Djibouti, and Somali jointly top the dimension on the free movement of people with perfect scores. In full adherence to the Free Movement of Persons Protocol of Kigali, the three countries have implemented visa-on-arrival systems for citizens from 53 African countries. This is followed by Mauritania (0.951) and Mozambique (0.944), who have also signed the protocol. On the free movement of person dimension, the least integrated countries are Ethiopia, Algeria, Libya, Burundi, Eritrea, Ethiopia, Burundi, and Algeria, with close to 0. None of these five poorly integrated countries have signed the Free Movement of Persons Protocol (Kigali). Still, they have requirements in place for the citizens of most African countries to obtain a visa before entering their territory (UNECA, AU, and AfDB, 2019).

Africa's most regionally integrated country in free movement, scoring 0.625, is South Africa. Kenya comes second, with a score of 0.444. The two countries are followed by Rwanda, Morocco, and Mauritius, with respective scores of 0.434, 0.430, and 0.424. The best overall performer on the continent, South Africa, is also the best performing on the infrastructure dimension and the productive, with a maximum score. The country is among the four best performers on the trade dimension, while it ranks as an average performer on the microeconomic size. On the free movement of people, South Africa ranks low. Coming second amongst the most integrated countries in Africa, Kenya enjoys outstanding performance in many dimensions, including free movement, productivity, and infrastructure.

Further, it is one of the top performers on the trade dimension and has ratified the AfCFTA Agreement. Kenya, however, records poor performance in the macroeconomic dimension. On the other hand, Rwanda ranks fourth in Africa on the macroeconomic dimension, where macroeconomic Integration is a strength. On the free movement of people, Rwanda boasts outstanding performance. The country has affected labor mobility by signing the Free Movement of Persons Protocol (Kigali) and promptly ratifying the AfCFTA agreement. However, even though it ranks third on overall regional Integration, Rwanda performs poorly on the productive dimension. On the macroeconomic dimension, Morocco and Mauritius are first and second.

Further, both countries enjoy good regional infrastructure. On the continent, Morocco ranks fourth while Mauritius holds the sixth position (UNECA, AU and AfDB (2019). South Sudan is the least integrated African country with 0.147, followed by Eritrea, scoring 0.161. Eritrea also falls among the bottom six in other dimensions, including trade, infrastructure, and the macroeconomic. South Sudan's weaknesses are in the infrastructure and macroeconomic dimensions, ranking last. Countries with the least scores include Sierra Leone, Sudan, and Burundi. The poor performance of Sierra Leone and Burundi is a factor of the lack of commitment to the liberalization of the movement of people. Sudan performs very poorly (UNECA, AU and AfDB, 2019).

THE LEVELS OF RECS ECONOMIC AND MONETARY INTEGRATION

Macroeconomic Integration

With an overall score of **0.537**, the **EAC** is relatively well integrated. The region's strongest performance is on the free movement of people dimension. Kenya is the best-performing country within the East African Community (EAC) and is followed by Uganda. Burundi and South Sudan are the worst performers. None of the EAC members has a bilateral treaty in force. However, the currency of Rwanda is easily convertible, making Rwanda the top performer under this dimension with a 0.991 score. With a score of 0.833, Tanzania has the EAC's best inflation differential. The productive dimension is where EAC countries perform the weakest, where the average score is 0.434. While the community has eliminated tariffs between its members, it is worth noting that the score of the regional economic community in trade integration is not high (0.440). The low trade score can be attributed to the low share of exports within the region (UNECA, AU, and AfDB, 2019).

An average score of 0.488 denotes moderate Integration in the AMU. The AMU is different from other RECS in that its performance on macroeconomic policies is relatively good. At the same time, it contends with a weakness in the dimension of the free movement of people. About the other three dimensions, the score of the AMU is moderate on trade (0.481); the members' trade outside of Africa with intra-regional trade remains low. On productive Integration, the score of the AMU is about the same (0.449). Even so, the scores of the members vary significantly, with Mauritania scoring next to zero against Tunisia's 0.796. Tunisia is also AMU's best performer on infrastructural Integration (0.906), scoring highly in the AfDB infrastructure index and with good flight connections in the region. The following three performers in infrastructural Integration within the AMU are Algeria, Libya, and Morocco, grouped around 0.550. The score held by Mauritania on this is zero, while Tunisia and Morocco are the strongest performers in the AMU overall. The weakest are Mauritania and Libya (UNECA, AU, and AfDB, 2019).

ECCAS, with an overall 0.442 score, is moderately integrated. Like most other RECs, ECCAS performs poorly on the productive dimension. However, in the macroeconomic dimension, the region records good performance. There are high disparities among the member states. The top performer within the Economic Community of Central African States (ECCAS) in the Republic of Congo. Cameroon or Gabon follows this. The region's bottom performance includes Angola, Burundi, and DRC (UNECA, AU, and AfDB, 2019).

IGADs overall regional integration score stands at 0.438, recording the best performance under the free movement of people, with a majority of its members demonstrating a commitment to the liberalization of mobility on the continent. Kenya and Uganda are the most successful IGAD member countries on regional Integration, while South Sudan and Eritrea are the least successful. On integrated trade and integrated production, Uganda leads IGAD and has the top score in the region to export intermediate goods. The lead on macroeconomic Integration is held by Ethiopia, which has an easily convertible. Along with Sudan, the two IGAD countries have enforced bilateral investment treaties. Kenya tops its peers in integrated infrastructure based on flight connections and the AfDB's Infrastructure Development Index (UNECA, AU, and AfDB, 2019).

The Economic Community of West African States (ECOWAS) holds a moderate average 0.425 score. The strongest ECOWAS performers include Burkina Faso, Côte d'Ivoire, and Senegal, while the weakest are Sierra Leone, Guinea-Bissau, and Liberia. The best performance of ECOWAS countries is within the dimension of the free movement of people, which is underpinned by its vision of creating a borderless vision and the subsequent fulfillment through the implementation of open visa policies by ECOWAS members. The performance of ECOWAS is buoyed by the top performer, Côte d'Ivoire, which has a respectable score of 0.718, Nigeria follows with a score of only 0.540. At the same time, Senegal fills the third position in the ranking with a 0.388 score. The lowest achievers are Sierra Leone, Gambia, and Sierra Leone (UNECA, AU, and AfDB, 2019).

The integration level in the Community of Sahel-Saharan States (CEN-SAD) only hits an average of 0.377. Morocco, Senegal, and Côte d'Ivoire (The latter two are also top performers in ECOWAS). The high performance recorded by Senegal and Côte d'Ivoire can be attributed partly to their mutual trade in fuels and lubricants. The third most integrated into CEN-SAD is Morocco, ahead of its other member countries on macroeconomic Integration with an almost perfect score of 0.941. Additionally, the country has enforced the most bilateral investment treaties. The least integrated countries in the CEN-SAD are Chad, Eritrea, and Sudan (UNECA, AU, and AfDB, 2019).

Common Market for Eastern and Southern Africa (COMESA) has a score of 0.367, average on the lower side. Trade is COMESA's best performance dimension, while performance within all the other dimensions, especially the productive dimension, holds tremendous improvement potentials. The three most integrated COMESA countries are Kenya, Rwanda, and Zambia. With a trade integration achievement of 0.951, which indicates its best share of exports and trade in the region, Zambia is an outlier. However, Zambia also scores highly on productive Integration (0.829). The other high performers in COMESA are Somalia, Djibouti, and Comoros, all with a perfect score in the dimension on the free movement of people, pulling their overall rankings to the above – average zone. The highest score achieved by these three countries on other regional integration dimensions is Djibouti's 0.443 in trade (UNECA, AU, and AfDB, 2019).

With 9 of its 16 members recording at an average level for this community, the Southern African Development Community (SADC) score is significantly low (0.337). The top performance of SADC is Zimbabwe, Mozambique, and South Africa, while at the bottom lies Angola, the Democratic Republic of Congo, and Eswatini (UNECA, AU, and AfDB, 2019).

FINANCIAL AND MONETARY INTEGRATION

There are currently three operational monetary unions in Africa. The Central African CFA franc covers six countries in Central Africa, the West African CFA franc, whose membership includes most francophone countries in West Africa; and the Common Monetary Area, which links Namibia, South Africa Lesotho, and Eswatini. The monetary unions are not conterminous with any of the eight RECS as recognized by the AU;

each forms its own deeper Integration within one of the RECS. AU envisions that there will be monetary unions for each of the blocks: the Economic Community of West African States (ECOWAS), the East African Community (EAC), the Southern African Development Community (SADC), Common Market for Eastern and Southern Africa (COMESA), and the Economic Community of Central African States (ECCAS) (UNECA, AU, UNCTAD and AfDB, 2019).

Evidence of Economic Performance Across Monetary Unions in Africa

Trends in Economic Growth Performance

Most regional economies have performed uniformly in the last few decades, making them indistinguishable in growth patterns, as depicted in Fig. 12.2a below. A few regions such as EAC and the IGAD have performed well, with an average annual GDP growth rate of 5%, above the African average of 3.5%, and the global average of 2.4%. However, performance has been more mixed within the regions, with Ethiopia growing rapidly at just over 10% per annum. In contrast, the fragile economies of Sudan, South Sudan, and Eritrea have grown more slowly and even contracted in some periods. Thus, no particular region can boast of the gains from Integration.

Patterns GDP and GDP Per Capita Among Regional Economies

The size of the regional economies is measured using the GDP of the individual countries in the group. The trends are shown in Fig. 12.2a; COMESA is the largest with US$2211.9 billion annually, dominated mainly by Egypt, taking up to 50% of the economy. The smallest economy is Comoros, at US$2.1 billion annually. The second-largest regional economy is GAFTA, at US$2200.9 billion annually. ECOWAS's economy has surpassed SADC in recent years. However, with the instability in the region, these gains cannot be attributed to integration benefits. The trends in GDP per capita (Fig. 12.2b) show that GDP is highest for SACU at US$5441.7, followed by GAFTA US$4728 and AMU US$4477.9, but lowest in the EAC at US$858.5. Notably, GDP per capita across the RECs

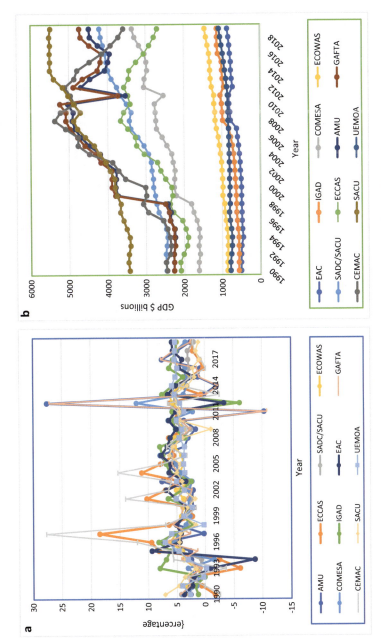

Fig. 12.2 (a) Trends in GDP growth rates across Africa's regional economies, 1990–2018. (b) Trends in average gross domestic product (2011 PPP$) 1990–2018. (Source: World Development Indicators and other sources)

tends to be diverse, unequal, and persistent over time, thereby showing no indications of convergence with time in terms of economic gains. In the EAC, the per capita income is highest for Kenya at US$1237, followed by Tanzania at US$985.

In comparison, the lowest is Burundi at US$208. In ECOWAS, the incomes are highest for Cabo Verde at US$3907, followed by Nigeria at US$2387. On the other hand, Sierra Leone has the lowest US$488.5 per capita income. For CEMAC, the incomes are highest for Gabon at US$9128.8, followed by Equatorial Guinea (US$9237.7), while the lowest is the Central African Republic (US$384.1) and Democratic Republic of Congo (US$423.6). In SACU, the incomes are highest in Botswana (US$8092) and South Africa (US$7346), while lowest in Lesotho (US$1384). In the UEMOA, Benin has an income of US$1259 while Senegal has US$695.5. Finally, in AMU, Libya has US$8122.2 as the highest, and Mauritania has US$1756.2 (Fig. 12.3).

Performance of Exports and Imports a Percentage of GDP

Trends and patterns of trade performance across regional economies are shown in Fig. 12.4. There is a distinct similarity in these trends as they appear to be influenced by global trending events. Trade seems to dominate SADC, ECOWAS, ECCAS, and COMESA, ranging between 70 and 90% of the GDP. However, the overall patterns are masked by individual countries' performance differences in the economic trading regions. In EAC – Rwanda, Uganda and Kenya hold large shares (36–52%); COMESA – Seychelles (189%), Djibouti (116%), and Mauritania (95%); ECOWAS – Cape Verde (116%), Guinea (132%) and Liberia (121%); SADC – Seychelles (189%), Mozambique (117%), and Mauritania (95%); and AMU – Libya (118%) and Mauritania (126%).

Trends in Net FDI Inflows Among the Economies

Several studies discuss several investment provisions in regional treaties (the scope, performance requirement, standard of treatment, dispute settlement, and expropriation) and the potential implications for FDI volume. These provisions at times apply to regional or extra-regional investors (Te Velde & Bezemer, 2004). From Fig. 12.5, the trends in net FDI inflows across different regional economies suggest no remarkable differences. However, variations are notable within regional economies, with

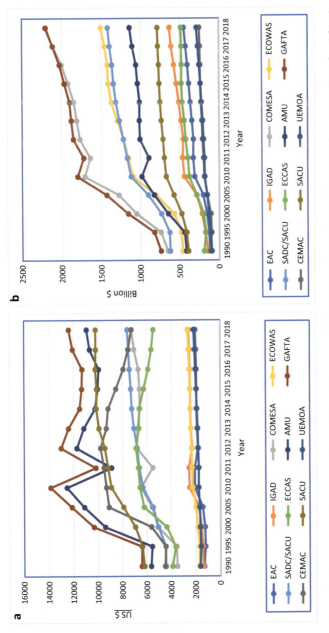

Fig. 12.3 (a) Trends in gross domestic product per capita (2011 PPP$) 1990–2018. (b) Trends in GDP for Africa's regional economies, (2011 PPP) 1990–2019. (Source: World Bank, World Development Indicators, Various years)

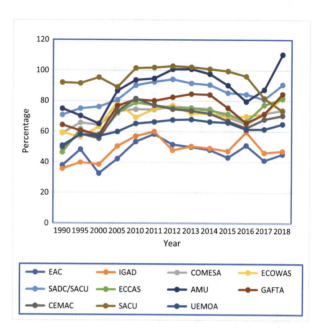

Fig. 12.4 Trends in exports and imports as % of GDP, 1990–2018. (Source: World Development Indicators and other sources)

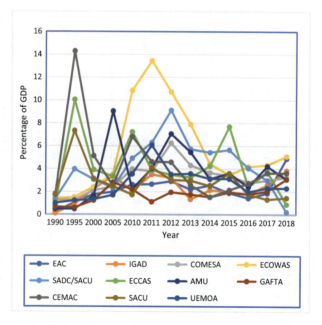

Fig. 12.5 Trends in Net FDI inflows among Africa's regional economies, 1990–2018

some countries showing stable patterns of net inflows. Within EAC, the flows are dominated by Rwanda and Uganda; In Comesa – Djibouti, Ethiopia, Zambia, and Uganda. In ECOWAS – Cape Verde, Ghana, Sierra Leone, and Mali. In SADC – Mozambique, Seychelles, Zambia, and Botswana dominate; AMU – Mauritania, Morocco; CEMAC-Gabon and Chad; UEMOA – Mali, Niger and Cote de Ivoire; and GAFTA – the flows are dominated by Egypt, Morocco, and Tunisia.

Performance in Human Development Indicators Among the Regions

There are some links between Integration and human development. First, there are regional integration initiatives in place to address distributional issues. Figure 12.6 shows the human development performance across the regional economies. The performance has been highest in GAFTA, increasing from 0.565 in 1990 to 0.716 in 2018, the highest average regional score for Africa. GAFTA also has the highest performance longevity at 75 years, educational performance, and has the

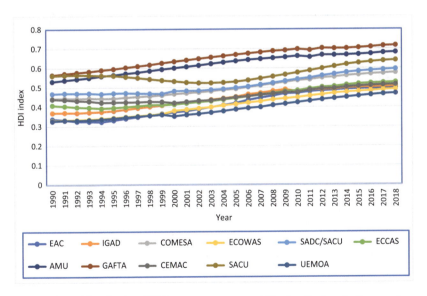

Fig. 12.6 Trends in HDI scores among Africa's Regional Economies, 1990–2018. (Source: World Development Indicators and other sources)

second-best average per capita income of US$4729 among regional economies.

AMU's second-highest HDI performance scores 0.532 in 1990 and steadily rises to 0.682 in 2018. SADC has the third-best HDI performance at 0.595 in 2018 from 0.468 in 1990, third in educational performance. The lowest score is in UEMOA, rising from 0.328 in 1990 to 0.470 in 2018. The region has the poorest longevity at 60.9 years, followed by EAC at 63 years. The region equally has one of the lowest averages per capita incomes of US$1075, with the EAC scoring the least at US$859. SACU has the highest average per capita, though ironically, longevity remains very low at 61 years while at the same time, educational performance is one of the highest. In addition, the EAC has poor human development performance while has the same time, the levels of macroeconomic Integration surpass the rest of Africa. On the other hand, AMU has high Integration at (0.488), longevity is high, and average per capita income is one of the highest at US$4478. Thus, there are persistent and widespread differences in human development performance over time within the same regional groupings.

CHALLENGES IN REGIONAL AND MONETARY INTEGRATION

Despite efforts to consolidate Integration in Africa, the region still contends many challenges. The challenges include multiple and overlapping memberships of RECs, limited financial resources to implement protocols, insecurity, and conflicts, poor sequencing of arrangements around regional Integration, and little infrastructure development. Also, five of the eight regional economic communities actively pursue monetary Integration. Macroeconomic convergence criteria have been adopted, but their member countries have experienced varying degrees of success in attaining the set criteria.

- Of the 16 SADC member states, nine are also members of COMESA, and one belongs to the EAC. As a result, confusion emanates from overlapping membership, duplication, competition, and a heavier burden on taxpayers (AUC, 2019).
- For EAC, the achievements around the implementation of the EAC programs and projects are accompanied by delays and inconsistent and declining disbursement from member states and development partners. This has been the diminished effectiveness of the organs

and institutions of the EAC. Besides, lengthy, tedious, and costly decision-making processes impede the implementation of policy decisions, programs, and projects (AUC, 2019).
- The IGAD faces insecurity, funding, inadequate coordination, poor implementation of projects and strategies, multiple memberships of RECs, and human resource deficit (AUC, 2019).
- The AMU faces various obstacles, the absence of harmonized norms and standards, and the failure to harmonize the regulations on customs, commercial operations, exchange, and transport. There is an ongoing high cost of intra-Maghreb transportation and telecommunication (AUC, 2019).
- The level of intra-COMESA trade has remained low, which is partly attributable to the existence of non-tariff barriers, the instability of electricity supply, and the poor transport network. In addition, there are limited transactions in the national currencies of COMESA by deposit banks and bureau de change as the stability of the exchange rates remains elusive, along with the absence of a mechanism for clearing and settling accumulated long positions by banks (AUC, 2019).
- In ECOWAS, the challenges include unstable regional security, low macroeconomic stability, and a lack of harmony in budgetary policies. There is a goal of the ECOWAS currency by 2020 (AUC, 2019).
- The ECCAS still faces internal political problems, economic extraversion, conflicts between national and regional interests, inadequate communication routes and infrastructure, and divergent appreciation of integration's costs and possible benefits (AUC, 2019).

Conclusions and Policy Suggestions

It is imperative to implement infrastructure projects towards more physical and economic integration. Whether at RECS or AU levels, African States should reinforce and allocate resources to their respective instruments that promote peace, security, and good governance. African countries should feel compelled to address implementation crises and work towards actioning promises and commitments at the regional and continental levels. This would entail adopting the Single African Air Transport Market, the ratification and implementation of the AfCFTA, monetary integration commitments, peace and security instruments, and the AU protocol on the movement of persons.

REFERENCES

Amurgo-Pacheo, A., & Pierola, M. D. (2007). *Patterns of export diversification in developing countries: Intensive and extensive margins* (Working Paper No. 20). Geneva, HEI.

AUC. (2019). *2019 African regional integration report: Towards an integrated and prosperous and peaceful Africa.* African Union Commission.

Berthelon Matias (2004). Growth Effects of Regional Integration Agreements, Working Papers Central Bank of Chile 278, Central Bank of Chile.

Conti, M. (2014). The introduction of the euro and economic growth: Some panel data evidence. *Journal of Applied Economics, 17,* 199–211.

Coulibaly, S. (2004). *On the assessment of trade creation and trade diversion effects of developing countries RTAs.* Paper presented at the annual meeting 2005 of the Swiss society of economics and statistics on resource economics, technology, and sustainable development. Available at http://www.wif.ethz.ch/resec/sgvs/078.pdf

Deme, M., & Ndrianasy, E. R. (2017). Trade-creation and trade-diversion effects of regional trade arrangements: Low-income countries. *Applied Economics, 49*(22), 2188–2202.

Dion, D. P. (2004). *Regional integration and economic development: A theoretical approach.* Discussion paper series of SFB/TR 15 governance and the efficiency of economic systems 20. Free University of Berlin.

Golit, P. D., & Adamu, Y. (2014). Regional integration models and Africa's growth in the 21st century: A fitness evaluation. *African Development Review, 26*(S1), 111–121.

Henrekson, M., Torstensson, J., & Torstensson (currently Gustavsson), R. (1997). Growth effects of European integration. *European Economic Review, 41*(8), 1537–1557.

Jong-Wha, L., Innwon, P., & Kwanho, S. (2008). Proliferating regional trade arrangements: Why and whither? *The World Economy, 31*(12), 1525–1557.

Kizito U. E., & Hooi H. L. (2019). Do economic and financial integration stimulate economic growth? A critical review. *Economics E-Journal 13*(1). DOI: 10.5018/economics-ejournal.ja.2019-4.

Klein, M. W., & Olivei, G. P. (2008). Capital account liberalization, financial depth, and economic growth. *Journal of International Money and Finance, 27,* 861–875.

Levine, R. (2001). International financial liberalization and economic growth. *Review of International Economics, 9,* 688–702.

Nwosu, O. E., Orji, A., Urama, N., & Amuka, J. I. (2013). Regional integration and foreign investment: The case of ASEAN countries. *Asian Economic and Financial Review, 3*(12), 1670–1680. www.ideas.repec.org/a/asi/aeafrj/2013p1670-1680.html

Ogbuabor, J. E., Anthony-Orji, O. I., Ogbonna, O. E., & Orji, A. (2019). Regional integration and growth: New empirical evidence from WAEMU. *Progress in Development Studies, 19*(2), 123–143. https://doi.org/10.1177/1464993418822883

Te Velde, W. D., & Dirk Bezemer (2004). Regional integration and foreign direct investment in developing countries.

Tumwebaze, H. K., & Ijjo, A. T. (2015). Regional economic integration and economic growth in the COMESA region, 1980–2010. *African Development Review, 27*(1), 67–77.

UNDP. (2011). Regional Integration and Human Development: A Pathway for Africa. United National Development Programme.

United Nations Economic Commission for Africa, African Union, African Development Bank and United Nations Conference on Trade and Development. (2019). *Africa regional integration index report 2019*. United Nations economic commission for Africa, African Union, and African development bank.

Vamvakidis, A. (1999). Regional trade agreements or broad liberalization: Which path leads to faster growth? *IMF Staff Papers, 46*(1), 42–68.

World Bank Data. (2020). World Development Indicators, The World Bank, Washington DC.

CHAPTER 13

Capital Markets' Development: Are African Countries Lagging?

Thaddee M. Badibanga

INTRODUCTION

African countries have been known until recently as the least developed and the poorest on earth. In the 1990s, the African economy grew annually on average at a rate of about 1.2 percent. In comparison, its population annual growth rate was 3 percent on average (Allen et al., 2011), contributing to increasing its poverty rate to 59.3 percent on average during the same period.[1]

---

[1] This poverty rate is the average headcount ratio at $1.90 per day (PPP, 2011) calculated from the World Development Indicators (World Bank, 2021) over the period 1990–2000. Increasing the poverty line from $1.9 per day (PPP, 2011) to $5.50 per day (PPP, 2011) yields a significantly higher average headcount ratio during the same period, 90.7%. The last figure seems unrealistic given other unidentified/unreported sources of income, including family assistance and all types of support from Non-government organizations. PPP is the Purchasing Power Parity.

T. M. Badibanga (✉)
Bowie State University, Bowie, MD, USA
e-mail: tbadibanga@bowiestate.edu

© The Author(s), under exclusive license to Springer Nature Switzerland AG 2022
A. A. Amin et al. (eds.), *Monetary and Financial Systems in Africa*,
https://doi.org/10.1007/978-3-030-96225-8_13

However, that poor growth performance was reversed in the early 2000s. Indeed, the African economy grew annually on average between 2003 and 2007 at a rate of 5 percent (Dahou et al., 2009). Such growth rate was not only greater than the annual average population growth rate for the first time in decades, but also, was higher than the world annual growth rate. As documented in Dahou et al. (2009), the high growth performance resulted from several factors, including

- the good performance of African exports, whose value increased 82% between 2000 and 2006.[2]
- High commitment of multilateral partners of the continent to its economic agenda noticeable through the increase of 300% in the value of their official development assistance to the continent between 2000 and 2006.[3]
- Massive capital flows to the continent in the early 2000s, mainly consisting of Foreign Direct Investments—FDI, Portfolio equity, bank debt, and bond flows. The value of capital inflows increased 500% between 2000 and 2006. In 2006, the flow of FDI, Portfolio equity, bank debt, and bonds to the continent were USD 36 billion, USD 13.5 billion, USD 10 billion, and USD 3 billion, respectively.
- A significant increase in the remittances to the continent which totaled a value of USD 22 billion in 2006.

This strong but short growth performance was ended by the 2007–2009 financial crisis, revealing thus the vulnerability of the African economy to external shocks and raising at the same time concerns about the sustainability of sources of funding that the continent has been relying on to finance its development. External funding sources such as remittances, development assistance, and commodity price hikes are unpredictable and thus limit the long-term development strategies for the continent.

Regardless of the economic upheaval described above, the continent can still develop internal fundraising mechanisms to achieve two primary goals. First, raising internal funds will allow the continent to finance its domestic-demand-based industries and thus reduce the importance of its commodity export sector, which is the main channel of transmission of external shocks.

---

[2] Export value increased from USD 159 billion in 2000 to USD 290 billion in 2006. Such an increase was explained mainly by the rise of commodity prices in international markets.

[3] The total value of the official development assistance to the continent in 2006 was USD 43.6 billion.

Second, financial independence will allow the continent to design and implement development strategies aimed at promoting the economic entities that produce to serve domestic needs rather than creating large firms to provide commodities to multinational enterprises that unfortunately have small or no impact on the continent's economy. The financial markets have the potential to achieve these goals. They serve as the internal channel of funding from savers to borrowers, and they improve the productivity of investment projects through the competitiveness they generate.

In this study, we investigate the performance of the capital markets in African countries to determine whether they have been lagging or not in comparison to the selected non-African countries that were economically similar to them about thirty years ago. We also construct a metric of the economic growth–capital market relationship and use it to assess the dynamics of African countries into this space and compare them to those of the aforementioned non-African countries over the period under analysis. African countries have had various experiences in developing their stock markets. However, most of them are still experiencing severe issues, including low capitalization, low liquidity, and a shortlist of participating companies on the stock exchange. Furthermore, their bond markets are either underdeveloped or in their infant stage.

Except for the introduction, this study is organized as follows. The second section reviews the literature on financial development and growth. The third section compares the economic performance of African countries over the period under analysis. The fourth section assesses the development of African countries' capital markets and compares it to that of the other selected countries outside Africa over 1990–2019. The fifth section investigates the relationship between economic growth and capital market development in African countries over 1990–2019. Finally, the sixth section presents concluding remarks and makes policy recommendations for the fast development of capital markets in African countries.

Literature Review: Financial Development and Economic Growth

Since the seminal work of Schumpeter (1911) on the importance of technological innovation in long-term economic growth, economists have devoted much effort to understand and describe the relationship between financial development and economic growth. Schumpeter's emphasis on the importance of the banking system in promoting investment in innovation and productive investment by the entrepreneurs was contradicted four decades later. Analyzing the same relationship, Robinson (1952) shows an opposite direction of causality: economic growth generates demand for financial services to which the financial system responds. Most of the research on the previous relationship in the neo-Schumpeterian era has been designed to address causality and related issues, which are formulated through the following questions (Pagano, 1993):

- **Question 1**—Is there any relationship between financial development and economic growth?
- **Questions 2**—If such a relationship exists, is it causal? Does such causality run from financial development to growth, from growth to financial development, or both ways?
- **Question 3**—If we concede that causality runs from financial development to growth, is such impact exerted through the efficiency of an investment or the rate of investment?

The answer to **Question 1** has been consistently provided since the early studies on this relationship, including Goldsmith (1969), McKinnon (1973), and Shaw (1973), which found a positive correlation between growth and financial development. However, their findings have been criticized for lacking analytical foundations (Pagano, ibidem). Subsequent works (Greenwood & Jovanovic, 1990; Saint-Paul, 1992) addressed those criticisms.

Accordingly, growth and financial development are jointly determined. Indeed, economic growth increases incentives for participation in financial markets, whose benefits increase with scales of funds invested while costs remain constant or increase slightly. Sussman (1991) considers even the possibility of decreasing the cost of participation in the financial markets as the economy grows due to the aggressive competition among financial intermediaries.

Empirical studies have found evidence of the correlation between growth and financial development. However, the nature of correlation varies across studies. For example, Levine and Renelt (1991), Atje and Jovanovic (1993), and King and Levine (1992) document positive correlations between growth and various indicators of financial development in cross countries data, while Roubini and Sala-i-Martin (1991) and Jappelli and Pagano (1992) report negative correlations between growth and financial development.[4]

Questions 2 and the attempts to answer them have dominated most research on the growth—financial development relationship in the post-Schumpeterian era. Nonetheless, the search for causality has been inconclusive regardless of the countries or regions analyzed, methods used, or the time horizon.

In cross-country analysis, Levine and Zervos (1998), Bist (2018), and Beck and Levine (2004) established the positive impact of financial development (i.e., stock markets and banks) on economic growth while such impact is found to be negative in De Gregorio and Guidotti (1995) for Latin American countries. Furthermore, Ductor and Grechyna (2015) found that such a positive impact exists up to the optimal level of financial development. Beyond that level, such impact becomes negative.[5]

In a time-series analysis of individual countries, the evidence of the impact of financial development on economic growth is mixed. Rahman et al. (2020) found in the case of Pakistan that financial development augments economic growth independently of the prevailing economic regime. Bist (2018) found in his time-series analyses of 16 low-income countries that the impact of financial development on economic growth is positive in 9 countries, negative in 3 countries, and non-existent in 4 countries. Chakraborty (2010) found no support of the impact of stock market development on growth in India, while Deb and Mukherjee (2008) found a positive impact of financial development on economic growth for the same country two years earlier.

The financial development—economic growth relationship has evidence in the long run (King & Levine, 1993a, 1993b; Levine, 1997; Demirgüç-Kunt & Maksimovic, 1998; Rajan & Zingales, 1998; and Christopoulos & Tsionas, 2004) but seems not to be established in the short run.

---

[4] These studies use disaggregated measures of financial development such as trading volume on the stock market, scaled by GDP (Atje & Jovanovic, 1993) or indicators of the importance of deposit bank credit relative to total credit (King & Levine, 1992) or bank reserve ratio - a proxy for financial repression (Roubini & Sala-i-Martin, 1991) or indicators of the development of household lending, such as the ratio of consumer credit to GDP and the maximum loan-to-value ratio in the mortgage market (Jappelli & Pagano, 1992).

[5] In this study, private credit is used as a measure of financial development.

Further, the direction of causality between economic growth and financial development seems also inconclusive. While causality in studies mentioned above runs from financial development to growth when established, some recent studies have demonstrated the opposite. For example, Arestis et al. (2001), in their study of the growth-financial development in 5 advanced countries, found that causality runs from financial development to growth for the cases of Germany, France, and Japan. However, causality runs from growth to financial development in the United States and the United Kingdom cases. Finally, causality between financial development and growth is found to be bidirectional in Demetriades and Hussein (1996), Luintel and Khan (1999), Calderon and Liu (2003), and Deb and Mukherjee (2008).

Furthermore, the impact of financial development on growth depends on the nature and operation of the financial institutions, according to Kassimatis and Spyrou (2001). It is positive in liberalized economies such as Chile and Mexico, negative in countries with speculative stock markets such as Taiwan, and neutral in financially repressed economies like India.

Question 3 is still largely unanswered today. Until recently, methods used to analyze the growth- financial development relationship had not appropriately described the transmission mechanisms of impact from financial development to growth (Pagano, 1993). Those methods are based on the exogenous growth literature, which prescribes that growth rate is exogenously determined.[6] As an implication, financial development can affect growth through the level capital stock per worker or the level of productivity but not through their growth rates. The rise of the endogenous literature in the 1980s has allowed more appropriate modeling of the financial development and growth relationship. In this model, financial development can have not only level effects but also growth effects.

A few studies have started to appropriately model the growth-financial development relationship to capture both the levels and growth effect. For example, de Gregorio and Guidotti (1995) found that financial development impacts growth through the efficiency of investment rather than the volume of investment. King and Levine (1992) document investment share as the transmission mechanism in the cross-country regression while the means of transmission in both the pooled cross-country and time-series regression are both the investment and efficiency channels.

---

[6]The endogenous growth literature is described in Badibanga and Ulimwengu (2019).

Economic Performance of African Countries (1990–2019)

Africa is today the most economically underdeveloped region globally, with a population estimated to 1.307 billion in 2019 and a Gross Domestic Product estimated to 2.6 Trillion USD in nominal terms. The annual growth rate of its population was 3% in 2019, while its economy's annual rate of growth in the same year was 3.7% (World Bank, 2021). The unemployment rate during the same year was 15%. The continent includes 54 countries grouped into four regional blocks: North Africa, West Africa, East and Central Africa, and Southern Africa. The economic performance of blocks and countries within those blocks has been different during the period under analysis.

We use data from the World Development Indicators—WDI 2021 (World Bank, ibidem) and the Penn World Tables 10.0 (Feenstra et al., 2015; Zeileis, 2021) to extract or construct indicators of interest for the economic assessment. We also use the New World Bank country classifications by income level: 2020–2021 (Serajuddin & Hamadeh, 2020) to track countries' movement into or out of income economic groups.

Starting with East and Central Africa, it is evident from Table 13.1—Panel 1 that this block has performed poorly on the economic ground compared to the world during the period under analysis. The average per capita GDP of the block (i.e., USD 1610.94) represented only 22.34% of the world average (i.e., 7194.21) in 1990. Thirty years later, this figure was only 18% of its world equivalent. This result comes without surprise, given that the average annual rate of growth of per capita GDP of the block over 1990–2019 (i.e., 1.8%) is the same as that of the world, preventing the block from achieving growth convergence.

Further investigation of data of this block reveals that out of 19 countries identified in this group in 1990, 11 were poor, four were lower-middle-income, one was upper-middle-income, and three were unclassified due to missing per capita GDP data.[7] Thirty years later, one county moved from low-income to lower-middle-income (i.e., Kenya) and the other from lower-middle-income to upper-middle-income (i.e., Mauritius). Plus, nine countries had favorable annual average growth rates over 1990–2019, while six countries had negative average yearly growth rates and one had zero rates over the same period. Of the nine countries with a

---

[7] The three unclassified countries include Djibouti, Eritrea, and Somalia.

Table 13.1 African countries' economic performance (1990–2019)

Panel 1—East and Central Africa

Country	Per capita GDP (Constant 2010 US$)		Average annual growth rate (%)
	1990	2019	
Burundi	327.99	208.07	-1.26
Cameroon	1343.51	1518.31	0.45
Central African Republic	488.55	384.15	-0.74
Comoros	1400.24	1399.39	0.00
Congo, Republic of	3016.52	2166.09	-0.97
Dem Republic of Congo	702.14	423.64	-1.37
Ethiopia	208.08	602.63	6.53
Gabon	11159.85	9177.52	-0.62
Kenya	917.41	1237.50	1.20
Madagascar	562.99	500.40	-0.38
Malawi	331.75	523.60	1.99
Mauritius	3805.21	10892.54	6.42
Mozambique	216.53	588.68	5.93
Rwanda	379.10	901.30	4.75
Tanzania	515.69	985.45	3.14
Uganda	399.44	962.54	4.86
Average	**1610.94**	**2029.49**	**1.87**
World (Average)	7194.21	11059.49	1.85

Panel 2—North Africa

Country	Per capita GDP (Constant 2010 US$)		Average annual growth rate (%)
	1990	2019	
Algeria	3571.14	4699.76	1.08
Egypt, Arab Republic	1557.55	3010.15	3.22
Libya	8779.89[a]	8122.17	-0.26
Morocco	1725.71	3396.06	3.34
Sudan	1733.09	3958.47	4.43
Tunisia	2224.85	4405.02	3.34
Average	**3265.37**	**4598.61**	**2.53**
World (Average)	7194.21	11059.49	1.85

[a]This figure is obtained from the Penn World Tables Version 10.0 and refers to the year 1993. The WDI 2021 database does not report per capita GDP for Libya until 1998

(continued)

Table 13.1 (continued)

Panel 3—Southern Africa

Country	Per capita GDP (Constant 2010 USR$)		Average annual growth rate (%)
	1990	2019	
Angola	2697.49	3111.16	0.52
Botswana	4113.45	8092.97	3.33
Comoros	1400.24	1399.39	0.00
Eswatini (former Swaziland)	2848.86	4818.19	2.38
Lesotho	642.30	1352.58	3.81
Namibia	3501.27	5766.00	2.23
Sao Tomé & Príncipe	219.88	784.53	8.86
Seychelles	7542.56	15048.75	3.43
South Africa	6059.80	7345.96	0.73
Zambia	1043.72	1653.83	2.02
Zimbabwe	1386.85	1183.10	-0.51
Average	**2860.76**	**4573.83**	**2.44**
World (Average)	7194.21	11059.49	1.85

Panel 4—Western Africa

Country	Per capita GDP (Constant 2010 US$)		Annual average growth rate (%)
	1990	2019	
Benin	833.61	1259.81	1.76
Burkina Faso	384.07	822.20	3.93
Cape Verde	952.76	3907.65	10.69
Chad	517.08	813.72	1.98
Cote d'Ivoire	1491.12	1727.28	0.55
The Gambia, The	830.75	815.22	-0.06
Ghana	816.08	1884.29	4.51
Guinea	541.89	920.88	2.41
Guinea-Bissau	637.22	635.53	0.00
Liberia	726.17[a]	516.26	-1.11
Mali	482.47	791.66	2.21
Mauritania	1568.20	1756.12	0.41
Niger	1124.92	1224.51	0.31
Nigeria	1507.08	2374.37	1.98
Senegal	1071.59	1584.47	1.65
Sierra Leonne	415.26	488.46	0.61
Togo	587.15	696.08	0.64
Average	**860.08**	**1306.97**	**1.91**
World (Average)	7194.21	11059.49	1.85

Source: Constructed by the author from the 2020 WDI and Penn World Table 10.0

[a] As for Libya, the WDI 2021 database does not report per capita GDP for Liberia until 2000. This figure is obtained from the Penn World Tables Version 10.0 and refers to the year 1993

positive growth rate, five grew their economies faster.[8] Those countries are Ethiopia, Mauritius, Mozambique, Rwanda, and Uganda.

Turning now on to the North Africa Block, we can see from Table 13.1—panel two that the per capita GDP's average growth rate was slightly greater than that of the world economy. However, such a rate was not enough for the economy of the block to converge toward the world economy. As a result, the block's per capita GDP was 42.0% of the world per capita in 2019, an 8% drop compared to the corresponding figure in 1990, that is, 45.4%.

As for the East and Central Africa blocks, there are no lots income dynamics in this block. In 1990, 5 of the six countries in this block were lower-middle-income, and one was upper-middle-income. In 2019, 3 countries were upper-middle-income, and three were lower-middle-income.

Furthermore, all countries grew on average at a moderate rate each. The exception is Libya which observed a negative average growth rate. On the other hand, Sudan achieved the highest growth rate in this group (i.e., 4.43%).

Next, the per capita income of Southern Africa grew during the period under analysis at a rate that was on average slightly greater than the average rate of growth of the world economy.

However, this block is surprisingly the only one that has achieved some economic convergence toward the world economy. In 1990, its average per capita income was 39.8% of the world's per capita income. In 2019, this proportion rose to 41.4%, or a 4% increase with respect to the 1990 figure.

Also, this block had diverse income dynamics. In 1990, 2 of its 12 countries were poor, six were lower-middle-income, three were upper-middle-income, and one (i.e., Equatorial Guinea) was unclassified due to missing data. In 2019, the block had one poor country, five lower-middle-income countries, four upper-middle-income countries, and one rich country (i.e., Seychelles).

Finally, Western Africa exhibits economic performance similar to Eastern and Central Africa. This block's per capita income grew on average over 1990–2019 at a rate close to the world's per capita income. Further, it failed to achieve convergence of its per capita income. Also, the per capita income of most block member countries grew on average over 1990–2019 at a rate lower than that of the world per capita income (i.e., 1.85%). Some observed even negative growth rates.

---

[8] The fast growth of the economy implies any growth of per capita income greater than 5%.

Finally, the only dynamics observed in this block consist of moving three countries from low-income group to lower-middle-income groups.

CAPITAL MARKETS DEVELOPMENT IN AFRICAN COUNTRIES

Capital Markets are the sources from which main entities such as local, state, and federal governments and companies seek to raise long-term funds. They include stock and bond markets.

Stock Markets

Stocks markets have existed in Africa for more than 100 years with the creation of Egyptian Exchange in 1883 and the JSE Limited (South Africa) in 1887. However, no more than ten countries had had stock markets activities by the year 1990. Recently, there has been an acceleration in the creation of stock markets in African countries, with the number of exchanges increasing to 29 by 2018. How have been the development processes of stock markets in African countries compared with the processes of other countries in the last 30 years?

To assess those processes, we classify the 10 African countries with operating stock markets by 1990 into three economic groups using the new World Bank country classification by income 2020–2021, namely, low-income, lower-middle-income, and upper-middle-income.[9] Next, we add a country or countries economically similar to the African countries in the group in 1990. Economic similarity implies that either country being compared has similar or close per capita GDP or belongs to the same economic group based on this new World Bank income classification. Lastly, we drop two countries for missing data: Zimbabwe in the lower-middle-income group and Botswana in the upper-middle-income group. Table 13.2 shows the classification of the selected countries by the income groups.

To assess the development of stock markets in African countries, we use the stock market capitalization to GDP ratio—SMCTOGDPR. This indicator measures the size of the stock markets, that is, the percentage of GDP that represents the stock market value. Also called the Buffet

---

[9] For the analysis, none of the selected African countries belonged to the high-income group in 1990 based on this new classification.

Table 13.2 Classification of selected countries by income groups

Economic status	Country	Per capita GDP in 1990 (Constant 2010 US$)
Low-Income Countries (Per Capita GDP ≤ 1025)	Ghana	816.08
	Kenya	917.41
	Bangladesh	411.17
Lower Middle income (1025 < Per Capita GDP ≤ 4038)	Egypt, Arab Republic	1557.55
	Mauritius	3805.21
	Morocco	1725.71
	Nigeria	1507.08
	Tunisia	2224.85
	Zimbabwe*	1386.85
	Indonesia	1707.82
	Sri Lanka	1189.66
	Philippines	1585.55
Upper Middle-Income Countries (4038 < Per Capita GDP ≤ 12,475)	Botswana*	4113.45
	South Africa	6059.80
	Malaysia	4536.97
	Brazil	7983.75
High-Income Countries Per Capita GDP > 12,475		

Source: Constructed by the author from the 2021 WDI and Penn World Table 10.0
*Countries dropped from the analysis for missing data

indicator, the SMCTOGDPR is the most used indicator for assessing the development of stock markets.

Besides the SMCTOGDPR, other indicators of stock market development include the ratio of the stock market total value traded as a percent of GDP, stock market turnover ratio, and the number of listed companies. The ratio of stock market total value traded to GDP measures the stock market trading activity relative to the size of the GDP. In contrast, the stock market turnover ratio measures the efficiency of stock markets. The number of listed companies indicated the number of companies whose securities are admitted to the exchange's trading platform. Admission to the trading platform provides opportunities to the accepted firm, including access to capital, enhanced visibility, liquidity, increasing employee morale, and transparency and efficiency.

Our data on stock market capitalization indicators or variables used to construct them are from the 2021 World Bank's World Development Indicators—WDI, Penn World Tables 10.0, Securities Exchanges of countries being analyzed, and the CEIC database. We use the stock market capitalization of listed domestic companies-to-GDP ratio and the number of listed domestic companies to assess the stock market development in African countries during the last 30 years, that is, over the period 1990–2019. Development of a stock market means a sustained expansion of the stock market over the period under analysis.

We depict in Fig. 13.1—Panels 1 to 3 the SMCTOGDPR for low-income, lower-middle- income, and upper-middle-income countries. As it can be seen from both figures, the performance on the stock market development based on the SMCTOGDPR seems mixed. Starting with the low-income group (Fig. 13.1—Panel 1), countries had different initial conditions and trends that make comparison difficult. Starting with different SMCTOGDPR in the early 1990s, Ghana and Kenya observed increases in this indicator up to 1995, followed by decreases in the same indicator until the early 2000s. During the same period, Bangladesh, which had initial conditions similar to those of Ghana had SMCTOGDPR with unclear trends until the early 2000s. However, the post-2000 trends in SMCTOGDPR show an increase for both countries until 2019. Nonetheless, Ghana's increases are moderate in comparison with Kenya and Bangladesh's. Furthermore, the overall trends of Kenya and Bangladesh do not reveal which country had a better performance.

Turning to the lower-middle-income group (Fig. 13.1—Panel 2), all countries started with similar or close SMCTOGDPRs except for The Philippines, which had the best conditions in 1990. Regardless of fluctuations observed in the behaviors of the SMCTOGDPR over 1990–2019 across countries, the overall trends indicate mixed performance. The Philippines, Mauritius, Indonesia, and Morocco had a good performance overall in capital market development over the period under analysis. Next, Sri Lanka, Nigeria, and Tunisia had either moderate or no increases in their SMCTOGDPRs. Finally, Egypt had less discernible trends. This country outperformed all other countries in the group over 2002–2007 on the capital market development. However, its SMCTOGDPR went through decreasing trends during the period under analysis, wiping out all the good performance achieved to bring down this indicator close to its initial level.

The upper-middle-income group's SMCTOGDPRs (Fig. 13.1—Panel 3) reveal that South Africa had the best process of capital market development over the period under analysis. Even though its initial condition was close to that of Malaysia, its SMCTOGDPR shows increasing

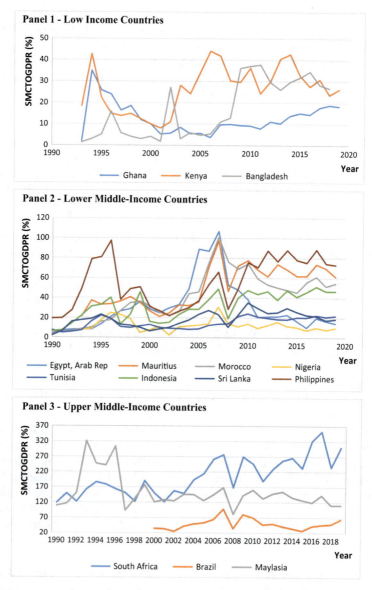

Fig. 13.1 Stock market capitalization of listed domestic companies-to-GDP ratio (1990–2019)

trends over 1990–2019, while the SMCTOGDPRs of the other two countries in this group reveal no clear trends during the same period.

The trends exhibited in Fig. 13.1 provide a broad view of the performance of countries on the capital markets development over the period under analysis. However, they are less precise and thus do not facilitate the assessment of each country's performance relative to the other countries in the group.

Therefore, we estimate the following trend line regression model for each country using the same data on SMCTOGDPR and the time variable to ease such assessment.

$$\text{SMCTOGDPR}_t = \beta_0 + \beta_1 \text{Time}_t + \varepsilon_t \quad (13.1)$$

where SMCTOGDPR is the stock market capitalization to GDP ratio, and ε_t is a random variable introduced in this model to capture all the non-trend related factors which are likely to influence SMCTOGDPR; Time is the trend variable that takes on successive values over 1990–2019 with a value of 1 in 1990 (initial year) and value of 30 in 2019 (ending year).[10] And β_0 and β_1 are respectively, the intercept and the slope coefficient, The Eq. (13.1) is expected to satisfy all the basic assumptions of a simple linear regression model, that is, linearity, normality, homoscedasticity, and non-autocorrelation.

The results of the estimation of Eq. (13.1) are displayed in Table 13.3. It is evident from this table that the coefficient of determination (R^2) is less than 50% for most countries, suggesting that the model in (13.1) barely or weakly explains the variability in SMCTOGDPR over time. Furthermore, the model fits data well only in one low-income country (i.e., Bangladesh), three lower-middle- income countries (i.e., Mauritius, Morocco, and Indonesia), and in one upper-middle-income country (South Africa). Next, the estimated slope coefficient is statistically significant for most countries (i.e., P-value is less than 0.05) except for Ghana, Egypt, Nigeria, and Brazil. However, it is questionable to interpret this slope regardless of its significance for countries where the model does not fit the data, namely, Kenya, Tunisia, Sri Lanka, Philippines, and Malaysia.

For countries with both the goodness of fit of the model (13.1) and significant slope coefficient (i.e., Bangladesh, Mauritius, Morocco, and

---

[10] Whenever SMCTOGDPR data were missing in 1990, the initial year is redefined as the year in which SMCTOGDPR data is available, and the Time variable is assigned value 1 in that year and successive values thereafter.

Table 13.3 Trend line regression of the stock market capitalization of listed companies to GDP ratio (1990–2019)

Dependent	LI-Country	Intercept	P-Value	Time	P-Value	R^2	Mean-Dependent	n
SMCTOGDPR	Ghana	14.22	0.00	-0.11	0.53	0.013	12.72	27
	Kenya	17.85	0.00	0.62	0.02	0.200	26.46	27
	Bangladesh	-1.99	0.57	1.38	0.00	0.608	16.61	26

Dependent	LMI-Country	Intercept	P-Value	Time	P-Value	R^2	Mean-Dependent	n
SMCTOGDPR	Egypt	23.30	0.02	0.46	0.39	0.026	30.44	30
	Mauritius	23.40	0.00	1.96	0.00	0.552	50.90	27
	Morocco	8.68	0.17	2.10	0.00	0.562	41.22	30
	Nigeria	14.73	0.00	-0.15	0.33	0.038	12.61	27
	Tunisia	7.46	0.00	0.47	0.00	0.487	14.78	30
	Indonesia	13.54	0.00	1.20	0.00	0.559	32.14	30
	Sri Lanka	10.36	0.00	0.53	0.00	0.341	18.50	30
	Philippines	32.50	0.00	1.49	0.00	0.281	50.60	30

Dependent	UMI-Country	Intercept	P-Value	Time	P-Value	R^2	Mean-Dependent	n
SMCTOGDPR	South Africa	113.79	0.00	5.85	0.00	0.659	204.39	30
	Brazil	46.41	0.00	0.28	0.71	0.008	49.30	20
	Malaysia	190.72	0.00	-2.49	0.03	0.155	152.05	30

Source: Constructed by the author from the results of estimation of the regression Eq. (13.1)

Indonesia), SMCTOGDPR increases each year moderately (between 1.2% and 2.1%), suggesting slow stock market development. Nevertheless, South Africa is the only country that has shown rapid growth of its stock markets. Its SMCTOGDPR increases by 5.85% each year.

Furthermore, the average SMCTOGDPR is below 50% for most countries except Mauritius, the Philippines, South Africa, and Malaysia. A low SMCTOGDPR may suggest that the stock markets are not sufficiently large to be a significant source of funds for households and firms in these countries.

The above results do not change when we use alternative stock market development indicators such as the total value of stocks traded to GDP ratio—TVSTTOGDPR—and the stock market turnover ratio—SMTR.[11] The results of TVSTTOGDPR indicate shallow trading activities for all low-income countries, and four lower-middle-income countries (i.e., Mauritius, Nigeria, Tunisia, and Sri Lanka), with this indicator stuck below 10% during the period under analysis. For the rest of the countries, the levels of activities were still low, with the TVSTTODGPR below 30% and 40% for the other lower-middle-income countries and upper-middle-income countries, respectively. On the other hand, South Africa's TVSTTOGDPR reached 50% in 2005 and even crossed the 100% bar since 2016, being the highest so far.

The SMTR tells the same story. This indicator gravitated around 10%, 20%, and 30% for the low-income, lower-middle-income, and upper-middle-income countries, respectively, reflecting low shares' trading respective to the market capitalization. The countries with an indicator above 50% are South Africa (2006 to 2019), Egypt (2006 to 2009), Indonesia (1997 to 1998), and the Philippines in 1997.

We finally plot in Fig. 13.2, Panels 1 to 3, the number of listed companies for the three income groups. Clearly, this figure shows that the number of listed domestic companies is not increasing for all African countries regardless of their income group. Furthermore, even countries that showed performance under the SMCTOGDPR, such as South Africa and Mauritius, had the number of listed domestic companies that did not match such performance. For example, this indicator had decreased for South Africa but remained constant for Mauritius.

---

[11] The results of these two indicators are not shown but are available upon request. Not showing them is because they do not add any information to those obtained under the SMCTOGDPR. In addition, they have several missing data.

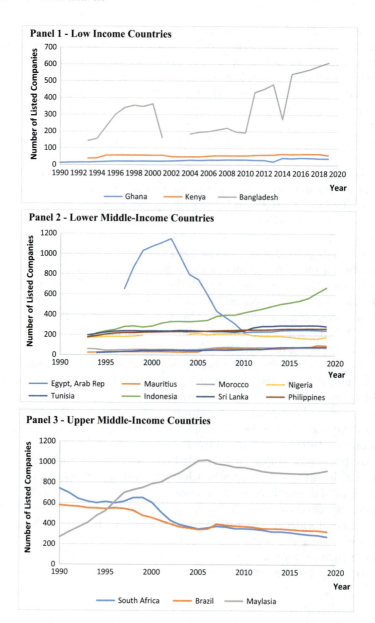

Fig. 13.2 Number of listed domestic companies (1990–2019)

The SMCTOGDPR and alternative indicators used in this study show clearly how difficult it is to accurately assess the performance of countries in their stock markets development. Those difficulties are not specific to this study only. Other studies have raised the same concerns. The SMCTOGDPR does not consider country-specific features of stock markets development such as macroeconomic, institutional, and financial characteristics. Consequently, the SMCTPGDPR does not consider countries' capacity and effort in the stock markets development process. In his analysis of the market capitalization of 104 countries over 1990–2012, Bayraktar (2014) reports an average SMCTOGDPR of 29% for 74 developing countries and an average SMCTOGDPR of 67% for 30 developed countries. Accordingly, the low SMCTOGDPR for most developing countries does not reflect the continued growth of their young but dynamic stock markets.

There is an ongoing effort to design and implement alternative indicators for assessing the gap between the SMCTOGDPR and the capacity of a country. Lynch (1996) suggests constructing stock market development measures that include country-specific structural measures, financial prices, product range, and transaction costs. Levine and Zervos (1998) propose an index that does not include country characteristics but combines the SMCTOGDPR, TVSTTOGDPR, SMTR, and the pricing error measure of stock market integration. Beck et al. (2008) suggest an estimate based on the financial possibility frontier constructed using socioeconomic factors (e.g., income, market size, population density, age dependency ratio, and conflict), macroeconomic management and credibility, available technology, and infrastructure. A country is classified as financially developed if its financial system is beyond the frontier and financially underdeveloped if it is below the boundary. Finally, Bayraktar (2014) constructs the effort index to measure the gap between actual market capitalization and the capacity in market capitalization based on country-specific characteristics.

We build on the above ideas to develop a measure to capture the effort in the market capitalization of the analyzed countries, which unfortunately is not reflected in SMCTOGDPR. We started by constructing the market capitalization of listed domestic companies in real terms.

We multiply the SMCTOGDPR by the GDP in 2010 constant US$. Next, we plot the Market capitalization in 2010 constant Billion US$ in Fig. 13.3 for the three income groups. As this chart shows, trends that were hardly discernible from the SMCTOGDPR can now be detected. Plus, those trends are increasing for most countries, although it is harder at this step to tell which trend lines have the steepest slopes.

We can ask at this step why those market capitalization trends are hardly reflected in the SMCTOGDPR? To answer this question, let us consider a fictional single-good economy called Mutefu. Suppose Mutefu produces donuts, and its GDP data in real terms for the five years is shown in Table 13.4 (column 2) below. Suppose that Mutefu has created the stock markets, and the market value of its outstanding shares of stocks for the five years is shown in Table 13.4 (column 3). Finally, let us assume that Mutefu uses the US$ in all its transactions.

We can determine the SMCTOGDPR of Mutefu by dividing its market capitalization by its GDP and multiply the results by 100 to express it in percent. The results are shown in column 4 of Table 13.4. We also add in columns 5 and 6 the percentage changes in GDP and market capitalization, respectively.

It is evident from Table 13.4—column 3 that the SMCTOGDPR does not reflect the sustained expansion of market capitalization. Indeed, both the GDP and market capitalization increase faster. However, the growth rate of market capitalization is at least 5% points greater than that of the GDP's, reflecting thus greater effort in market capitalization.

We can learn from the above example that the market capitalization effort in the early stage of stock market development is not reflected in the SMCTOGDPR due mainly to the size of the GDP that engulfs such effort.

To assess the effort in market capitalization, we use the 3-step process described below. First, we use the inputs of SMCTOGDPR to assess the trend-line effect on market capitalization and the trend-line effect on GDP separately. Both variables are expressed in 2010 constant US$. The trend line regression models for the market capitalization (MK) and the GDP are respectively:

$$MK_t = \alpha_0 + \alpha_1 \text{Time}_t + \epsilon_t \qquad (13.2)$$

$$\text{GDP}_t = \gamma_0 + \gamma \text{Time}_t + \tau_t \qquad (13.3)$$

where MK, GDP, and Time are defined as before, ϵ_t *and* τ_t are random variables associated with MK and GDP equations; α_0 and α_1 are respectively the intercept and the slope coefficients of the MK equation; and γ_0

13 CAPITAL MARKETS' DEVELOPMENT: ARE AFRICAN COUNTRIES LAGGING?

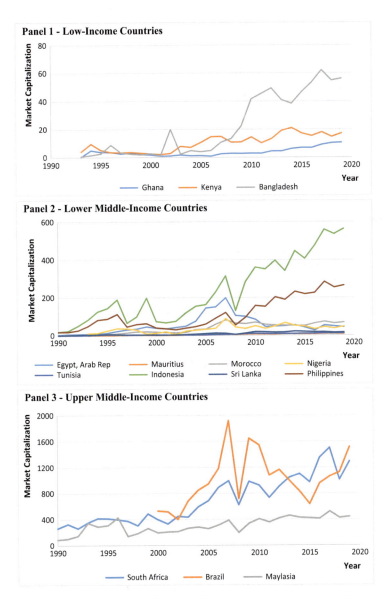

Fig. 13.3 Stock market capitalization of listed domestic companies—2010 constant billion US$ (1990–2019)

Table 13.4 Stock market capitalization of listed companies in Mutefu

Year	GDP (constant $)	Market capitalization (constant $)	SMCTOGDPR (%)	% Change GDP	% Change SMKTOGDPR
1	1000.00	100.00	10.00	–	–
2	1500.00	175.00	11.7	50.0	75.0
3	1800.00	220.00	12.2	20.0	25.7
4	2100.00	270.00	12.9	16.7	22.7
5	2420.00	330.00	13.6	15.2	22.2

The author from fictional data created them

and γ_1 are respectively the intercept and the slope coefficients of the GDP equation. Equations (13.2) and (13.3) are expected to satisfy all the basic assumptions of a simple linear regression model: linearity, normality, homoscedasticity, and non-autocorrelation.

Next, we estimate Eqs. (13.2) and (13.3) to obtain the estimated values of α_1 and γ_1. Lastly, we use the estimated values of α_1 and γ_1 to calculate the ratio α_1/γ_1.

What is this ratio? This ratio of the effect of Time on MK to the effect of Time on GDP can be expressed as follows:

$$\alpha_1 / \gamma_1 = \frac{d(MK)}{d(\text{Time})} / \frac{d(GDP)}{d(\text{Time})} \quad (13.4)$$

We can manipulate the Eq. (13.4) and rewrite it as:

$$\alpha_1 / \gamma_1 = \frac{d(MK)}{d(\text{Time})} \times \frac{d(\text{Time})}{d(GDP)} = \frac{d(MK)}{d(GDP)} \quad (13.5)$$

It is evident from (13.5) that α_1/γ_1 is the change in market capitalization to the change in GDP. We will call this ratio CMKTOCGDPR.

The results of the estimation of Eqs. (13.2) and (13.3) are shown in Table 13.5. Starting with regression model (13.2), R^2 (column 7, Panel 1, Table 13.5) indicates that the trendline of the market capitalization is reliable for all countries except for Ghana, Egypt, Nigeria, and Brazil. The R^2 in the regressions of those countries is less than 50%. Furthermore, the estimated coefficient of the time variable (α_1) is statistically significant at a

Table 13.5 Trendline Regressions of Market Capitalization and GDP (1990–2019)

Panel 1: MK	Country	Intercept	P-Value	Time	P-Value	R^2	SMCTOGDPR	n
	Ghana	0.37	0.66	0.24	0.00	0.478	12.72	27
MK—LI	Kenya	1.51	0.24	0.63	0.00	0.719	26.46	27
	Bangladesh	-12.78	0.00	2.48	0.00	0.806	16.61	27
	Egypt	22.46	0.18	2.05	0.04	0.149	30.44	30
	Mauritius	0.01	0.98	0.35	0.00	0.841	50.90	27
	Morocco	-5.44	0.23	2.70	0.00	0.806	41.22	30
MK—LMI	Nigeria	16.30	0.01	1.36	0.00	0.341	12.61	27
	Tunisia	0.08	0.89	0.36	0.00	0.824	14.78	30
	Indonesia	-38.84	0.16	17.65	0.00	0.831	32.14	30
	Sri Lanka	-0.87	0.48	0.68	0.00	0.779	18.50	30
	Philippines	-14.19	0.37	8.13	0.00	0.739	50.60	30
	South Africa	116.87	0.04	37.25	0.00	0.836	204.39	30
MK—ULI	Brazil	738.96	0.00	26.33	0.09	0.149	49.30	20
	Malaysia	151.85	0.00	10.11	0.00	0.583	152.05	30

Panel 2: GDP	Country	Intercept	P-Value	Time	P-Value	R^2	SMCTOGDPR	n
	Ghana	6.19	0.00	1.66	0.00	0.934	12.72	27
GDP-LI	Kenya	14.79	0.00	1.58	0.00	0.921	26.46	27
	Bangladesh	23.51	0.00	5.75	0.00	0.933	16.61	26
	Egypt	58.45	0.00	7.47	0.00	0.974	30.44	30
	Mauritius	3.85	0.00	0.35	0.00	0.991	50.90	27
	Morocco	30.62	0.00	3.03	0.00	0.971	41.22	30
GDP-LMI	Nigeria	77.25	0.00	15.31	0.00	0.963	12.61	27
	Tunisia	15.89	0.00	1.24	0.00	0.992	14.78	30
	Indonesia	201.58	0.00	28.77	0.00	0.924	32.14	30
	Sri Lanka	10.35	0.00	2.38	0.00	0.950	18.50	30
	Philippines	50.38	0.00	8.50	0.00	0.912	50.60	30
	South Africa	185.50	0.00	8.72	0.00	0.975	204.39	30
GDP-UMI	Brazil	1526.46	0.00	49.76	0.00	0.867	49.30	20
	Malaysia	55.24	0.00	10.30	0.00	0.971	152.05	30

Source: Constructed by the author from the estimation results of the regression Eqs. (13.2) and (13.3).
LI, LMI, and UMI stand for low-income, lower-middle-income, and upper-middle-income, respectively

5% significance level for all countries except for Brazil, where it is statistically significant at 10%.[12] Turning now on to the regression model (13.3), R^2 (column 7, Table 13.5) indicates that the trendline of the GDP fits data better for all countries. Moreover, the estimated coefficient of the Time variable is statistically significant at a 1% significance level for all countries.

We next calculate the CMKTOCGDPR and display the results in Table 13.6. The results reveal low market capitalization efforts for low-income African countries (i.e., Ghana and Kenya) and lower-middle-income African countries (i.e., Egypt, Nigeria, and Tunisia). Indeed, per 1 USD increase in the GDP, the value of each outstanding share of a publicly traded company in those countries increases by less than 0.5 USD. However, great effort in market capitalization is observed in the lower-middle-income African countries (i.e., Mauritius and Morocco) and in the upper middle income (i.e., South Africa), where the value of an outstanding share of a publicly-traded company increase by almost 1 USD or more per 1 USD increase in the GDP.

How is the performance of African countries compared with the non-African countries in their respective economic groups? For the low-income

Table 13.6 Effort in stock market capitalization (1990–2019)

Income group	Country	CMKTOCGDPR
Low-income	Ghana	0.147
	Kenya	0.395
	Bangladesh	0.433
Lower Mid-income	Egypt	0.274
	Mauritius	0.995
	Morocco	0.892
	Nigeria	0.089
	Tunisia	0.289
	Indonesia	0.614
	Sri Lanka	0.285
	Philippines	0.957
Upper Mid-income	South Africa	4.274
	Brazil	0.529
	Malaysia	0.982

Source: Constructed by the author from the estimation results of the regression Eqs. (13.2) and (13.3)

---

[12] See the P-values associated with the estimated coefficient of the Tome variable in column 6 of Table 13.3.

group, the effort in market capitalization for Bangladesh is not different. As for the African countries, its CMCTOCGDPR is less than 0.5 USD, indicating a low effort in market capitalization. On the other hand, for the lower-middle- income countries, the performance is mixed. For example, Sri Lanka aligns with Egypt, Nigeria, and Tunisia (i.e., low MK effort), while the Philippines and Indonesia align with Mauritius and Morocco (i.e., moderate to high MK effort).

For the upper middle-income group, Brazil performed moderately with a CMKTOCGDPR slightly greater than 0.5 USD, while Malaysia performed strongly with a CMKTOCGDPR close to 1 USD. On the other hand, South Africa did outperform the two countries in its group, with a CMKTOCGDPR greater than 4 USD indicating an extreme effort in market capitalization.

Bond Markets

In recent years, there has been a proliferation of bond markets in African countries. As a result, there were three types of bond markets in 2020: the local SSA bond markets, international SSA bond markets, and corporate bond markets. SSA is the acronym referring to Sovereigns, Supranational, and Agencies.

According to the International Capital Market Association—ICMA (2020), the estimated total notional value of the outstanding SSA and corporate bonds was 836.6 Billion USD by July 2020. The domestic SSA bond markets are identified in 36 countries. They are the largest component of these markets, with 58.3% representing an estimated notional value of 488.1 Billion USD and with 4720 issues.[13] The international SSA bond markets are the next largest component, with 23.8% representing 199.1 Billion USD and 470 issues. They are identified in 21 countries.[14]

---

[13] The list of countries with domestic SSA bond markets includes Egypt, Algeria, Angola, Morocco, Kenya, Ghana, Mauritius, Lesotho, Tunisia, Uganda, Namibia, Tanzania, Cote d'Ivoire, Zambia, Mozambique, Benin, Togo, Senegal, Botswana, Mali, Burkina Faso, Niger, Cameroon, Gabon, Rwanda, Burundi, Eswatini (former Swaziland), Sierra Leonne, Tchad, Gambia, Congo, Malawi, Madagascar, Seychelles, Equatorial Guinea, and Guinea-Bissau. The order of countries is determined by the size. Egypt has the largest market while Guinea-Bissau has the smallest market.

[14] The list of countries with international SSA bond markets includes Egypt, Nigeria, Ghana, South Africa, Angola, Cote d'Ivoire, Kenya, Morocco, Tunisia, Senegal, Zambia, Gabon, Namibia, Ethiopia, Mozambique, Cameroon, Benin, Rwanda, Congo, Seychelles,

The corporate bond markets are the smallest since they represent 17.8% of the total value or an estimated 149.5 Billion USD and 465 issues. Those markets are integrated in 17 countries.[15]

Regardless of the seemingly atomization of those bond markets, they are primarily underdeveloped or still in an infant stage. Indeed, the bond market capitalization to GDP ratio in 2020 was only 12.5%, indicating those markets are not reliable sources of funding for capital spending and government deficits.[16] The market capitalization of SSA bonds was 10.2%, while that of the corporate bond was 2.2%.

In addition to the size issue, the bond markets in African countries are confronted with several issues that impede their development. Allen et al. (2011) and Mu et al. (2013) document some deficiencies: the lack of secondary markets for bonds, short maturity for bonds (i.e., less than ten years), absence of an extensive range of treasury bills and bonds, lack of effective intermediate channels for absorbing domestic saving, and others.

Growth: Financial Development Relationship

The relationship between capital market development and economic growth has been the subject of much investigation. The regularity emerging from such a study is a positive relationship between capital market development and economic growth. However, the direction of causality in that relationship is still missing any substantive evidence.

We test in this section the existence of the positive relationship between indicators of stock markets' development and those of economic growth. We use the SMCTOGDPR and the market capitalization in real terms for the indicators of stock markets' development and the GDP in real terms and the annual rate of growth of GDP in real terms for the indicators of

---

and Zimbabwe. The order of countries is determined by the size. Egypt has the largest market while Zimbabwe has the smallest market.

[15] The list of countries in which corporate bond markets are integrated includes Mauritius, Liberia, Morocco, Nigeria, Ghana, Togo, Namibia, Botswana, Tunisia, Kenya, Mozambique, Eswatini (former Swaziland), Cote d'Ivoire, Burkina Faso, Uganda, and Djibouti. The order of countries is determined by the size. Mauritius has the largest market while Djibouti has the smallest market.

[16] This market capitalization figure is obtained by dividing the estimated total value of all outstanding bonds in 2020 by t the GDP of the continent in 2020.

economic growth. We present the correlation coefficients of those relationships in Table 13.7, columns 3 to 6.

Starting with the relationship between market capitalization in real terms and GDP in real terms, the correlation coefficients depicted in column 4 of Table 13.5 indicate a strong linear relationship between the two indicators for all countries. Egypt and Brazil were the exceptions. Their correlation coefficients are less than 40% each. The correlation coefficients are the range 69.2% to 92.8% for all those countries.

The other indicators yield similar or mixed results. Similar results for the SMCTOGDPR are used in place of market capitalization against GDP in real terms. However, the list of countries whose growth–market capitalization relationship is nonexistent now includes Ghana, Kenya, Nigeria, Malaysia, Egypt, and Brazil. For the indicators GDP_RG (i.e., the annual rate of growth of GDP) and SMCTOGDPR, the relationship exists only for Ghana and The Philippines; and is even controversial (i.e., negative) in the case of Tunisia. For the indicators GDP_RG and market capitalization in real terms, the relationship exists only for Kenya, Bangladesh, and The Philippines; and is also controversial (i.e., negative) in Tunisia.

Table 13.7 Correlation coefficients between economic growth and stock markets' development (1990–2019)

Income group	Country	GDP-SMCTOGDPR	GDP-MK	GDP_RG SMCTOGDPR	GDP_RG MK
LI	Ghana	0.050	0.825	-0.253	0.032
	Kenya	0.385	0.830	0.582	0.677
	Bangladesh	0.764	0.928	0.440	0.709
LMI	Egypt	0.075	0.307	0.467	0.440
	Mauritius	0.729	0.918	-0.103	-0.227
	Morocco	0.693	0.882	0.092	0.055
	Nigeria	-0.184	0.692	0.027	0.127
	Tunisia	0.697	0.912	-0.533	-0.588
	Indonesia	0.742	0.956	0.056	0.079
	Sri Lanka	0.554	0.896	0.349	0.138
	Philippines	0.556	0.928	0.591	0.654
ULI	South Africa	0.819	0.924	0.022	-0.043
	Brazil	0.098	0.371	0.354	0.230
	Malaysia	-0.367	0.779	0.362	-0.039

Source: Constructed by the author from the results of correlation coefficients between indicators. LI, LMI, and UMI stand for low-income, lower-middle-income, and upper-middle-income, respectively

Conclusion

In this study, we assessed the capital market development in African countries and compared their performances to those of non-African countries that were in similar positions thirty years ago. The results show a mixed performance in the capital market development.

Starting with the low-income group, Ghana and Kenya had poor performance in capital market development. However, the non-African country included in their economic group for comparison reasons (i.e., Bangladesh) had not done well either. A low effort in market capitalization had characterized both three countries. For each increase of 1 USD in their GDP, the market value of a company's outstanding shares of stock improves only by less than 0.5 USD.

Furthermore, the performance of some lower-middle-income countries seems no different. As for the low-income countries, Egypt, Nigeria, Tunisia, and the other lower-middle-income countries included in their group for comparison reasons (i.e., Sri Lanka) had a low market capitalization effort. However, Mauritius and Morocco are the only lower-middle-income African countries with excellent market capitalization efforts. That is, per each increase of 1 USD in GDP, the market value of a company's outstanding shares of stock improved by almost the same value.

Moreover, their comparison to the other two lower-middle-income countries reveals they had matched the performance of The Philippines and even outperformed Indonesia, which had just an average effort.

Turning to the upper-middle-income group, South Africa is the only African country in this group that had performed exceptionally well with a considerable effort in market capitalization. Indeed, per each 1 USD increase in GDP, the market value of a company's outstanding shares of stock improves by 4.274 USD.

Moreover, South Africa had outperformed the other two upper-middle-income countries included for comparison reasons. It had surpassed Malaysia, which had a great effort of 0.982, and Brazil, which had just an average effort of 0.529.

Regardless of some effort/performance of some African countries in stock market capitalization, overall, they are still experiencing severe issues, including low capitalization, low liquidity, and a shortlist of participating companies on the stock exchange. Except for South Africa and Mauritius, the rest of the African countries investigated barely reached the average SMCTOGDPR of 50%, raising thus concerns about the ability of such small stock markets to be viable sources for government deficit and private sector capital funding. Some countries such as Ghana, Nigeria, and Tunisia have average SMCTOGDPR in the range of 10 to 15% only. Even South Africa, which has had SMCTOGDPR in the ranges of developed countries, is not immune from issues. Indeed, the number of listed domestic companies is unmatched with the country's potential for stock markets' development. This number decreased to 274 companies in 2019 from 740 companies in 1990 or a 62.5% decrease.

More sensible policies have the potential of speeding the development of capital markets, improving their efficiency, and channeling resources into productive investment and fostering growth. The most urgent policies are ones that: emphasize the reinforcement of institutional capacity to enforce contracts and commercial regulations, the creation of electronic registry systems of property ownership, the reinforcement of monetary policy, the diversification of financial portfolio options, the use electronic trading and clearing systems, and the creation of secondary markets.

REFERENCES

Allen, F., Otchere, I., & Senbet, L. W. (2011). African financial systems: A review. *Review of Development Finance, 1*(2011), 79–113.

Arestis, P., Demetriades, P. O., & Luintel, K. B. (2001). Financial development and economic growth: The role of stock markets. *Journal of Money, Credit and Banking, 33*(1), 16–41.

Atje, R., & Jovanovic, B. (1993). Stock markets and development. *European Economic Review, 37*(2–3), 632–640.

Badibanga, T., & Ulimwengu, J. (2019). Optimal investment for agricultural growth and poverty reduction in the Democratic Republic of Congo – A two-sector economic growth model. *Applied Economics*. https://doi.org/10.1080/00036846.2019.1630709

Bayraktar, N. (2014). Measuring relative development level of stock markets: Capacity and effort of countries. *Borsa Istanbul Review, 14*(2), 74–95.

Beck, T., Feyen, E., Ize, A., & Moizeszowicz, F. (2008). *Benchmarking financial development*. Policy Research Working Paper No. 4638. World Bank, Washington, DC.

Beck, T., & Levine, R. (2004). Stock markets, banks, and growth: panel evidence. *Journal of Banking and Finance, 28*(3), 423–442.

Bist, J. P. (2018). Financial development and economic growth: Evidence from a panel of 16 African and non-African low-income countries. *Cogent Economics & Finance, 6*(1). https://doi.org/10.1080/23322039.2018.1449780

Calderon, C., & Liu, L. (2003). The direction of causality between financial development and economic growth. *Journal of Development Economics*, 72(1), 321–334.
Chakraborty, I. (2010). Financial development and economic growth in India: An analysis of the post-reform period. *South Asia Economic Journal*, 11(2), 287–308.
Christopoulos, D. K., & Tsionas, E. G. (2004). Financial development and economic growth: Evidence from panel unit root and cointegration tests. *Journal of Development Economics*, 73(1), 55–74.
Dahou, K., Omar, H. I, & Pfister, M. (2009). *Deepening African financial markets for growth and investment*. Paper presented at the Ministerial and Expert Roundtable of the NEPAD-OECD Africa Investment Initiative on November 11–12, 2009.
De Gregorio, J., & Guidotti, P. E. (1995). Financial development and economic growth. *World Development, Elsevier*, 23(3), 433–448.
Deb, S. G., & Mukherjee, J. (2008). Does stock market development cause economic growth? A time series analysis for Indian Economy. *International Research Journal of Finance and Economics—Issue*, 21(2008).
Demetriades, P., & Hussein, K. (1996). Does financial development cause economic growth? time-series evidence from 16 countries. *Journal of Development Economics*, 51(2), 387–411.
Demirgüç-Kunt, A., & Maksimovic, V. (1998). Law, finance and firm growth. *Journal of Finance*, 53(6), 2107–2137.
Ductor, L., & Grechyna, D. (2015). Financial development, real sector, and economic growth. *International Review of Economics & Finance*, 37(C), 393–405.
Feenstra, R. C., Inklaar, R., & Timmer, M. P. (2015). The Next Generation of the Penn World Table. *American Economic Review*, 105(10), 3150–3182. http://www.ggdc.net/pwt/.
Ghana Stock Exchange website: https://gse.com.gh.
Goldsmith, R. W. (1969). *Financial structure and development*. Yale University Press.
Greenwood, J., & Jovanovic, B. (1990). Financial development, growth and the distribution of income. *Journal of Political Economy*, 98, 1076–1107.
Indonesia Stock Exchange website: https://www.idx.co.id.
International Capital Market Association – ICMA. (2020). *African SSA and corporate bond markets*. https://www.icmagroup.org/About-ICMA/icma-regions/africa/african-corporate-bond-markets/
Jappelli, T., & Pagano, M. (1992). *Saving, growth, and liquidity constraints*. Discussion paper no. 662. CEPR, London.
Kassimatis, K., & Spyrou, S. I. (2001). Stock and credit market expansion and economic development in emerging markets: further evidence utilizing cointegration analysis. *Applied Economics*, 33(8), 1057–1064.

King, R., & Levine, R. (1992). *Financial indicators and growth in a cross-section of countries*. Working paper no. 819. The World Bank, Washington, DC.

King, R. G., & Levine, R. (1993a). Finance and growth: Schumpeter might be right. *Quarterly Journal of Economics, 108*(3), 717–737.

King, R. G., & Levine, R. (1993b). Finance, entrepreneurship and growth. *Journal of Monetary Economics, 32*(3), 1–30.

Levine, R., & Renelt, D. (1991). *A sensitivity analysts of cross-country growth regressions*. Working paper no. 609. The World Bank, Washington, DC.

Levine, R. (1997). Financial development and economic growth: views and agenda. *Journal of Economic Literature, 35*(2), 688–726.

Levine, R., & Zervos, S. (1998). Stock markets, banks, and growth. *American Economic Review, 88*(3), 537–558.

Luintel, K. B., & Khan, M. (1999). A quantitative reassessment of the finance-growth nexus: evidence from a multivariate VAR. *Journal of Development Economics, 60*(2), 381–405.

Lynch, D. (1996). Measuring financial sector development: a study of selected Asia-Pacific countries. *Developing Economies, 34*(1), 3–33.

McKinnon, R. I. (1973). *Money and capital in economic development*. Brookings Institution.

Mu, Y., Phelps, P., & Stotsky, J. G. (2013). Bond markets in Africa. *Review of Development Finance, 3*(2013), 121–135.

Nairobi Securities Exchange – NSE Kenya website: http://www.nse.co.ke.

Pagano, M. (1993). Financial markets and growth – An overview. *European Economic Review, 37*(1993), 613–622.

Rahman, A., Khan, M. A., & Charfeddine, L. (2020). Financial development–economic growth nexus in Pakistan: New evidence from the Markov switching model. *Cogent Economics & Finance, 8*(1). https://doi.org/10.1080/23322039.2020.1716446

Rajan, R. G., & Zingales, L. (1998). Financial dependence and growth. *American Economic Review, 88*(3), 559–586.

Robinson, J. (1952). *The Rate of Interest and Other Essays*. Macmillan.

Roubini, N., & Sala-i-Martin, X. (1991). *Financial development, the trade regime, and economic growth*. Discussion papers no. 654. https://elischolar.library.yale.edu/egcenter-discussion-paper-series/654.

Saint-Paul, G. (1992). Technological choice, Financial markets, and economic development. *European Economic Review, 36*, 763–781.

Schumpeter, J. A. (1911). *The Theory of Economic Development*. Harvard University Press.

Serajuddin, U., & Hamadeh, N. (2020). *New World Bank country classifications by income level: 2020–2021*. The World Bank Group.

Shaw, E. S. (1973). *Financial deepening in economic development*. Oxford University Press.

Sussman, O. (1991). *A theory of financial development*. Working paper no. 233. The Hebrew University of Jerusalem, Jerusalem.

World Bank. (2021). *World Development Indicators -WDI 2020*. The World Bank Group.

Zeileis, A. (2021). pwt10: Penn World Table (Version 10.x). R package version 10.0-0, https://CRAN.R-project.org/package=pwt10

CHAPTER 14

African Monetary Unions and Competitiveness

Oluremi Davies Ogun

INTRODUCTION

Assessing a country's competitiveness is of much interest to policymakers within and outside the local economy. Evaluating international competitiveness enables policymakers to ascertain how their exports compare with their competitors in the global market (Bayoumi et al., 2018). Also, maintaining national competitiveness is important for small open economies that desire to provide opportunities for their people to improve their living standards and quality of life by providing employment and raising incomes via productivity gains (Ramirez & Tsangarides, 2007).

With the successful formation of the European Monetary Union (EMU), the launch of the Euro, and its relative success in improving the macroeconomic performance of the member states, several economic groups have contemplated the formation of their monetary Union (Coulibaly & Gnimassoun, 2013; Razzaghi et al., 2018). The aim is usually to reap the benefits afforded by the membership of a Single Market such as the direct competitiveness arising from the availability of huge

O. D. Ogun (✉)
Department of Economics, University of Ibadan, Ibadan, Nigeria

market. The high degree of internal heterogeneity allows companies to create regional value chains that take advantage of differences in local circumstances to achieve higher productivity as well as cost efficiency such as in the European Union (E.U.) (Ketels & Porter, 2018). Although there are costs associated with membership of a monetary union e.g. the loss of independence in the use of exchange rate and monetary policies by the sovereign national government to address the nation's international competitiveness challenges and other national economic shocks, the encouragement from the success of the E.U. appeared to have been more influential.

This chapter evaluates the impact of the formation of monetary unions by African countries on the international competitiveness of the member states. For data unavailability, the approach in the study is to compute relevant indices of competitiveness for affected African countries compared to countries of the Eurozone. The results suggested that while the African countries lagged the countries in the EMU on some fronts, they seemed to be relatively faster on the technological index, raising prospects of a brighter future.

The rest of the chapter is organized as follows. Following the introduction is the literature review, next is the method of analysis and the data employed. Section "Comparative Evaluation of Performances of Monetary Unions" documents the comparison of the performances of the currency zones, while the last section concludes the chapter.

Literature Review

Conceptual Issues

Definitions and Concept of Competitiveness There is no consensus on the definition of competitiveness (Ketels, 2016; Siudek & Zawojska, 2014); likewise, no single measure of competitiveness can entirely capture all relevant dimensions of competitiveness (Siudek & Zawojska, 2014). However, there are two main competing views on the definition of competitiveness: The cost/market share-view and the productivity-based view of competitiveness (Ketels, 2016). While the former "looks at competitiveness as a location's unit cost level, driving companies' ability to compete successfully on global markets," the latter sees "competitiveness as a location's productivity level, driving the standard of living the individuals in that location can sustain." Specific definitions include OECD (1992) that defined competitiveness from a macroeconomic viewpoint as the extent to which a nation can compete internationally while at the same time be able to sustain high income for its people under free trade and fair market conditions. Cockburn et al. (1999) defined competitiveness at the microeconomic level as being the capacity to sell products profitably. To be competitive, a firm must charge lower prices for its products or offer products of better quality or better service than its competitors. Ramirez and Tsangarides (2007) then gave a general definition of competitiveness, as the ability of a country to operate efficiently and productively with other countries while keeping living standards of its citizens high.

Porter et al. (2007) noted that, although the most intuitive definition of competitiveness is a country's share of world markets for its products, thus justifying interventions to alter market outcomes in a nation's favor using strategies such as subsidies, artificial restraints on local wages, and intervention to devalue the nation's currency in order to "make a nation more competitive." However, they criticized this view because low wages reveal a lack of competitiveness and depress prosperity for citizens. Also, subsidies drain national income and bias choices away from the most productive use of the nation's resources. In addition, the need for devaluation discounts products and services sold in the international market while raising the cost of imports. Therefore, exports based on low wages or a cheap currency do not support an attractive standard of living.

Consequently, they opined that true competitiveness is measured by productivity (traded and non- traded sectors). Furthermore, they argued that since productivity is real high wages, a strong currency, attracts high returns to capital leading to a high standard of living and high productivity. Still, in line with the market share view, competitiveness according to the Irish National Competitiveness Council is defined as the ability of firms to compete in markets (Ketels, 2016). Hence, a country's national competitiveness refers to the ability of the enterprise based in the country to compete in international markets.

The goal of competitiveness in an economy is the level of productivity. Hence competitive economies have the capacity for high and rising living standards, granting all members of a society the ability to contribute to and benefit from these levels of prosperity. Furthermore, competitive economies are sustainable—being able to cater to the present generation's needs without compromising the ability and hopes of future generations to meet their needs (WEF, 2014). Also, Schwab (2017) defines competitiveness as the set of factors as well as policies, and institutions that determine the productivity of an economy, which in turn sets the level of prosperity that the economy can achieve.

Measuring Competitiveness According to Coulibaly and Gnimassoun (2013), "Since the equilibrium exchange rate is defined as the real exchange rate that allows an economy to reach its internal and external equilibriums, exchange rate misalignments constitute not only an indicator of competitiveness but also a useful indicator of the viability of a monetary union." Likewise, Razzaghi et al. (2018) justified real exchange rate misalignment as a suitable index to measure economic competitiveness by noting that many macroeconomic fundamentals will affect the real exchange rate. However, the real exchange rate misalignments were usually computed as the difference between the current real effective exchange rate level and the estimated long-run equilibrium exchange rate. Also, real effective exchange rates have become a standard metric for measuring competitiveness (Bayoumi et al., 2018). However, confusion arises when different real effective exchange rate measures are used to indicate competitiveness (Hallwirth, 2015). Collignon (2013) criticized the use of relative unit labor costs (ULC) as a competitiveness measure, arguing that cost competitiveness goes beyond wages and labor productivity. Accordingly, the concept of competitiveness must describe the conditions under which the return on capital can attract new investment. Collignon, hence, proposed the "equilibrium unit labor costs" measure, which assumes that the relative return on capital is equal to the euro area averages and takes equal returns on capital as a benchmark. It argues that the relative return on capital in different member states would indicate whether labor costs are overvalued when the return on capital in one country is below the euro area average or undervalued if it is above this average. Sinn (2014a) also argued against using ULC as an alternative measure of competitiveness since it erroneously suggests improved competitiveness when jobs and businesses with high labor costs exit the market. The phenomenon is known as 'dismissal productivity' (Hallwirth, 2015).

Issues on Competitiveness of Member States in a Monetary Union Ketels and Porter (2018) pointed out that Single Market and Common Currency remove many barriers for cross-border trade, investment, and migration, transforming European competitiveness. Kowalski and Pietrzykowski (2010) identified these barriers as a reduction in transaction costs, absence of currency risk, greater monetary stability and predictability, and growth of macroeconomic credibility that resulted in lower market interest rates in some countries. However, Common Currency has incapacitated domestic economies by using key national policy tools traditionally employed to combat economic downturns and volatility while increasing the potential for cross- border spillover from macroeconomic crises in Europe. Consequently, what adversely affects competitiveness in Europe is not removing traditional barriers to trade and investment or strengthening linkages across Europe. Rather, what is crucial the ability of individual regions and countries within the E.U. to successfully compete in the common European market and the broader global economy. Hence, emphasis should be on microeconomic competitiveness (Ketels & Porter, 2018). The microeconomic competitiveness should be anchored on the domestic competitive advantages that empower local firms to compete successfully within and outside the union. More importantly is the efficiency potential and adaptive capabilities of firms, product and process innovation capacity of businesses, including cost control and cost reduction (Kowalski & Pietrzykowski, 2010). In a common currency area, the competitiveness level among members is quite important. Large differences in competitiveness among member countries will cause current account imbalances across countries and threaten the stability of the optimal currency area (OCA) itself. Under this situation, the central bank faces difficulties formulating standard and consensus policies (monetary and exchange rate) in the monetary Union (Coudert et al., 2013). Therefore, for a viable and sustainable monetary union, member states should have relative competitiveness levels (Coulibaly & Gnimassoun, 2013).

In line with the above, Sinn (2014b) cited in Cid (2016) observed that European Monetary Union (EMU), although, has reduced protection and increased competition in the internal market, it has exacerbated macroeconomic imbalance among member states since the financial crisis of 2007. This was due to credit financing in the EMU. In addition, the strengthening of integration by the EMU elicited different outcomes among member states depending on their imbalances and capabilities for adjustment or ability to reform; accordingly, there exists a strong link between the EMU and the European imbalance (Cid, 2016). Also, structural limitations facing the member states had manifested in a limited capacity for competitiveness (Cid, 2013), which in turn, compounded the European imbalance that manifested as current and capital accounts, external and internal public debt, unemployment, and other current and structural imbalances (Cid, 2016).

Another significant issue affecting competitiveness in a monetary union, as evidenced in the EMU, is that major divergences such as persistent inflation rate differences lead to significant macroeconomic imbalances (Hallwirth, 2015). With nominal exchange rates completely pegged between the Euro Area members since January 1, 1999, the real exchange rates have continued to vary as inflation rates have still differed across countries (Coudert et al., 2013). Mongelli and Wyplosz (2008) observed that higher inflation in peripheral countries has led to an appreciation of their real exchange rates more than the expected Balassa–Samuelson effect, eroding their competitiveness and external trade.

Summarizing the mechanism, Lane (2006) noted that "membership in a monetary union can amplify the asymmetric impact of certain shocks. A common nominal interest rate implies that persistent differences in national inflation rates translate into real interest rates across member countries. The countries with relatively higher medium-term inflation enjoy lower real interest rates than those with below-average inflation—stimulating demand, credit growth, and housing markets in the former group. Over time, there is an offsetting corrective mechanism as the higher- inflation countries experience higher labor and other costs, leading to a loss of competitiveness *vis-à-vis* the lower-inflation group in the currency union".

Consequently, the later crisis in the Euro Area, especially as it relates to its competitiveness challenges, have led to further studies on competitiveness in a monetary union or the optimality of currency area based on analyses of competitiveness of member states or potential member states. (Collignon, 2013; Cid, 2013, 2016; Ketels & Porter, 2018).

Theoretical Review

We trace the investigations into the cost and benefits of monetary union to the seminal work of Mundell (1961), who originated the concept of optimal currency area (OCA). It was formulated based on the debate on the relative merits of fixed versus flexible exchange rates. A currency area refers to a geographical entity of a group of countries with a single currency or countries maintaining their separate national currencies with the currencies fully convertible into one another under permanently fixed exchange rates. "Optimum" is used to describe the maintenance of external and internal equilibrium by members of the currency area. The former reflects a sustainable balance of payments while the latter implies full employment with a stable domestic price level, low inflation. In his seminal work, Mundell noted that economies with a similar balance of payments shocks are better suitable for an OCA than those with asymmetric shocks. The explanation is that the implementation of common monetary policy will be beneficial to all without adjusting the exchange rate between the economies. At the same time, the countries with a high probability of asymmetric shocks should preserve the exchange rate as an adjustment mechanism to stabilize growth, assuming short-run rigidity in nominal wage and prices. However, in asymmetric shocks within the monetary union, factor mobility, especially labor and wage-price flexibility, becomes important since, with limited factor mobility and rigid wages, member states face difficulty adjusting to asymmetric shocks with the fixed exchange rate.

Building on Mundell's work, McKinnon (1963) argued that in small and highly open economies, all things being equal, the flexible exchange rate is less effective in influencing external balance, hence competitiveness, and more damaging to domestic price level stability. Therefore, such economies are better suited for monetary unions than are relatively closed economies. Kenen (1969), cited in Kunroo (2016),[1] contributed that more diversified economies are better candidates for OCA membership than less diversified economies because the diversification provides insulation against various shocks, forestalling the necessity of frequent changes in terms of trade via the exchange rate. Kenen argues that a less diversified economy that produces only one exportable good would require a flexible exchange rate to mitigate the effects of a shock to the terms of trade. Alternatively, adjust the economy by reducing wages and prices, increasing unemployment for the fixed exchange rate. However, a high diversification confers an economy with the capacity to withstand sector-specific shocks. Therefore, it negates the need to effect frequent changes in terms of trade through exchange rate adjustment. Hence, highly diversified economies are better candidates for currency areas.

Mundell, McKinnon, and Kenen all proposed *ex-ante* criteria for entry into monetary union. However, there have been documented arguments exploiting the Lucas Critique to favor *ex-post* criteria (e.g., Kunroo, 2016).

---

[1] Kunroo (2016) is an excellent review of the recent developments in the OCA theory.

Methodological Review

The analysis and assessment of the competitiveness of a given economy are usually based on two approaches (Kowalski & Pietrzykowski, 2010). The first involves using econometric models of the scale and variations of real effective exchange rate misalignment from its equilibrium. The second approach constitutes a comparative analysis of measures of competitiveness using descriptive tools, usually graphs.

Ramirez and Tsangarides (2007) used a vast competitiveness framework to evaluate the competitiveness of the CFA zone: the West African Economic and Monetary Union (WAEMU) and Central African Economic and Monetary Union (CEMAC) regions using their performance as a benchmark against other countries and similar groups, which included Sub-Sahara Africa (SSA), Latin America, emerging Asia and the Organization for Economic Cooperation and Development (OECD). In their framework, competitiveness was viewed as comprising two interlinked components: environment and policy. The environment component was made up of measures of productivity, labor markets, costs, prices, exchange rates, and wages that affect the country's exports, enough to pay for its import requirements and maintain full employment. In contrast, the policy component consisted of factors that impact innovation and productivity for better business performance, such as the business environment, governance, and physical and human capital. These were aimed at improving economic growth and the quality of life of the people, measured using the United Nations' Human Development Index. The study was conducted using various descriptive tools and depending on data availability for the different measures for various periods.

Kowalski and Pietrzykowski (2010) carried out a comparative analysis, with graphs, of economies within the European Monetary Union (EMU) to determine the level and shifts in their competitiveness between 1999 and 2009 using real effective exchange rate (REER) deflated by the consumer price index (CPI) and unit labor costs (ULC) separately. Collignon (2013) constructed an equilibrium unit labor cost and then assessed changes in the positions of competitiveness levels of member states of the Euro Area by taking the difference between the actual and equilibrium unit labor costs relative to the euro area for each country. This was then computed into a single competitiveness index whose movement was analyzed with a graph from 1990 to 2010. The zero lines indicated that the average return on the capital stock in a given Member State was equal to the Euro Area. Therefore, an index number above the zero line shows that the ULCs of a Member State were above equilibrium, which means an overvaluation. Conversely, an increase in the index indicated a loss of competitiveness.

Coudert et al. (2013) assessed real exchange rate misalignments for eleven Eurozone countries: Austria, Belgium, Finland, France, Germany, Greece, Ireland, Italy, the Netherlands, Portugal, and Spain, as well as for the whole euro area countries based on the Behavioral Equilibrium Exchange Rate (BEER) approach. The study used a parsimonious model. The real equilibrium exchange rate depends on a productivity variable to account for a Balassa–Samuelson effect and the net foreign asset position. The estimation was done using panel cointegration analysis, precisely the dynamic OLS (DOLS) rates over the period 1980–2010. After the estimations, we computed the misalignments. Finally, we examine the persistence of the misalignments using the autocorrelation coefficients of misalignments for the whole period and sub-samples. The sub-sample was included before and after the formation of the monetary union. The panel VECM was also estimated with GMM estimator to verify the result of the autocorrelation analysis.

Couharde et al. (2013) studied the convergence process of CFA franc zone real exchange rates towards equilibrium. Furthermore, the role played by the anchor currency in their adjustment process and its implication for a shift in competitiveness. The study employed the panel cointegration technique, using the Dynamic Least Squares estimator for panel data to estimate a Behavioral Equilibrium Exchange Rate (BEER) model. The model captures the long-run relationship between REER and terms of trade, relative purchasing power parity (PPP), GDP per capita (productivity differential), openness, public spending relative to GDP, and net foreign assets (NFA) relative to GDP from 1985 to 2009. After that, VECM was used to analyze the convergence process towards equilibrium.

Coulibaly and Gnimassoun (2013) investigated the optimality of a monetary union in West Africa (ECOWAS), emphasizing the economic competitiveness of member countries using a proxy of competitiveness, exchange rate misalignments, which they opined constitute a useful indicator of the viability of a monetary union. Firstly, the Behavioral Equilibrium Exchange Rate (BEER) model, as above, was estimated for CFA and WAMZ countries covering 17 countries under four regions (WAEMU, CAEMC, WAMZ, and WAMZ without Nigeria

(WAMZ_WNGA)),[2] from which the corresponding misalignments were computed. The regional misalignments were calculated as the weighted averages of misalignments of countries belonging to the area. The weights used corresponded to each country's share in the considered region's real GDP. The dynamics of the regional misalignments were analyzed in terms of sigma-convergence and co- movements. We use varied methods to estimate the long-run relationship. First, the methods included panel cointegration techniques (Pool Mean Group, Dynamic OLS, and Fully-Modified OLS estimators). Secondly, further investigation was carried by a cluster analysis, which enabled them to examine the similarities and dissimilarities of the CFA and WAMZ countries in terms of economic competitiveness. Data used was annual data over the period 1985–2009.

Razzaghi et al. (2018) evaluated the practicability of establishing a common currency among Organization of Islamic Countries (OIC) member countries by analyzing the economic competitiveness differentials as a benchmark for Optimum Currency Area criterion. The study adopted the panel cointegration techniques and the Pooled Mean Group method. First, real exchange rate misalignment was used as an index to measure economic competitiveness because real exchange rate affects and will be affected by many macroeconomic fundamentals. The explanatory variables used to estimate the long-run equilibrium include: real exchange rate, productivity differential, net foreign assets, terms of trade, openness, and government expenditure. The weighted average regional (economic bodies that make up the OIC) real exchange rate misalignments were then analyzed from 1980–2014 using correlation and sigma convergence analysis.

Henry (2018) analyzed macroeconomic interactions in SSA countries, especially in the franc CFA zone.[3] The investigation used a sample of 25 SSA countries, 14 of which belonged to the CFA zone, five belonged to

---

[2] CAEMU: Central African Economic and Monetary Union; WAMZ: West African Monetary Zone.

[3] The CFA zone is unique in that it is the only monetary union that uses a common currency that is itself pegged to another one, subjecting its members to a double constraint regarding their monetary policy. The currency is not only being constrained by the common policy determined by their common central bank (respectively, the BCEAO— Banque Centrale des Etats de l'Afrique de l'Ouest—for the West and the BEAC— Banque des Etats de l'Afrique Centrale—for the Central region) but they are also required to align their common monetary policy to that of the Eurozone (Henry, 2018).

the Economic Community of Central African States (ECCAS) but not to the CFA zone, and six belonged to WAMZ. We examine the findings between the CFA zone and the non-CFA zone. The study examined how monetary policy constraints, specifically nominal exchange rate devaluation, affect trade, competitiveness, and growth level of commodity-dependent economies using a Panel Vector Auto-Regressive model with four key macroeconomic variables: growth, current account balance, real effective exchange rate, foreign direct investment, and commodity terms of trade as an exogenous variable.

Amaefule's (2019) study was different from the above studies in that it did not analyze changes in competitiveness. Rather the study examined the impact of capital movement inward on the internal competitiveness (productivity proxy by RGDP) and external competitiveness (proxy by trade percentage of GDP and trade robustness as openness) of WAMZ from 1970 to 2017. Following the literature, the proxies arose from the conceptualization of competitiveness as the capacity to expand domestic output and improve the market share of locally produced goods in the global market ceteris paribus. Therefore, the following explanatory variables were used in each of the equations: Foreign Direct Investment (FDI) Inflow, Official Development Assistance (ODA) Inflow, loans from International Bank for Reconstruction and Development (IBRD), and population. In addition, the study employed a dynamic heterogeneous panel estimator, Pooled Mean Group (panel ARDL) estimator, in an unbalanced panel study and controlled for seasonal variation in country-specific effect dummy variables.

Empirical Review

Analyzing the two main objectives of competitiveness based on their framework, Ramirez and Tsangarides (2007) showed that WAEMU and CEMAC output per capita in nominal terms did not compare favorably with other groups. The GDP per capita (both in U.S. dollar and PPP adjusted terms), were lower than the other developing country groups. However, since 1994 CFA devaluation, except a marked drop of 1999 due to oil price burst, real GDP growth in the CEMAC averaged about 5 percent per annum. In the WAEMU, real growth was lower and more volatile, with an annual average of about 4 percent. Real growth in both groups exceeded growth in Latin America and OECD. In the CEMAC, growth was also higher than that of emerging Asia and was almost double the SSA average from 2001 to 2006. Despite the improved performances in economic growth in both regions, these have largely failed to translate into a better quality of life and sustainable improvements in living standards.

The analyzed environmental component indicated that productivity compared with trading partners for WAEMU and CEMAC was falling. In addition, while high population growth rates exerted a resource constraint, some labor market conditions, such as labor force participation, showed some promise compared to others. The various real exchange rate measures suggested a loss of competitiveness due to an appreciation of the CFA franc in both WAEMU and CEMAC. However, the cost measure proxy by constructed nominal wage indices showed that nominal wages grew slower than other domestic prices in the majority of the countries in both regions. Examining the macroeconomic performance revealed that export volumes improved in both regions, with the oil sector dominating the CEMAC. In WAEMU, the export growth rate was much lower when compared with CEMAC but more diversified. The foreign direct investment (FDI) was found to be rising in CEMAC and compared favorably with the rest of the SSA but remained unchanged in WAEMU.

The policy component examined using the business environment showed that the profitability of exports improved in the CEMAC owing largely to the rise in oil prices but declined in the later period of the analysis in the WAEMU. Survey-based business environment indicators revealed structural impediments to developing a competitive private sector in both regions. In addition, the World Bank's Worldwide Governance Indicators (WGI) suggested that countries in the two groups tended to rank below average on important dimensions of governance. The dimension of governance included government effectiveness, regulatory quality, the rule of law, and control of corruption, compared to other countries at a similar level of development. Although infrastructure and technology indicators showed some improvements over SSA averages while selected physical capital indicators pointed to improvement, particularly for the CEMAC, the two regions were seriously deficient according to human capital indicators.

Kowalski and Pietrzykowski's (2010) study found that the REER depreciated between 1999 and 2000 in all EMU countries and Greece, implying that the countries' relative price competitiveness in this grouping improved. However, starting from 2001 in the Netherlands and Portugal, and subsequently, in most of the remaining countries, the REER began to grow, reflecting the downward shifts of competitiveness both in relation to third parties and within the EMU. Throughout the period under study, only Germany and Austria reported systematic improvement in competitiveness expressed in REER. Moreover, the analysis of their export of goods and services with 1999 values indicated that Germany and Austria had the greatest increase in their capacity for export, as reflected by their price-cost competitiveness, followed by Luxembourg, Belgium, and the Netherlands.

Similarly, based on cost competitiveness, Collignon's (2013) examination of the competitiveness index showed that Germany increased their competitive advantage the most, from +10 in 2000 to -5 percent in 2008. On the other hand, the Netherlands' index fell from zero in 1999 to -10 percent in 2008, increasing competitiveness. Other countries that improved their competitiveness were Greece (although this was not enough to eliminate the wage overvaluation), Luxembourg, Belgium, and Austria. Concerning loss in competitiveness, Ireland's index rose from an undervaluation close to -30 percent in 2002 to -5 percent in 2007. Finland followed by reducing its competitiveness from -20 to -10 percent. Italy's advantage also declined from -11 percent to -2.5 percent. On the whole, other countries that experienced loss in competitiveness between 1999 and 2008 were France, Portugal, and Spain.

Coudert et al. (2013) showed that exchange rate misalignments had been larger since the monetary union for 8 out of the 11 Euro Area members studied. Also, they pointed out that the increase in misalignments since the currency union was markedly higher in the three peripheral countries (Greece, Ireland, and Portugal) that experienced the sovereign debt crisis in 2010–2011, suggesting that their debt crisis was not only due to their deteriorating public finances (or to a bank crisis in the case of Ireland), but also due to loss of competitiveness. The findings indicated that the core countries: Germany, France, the Netherlands, Austria, Belgium, and Finland gained competitiveness in the early 2000s due to the weakness of the Euro. However, the appreciation of the Euro against third currencies since the mid-2000s resulted in the whole area's loss of competitiveness relative to third countries.

Couharde et al. (2013) found that the movement in the real exchange rate of the CFA zone was influenced by the Euro and exhibited persistence in its adjustment towards equilibrium when the Euro appreciated. The implications are that given wage and price rigidity and the absence of nominal exchange rate adjustment, shifts in the competitiveness of the

CFA Franc zone driven by the fluctuations of the real exchange rate of the Euro are likely to be persistent.

Coulibaly and Gnimassoun's (2013) findings indicated that, among the four areas, WAEMU was more homogeneous than any of the other zones, with a high correlation between competitiveness levels of its members. The member countries showed a high bilateral correlation of their misalignment. The results also suggested that this area could be joined by Ghana, Gambia, and, to a lesser extent, Sierra Leone from the WAMZ area because of a more homogeneous competitiveness level. In addition, the study highlighted interesting similarities between Nigeria's misalignments and those of the CAEMC area, indicating that Nigeria would find it more beneficial to join the CAEMC area than the WAEMU area. The correlation of misalignments between WAEMU and WAMZ was negative but positive with WAMZ_WNGA (WAMZ without Nigeria), implying a different competitiveness level between Nigeria and WAEMU countries. Concerning the formation of the monetary union of ECOWAS, Ghana and Senegal were found to be the best references for the area. They argued that in addition to being institutionally stable and economically relatively strong countries, their misalignments were positively correlated to most ECOWAS member states.

The dynamics of regional misalignments showed similar results to those of correlation analysis. The findings indicated that generally, while their economies' features differ, the WAEMU and CAEMC areas had relatively close misalignments, which highlighted the influence of their common anchor currency. Compared to the CFA zone's monetary unions, the misalignment within the WAMZ area was significantly larger because Nigeria constituted 90% of the misalignment area. Still, without Nigeria, the misalignment was closer to WAEMU. Also, before 1999, especially from 1994 to 1999, the real exchange rate of the CFA zone countries was markedly undervalued due to the effects of the CFA franc devaluation of 1994, while real exchange rates in the WAMZ area exhibited a substantial overvaluation. However, from early 2000, the misalignments of all four regions were undervalued, although there remained significant differences in levels. The synchronization of misalignments' cycles in the latter years was partly explained as emanating from the significant improvement of the regions' terms of trade in the 2000s through increasing commodity prices and better net foreign asset positions in recent years. The improved terms of trade and net foreign asset position led to a more appreciated equilibrium exchange rate. It increased, therefore, the probability of having an undervalued exchange rate.

Razzaghi et al.'s (2018) findings showed no significant negative correlation coefficient of misalignment among OIC regions. The results showed undervalued real effective exchange rates in most OIC regions within the last decade, implying improved economic competitiveness in these regions. In addition, the OIC regions experienced different but co-moved and converged misalignment. The results of sigma convergence analysis indicated that the misalignments in the whole set of OIC regions were not persistent, and the standard deviations of exchange rate misalignments had reduced over the last decade on average for all the regions. The authors interpreted this to mean that the competitiveness differentials have diminished through OIC regions, especially among various regions within the last decade.

Henry (2018) found that foreign investment in the CFA zone did not generate strong and persistent effects on growth as observed in the other countries outside the zone and suggested that the CFA economies should monitor the inflow of foreign investment as well as promote domestic investment into sectors contributing to long-term growth to spur diversification of their export structure. The negative effect of the real exchange rate on growth was much stronger in the CFA zone than in other zones. Also, the results indicated that the REER's appreciation positively impacted the current account balance in the CFA zone, unlike what was obtained in the member countries of other zones, implying that the Marshall–Lerner condition was not verified in the CFA sample. Therefore, according to the author, the competitiveness of CFA members was not impacted by the monetary constraint of not being able to stimulate exports through the nominal exchange rate tool, as opposed to other monetary zone members; rather, the obstacle to competitiveness in this zone lied in the dependence on raw commodities for which CFA countries acted as price takers. Furthermore, for countries outside the CFA monetary zone, FDI created positive spillover effects that improved trade balance with a persistent effect over a few years. This was not the case for the CFA countries as investment had an insignificant negative effect on the current account balance.

Amaefule (2019) findings showed that in the long run, while ODA inflows (although insignificant) and IBRD inflows result in a decline in internal competitiveness (productivity) and external competitiveness (in terms of trade robustness) in WAMZ, FDI indicated a positive and significant effect on internal and external competitiveness (on both trade volume and trade robustness). IBRD, however, improved trade as a percentage of GDP. Only ODA positively and significantly affected productivity and trade volume in the short run. Of note is that the speed of adjustment, although negative, was insignificant in all the three equations estimated.

METHODOLOGY AND DATA

One main approach to analyzing competitiveness is comparing composite and uniform performance measures (Kowalski & Pietrzykowski, 2010). These measures point to economies' competitiveness levels and shifts. For this study, the measures were analyzed by comparing how the countries of the CFA monetary zone fared relative to those of the European Monetary Union (EMU), whose currency, the Euro, was the anchor currency of the CFA franc. Monetary Union was expected to provide a huge market for its members, and the use of common currency removed the barrier to cross-border trade and investment, so a reduction in transaction costs, absence of currency risk, greater monetary stability and predictability, and growth of macroeconomic credibility would result into lower market interest rates in some countries. Hence, the measures adopted for this study included real effective exchange rate (REER), exports-GDP ratio, exports- imports ratio, and technological development (proxy by permanent income). In addition, all measures were analyzed relative to 1999 (base year) when the Euro was launched and European Monetary Union was created. This helped evaluate the competitiveness before and after the formation of the European Monetary Union.

For the construction of the index for technological development, nominal GDPs were regressed against time and decomposed into actual, residual, and fitted components. The fitted component, which approximated permanent income, was the proxy for technological development.[4]

Data on REER were sourced from the International Financial Statistics (IFS) online, while exports, imports, exports to GDP, and nominal GDP data were from the World Development Indicator database. The exports and imports values were in constant U.S. dollars. It is helpful to point out that for some measures, due to data unavailability, some countries (in the CFA zone especially) were dropped from the analysis.[5]

---

[4](Ogun, 2014).
[5]Ten countries were, however, sampled for the EMU. These were Austria, Belgium, France, Germany, Greece, Ireland, Italy, the Netherlands, Portugal, and Spain.

COMPARATIVE EVALUATION OF PERFORMANCES OF MONETARY UNIONS

Brief Background on the CFA Monetary Zone and the European Monetary Union

Eleven E.U. member states adopted the Euro as a single currency on January 1, 1999, following the establishment of the European Central Bank on June 1, 1998, after a long process of political and economic integration: Austria, Belgium, Finland, France, Germany, Ireland, Italy, Luxembourg, Netherlands, Portugal, and Spain. Subsequently, the following countries joined in the relevant dates: Greece, 2001; Slovenia, 2007; Cyprus and Malta, 2008; Slovakia, 2009; Estonia, 2011; Latvia, 2014 and Lithuania, 2015. Amongst others, price stability was an expected benefit of the Euro. Notably, one early argument for the Euro was the expectation of competitive pressure through, for example, more transparency about prices and the elimination of the possibility to devalue the exchange rate (Beetsma & Giuliodori, 2010).

Likewise, the CFA zone was created in 1945 as a monetary arrangement between former French colonies and France, ensuring monetary and financial stability for its members, with its currency CFA franc anchored against the French franc. However, with the formation of the European Monetary Union in 1999 to which France is a member, the CFA franc was then pegged to the Euro with the French Treasury providing unlimited guarantee for the convertibility of the CFA franc into Euro. As a result of this pegging, the CFA franc is much more influenced by the economic realities within the euro area than those within the franc zone (Nubukpo, 2015). The CFA zone is made up of two independent monetary blocks: the West African Economic and Monetary Union (WAEMU) and the Central African Economic and Monetary Union (CAEMU).[6]

Analysis and Discussion

Real Effective Exchange Rate (REER) The real effective exchange rate has been a standard measure of international competitiveness. It measures

---

[6]WAEMU is made up of eight (8) countries: Benin, Burkina Faso, Cote d'Ivoire, Guinea Bissau, Mali, Niger, Senegal and Togo while the six (6) members of CAEMU are Cameroon, Chad, Republic of Congo, the Central African Republic, Equatorial Guinea and Gabon.

the price competitiveness of world economies. For this study, a rise in the real effective exchange rate signifies a loss in competitiveness. The analysis of the trend of REER in Fig. 14.1a showed an initial gain in competitiveness for the EMU members; however, from 2001, the REER began to rise and peaked in 2008/2009, coinciding with the global financial crisis. The trend suggested more synchronized exchange rate behavior than before 1999. With the 1999 level set at 100, Ireland lost the most in competitiveness with a REER of 132.2% followed by Spain with 115% in 2008. Only Germany, France, and Austria maintained high relative competitiveness following the establishment of the European Monetary Union with low REERs. They gained the most competitiveness among the ten countries assessed compared to the pre-EMU period. Ireland, Spain, and Portugal experienced worsening competitiveness compared to the pre-EMU period, although their competitiveness improved in 2009. Ireland was the worst hit as its competitive price gains were reversed immediately after 1999. In comparison to 1999, the economies that were more competitive in 2018, in terms of REER, were Germany, 90.75%, France, 93.06%, Italy, 98.81%, and Greece, 99.34%.

For the WAEMU members with available REER data, in Fig. 14.1b, the devaluation of the CFA franc in 1994 improved their competitiveness. However, between 1994 and 1998, there was an average rise in their REERs. However, like the EMU members, the WAEMU members experienced rapid deterioration of their competitive strength from 2000, a year earlier than their counterparts in EMU, which also climaxed during the global financial crisis with the REERs of Cote d'Ivoire and Togo standing at 117.31% and 115.56%, respectively. Nevertheless, these REERs were a little higher than the 1999 values. In 2018, their REERs were 106.44 and 103.37%, respectively.

Figure 14.1c reflects the trend in the REERs of CAEMU countries. Like the WAEMU countries, the CAEMU members gained competitiveness following the devaluation of the CFA currency in 1994, but the REERs rose after that. Although competitiveness was restored in 1999 for similar reasons as the previous two unions, only Gabon and Cameroon have maintained their price competitiveness since then while the Central African Republic and Equatorial Guinea kept declining. In 2018, the REERs of Gabon and Cameroon were 100.83% and 98.51%, respectively, relative to 1999, while those of the Central African Republic and Equatorial Guinea stood at 141.96% 163.54%, respectively.

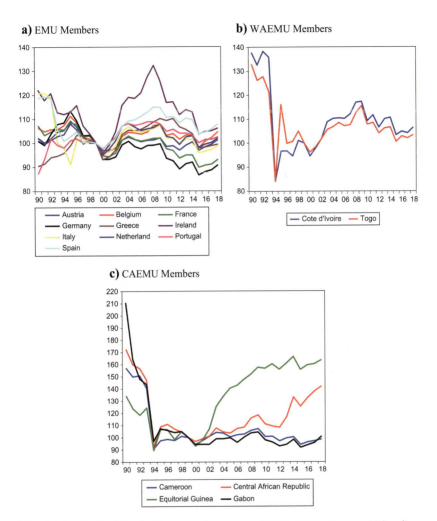

Fig. 14.1 (**a, b, c**) Real effective exchange rate (1999=100). (Source: IFS online database)

Exports of Goods and Services (% of GDP) Assessing the effects of the REER trend on export competitiveness is the focus of this section and the next. With the base year of 1999 = 100, for the EMU members in Fig. 14.2a, the exports of goods and services as a percent of GDP showed a positive trend from the pre-EMU period and a marked dip in 2009. The exception was Ireland that posted a decline in its export from 2003 to 2008. From 2001, Germany and Austria led on improved exports growth, which also reflected their price competitiveness during this period until 2011 when Austria began losing its competitive price edge while Greece and Portugal were gaining. However, the export competitiveness of France did not match its price competitiveness as it became the least competitive in 2010. In 2018, France only gained 20.18% over the 1999 exports value compared with Portugal's gain of 164.34%, Germany's 75.88%, and Greece's 187.62%. Relative to GDP, the exports of Greece and Portugal rose sharply after the global financial crisis. The figure also confirmed that Ireland's competitiveness which was improving before 1999, suffered. From 2003 until 2009, it lost its competitive edge and was the least competitive due to rising REER. Compared with the EMU member states, the WAEMU members in Fig. 14.2b, generally did not show any consistent and appreciable growth of exports-GDP ratio post-1999. The exception to this was Burkina Faso from 2009. Relative to 1999, its exports ratio rose remarkably from 133% in 2009 to 202% in 2010 and 323% in 2018. In relation to 1999, Benin's average exports to GDP ratio was 114% from 1994–1998 following the devaluation of the CFA franc but fell to an average of 87.77% from 2000–2012 before rising to an average of 120% between 2013 and 2018. It performed far better in 2018, with a value of 149.08%.

In contrast, Cote d'Ivoire had an improving export competitiveness post-1999 compared to pre- 1999 until 2013, when its exports-GDP started declining. Its value was 70.27% in 2018 compared to 97.63% in 1998, suggesting a much worse scenario than before Euro. Guinea Bissau, which witnessed growth in exports in the run-up to 1999, also witnessed a decline in its exports as a percent of GDP after the reference year but recovered in 2012.

Figure 14.2c showed that the competitiveness of the exports of CAEMU countries was dissimilar to the EMU members but comparable to the WAEMU members. The movement showed a wave- like pattern. A closer look reveals that only the Republic of Congo and Cameroon improved their export-GDP ratio after 1999. Although their performances declined from 2013, that of the Republic of Congo rose again in 2017. From 2016, Cameroon's ratio fell below the 1999 level of 96.33%, and remained so till 2018, while Congo rose from 130% in 201 to 136.8% in

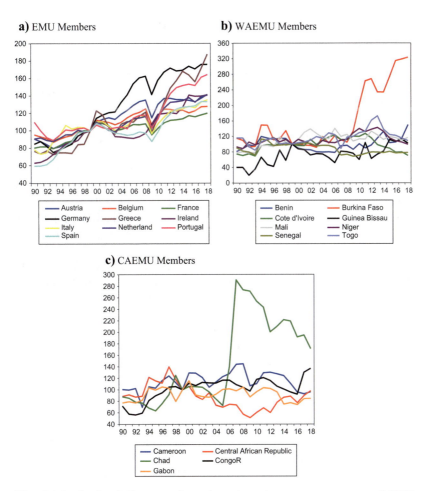

Fig. 14.2 (**a, b, c**) Exports of goods and services as a percentage of GDP (1999=100). (Source: WDI database)

2018. Another country that became more competitive post-1999 was Chad, although, from 2006, its performance had been on the decline.

Export-Import Ratio (%) The ratio of exports to imports is used to examine the competitive ability of an economy and the capacity of its firms to compete locally and internationally and could signal REER (dis) equilibrium (Kowalski & Pietrzykowski, 2010). Figure 14.3a is the exports-imports ratio of EMU members. It again shows the high competitiveness of Germany, which is much improved after the establishment of the monetary union. Austria also confirmed an improvement in competitiveness post-1999. Spain's competitive ability slowed after 2000 and only exhibited a high and persistent growth from 2008. Greece also experienced a fluctuating and declining competitiveness until 2010 when its competitiveness exceeded the 1999 level and had risen to 140.5% of the 1999 level. Portugal's exports-imports ratio, which declined before the EMU was established, picked up after its establishment and rose rapidly to 139% in 2012. Ireland's value was almost level with 1999 and fell below it between 2004 and 2009 before rising, reflecting its high REER. Whereas Belgium and the Netherlands did not improve appreciably post-1999 in this measure, France's exports-imports ratio was on a steady decline.

Figure 14.3b is the WAEMU members' exports-imports ratio. As could be observed, the 1994 devaluation improved the competitiveness of WAEMU countries; however, the gain was short-lived. Though other countries gained competitiveness in the early years of the formation of the EMU, Senegal's competitiveness was on a free fall. At the same time, Burkina Faso stopped its slide in competitiveness and started to rise in 2006 even with a fluctuating performance. Mali's exports- imports ratio rose to its highest level of 153.3% in 1999 in 2002 but declined. Similarly, Togo improved tremendously to record a gain of 186.1% in competitiveness over the 1999 level in 2012 before suffering a sharp loss in its competitive ability to remain below the 1999 level. Since 2016, Benin has performed better than the 1999 level exceeding the reference level by 25.5% in 2018. Again, similar to the WAEMU members, the CAEMU countries in Fig. 14.3a improved in 1994 but their performances had nose-dived below the 1999 level, except in year 2000 when the ratio was 106% for Gabon.

TECHNOLOGICAL DEVELOPMENT

The index of technological development was compared for the three monetary unions using permanent income as a proxy. This is used to assess the technological competitiveness of the countries in the monetary unions. Figure 14.4a captured the technological development of EMU members. Ireland was the smallest economy among the sampled countries and stood

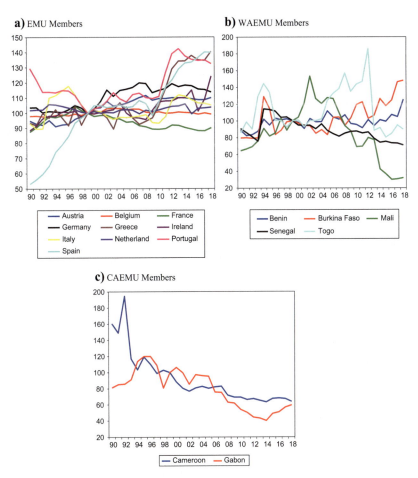

Fig. 14.3 (**a, b, c**) Exports-import ratio (1999=100). (Source: Computed from WDI database)

out quite remarkably under this measure of competitiveness. Its nominal GDP was 98.7 billion in 1999, but its development index in 2018 was 277.1% of the 1999 value. It developed the most rapidly in pre- and post-1999. Spain was next to Ireland. Germany, the biggest economy among the group, with a nominal GDP of €2194 billion in 1999, was among the least developed. Likewise, Italy performing very well before establishing the European Monetary Union, had the worst competitiveness after its establishment. It is the third-largest economy in the EMU after Germany and France. France was the most competitive among the three. In 2018, Germany, France, and Italy's technological development indexes were 150%, 171.8%, and 158% in 1999, respectively.

Figure 14.4b shows the technological development of WAEMU countries. It suggested that WAEMU countries improved more than the EMU

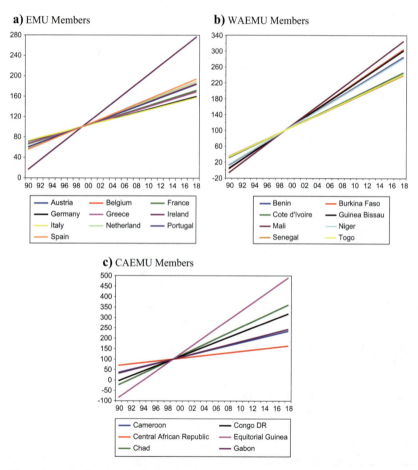

Fig. 14.4 (a, b, c) Index of technological development (1999=100). (Source: Computed from WDI database)

members. It reveals different development clusters among the members, with Mali standing out. Mali improved the most relative to the 1999 level and compared with the years before the formation of the European Monetary Union. It is the third-largest economy in the Union after Cote d'Ivoire and Senegal. In 2018, its technological development index was 326% that of 1999 level. Following Mali were Burkina Faso and Guinea Bissau with 304.8% and 301.8% of 1999 level. Senegal, Togo, and Cote d'Ivoire's performances were the worst compared to the pre-1999 period.

Similar to the previous two unions, Fig. 14.4c indicated that relative to their 1999 levels, CAEMU countries with lower technological development indexes improved more than others. Equatorial Guinean, for instance, improved its technological competitiveness the most from its pre-1999 level and followed by Chad, while the Central African Republic was the least competitive after 1999, followed by Cameroon and Gabon. CAEMU members also improved their competitiveness technologically more than the EMU members relative to 1999.

Conclusion

This study had examined the competitiveness of the European Monetary Union (EMU), and the CFA zone, made up of two monetary unions: the West African Economic and Monetary Union (WAEMU) and Central African Economic and Monetary Union (CAEMU). However, with the unavailability of aggregated data for the monetary unions under the CFA zone and the limitation of data for some countries, aggregation at the union level would be misleading. Hence, the analysis was based on the country level.

Using a comparative method based on the country level, all the measures were examined relative to 1999 when the European Monetary Union was formed. The analysis was conducted in terms of pre- and post-1999. The finding suggested that the competitiveness levels of the countries in the different unions since the establishment of the European Monetary Union depended on the measure used. Based on the trend of REER, the EMU and WAEMU members followed a similar pattern with initial gain in competitiveness short-lived. This gain was followed by a loss of competitiveness that peaked at the global financial crisis. However, from 2015, the countries in both unions started losing competitiveness once more. This pattern was less pronounced for the CAEMU member states. Using the Exports of goods and services as a percentage of GDP, the EMU members showed a more general positive trend than the other two unions after adopting the Euro in 1999, ignoring the peculiarity of 2009. Their entry into a monetary union seemed to have improved their export-GDP ratio. However, the WAEMU economies are generally more turbulent than the EMU members in the export-imports ratio. As a result, the gains in competitiveness were rapidly eroded. For the CAEMU countries, there was a persistent loss of competitiveness. The permanent income used to proxy index of technological development suggested that the West African Economic and Monetary Union (WAEMU) and Central African Economic and Monetary Union (CAEMU) had a more rapid technological development than their counterparts in the European Monetary Union (EMU)—an outcome that in a way seemed to fit the dictate of the conditional convergence principle.

Individually, some countries were found to have gained more competitiveness after 1999 than others. Some countries took advantage of entry into the monetary union to improve their economy, while some suffered more. For instance, in the EMU Germany became more competitive after 1999 than before EMU; likewise, Austria. For the CFA monetary zone, Burkina Faso, Togo, and Mali in the WAEMU while Cameroon, Chad, and the Republic of Congo in CAEMU performed better after post-1999 the export-GDP ratio.

References

Amaefule, C. (2019). Competitiveness, capital movement inward, and eco economic and monetary union in WAMZ. *International Journal of Research and Scientific Innovation*, 6(12), 254–262.

Bayoumi, T., Appendino, M., Barkema, J., & Cerdeiro, D. A. (2018). *Measuring competitiveness in a world of global value chains.* IMF Working Papers 18/229. International Monetary Fund, Washington, DC.

Beetsma, R., & Giuliodori, M. (2010). The macroeconomic costs and benefits of the EMU and other monetary U–Ions: An overview of recent research. *Journal of Economic Literature*, 48(3), 603–641.

Cid, F. B. (2013). Stability and competitiveness in the european monetary union. *Ekonomiaz, Revista vasca de economia*, 82(01), 81–106.

Cid, F. B. (2016). The European imbalances: Competitiveness and economic policy in a non- optimal monetary union and a global recession. *Cuadernos Económicos de Ice*, (91), 27–54.

Cockburn, J., Siggel, E., Coulibaly, M., & Vézina, S. (1999). Measuring competitiveness and its sources: The case of Mali's manufacturing sector. *Canadian*

Journal of Development Studies / Revue canadienne d'études du développement, 20(3), 491–519.
Collignon, S. (2013). Macroeconomic imbalances and competitiveness in the Euro area. *Transfer, 19*(1), 63–87.
Coudert, V., Couharde, C. & Mignon, V. (2013). On currency misalignments within the euro area. *Review of International Economics, 21*(1), 35–48.
Couharde, C., Coulibaly, I., & Damette, O. (2013). Anchor currency and real exchange rate dynamics in the CFA franc zone. *Economic Modelling, 33*(3), 722–732.
Coulibaly, I., & Gnimassoun, B. (2013). Optimality of a monetary union: New evidence from exchange rate misalignments in West Africa. *Economic Modelling, 32*(3), 463–482.
Hallwirth, V. (2015). *Monitoring competitiveness in the European economic and monetary union*. IMK Study, No. 44, Hans-Böckler-Stiftung, Institut für Makroökonomie und Konjunkturforschung (IMK), Düsseldorf.
Henry, A. (2018). Monetary union, competitiveness and raw commodity dependence: Insights from Africa. *Comparative Economic Studies*. https://doi.org/10.1057/s41294-018-0080-6
Kenen, P. B. (1969). The optimum currency area: An eclectic view. In R. A. Mundell & A. K. Swoboda (Eds.), *Monetary problems of the international economy*. University of Chicago Press.
Ketels, C. (2016). Review of competitiveness frameworks. In *An analysis conducted for the Irish National Competitiveness Council*. National Competitiveness Council.
Ketels, C., & Porter, M. E. (2018). *Towards a new approach for upgrading Europe's competitiveness*. Harvard Business School Working Paper 19–033.
Kowalski, T., & Pietrzykowski, M. (2010). *The economic and monetary union vs. shifts in competitiveness of member states*. MPRA Paper No. 33995.
Kunroo, M. H. (2016). Theory of optimum currency areas: A literature survey. *Review of Market Integration, 7*(2), 1–30.
Lane, P. R. (2006). The real effects of european monetary union. *Journal of Economic Perspectives, 20*(4), 47–66.
McKinnon, R. I. (1963). Optimum currency areas. *The American Economic Review, 53*(4), 717–725.
Mongelli, F. P., & Wyplosz, C. (2008). *The Euro at ten – Unfulfilled threats and unexpected challenges*. A Paper Presented at the Fifth ECB Central Banking Conference, 13–14 November, Frankfurt am Main.
Mundell, R. A. (1961). A theory of optimum currency areas. *The American Economic Review, 51*(4), 657–665.
Nubukpo, N. (2015). The CFA franc: An obstacle to the emergence of African economies? *L'Économie Politique, 68*(4), 71–79.

OECD. (1992). *Technology and the economy: The key relationships.* Organization for Economic Cooperation and Development.

Ogun, O. (2014). Modeling Africa's economic growth. *Journal of Economics and Economic Education Research, 15*(2), 143–163.

Porter, M. E., Ketels, C., & Delgado, M. (2007). The microeconomic foundations of prosperity: Findings from the business competitiveness index. *Global Competitiveness Index 2007–2008,* 51–81.

Ramirez, G., & Tsangarides, C. G. (2007). *Competitiveness in the CFA Franc zone.* IMF Working Papers 18/212. International Monetary Fund, Washington, DC.

Razzaghi, S., Salmani, B., & Kazerooni, A. (2018). Feasibility of a monetary union in Islamic regions of OIC countries: New evidence from competitiveness differentials. *International Journal of Economics, Management and Accounting, 26*(1), 229–245.

Schwab, K. (2017). *Global competitiveness index 2017–2018.* World Economic Forum.

Sinn, H.-W. (2014a). Austerity, growth and inflation: Remarks on the Eurozone's unresolved competitiveness problem. *The World Economy.* https://doi.org/10.1111/twec.12130

Sinn, H.-W. (2014b). *The Euro Trap. On bursting bubbles, budgets, and beliefs.* Oxford University Press.

Siudek, T., & Zawojska, A. (2014). Competitiveness in the economic concepts, theories and empirical research. *Oeconomia, 13*(1), 91–108.

WEF. (2014). *The Europe 2020 competitiveness report: Building a more competitive Europe.* World Economic Forum.

CHAPTER 15

Financial Institutions Versus Trade and Infrastructural Development in Africa

Bruno L. Yawe, J. Ddumba-Ssentamu, Yusuf Kiwala, and Ibrahim Mukisa

Introduction

The importance of short-term financing of international trade, known as trade finance, is explicitly recognized in the Addis Ababa Action Agenda as an essential means of implementing the Sustainable Development Goals (SDGs). The World Trade Organization (2016) has noted that the availability of finance is essential for a healthy trading system. Nevertheless, there are significant gaps in its provision, and therefore many companies cannot access the financial tools they need. As a consequence of inadequate trade finance, opportunities for growth and development are missed; businesses are deprived of a vital ingredient they need to trade and expand. The post-2015 development agenda "Transforming Our World: The 2030 Agenda for Sustainable Development" outlines 17 Sustainable

---

B. L. Yawe (✉) • J. Ddumba-Ssentamu • I. Mukisa
School of Economics, Makerere University, Kampala, Uganda

Y. Kiwala
School of Business, Makerere University, Kampala, Uganda

© The Author(s), under exclusive license to Springer Nature Switzerland AG 2022
A. A. Amin et al. (eds.), *Monetary and Financial Systems in Africa*,
https://doi.org/10.1007/978-3-030-96225-8_15

Development Goals, each with its respective targets and indicators and an implementation plan. Sustainable Development Goal 9 seeks to build resilient infrastructure, promote inclusive and sustainable industrialization, and foster innovation. Technological progress helps address significant global challenges of unemployment and attaining higher levels of energy efficiency. For instance, the internet has enabled a more interconnected and prosperous world. The more connected the world gets, the more all could benefit from the wisdom and contributions of people everywhere on the planet. The more investment in innovation and **infrastructure**, the better off we will all be. Bridging the digital divide, promoting sustainable industries, and investing in scientific research and innovation are important ways to facilitate sustainable development. Infrastructure is an explicit goal and an implicit means to implement and achieve all the other SDGs.

This chapter covers trade finance and the role of financial institutions in infrastructural development in Africa contains six sections and unfolds as follows: financing of international trade; status of trade finance in Africa and other challenges to trade financial institutions and infrastructural development in Africa; models for financing infrastructure; status of financing infrastructure development in Africa; as well as conclusion and policy implications.

Financing of International Trade

Financial institutions facilitate trade through trade finance, which facilitates both national and international trade. LlewellynConsulting (2016) defines trade finance generally as financial products that are explicitly linked to underlying international trade transactions (whether exports or imports), a significant portion of which is provided by banks. Thus, trade finance is often described as a lubricant of trade. These facilities usually have short-term maturity of six months or less. About 80 percent of global trade is currently supported by financing or credit insurance.[1]

The availability of credit or payment guarantees are critical for trade, especially considering that cash advances cover only a small part of international trade. Importers generally wish to verify the physical integrity of merchandise on arrival before they pay, while exporters would instead be paid upon shipment. Available credit or a payment guarantee is required to bridge the gap between the interests of exporters and the importers.

[1] https://www.wto.org/english/res_e/booksp_e/tradefinsme_e.pdf

Trade finance serves this purpose, providing the needed credit, guarantees of payment, and insurance for the merchandise or service on terms satisfactory to both the exporter and the importer. Trade finance thus mitigates the risk of cashless trade transactions and is often described as a lubricant of trade (World Trade Organization, 2016).

However, most trade credit, payment guarantees, and insurance are short-term, with a standard maturity of 90 days. Nonetheless, trade credit can be extended beyond these standard periods for aircraft, capital equipment, and other such goods requiring longer production and delivery cycles. There are two primary forms of trade finance: bank-intermediated finance and inter-company credit or inter-firm credit.

Myriad bank-intermediated trade finance products are employed to reduce risks related to international payments between importers and exporters (Bank for International Settlements, 2014). These include Letters of credit; performance guarantees or performance standby L/Cs; Documentary collections; Pre-export finance; Supplier credit; Receivables discounting; Import and export loans; and Supply chain finance (SCF).

Trade finance obtained through bank intermediation performs two vital roles: providing for working capital to fund international trade transactions and providing means to reduce payment risk. The principal alternative to bank-intermediated products is inter-firm trade credit. Firms' ability to directly extend credit is supported by possibilities to discount their receivables and the availability of financing not directly tied to trade transactions. In addition, the possibility is to mitigate payment risk by purchasing trade credit insurance (Bank for International Settlements, 2014).

Developing countries widely use letters of credit in commodity trading. They are typically bank written payment guarantees due from the buyer (the importer, company A) to the seller (the exporter, company B) or its bank (see Fig. 15.1). The letter of credit specifies the conditions of payment, including the obligations of the seller, such as delivery conditions, documents to be submitted, and those of the buyer, notably the guarantee that the bank will pay the outstanding amount if the buyer fails to do so (World Trade Organization, 2016). Most letters of credit are governed by Uniform Customs and Practice for Documentary Credits, promulgated by the International Chamber of Commerce. They are routinely used by importing and exporting companies when large purchases are involved and alleviate the buyer's burden to pay a deposit before delivery. Thus, a letter of credit substitutes the creditworthiness of a bank for the buyer's creditworthiness.

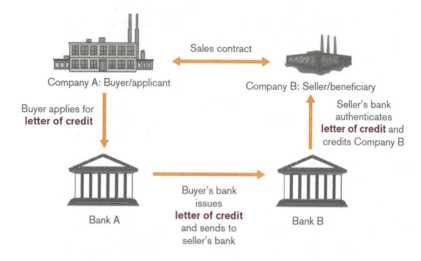

Fig. 15.1 Letters of credit. (Source: World Trade Organization (2016))

It is noteworthy that there are other types of bank-intermediated trade finance apart from letters of credit. For example, outright lending by banks can involve pre-shipment export finance either in the form of working capital for the exporter to purchase the raw material needed for subsequent manufacturing of final goods or on a with-recourse basis against a confirmed export order from the buyer or a letter of credit.

Letters of credit (L/C) are among the most common bank-intermediated trade finance instruments. Typically they have short-term tenors (less than 90 days). An *import L/C* is a commitment by a bank on behalf of the importer that the exporter will be paid, provided that the terms and conditions stated in the L/C are met, as verified through the presentation of all required documents. The importer pays his bank a fee to render this service, while the goods transacted serve as the bank's collateral. The exporter, in turn, may engage her bank to provide an *export confirmed L/C*, which would guarantee the payment from the importer's bank. L/Cs may be funded or unfunded depending on the point within the trade transaction cycle (Bank for International Settlements, 2014).

Inter-firm trade credit or the delayed payment a supplier allows its downstream customer on a product sale. Delivering inputs to a firm may sometimes not come with immediate payments, depending on whether the supplier requires the buyer to prepay or allows delayed payment. A short-term delay in payments is a widely observed form of inter-firm credit. The delayed payments granted are referred to as trade credit (Daripa & Nilsen, 2011). Much of inter-firm credit is interest-free and so too are pure cash prepayments. In the case of trade credit, "net" terms are in widespread use. The most frequently used terms are "net 30," requiring the buyer to repay within 30 days, again at zero interest cost to the buyer. Trade credit has an implicit interest cost for the buyer only when the seller sets up a discount for early repayment, and the buyer does not repay within the discount period (ibid.).

Status of Trade Finance in Africa and Other Challenges to Trade

For the period 2015–2013, the average monetary value of trade in Africa stood at US$ 760 billion per year, which represents 29% of the continent's Gross Domestic Product. Although trade is an essential growth driver, Africa appears to be missing out. Its share of global trade is estimated at only 3%, and compared to other regions, Africa's intra-regional share of trade is much lower (Africa: 15%, European Union: 63%, North America: 50%, and Asia: 52%). Increased intra-African trade can contribute to developing cross-border infrastructure, catalyzing intra-regional investment, and reducing the constraints of unfavorable boundaries for landlocked countries. Nevertheless, Africa is yet to sufficiently address existing trade constraints and fully secure the growth-enhancing benefits of trade. One of the constraints for expanding trade within Africa and with the rest of the world is a trade finance gap estimated at US$ 82 billion in 2019. Filling this gap means addressing the obstacles African banks face in expanding access to trade finance. It is worth noting that the lack of trade finance is a significant non-tariff barrier to trade and limits the full trade potential of the African Continental Free Trade Area and the Tripartite Free Trade Area (Zeidy, 2020).

The onset and rapid spread of the COVID-19 pandemic pose serious public health and economic threat across the global economy. In response, many African countries, like the rest of the world, have adopted measures to slow down the spread of the virus. These have curbed physical interactions, closed borders, and shut businesses. However, while the measures are meant to save lives and limit the impact of the pandemic on the already weak public health infrastructure, they are also expected to dampen the region's GDP growth. As a result, current projections of the potential impact of Covid-19 reveal economic growth falling -3.4% to -1.7% in 2020, and hence that Africa could experience its first recession in 25 years. While the disruptions to domestic economic activities due to the pandemic containment measures would explain a large part of that decline, the pandemic's potential risks to African trade and the trade finance that underpins it could also amplify the effects (Nyantakyi & Drammeh, 2020). The risks to trade stem from two fronts. First, close to half of Africa's merchandise trade is with economies and regions highly impacted by the pandemic, including China, the EU, and the USA (see Fig. 15.2). Second, commodity trade has been particularly affected, which has left some of the region's leading economies vulnerable.

Nyantakyi and Drammeh (2020) have observed that to mitigate the potential impact of COVID- 19 on African trade and keep market access channels open, an uninterrupted supply of trade finance by banks is vital. Nevertheless, the measures governments have likely adopted to fight the pandemic may also affect firms' ability to obtain trade finance when they need it the most. In the short term, the low digitization rate of trade finance transactions could slow down approval rates and decrease trade finance supply during the pandemic. In addition, the pandemic may expose one of Africa's most significant weaknesses in trade finance supply—non-digitalization and hence the high level of dependence on manual transaction processes. As Fig. 15.3 shows, the African region has been slow to adopt digital and electronic business processes, including trade finance, relative to the rest of the world.

The adoption of digital solutions to trade finance transactions could reduce the time and monetary costs of document processing by banks and increase the supply of trade finance. Figure 15.4 shows a positive correlation between the average level of trade finance (funded and unfunded) and the business digital adoption index.

Additionally, the pandemic is expected to increase the trade finance gap by limiting the foreign exchange available for the financing of African trade. The trade finance gap in Africa in 2019 was estimated at USD 82 billion. If the pandemic persists, it could worsen the shortfall in liquidity experienced by banks engaged in trade finance in Africa. In regular times, close to 20% of African- based banks cite inadequate foreign exchange liquidity as a critical barrier to increasing trade finance supply (see Fig. 15.5). Moreover, in terms of value, more than half of world trade is

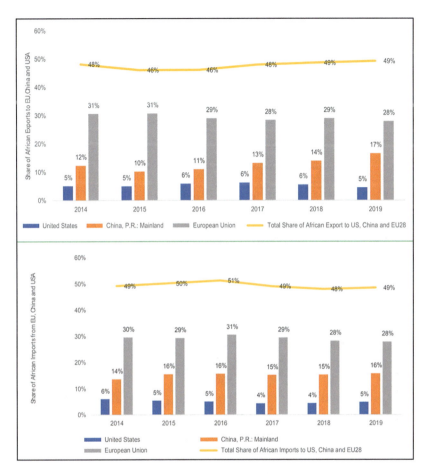

Fig. 15.2 Share of African trade (exports and imports) to China, European Union, and United States. (Source: Nyantakyi and Drammeh (2020))

denominated in US dollars, and 80% of letters of credit are priced in US dollars. Therefore, foreign exchange liquidity shortages in the region could encourage global banks to reduce correspondent banking lines for African domestic banks. This could potentially restrict the dollar liquidity available to firms for trade, increase rejection rates for trade finance, and increase the size of the trade finance gap in Africa above the USD 82 billion recorded in 2019 (Nyantakyi & Drammeh, 2020).

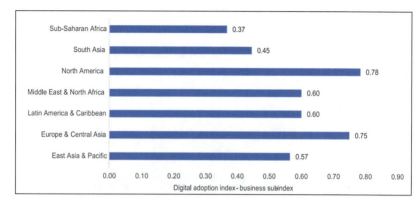

Fig. 15.3 Digital adoption—Business sub-index (DIA) by region. (Source: Nyantakyi and Drammeh (2020))

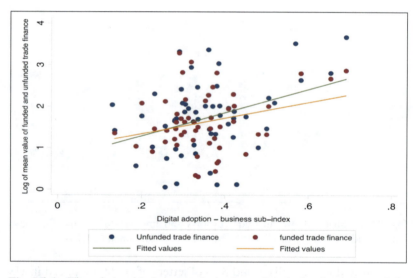

Fig. 15.4 The relationship between the business digital adoption index and the average values of funded and unfunded trade finance assets in Africa (2014 and 2016). (Source: Nyantakyi and Drammeh (2020))

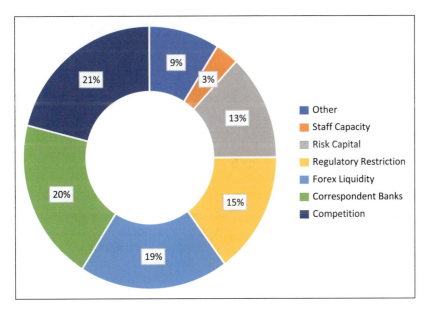

Fig. 15.5 Constraints to trade finance supply in Africa. (Source: Nyantakyi and Drammeh (2020))

Financial Institutions and Infrastructural Development in Africa

The stock and the quality of infrastructure are a principal input into growth and development in all countries, especially in emerging and developing countries. More infrastructure can support aggregate demand during the construction phase and complement other inputs over the long term by raising their productive capacity. Consequently, many countries have turned their attention to public investment in infrastructure while encouraging the participation of the private sector. Thus, there is a growing and renewed interest in infrastructure financing (Cerra et al., 2017).

Infrastructure is characterized by two attributes, namely, "capitalness" and "publicness" (Palei, 2015). Table 15.1 classifies the degree of the capital intensity of infrastructure and social significance.

Infrastructure may be capital-intensive facilities that are not of public interest even though the public extensively uses them. To Economists, such objects are physical infrastructure or infrastructure capital. In

Table 15.1 Classification of the degree of the capital intensity of infrastructure and public works

		Capital High level	Low level
Publicity	High level	Roads, highways, airports, ports, electricity, water and sewerage, telecommunications	Schools, hospitals, parks, courts, museums, theatres, libraries, universities, hospitals
	Low level	Industrial infrastructure	Fountains and statues

Source: Palei (2015)

scientific literature, the role of infrastructure is evaluated by the services provided by the physical infrastructure assets. Infrastructure services, such as energy, transport, telecommunications, water, sanitation, and safe waste disposal, are fundamental to various household activities and economic production. Infrastructure is generally a long-term, spatially bound, a capital-intensive asset with a long life cycle. The return on such investment takes so long that this long turnaround period is often associated with a "market failure" (a situation in which the market system crashes, and economic efficiency is not achieved) (ibid).

Infrastructure has often been viewed as facilitating economic growth, considering it could increase productivity, motivate business activity by reducing transport and production costs, and facilitate market access. However, some of these effects cancel out at the aggregate level, given that infrastructure comes at a high cost. Moreover, even when there is no "free input" effect, the effects of infrastructure on output at the aggregate level may still not be the same as the effects of total capital for several reasons (OECD, 2009). These include the possibly significant economies of scale and network externalities that may characterize infrastructural investments by linking countries and regions. In addition, infrastructure may have a competition-enhancing effect, thereby improving market access by lowering transport costs. Nevertheless, the causal link between infrastructure and growth may operate in the opposite direction, as countries with high output levels will also be able to fund higher infrastructure investments, which may be desirable for social reasons. Besides, infrastructure investment will, to some extent, reflect expectations of future capacity utilization.

Models for Financing Infrastructure

The OECD (2015) has highlighted the models of financing infrastructure, including private financing, official development assistance; national development banks; resource financed infrastructure; public-private partnerships, and blended finance.

Private Financing of Infrastructure in Africa

Batley (2009) notes that although there is a clear rationale for Private Participation in Infrastructure (PPI), experience shows that, in practice, the poor often benefit least from it. It is worth noting that private investment is lowest in the poorest countries of Africa and the services most essential to the poor, such as water and sanitation. On the one hand, much of the literature suggests that these failures justify the work of the facilities in seeking innovative ways to facilitate PPI and ensure that the benefits are genuinely pro-poor. Conversely, some have used the evidence to assert that, despite the need for infrastructure development, the rationale for private investment, in particular, is misguided. In any case, the donor and the broader literature generally consider the private investment as a complement to, rather than a substitute for, public infrastructural investment.

Private investment has been concentrated in commercially attractive sectors and countries, so it has not always matched development needs (Tyson, 2018). However, private finance in Africa has primarily financed the telecommunications sector, with some minor financing of power plants and container terminals. Further effort is needed to leverage private capital (United Nations Economic Commission for Africa, 2017).

OECD (2015) presents a taxonomy of instruments and vehicles for infrastructure financing (see Table 15.2). The taxonomy sorts the instruments based on several dimensions. The left-hand margin describes modes of investment, recognizing that there are broad asset categories (fixed income, mixed, equity), followed by principal instruments. Besides the fact that investors can either be creditors or equity-holders, some investments, particularly PPP contracts and concessions, may have debt-like characteristics due to contracted cash flows. Categories are defined by their nature (creditors, equity-holders, or creditors with equity options and participation rights), with the distinction drawn from whether an investor receives priority claims incorporate or project cash flows (the creditor) or residual claims to cash flows (equity).

Table 15.2 Taxonomy of instruments and vehicles for infrastructure financing

Modes		Infrastructure finance instruments		Market vehicles
Asset category	Instrument	Infrastructure project	Corporate balance sheet/other entities	Capital pool
Fixed income	Bonds	Project bonds Municipal, sub-sovereign bonds Green bonds, Sukuk	Corporate bonds, Green bonds Subordinated bonds	Bond indices, bond funds, EFTs
	Loans	Direct/co-investment lending to an infrastructure project, syndicated project loans	Direct/co-investment lending to infrastructure corporate	Debt funds (GPs)
			Syndicated loans, securitized loans (ABS), CLOs	Loan indices, loan funds
Mixed	Hybrid	Subordinated loans/bonds, mezzanine finance	Subordinated bonds, convertible bonds, preferred stock	Mezzanine debt funds (GPs), hybrid debt funds
Equity	Listed	YieldCos	Listed infrastructure & utility stocks, closed-end funds, REITs, IITs, MLPs	Listed infrastructure equity funds, indices, trusts, ETFs
	Unlisted	Direct/co-investment in infrastructure project equity, PPP	Direct/co-investment in infrastructure corporate equity	Unlisted infrastructure funds

Source: OECD (2015)

Along the top of Table 15.2 are the finance instruments followed by market channels. There are essentially two ways to finance infrastructure through private investment: stand-alone infrastructure projects or corporate balance sheet finance and other balance sheet-based structures. From an investor's perspective, the instruments and pooling mechanisms selected for investment depends on the type of asset (debt, equity, listed or unlisted), regulatory and tax factors, and the investors' definition and allocation of infrastructure in their portfolios, based on their asset/liability framework. Other considerations are diversification and investor sophistication: small investors with limited resources and small amounts of capital allocated to infrastructure are limited to capital pool channels and corporate investments. At the same time, significant funds may be able to commit capital directly to projects.

The instrument column divides the asset categories into the principal modes—fixed income into bonds and loans, equity into listed and unlisted shares, and hybrids being combinations of both. These instruments can further define the level of control in an investment, liquidity, and the types of contractual claims on cash flows. Together, loans and bonds form the largest categories of infrastructure finance, mirroring the broader fixed income markets: global debt markets are the deepest capital markets in the world. Debt instruments can be structured into long-term maturities that extend over the life of long-term assets. Moreover, debt financing can be provided through multiple instruments. Debt instruments can take the form of direct loans held on the balance sheets of financial institutions or may be structured for resale to investors. They could also be distributed in markets, be it private markets (such as private-placement debt) or public markets through registered corporate and government bonds.

Furthermore, financiers of infrastructure projects can take advantage of clientele effects in debt markets. For instance, issues can be tailored to fit the demands and preferences of confident investors such as pension funds and insurance companies, thereby broadening the appeal of infrastructure finance to a larger potential pool of capital. In addition, hybrid instruments such as mezzanine finance are debt instruments with equity-like participation, thus forming a bridge between debt and equity.

Equity finance comprises all financial resources provided in return for shares in the firm. Investors may sell their shares in the firm/project if a market exists, or they may get a share of the proceeds if the asset is sold. Investors are vital in financing infrastructure investments as risk capital providers to initiate a project or refinancing. Listed shares are indirect participation rights in corporations, projects, and other entities; investors hold minority positions with limited influence management. Unlisted shares often confer direct ownership, control, and operation of the corporate entity or project asset due to concentrated shareholder positions and closer ties to managers. Equity investors are interested in maximizing total return on equity—in the case of infrastructure, and these objectives can be met through maximizing dividend yield since many projects lack a vital growth component. Other investor requirements (private equity) such as exit strategy are essential considerations.

National Development Banks and Infrastructure Development in Africa

For African countries, the transformation into modern economies will be impossible without infrastructure. Firms cannot produce goods and services without a reliable supply of inputs, such as power and water. Without transportation and communications infrastructure, they cannot get goods to the market or communicate with customers. Thus, Africa's infrastructure development and integration benefits are high, and increasing trade would contribute to market efficiency and economic growth. However, low-quality infrastructure acts as a constraint on trade (United Nations Economic Commission for Africa, 2017).

Resource Financed Infrastructure

Resource-rich developing countries are known to have been using their natural resources as collateral to obtain financing for investment. This enables them to counterbalance the barriers to conventional bank lending and capital markets and thus has given rise to the Resource Financed Infrastructure (RFI) model. The RFI model derives from previous oil-backed lending models pioneered by several Western banks in Africa. Under a Resource Financed Infrastructure (RFI) arrangement, a loan for current infrastructure construction is securitized against the net present value of a future revenue stream from oil or mineral extraction (World Bank, 2014). Thus, the RFI model allows countries with recent natural resource discoveries to accelerate infrastructure investments by pledging future government revenue from resources flows. In some circumstances, the resource financed infrastructure model could be a helpful commitment device if governments would otherwise find it hard to invest resource revenue productively once cash has started flowing (United Nations Economic Commission for Africa, 2017).

Public-Private Partnerships

The potential for market failures in infrastructure calls for government intervention. Nevertheless, the potential for government failure also suggests that state intervention must be undertaken carefully. However, what is clear is the need for a synergy between the private and the public sectors in building infrastructure. Public-Private Partnerships (PPPs), as the term insinuates, aim to provide a mechanism by which such synergy between the two sectors may be achieved in reality. Despite its popularity worldwide, a unanimous definition of PPPs is yet to be agreed upon. Indeed, the definition of PPP usually varies from one PPP project to another, and there are widespread differences in what the term is taken to encapsulate. The OECD has defined PPPs from traditional procurement methods based on risk transferred to the private sector. Thus, one can define a public- private partnership as an agreement between the government and one or more private sector partners. The agreement outlines how delivery of service by both parties would align with the objectives of the government and the private partners, along with a sufficient transfer of risk to the private sector partners (Meaney & Hope, 2012).

Different models fit within the broad PPP concept, but, in line with the definition mentioned earlier, the asset's operation is always the private sector's responsibility. Each of these models allocates different levels of risk to the private sector. Three models within the PPP concept include: Build–Develop–Operate; Build–Own–Operate; and Build–Operate–Transfer (Meaney & Hope, 2012). Under the Build–Develop–Operate model, the private sector partner buys or leases an existing asset from a public agency, invests capital in enhancing and developing the infrastructure, and then operates it according to the terms of a contract with a public agency. While under the Build–Own–Operate model, the public agency awards a single contract—which bundles the construction and operation of the infrastructure—to a private sector partner. The public agency is responsible for specifying the project's design, but ownership of the asset remains with the private agency once it is built. Finally, under the Build–Operate–Transfer model, the private sector entity is responsible for constructing the infrastructure according to the design specifications agreed to by the public agency—and subsequently operates the infrastructure for a specified period under a contract or contract franchise agreement with the agency. At the end of the contract, ownership and operation of the infrastructure are transferred to the public agency.

While potentially useful, PPPs also raise concerns that need attention. Regardless of the chosen infrastructure delivery tool, infrastructure projects, typically large-scale and long-term, pose some risks-technical, construction, operating, financial, force majeure, regulatory/political, project default, environmental and social. PPPs are not immune to these issues, requiring in all cases a solid analytical framework that could avoid extra costs and maximize value to all parties, with the long-term goal of providing better infrastructure to the region. PPPs are not easy fixes for governments seeking to scale up infrastructure investment. They require institutional developments (including project preparation capacity) that consolidate before delivering their potential. If done poorly, they can result in higher costs and fewer and worse services (Inter- American Development Bank, 2017).

PPPs combine the skills and resources of both the public and private sectors and distribute risks and responsibilities among the stakeholders. This partnership affords governments expertise from the private sector and, most importantly, new funding sources for public services that otherwise could not have been funded due to a shortage of capital or funds (The International Institute for Sustainable Development, 2015). The International Institute for Sustainable Development (2015) highlights some of the most common financing/funding mechanisms for PPPs and infrastructure projects: Government Funding; Corporate or On-Balance Sheet Finance, and Project Finance.

Government funding entails the government financing some or all of the capital investment in a project while the private sector ensures the efficient running of the project. The government, for example, procures civil works for the project. However, the private operator takes charge of the operation and maintenance of the facilities or provides the service to the private operator. Meanwhile, in build-operate-transfer and design-build-operate models of project financing, lump- sum payments are made to the operator for completed stages of construction and then receive an operating fee to cover the operation and maintenance of the project.

While under the Corporate or On-Balance Sheet Finance, the private participant would finance part of the capital investment for the project and source the remaining part through corporate financing. This entails financing the project based on the private operator's balance sheet. This method is generally deployed when the cost of the financing is not high or when the private participant involved is large enough to fund the project from its balance sheet.

Under project finance, the financing usually would be limited recourse lending to a special project vehicle (special purpose vehicle—SPV) with the right to execute the project. The SPV depends on revenue streams based on the contractual arrangements and/or on tariffs paid by end-users that will only commence once construction has been completed and the project is in operation. It is, therefore, a risky enterprise. Consequently, the lenders would conduct extensive due diligence to ascertain the potential viability of the project before committing to financing it. They would also review the sufficiency of the protection of the company undertaking the project given its risk allocation.

In terms of familiar sources of financing for PPPs, a PPP project involves both equity and debt financing. The primary sources of financing PPPs include equity contributions; Debt Contributions; Bank Guarantees/Letters of Credit/Performance Guarantees; Bond/Capital Markets financing; and Mezzanine/Subordinated Contributions (The International Institute for Sustainable Development, 2015).

Under equity contributions, project sponsors are the investors investing in the company that would likely provide expertise and the required services such as construction and related operations. Sponsor funding is equity contributions in the project as share capital and or other shareholder funds. Equity generally is the lowest priority funding of the project and potentially bears the highest risk even though it could also result in the highest returns. Equity contributors in project- financed transactions might include the project participants, local investors, the host government, the grantor, other interested governments, institutional investors, and bilateral or multilateral organizations.

In terms of debt contributions, debt can be obtained from many sources, including commercial lenders, institutional investors, export credit agencies, bilateral or multilateral organizations, bondholders, and sometimes the host country government. Debt contributions have the highest priority among the invested funds, and debt repayment specifies whether the interest rate would be fixed or variable and payment periods. The source and type of debt will have an important influence on the nature of the debt provided. For example, commercial banks are desirable long-term debt providers, given flexibility in renegotiating loans considering new or unforeseen conditions. Such flexibility may not be familiar with other sources of funds, for example, from bondholders. Another source of project debt is suppliers of equipment. Suppliers benefit from such financing because they sell their equipment despite the more aggressive terms by supplying on credit.

Under bank guarantees/letters of credit/performance guarantees, bank guarantees form an essential part of project financing, thereby allowing counter-parties immediate access to payment without the cost of locking up cash. Such guarantees may be "on-demand" or may only be payable if the courts determine a default or through adjudication. A bank-issued guarantee, letter of credit or performance bond fixes the amount and obtains a counter indemnity, possibly secured against fixed or variable charges or cash deposits. The issuer is entitled to convert the counter indemnity payments into loans or demand immediate repayment.

Bond financing allows borrowers to access debt directly from individuals and institutions rather than through intermediaries such as commercial lenders. The bond issuer (the borrower) sells the bonds to the investors (bond buyers). Rating agencies assess the riskiness of the project and assign a credit rating to the bonds. The credit rating then signals bond buyers on the attractiveness of the investment and the price they should pay. Bond financing generally is associated with lower borrowing costs when the project gets a sufficiently strong credit rating. Rating agencies may be consulted when structuring the project to maximize its credit rating. Bond financing benefits projects in terms of lower interest rates, longer maturity (which can be very helpful given the duration of most of these projects), and more liquidity.

Mezzanine/Subordinated Contributions are located somewhere between equity and debt. Mezzanine contributions are accorded lower priority than debt but higher priority than equity. The use of mezzanine contributions (which can also be characterized as quasi-equity) allows the project company to maintain a higher debt-to-equity ratio. Mezzanine financing for project financing can be obtained from shareholders, commercial lenders, institutional investors, and bilateral and multilateral organizations. Mezzanine contributors are entitled to compensation for the added risk they take either by receiving higher interest rates on loans than the senior debt contributors and by receiving partial participation in the project profits or the capital gains achieved by project equity.

Blended Finance

The term "blended finance" has been used for more than a decade in international development and broader practice. Different uses of the term reflect different and valid rationales, usually conditioned by the context in which they are applied. In broad discussions on financing for development, blended finance combines public development finance and private investment to support investments in developing countries. Building on previous definitions and focusing on the central rationale for blending, OECD (2018) defines blended finance as the strategic use of development finance to mobilize additional finance towards sustainable development in developing countries. In the context of this definition, development finance includes official development finance (i.e., both concessional and non-concessional development finance from official sources) and private funds governed by a development mandate (e.g., financing provided by philanthropic organizations). Additional finance includes commercial finance from public and private sources whose principal purpose is commercial rather than developmental (includes but is not limited to investment by public or privately owned pension funds or insurance companies, banks, and businesses).

The OECD definition of blended finance reflects an overarching policy perspective that derives from the importance of enhanced mobilization of financing for development. The OECD approach supports development finance to increase the mobilization of additional financing for development, particularly from commercial sources. Under this broad approach, finance providers may be governments, foundations, development finance institutions (DFIs), among others; resources may be concessional or non-concessional, and the investee may be public or private. The OECD framework for blended finance thus considers development finance as only one part of the total financing for a project, but one that is deployed to enable overall financing needs to be met mainly through non-development finance. The funding and financing can be within the financing structure of a transaction (blending of development and commercial finance at the debt or equity level); outside the financial transaction (risk mitigation instruments such as foreign exchange risk, political risk insurance, or performance-based payments); or a combination of both. The DFI approach to blended concessional finance for private sector operations is outlined in the DFI Working Group's enhanced guidelines (OECD, 2018). The approach reflects their role as financial institutions with an operational mandate in financing private investment projects. The specific focus of the guidelines is on blending concessional funds with non-concessional resources deployed by DFIs and multilateral development banks (MDBs) to support private sector operations. MDBs and DFIs have developed specific systems, processes, and principles for deploying concessional finance in private sector projects to minimize the potential risk of competitive distortion that might hinder rather than reinforce market solutions. Table 15.3 highlights the common areas and differences between the two frameworks for blended finance.

Table 15.3 Comparing definitions of blended finance (BF)

		OECD DAC Blended Finance Principles		DFI working Group Guidelines	
		Development Finance used in BF	Finance mobilized in BF	Development Finance used in BF	Finance mobilized in BF
Source of finance	Motivation/mandate	Development only	Commercial only	Development only	Development and/or commercial
	Ownership	Public and private	Public and private	Public and private	Public and private
	Terms of finance	Concessional and non-concessional	Non-concessional only	Concessional only	Non-concessional only
Use of finance	Investee	Public and private		Private only	

Note: Shaded cells highlight the main differences—source: OECD (2018)

Status of Financing Infrastructure Development in Africa

The Infrastructure Consortium for Africa (ICA) recorded that new financial commitments to African infrastructure in 2018 totaled US$ 101 billion. The origin of these new commitments was as follows: 37% from African governments; 26% from China; 22% from ICA members; 12% from the private sector; and 2% from the Arab Co-ordination Group (see Fig. 15.6). Compared to 2017, additional commitments in 2018 increased by approximately 12%. These came from financing by African governments and the inclusion of some sub-national financing, along with a significant increase in new commitments from Chinese sources, which rose from US$ 19 billion in 2017 to US$ 26 billion in 2018, including a US$ 5.8 billion commitment to a 3.5 GW hydro complex in Nigeria which will take six years to complete. The sectoral distribution of total new commitments in 2018 was: 44% energy, 33% transport, 13% water, 7% ICT, and 4% multisector (OECD/ACET, 2020).

Nevertheless, given the oscillations from year to year, Fig. 15.6 needs to be complemented with moving averages. Thus the 2018 data in Fig. 15.6 of US$ 38 billion from African government sources compares with a US$ 28 billion average over the period 2015–17; the US$ 26 billion from Chinese sources in 2018 compares with an average of US$ 16 billion in the preceding three years, and the US$ 20 billion from ICA members in 2018 compares with average commitments of US$ 19 billion in 2015–17. Thus, Chinese financing for African infrastructure has been

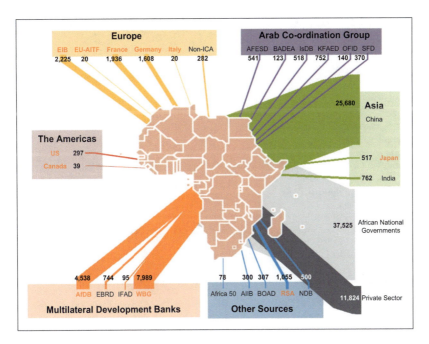

Fig. 15.6 Sources of infrastructure financing in Africa in 2018, commitments in US$ million. (Source: OECD/ACET (2020))

running at levels comparable to, or higher than, financing from all G7 members and multilateral development banks combined (OECD/ACET, 2020).

Table 15.4 and Fig. 15.7 present investment by sector in Sub-Saharan Africa in US$ million over the period 1990–2019.

Conclusion and Policy Implications

One way to overcome Africa's trade finance gap is to respond swiftly and implement regulatory measures should be implemented. For a start, regulators (domestic and international) should work with banks to put measures to allow digital approval and transmission of the required documents for trade finance. Although some banks have already streamlined internal processes to promote the electronic processing of trade finance transactions, others note that these measures will have limited impact without

Table 15.4 Investment by sector in Sub-Saharan Africa (US$ million): 1990–2019

Sector	Investment (US$ million)
Airports	1919
Electricity	46,451
ICT	9083
Integrated municipal solid waste	7
Natural gas	2219
Ports	13,643
Railways	5590
Roads	3368
Treatment and disposal	285
Water and sewerage	779

Source: https://ppi.worldbank.org/en/snapshots/region/sub-saharan-africa

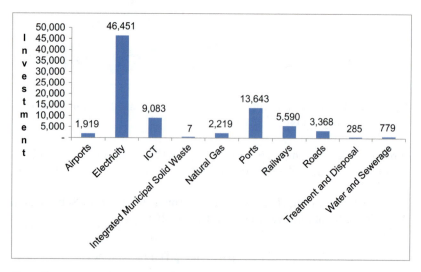

Fig. 15.7 Investment by sector in Sub-Saharan Africa (US$ million): 1990–2019. (Source: https://ppi.worldbank.org/en/snapshots/region/sub-saharan-africa)

appropriate national and global regulatory support. In addition, development finance institutions and governments that intend to provide financial facilities to support businesses and other critical sectors should include rapid emergency facilities such as trade finance lines coupled with risk mitigation instruments earmarked to support banks, SMEs, and other local corporates. It is noteworthy that Development Finance Institutions have responded swiftly to support African trade. For example, of the US$ 1.35 billion set aside by the African Development Bank for COVID-19's rapid response to the private sector, US$ 270 million is set aside for supporting trade finance. This comes to add to the existing guarantee capacity of more than US$ 700 million. The Global Trade Finance Program International Finance Corporation's, on its part, has at least US$ 2 billion additional capacity earmarked as a guard against repayment risks associated with trade finance globally. While these are reasonable steps, it is essential to ensure that firms in more vulnerable economies and sub-regions benefit from this support (Nyantakyi & Drammeh, 2020).

There is a tendency in Political discourse tends to assume that all spending labeled "infrastructure" is necessarily good and that the government is best placed to deliver these projects in many countries. However, it is clear from the academic literature that this is far from the consensus view. Although there are potentially significant gains from infrastructure investment for economic growth theoretically, the efficacy of infrastructure spending at best is mixed in practice. To enhance the returns to infrastructure investment, myriad issues in both developed and developing economies need to be addressed. These include the measurement of the returns to infrastructure, the evaluation methods for the projects, the delivery mechanisms, and the existing and evolving regulatory environment. A rigorous analysis of infrastructure spending is needed to improve the disappointing performance so far. Perhaps the worst time to address the under-provision of infrastructure is during a crisis, especially when evaluation and delivery have not been adequately done well in advance. A more transparent process of evaluation and delivery and an improved understanding of the complexities of infrastructure are investments in policy infrastructure that are well worth making (Henchel & McKibbin, 2017).

References

African Union and United Nations Economic Commission for Africa. (2017). *Development financing in Africa*, available at: https://www.uneca.org/sites/default/files/PublicationFiles/development_financing_in_africa_eng_2017.pdf

Bank for International Settlements. (2014). *Trade finance: Developments and issues*. CGFS Papers No 50. Available at: https://www.bis.org/publ/cgfs50.pdf

Batley, R. (2009). Private-sector investment in infrastructure: Rationale and causality for pro- poor impacts. *Development Policy Review*, 27(4), 397–417.

Cerra, V., Cuevas, A., Goes, C., et al. (2017). Determinants of infrastructure and its financing. *Emerging Economy Studies*, 3(2), 1–14. Available at: https://www.researchgate.net/publication/321634038_Determinants_of_I–frastructure_and_Its_Financing

Daripa, A., & Nilsen, J. (2011). Ensuring sales: A theory of inter-firm credit. *American Economic Journal: Microeconomics*, 3(February 2011), 245–279. https://www.trafigura.com/media/1226/2016_trafigura_llewellyn_trade_finance_and_regulation_en.pdf.

Henchel, T., & McKibbin, W. J. (2017). The economics of infrastructure in a globalized world: Issues, lessons and future challenges. *Journal of Infrastructure, Policy and Development*, 1(2).

Inter-American Development Bank. (2017). *Evaluation of public-private partnerships in infrastructure.* Available at: https://publications.iadb.org/publications/english/document/Evaluation-of-Public-Private-Partnerships-in-Infrastructure.pdf

LlewellynConsulting. (2016). *Trade finance and regulation: The risk of unintended consequences*, available at: https://www.trafigura.com/media/1226/2016_trafigura_llewellyn_trade_finance_and_regulation_en.pdf

Meaney, A., & Hope, P. (2012). *Alternative ways of financing infrastructure investment: Potential for 'Novel' financing models.* International Transportation Forum, Discussion Paper No. 2012.07. Available at: https://www.oecd-ilibrary.org/docserver/5k8zvv4vqj9s-en.pdf?expires=1594009492&id=id&accname=guest&checksum=A5EC891F48B191DB7FDA82F5033A524E

Nyantakyi, E. B., & Drammeh, L. M. (2020). COVID-19 pandemic potential risks for trade and trade finance in Africa. African. *Economic Review*, 11(6).

OECD. (2009). *Infrastructure and growth: Empirical evidence.* OECD Economics Department Working Papers No. 685. Available at: https://www.oecd-ilibrary.org/docserver/225682848268.pdf?expires=1593583437&id=id&accname=guest&checksum=8FBFCE9838CB7E6F69B474CDCAC83D33

OECD. (2015). *Infrastructure financing instruments and incentives.* Available at: http://www.oecd.org/finance/private-pensions/Infrastructure-Financing-Instruments-and-Incentives.pdf

OECD. (2018). *Making blended finance work for sustainable development goals.* OECD Publishing. https://doi.org/10.1787/9789264288768-en

OECD/ACET. (2020). *Quality infrastructure in 21st century Africa: Prioritizing, accelerating and scaling up in the context of Pida (2021–30).* Available at: https://www.oecd.org/dev/Africa-Quality-infrastructure-21st-century.pdf

Palei, T. (2015). Assessing the impact of infrastructure on economic growth and global competitiveness. *Procedia Economics and Finance*, 23(2015), 168–175.

The International Institute for Sustainable Development. (2015). *Green bonds in public-private partnerships*. Available at: https://www.iisd.org/sites/default/files/publications/green-bonds-public-private-partnerships.pdf

Tyson, J. E. (2018). *Private infrastructure financing in developing countries: Five challenges, five solutions*. Available at: https://www.odi.org/sites/odi.org.uk/files/resource-documents/12366.pdf

World Bank. (2014). *Resource financed infrastructure: A discussion on a new form of infrastructure financing*. Available at: https://elibrary.worldbank.org/doi/abs/10.1596/978-1-4648-0239-3

World Trade Organization. (2016). *Trade finance and SMEs: Bridging the gaps in provision*. Available at: http://invenio.unidep.org/invenio//record/20486/files/tradefinsme_e.pdf

Zeidy, I. A. (2020). *The role of trade finance in promoting trade: The implications of COVID 19 on trade finance in Africa*. Available at: https://www.comesa.int/wp-content/uploads/2020/07/The-Role-of-Trade-Finance-in-Promoting-Trade-and-the-Implications-of-Covid-192.pdf

CHAPTER 16

Prospect of Economic Unions on Intra-regional Trade in Africa

Grace Nkansa Asante

INTRODUCTION

The Abuja Treaty signed in 1991 complements the Lagos Plan of Action to integrate African countries in order to stimulate trade for the development of Africa. Out of this, the entire continent was divided into eight Regional Economic Communities (REC), namely; the East African Community (EAC), the Economic Community of Central African States (ECCAS), the Economic Community of West Africa States (ECOWAS), Arab Maghreb Union (UMA), Common Market for Eastern and Southern Africa (COMESA), Community of Sahel-Saharan States (CEN-SAD) Southern African Development Community (SADC), and Intergovernmental Authority on Development (IGAD). The formation of these RECs was to pursue policies towards integrating countries by 1999, harmonize and increase intraregional trade by 2007, create Free Trade Area (FTA) and Customs Union by 2017, form the African Customs Union by 2019, create a Common Market by 2023 and finally an African

---

G. N. Asante (✉)
Department of Economics, KNUST, Kumasi, Ghana
e-mail: graceoforiabebrese@knust.edu.gh

Economic and Monetary Union by 2028. Currently, there are two currency unions in Africa, namely the West African Economic and Monetary Union (WAEMU), which consists of eight West African countries, and the Central African Economic and Monetary Union (CEMAC), which comprises six Central African countries.

The ECOWAS was established on 28 May 1975 under the Treaty of Lagos. It was established as a free trade area (FTA) to achieve intraregional commerce and economic integration. The FTA treaty was signed by 16 member countries and included the following members: Nigeria, Cote D'Ivoire, Ghana, Burkina Faso, Togo, Benin, Niger Mali, Guinea Bissau, Senegal, Guinea, Liberia, Sierra Leone, Gambia, Cape Verde, and Mauritania. ECOWAS sub-region is characterized by two zones, namely, the West Africa Economic and Monetary Union (WAEMU) and the West Africa Monetary Zone (WAMZ). The two zones were to merge in 2020, following the adoption of a single currency in the WAMZ in 2003. Countries in the WAEMU are La Cote d'Ivoire, Burkina Faso, Togo, Mali, Benin, Guinea Bissau, Senegal, and Niger. The expected members of the WAMZ consist of Nigeria, Ghana, Guinea, Sierra Leone, The Gambia, and Liberia. The ECOWAS Trade Liberation Scheme (ETLS) was implemented in 1979 to enhance trade, and the ECOWAS Monetary Cooperation Programme (EMCP) was set up in 1987 to reduce currency convertibility among member states and bring about a single currency. However, despite the rattling effort of ECOWAS, the level of trade between member states remained below 12% of total trade (UNCTAD database, 2018).

The South Africa Customs Union (SACU) is the oldest globally and most successful union in the continent. It was formed with Botswana, Lesotho, Kingdom of Eswatini, then Swaziland, South Africa, and Lesotho to integrate the British colonies and coordinate economic policies in 1910. The South African pound was used as the single currency but substituted with the Rand after independence, except for Namibia. However, the treaty was renegotiated, and South Africa Customs Union (SACU) was cemented as the union's official name. In 1976, Botswana withdrew from the use of the Rand when its exports revenues in diamond and beef increased and managed its currency based on a basket of currencies which the South African Rand held approximately 60%. In 1980, Lesotho established its central bank and issued its currency. Namibia gained its independence in 1990 and joined the union in 1992, which led to the introduction of the Namibian dollar in 1993, pegged to the South African Rand.

The South African Union treaty established six institutions in the SACU to facilitate trade-related activities in the trade bloc. The treaty also led to the signing a free trade agreement with the European Union Free Trade Association (EFTA). The agreement's purpose was to create an enabling business environment in 2008. The most performing regional economic communities in the continent compared to ECOWAS have currency arrangements that favor trade. For example, the convertibility of the Kenyan shilling facilitates trade in East Africa Community (EAC), and that of the SADC is because some currencies are pegged to the South African Rand in the South African Customs Union (SACU). Trade in the EAC and SADC on average 19.1% and 15.1%, respectively, compared to 9.0% for the ECOWAS as averaged intra-trade data from 2000 to 2017 (UNCTAD, 2018). More so, the WAEMU, part of the ECOWAS, averages at 13.7% due to the use of a common currency (UNCTAD, 2018).

Studies such as Patroba and Nene (2013) and Rametsi (2015) have evaluated the feasibility of a monetary union in SACU using the OCA criteria and concluded that countries in the community are not prepared to adopt a common currency. However, these studies evaluated the suitability of currency unions without evaluating the common currency's impact in stimulating trade in line with attenuating shocks and unveiling greater trade potential. Studies such as Amoah (2013), Kamara (2015), among others, Mensah (2015) have assessed the feasibility of creating a West African currency union by testing the macroeconomic convergence of ECOWAS countries. The results showed that West African countries are not prepared to adopt a common currency; and that such a move would be costly.

However, empirical studies using the OCA criteria have shown that the European Monetary Union (EMU) was never an Optimal Currency Area, before the currency union (Komárek & Horvath, 2002; Vrňáková & Bartušková, 2013). That notwithstanding, the currency union generated trade among member states (UNCTAD database, 2018). A recent evaluation of the EMU based on OCA criteria showed countries are converging with the introduction of the Euro (Rose, 2008; Crowley et al., 2013). Given this, evaluating the feasibility of currency unions in West and South Africa using the OCA criteria would not adequately predict the trade effect of the policy. These studies mentioned failed to acknowledge the effect of a common currency on trade and how this will manage shock among member States as rightly reported by Ncube et al. (2014) that intra-regional trade has helped attenuate the effect of global shocks in SACU. In this context, Anokye and Imran (2014) estimated the prospect of ECOWAS currency union on intra-regional trade and reported that currency union would improve trade in the sub-region using a linear model. Contrarily, Monte Carlo simulation tests have shown that the gravity model of international trade is best estimated as a nonlinear model (Bobková, 2012; Vavrek, 2018).

Therefore, this study seeks to evaluate the prospect of ECOWAS currency union on intra-regional trade potential and specifically evaluate whether the adoption of the common currency would lead to trade creation or diversion using the Poisson Pseudo Maximum Likelihood (PPML) estimator, which is a nonlinear estimator. The study further estimates the trade effect of adopting a common currency to unveil whether it will lead to regional trade or not in the Southern Africa Customs Union (SACU). Finally, the study further evaluates whether countries are overtrading or under- trading.

Literature Review

Theoretically, Mundell (1961) and McKinnon (1963) developed the Optimal Currency Area (OCA) theory to postulate that countries with high labor mobility, substantial product diversification, high degree of openness, flexible prices and wages, effective monetary policy, close inflation rates and the will to give up their currencies will benefit from a currency union. Kenen (1969) held that product diversification is an important criterion for an OCA and that product diversity was a key factor for labor to move within a region. In addition, Mundell (1961) focused on the cost of joining a currency union, whereas McKinnon (1963) and Kenen (1969) centered on the conditions for enhancing the benefit for an optimal currency area. Critical issues concerning OCAs include reduced cost as a benefit versus the cost of giving up monetary sovereignty and dealing with synchronizing member states' business cycles. The theory concludes that there is the need to experience symmetric reactions to external shocks to lower the cost of regionally coordinated policies.

In 1962, Tinbergen advanced the gravity model of international trade with intuition based on Newton's law of gravity. According to the gravity model, trade between two countries depends on their economic strength (GDP or GNP) and is inversely related to the trade cost. Thus, trade depends on income and distance. The theory of trade creation-trade diversion, propounded by Viner (1950), states that trade creation leads to unleashing untapped trade potentials among trading member states and therefore improve welfare. However, trade diversion is problematic because it diverts trade from the cheapest supplier nation to a member state within the union making it cheaper only due to the removal of tariffs but is expensive for non-members. Theoretically, exchange rate volatility shows the level of risk involved with changes in the exchange rate. Depending on the assumptions, by increasing the risk or shock in international trade, exchange rate volatility could hurt exports. However, according to Sercu and Vanhulle (1992), exchange rate volatility can stimulate trade on average given that it shows a higher probability that ex-post deviations from the commodity price parity will be more significant than tariffs and transportation costs.

Rose (2000a) assessed the impact of exchange rate volatility and currency union on trade within the European Monetary Union from 1970 to 1990 using ordinary least squares with country fixed effects. The results showed that countries in a currency union would trade three times more than countries using their sovereign currency. Ofori-Abebrese (2006) presents another study of the Eco and the Economic Development of West Africa by analyzing the macroeconomic convergence and the state of the member countries in the zone and concluded that when the nominal convergence is achieved, West African countries will ensure the maximum benefit of the union. Qureshi and Tsangarides (2009) clustered three overlapping periods (1990 to 2004, 1995 to 2004, and 2000 to 2004) with multivariate data to analyze the suitability of common currency for West African countries. The study raises doubts on the possibility of establishing a monetary union for the WAMZ and integrating with the WAEMU. Finally, Amoah (2013) used the Macroeconomic Convergence Criteria to assess the performance of Ghana, Nigeria, and Gambia to ascertain the feasibility of a single currency for WAMZ with time-series data from 1980 to 2011. It was reported that the WAMZ is not ready to form a monetary Union, hitherto not an optimum currency area.

Anokye and Imran (2014) evaluated the impact of the ECOWAS currency union on intra- regional trade from 1995 to 2010 using an augmented gravity model and a dynamic OLS estimation technique. The results showed that currency unions have a significant positive impact in the sub-region, particularly Benin, Burkina Faso, Niger, Togo, and Senegal trade more with countries with a common currency. Kamara (2015) adopted the cluster analysis to evaluate the proposed Currency Union in the ECOWAS zone and establish whether the countries have common characteristics. The study showed that countries are heterogeneous, and intra-trade among the countries is insufficient to generate the benefits expected from the union. The study further points out that ECOWAS is not an optimal currency area and, therefore, could be risky to form a currency union.

Bhowmik and Sen (2013) adopted the optimal convergence criteria to evaluate the feasibility of a common currency in SACU spanning 1985 to 2012. The paper concludes that SACU has the potential to introduce a common currency. Finally, Rametsi (2015) used the Error Correction Model, central tendencies, and standard deviation to examine the possibility of SACU as an Optimal Currency Area (OCA) with data spanning from 1980 to 2015. The study showed convergence of macroeconomic indicators; therefore, the trade bloc is an Optimal Currency Area and can adopt a common currency.

METHODOLOGY

Data Type and Source

The study utilized a dataset of 4320 bilateral trade observations for 2000 to 2017, although the dependent variables have some missing observation. Data for bilateral trade are from IMF Direction of Trade Statistics (DOTs) and U.N. Comtrade, real GDP and GDP per capita were sourced from World Bank's World Development Indicators (WDI), distance from CEPII, Real Effective Exchange Rate (REER) from World Bank's WDI and Freedom House's Polity V.

Specification of Model

Following the works of Rose (2000a), Rose and Van Wincoop (2001), and Micco et al. (2003), the current study investigates the impact of the proposed currency union on trade in the ECOWAS and SACU using the augmented gravity model of international trade. The augmented model is specified as follows;

(i) Currency union (C.U.) effect on trade

$$X_{ijt} = \beta_o + \beta_1 \ln(Y_i Y_j)_t + \beta_2 \ln(Y_i Y_j / Pop_i Pop_j)_t + \beta_3 \ln D_{ij}$$
$$+ \beta_4 Cont_{ij} + \beta_5 Lang_{ij}$$
$$+ \ln \beta_6 ComCol_{ijt} + \tau CU + r(V_{ij})_t + \delta Volat_{ij} + \varepsilon_{ijt} \quad (16.1)$$

(ii) Trade Creation-Trade Diversion

$$X_{ijt} = \beta_o + \beta_1 \ln(Y_i Y_j)_t + \beta_2 \ln(Y_i Y_j / Pop_i Pop_j)_t + \beta_3 \ln D_{ij}$$
$$+ \beta_4 Cont_{ij} + \beta_5 Lang_{ij}$$
$$+ \ln \beta_6 ComCol_{ijt} + \tau CU + r(V_{ij})_t + \delta Volat_{ij} + \gamma Deffect_{ijt} + \varepsilon_{ijt}$$
(16.2)

where i and j denotes countries, t denotes time, and the variables are defined as X_{ij} denotes the value of bilateral trade (exports) between ij and, Y is real GDP, Pop is population, D_{ij} is the distance between i and, $j$cont$_{ij}$ is a binary variable with value equal to 1 if i and j share a land border, Lang$_{ij}$is a binary variable which is unity if i and j have a common official language, ComCol$_{ij}$ is a binary variable which is unity if i and j were colonized by the same colonial master. CU_{ijt} is a binary variable which is unity if i and j use the same currency at the time t, $V_{t(ij)}$ is the volatility of the bilateral (between i and j) real effective exchange rate in the period before t, ε_{ij} is a vector of nuisance coefficients, and represents the myriad other influences on bilateral exports, assumed to be well behaved. Volat$_{ij}$ is a binary variable that is unitary if the exchange rate is low peaked in the period t(PEAKNESS). Incolo$_{ij}$ is a binary variable that is equal to 1 if a country colonized the other in the SACU model due to its instances in the bloc. Deffect$_{ij}$ Trade creation or trade diversion effect is a binary variable that is equal to 1 if a country is a member of a currency union. Thus, a significant positive value depicts trade creation and otherwise trade diversion. The total number of countries used in the study $N = 16t$ is the time-series dimension of the data ($T = 18$ years), the coefficients $\beta_0 \beta_1 \beta_2 \beta_3 \beta_4 \beta_5 \beta_6$ are parameters for their respective variables where β_0 is the constant and ε is the error term. Thus, the coefficient of interest is τ, γ and r.

Definition of Variables and Expected Signs

Export of goods proxied for bilateral trade between the reporting country and the partner since imports are usually underestimated. The data on exports were reported at the levels to suit the nonlinear estimation technique procedure. Border is defined as the geographic boundaries of countries. The coefficient of sharing a land border is expected to have a positive relationship with trade. The spatial theory of trade depicts that countries sharing border tends to cooperate to enhance trade. The dummy was represented with 1 if country-pairs share the same border and 0 otherwise. The proxy for infrastructure development in the countries is per capita income. According to Sharma and Chau (2010), GDP per capita serves as a good proxy to depict the level of development to facilitate trade. The coefficient of GDP per capita used is expected to have a positive relationship with the trade. It was measured as the log product of GDP per capita of the country-pairs in the model.

GDP is a proxy for economic mass of the country in the model. The study expected GDP to have a positive relationship with trade. It was measured as the log product of the GDP of country-pairs. The coefficient of language is expected to have a positive relationship with trade. In his book the Wealth of Nations, Adam Smith argued that common language enhances trade. The dummy was represented 1 if country-pair shared a common official language and 0 otherwise. Distance is the transportation cost involved in trading between the two countries. The coefficient of distance is expected to have a negative relationship with trade because, as distance increases, the cost of trading among countries ostensibly increases, thereby reducing the volume of trade. The dummy was represented 1 if the country-pair are currently in a currency union and 0 otherwise. The coefficient of the common currency is expected to have a positive effect on trade because countries using the same currency tend to trade more than countries with independent currencies (Rose, 2000a).

Exchange rate volatility was computed as the standard deviation of the moving average of the logarithm of the real effective exchange rate (REER) (Serenis & Tsounis, 2014). The real effective exchange rate is the nominal effective exchange rate which is measures the value of several foreign currencies divided by a price deflator or index of costs. The coefficient of exchange rate volatility between the countries is expected to have a negative relationship with bilateral trade. Gagnon (1993) asserted that exchange rate volatility hurts international trade.

The peak of exchange rate volatility is a dichotomous variable computed as average volatility, deducted from various values and represented by 1 if low peaked and 0 otherwise. Highly peaked exchange rate discourages trade by increasing the cost of trading among trading partners, whereas low peaked exchange rate volatility encourages trade. The coefficient of exchange rate peak ($Volat_{ij}$) is expected to have a negative relationship with trade. Incolo was a dummy that represented if the country pair has one colonizing the other. If a country colonized the other, it is 1 and zero otherwise.

Estimation Technique and Empirical Application

Monte Carlo simulation shows that the gravity model of international trade is best estimated using a nonlinear model (Silva & Tenreyro, 2011). The Poisson Pseudo Maximum likelihood (PPML) is the best estimator for the gravity model due to its ability to eliminate heteroscedasticity, autcorrelation and cater for model misspecification. Sampling bias in the specification will results from the PPML having observations with zero trade values, not suitable for linear estimation techniques because the logarithm of zero is undefined, resulting in sampling bias. Omitting relevant observations poses serious problems, and information is lost (Eichengreen & Irwin, 1996). Furthermore, unlike other estimators, the PPML estimates real data with zero trade and is efficient in small or large sample sizes (Silva & Tenreyro, 2006).

The robust standard error eliminates problems related to panel data estimation such as autocorrelation. In addition, PPML fits the data better by controlling the non-uniform variance than the log-linear model. This is because the error term has a variance that occurs at a higher point in time, which can be affected by one or more explanatory variables (Silva & Tenreyro, 2006). The conditions for the second and highest moments are missing in the estimation process. Therefore, the coefficients of the loglinear model can be very misleading due to the presence of non-uniform variance. Moreover, unlike log-linear estimators, PPML estimates the effect of policy variables on transactions, which can be misleading because log-linear estimators estimate policy variables. Further research on the best estimators of the coefficients of the gravity model is PPML (Bobková, 2012; Vavrek, 2018). For this reason, the PPML estimation method is the best option for estimating parameters.

ANALYSIS AND DISCUSSIONS

This section presents the empirical estimates and the results of the study. The section begins with the trend analysis of exchange rate volatility and intra-regional trade in the ECOWAS sub-region. It then discusses the estimated relationship between currency union and trade and the controls that affect the level of trade between countries. Finally, it presents the same analysis for the SADC countries.

Trend Analysis of Intra-Regional Trade and Exchange Rate Volatility on the ECOWAS Sub-Region

The trend analysis shows a relationship between exchange rate volatility of the ECOWAS countries' sovereign currencies and intra-regional trade.

In Fig. 16.1, fluctuations in the exchange rate of the ECOWAS currency adversely affected the trade levels of the subregions. Fluctuations in West African currency exchange rates peaked in 2003, 2005, 2012 and 2016, while intra-regional trade peaked in 2004, 2006, 2009 and 2013, at high levels in West Africa. In addition, in 2002, 2007 and 2014, exchange rate fluctuations increased in West African countries, but trade flows within the region decreased. In 2008, 2010 and 2015, the depreciation of the US dollar caused both exchange rate volatility and intra-regional trade to be high.

The analysis shows that countries that use sovereign currencies have a greater adverse effect on trade in the sub-region. In light of this, the high demand for the U.S. dollar has a negative effect on the returns on international markets and growth in the sub-region. In conclusion, sovereign currencies represent major obstacles to trade in the sub-region compared to other trading blocs. The reason is that the sovereign currencies are non-convertible and the compounding effect of the demand for foreign currencies to trade with another.

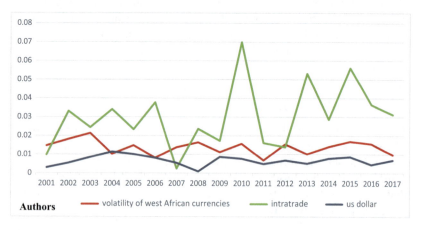

Fig. 16.1 The trend of exchange rate volatility and intra-regional trade on ECOWAS sub-region from 2000 to 2017

Table 16.1 Descriptive statistics for ECOWAS

Variable	Obs	Mean	Std.Dev.	Min	Max
Trade	4320	3.3307	1.5608	0	4.5909
GDP	4320	10.131	0.782	0.619	11.71
GDP per capita	4320	3.224	0.21	2.776	3.774
Distance	4320	1334.146	768.75	105.181	5294.028
Volatility	4314	0.189	0.204	0	1.916

Descriptive Statistics

Before estimating the effect of the proposed common currency union on trade in the ECOWAS sub-region, descriptive statistics were employed to present quantitative descriptions of the data used in the study. Summary of the sample measures which include, mean, standard deviation, minimum and maximum values of the variables are presented in Table 16.1.

The data was strongly balanced using Stata (v14). The descriptive statistic for the dummies was eliminated from the table. Trade averaged 3.3307 and ranges between 0 and 4.5909. Trade also had a standard deviation of 1.5608. The GDP variable averaged 10.131 and ranged between 0.619 and 11.71. GDP also had a standard deviation of 0.782. The GDP per capita variable averaged 3.224 with a maximum of 3.774 and a minimum of 2.776. The distance variable averaged 1334.146 with a maximum of 5294.028, a minimum of 105.181, and a standard deviation of 768.75. The volatility variable had a mean value of 0.189 with a maximum of 1.916 and a minimum of 0. The volatility variable reported a standard deviation of 0.204.

Results for Currency Union Effect on Trade

The study estimates the effect of the proposed common currency union on trade in the ECOWAS sub-region.

In Table 16.2, the estimated coefficient for GDP is 1.274, and it is statistically significant at 1%. This implies that a 1% increase in GDP leads to a 1.274% increase in the level of trade. Interpreting the coefficient as semi-elasticity, a 1% increase in GDP leads to a 0.013% increase in the level of trade. Specifically, this finding is not startling because a higher GDP will make it possible to raise the level of trade in the sub-region. Vijayasri (2013) argues that countries will produce relatively more of a particular commodity to trade with other countries for what with their existing

Table 16.2 Currency union effect on trade

Variables	Coefficients	Standard errors
GDP	1.274***	0.2107193
GDP per capita	1.497***	0.3967805
Distance	-0.001***	0.0002609
Border	0.278	0.3259134
Language	0.996**	0.4216771
Colonizer	-1.049 **	0.4876522
Common currency	1.487***	0.416091
Exchange rate volatility	-0.281*	0.1459928
Exchange rate peak	-4.080***	0.298774
Constant	-16.928***	-3.716512

Note: *, ** and *** represent rejection of null hypothesis at 10%, 5% and 1%. Authors' estimates

resources they cannot produce. As the countries produce more, economic activities increase with GDP, stimulating more trade effects.

GDP per capita exhibits a positive relationship with trade as the estimated coefficient is 1.497 and statistically significant at 1%. Interpreting the coefficient as semi-elasticity, 1% increase in GDP per capita leads to a 0.015% increase in trade. GDP per capita is used in the study as a proxy for all other variables not specified in the model, and the result shows that other relevant factors facilitated trade in the sub-region. This explains that the existing infrastructural development, institutional quality, and others contribute immensely to trade in the sub-region. Moreover, the result reflects Osabuohien and Efobi's (2013) argument that the existing institutional quality facilitates trade even though low in the sub-region. In addition, countries are struggling to improve institutional infrastructure as they are constrained by insufficient public expenditures (Ngwenya, 2015).

Distance is negatively related to trade with an estimated coefficient of -0.001 and is statistically significant at 1%. Interpreting the coefficient as semi-elasticity, an increase in distance between countries is associated with about 0.00001% decrease in trade. The result implies that as distance increases, trading costs increase, reducing trade among member states. The result confirms that of Torres and van Seters (2016), who argued that the prevalence of barriers hampers trade in the sub- region over long distances due to increased trade cost, therefore generating greater incentives for informal trade in the sub-region.

Border is found to have a positive but insignificant impact on the level of trade among countries. The estimated coefficient is 0.278, but the insignificance of the impact of border on trade indicates that borders among countries have not played any significant role in trade in the ECOWAS zone. This result buttresses the conclusion of Masson (2008) that intra-regional trade tends to increase if countries, on average, shares border with four other countries.

Language is found to have a positive and significant impact on trade at 5% level of significance. The estimated coefficient of 0.996 shows that countries in the sub-region trade more with countries with the same official language. This finding partly reinstates that countries in the WAEMU region trade more than countries in the WAMZ (Africa Development Report, 2017).

Countries sharing the same colonizer have a negative and significant effect on trade at a 5% significance level. The estimated coefficient is -1.049, indicating that countries barely trade with other countries mainly due to a common colonizer. The result is startling but intuitively plausible since countries trade more with their colonial masters than countries of the same sub-region. Also, trading based on having a common colonizer ties members into other treaties, therefore, suppressing the gains from trade. According to the WTO database, countries in the ECOWAS sub- region trade more with their colonial masters than themselves hitherto the rest of the world. In this background, Settles (1996) argued that colonization led to Africa's current political, cultural, social, and economic structure, especially West Africa, where the trans-Atlantic slave trade was executed.

The use of common currency is found to have a strong positive and significant impact on trade. The estimated coefficient is 1.487 and statistically significant at 1%. The result shows that adopting a common currency reduces transaction costs, stimulating trade through saving. The model delivers τ of 1.487, an estimate greater than that of Glick and Rose's (2002) estimation of 1.4 due to the low level of trade among countries in the ECOWAS sub-region. The high estimate of the currency union effect on trade in the sub-region can be partly attributed to greater trade potential to be unearthed in the sub-region.

The study shows that the effect of exchange rate volatility on trade in the sub-region is negative but significant. The estimated coefficient is -0.281 and statistically significant at 10%. Interpreting as semi-elasticity, exchange rate volatility is associated with a decline in trade considerably of about 0.028%. The result shows that the exchange rate plays a far more expected role in the level of trade in the sub-region. Thus, when exchange rate volatility is high, trade levels decline among member states since it increases the cost of trading. This result also confirms the outcome of the trend analysis. According to Tchokote et al. (2015), exchange rate volatility casts down net-export in the sub-region, adversely affecting trade flows.

The exchange rate peak is found to have a negative and significant effect on trade. The estimated coefficient is -4.080 at a 1% significance level. The result shows that the exchange rate peaked for most trading periods in the years under study. The result partly accounts for the low level of trade among member states in the sub-region. The high or low peak captures the unpredicted variation of exchange rate volatility that affected exports. The higher the value of unpredicted factors, the greater the adverse effect of volatility on exports hitherto trade. The higher the volatility (high peak), the greater the adverse effect on the level of exports (Serenis & Tsounis, 2014; Panda & Mohanty, 2015).

Results for Trade Creation-Trade Diversion

The study estimates whether the trade effect resulting from a common currency will significantly affect welfare (Table 16.3).

Deffect is found to have a positive and significant effect on trade and statistically significant at a 5% significance level. The estimated coefficient is 0.940, which shows that adopting a common currency will lead to trade creation. This implies that using a common currency in the ECOWAS sub-region will facilitate trade flow among member states to stimulate economic growth and development.

Table 16.3 Trade creation-trade diversion

Variables	Coefficients	Standard errors
GDP	1.230***	0.1874022
GDP per capita	1.749***	0.4050678
Distance	-0.0001***	0.0002611
Border	0.196	0.3152525
Language	1.391***	0.3740225
Colonizer	-0.789**	0.3955442
Common currency	1.755***	0.4142515
Exchange rate volatility	-0.283*	0.1445755
Exchange rate peak	-4.004***	0.2971851
(Trade Creation or diversion)	0.940 **	0.3670803
Cons	-18.419***	3.687848

Note: *, ** and *** represent rejection of null hypothesis at 10%, 5% and 1%. Authors' estimates

Results for Trade Potential in the ECOWAS Sub-Region

The study seeks to determine whether countries are over-trading or under-trading empirically (Table 16.4). The positive mean value depicts trade potential in the sub-region to be minimal. Comparing the mean value to the maximum value hammers home the fact that the countries are not maximizing trade. The results indicate that countries could trade more based on their geographical and economic fundamentals. Intuitively, the greater trade potential will unleash larger positive effects on the trade creation effect of adopting a common currency.

Empirical Results and Interpretation for the SACU

Descriptive Statistics

Before estimating the effect of the proposed common currency union on trade in the SACU sub- region, descriptive statistics were carried out to present quantitative descriptions of the data used in the study. Descriptive summary of the sample: mean, standard deviation, minimum and maximum values of the variables are presented in Table 16.5.

The data was strongly balanced using Stata (v14). The descriptive statistic for the dummies was eliminated from Table 16.5. Trade averaged 4.4408 and ranged between 12 and 5.0509. Trade also had a standard

Table 16.4 Trade potential in the ECOWAS sub-region

Variable	Observation	Mean	Standard deviation	Minimum	Maximum
Trade potential	4314	0.1626602	1.0808	-1.8909	4.1609

Note: The Minimum and Maximum depicts the range for trading. Authors' Estimates

Table 16.5 Descriptive statistics of data for SACU

Variable	Obs	Mean	Std.Dev.	Min	Max
Trade	294	4.4408	1.0009	12	5.0509
GDP	360	20.25261	0.9495888	18.70796	21.8668
Per capita	360	7.166401	0.372993	6.410511	7.759216
Distance	360	2.97756	0.1803511	2.68944	3.170836
Volatility	360	0.1897921	0.186033	0.0015824	1.144315

deviation of 1.0009. The GDP variable averaged 20.25261 and ranged between 18.70796 and 21.8668. GDP also had a standard deviation of 0.9495888. The per capita variable averaged 7.166401 with a maximum of 7.759216 and a minimum of 6.410511. The distance variable averaged 2.97756 with a maximum of 3.170836, a minimum of 2.68944, and a standard deviation of 0.1803511. The volatility variable had a mean value of 0.1897921 with a maximum of 1.144315 and a minimum of 0.0015824. The volatility variable reported a standard deviation of 0.186033.

Trend Analysis of Intra-Regional Trade and Exchange Rate Volatility on the SACU Sub-Region

Figure 16.2 shows the relationship between exchange rate volatility and intra-regional trade in SACU. From the diagram, the exchange rate was low peaked for most trading periods. There were periods characterized by highly peaked exchange rate volatility coupled with high intra-trade in the trade bloc. During these periods, the financial market of South Africa was performing well to attenuate the volatility of the Rand in line with increasing investment in the financial market. In the year 2002, exchange rate volatility and intra-trade peaked high at 0.07, which can be partly attributed to the high inflation experienced from 2001, which could not meet the target set in 2002, notably in South Africa, coupled with a rise in the price of primary exports. In the same vein, 2010 recorded the highest volume of trade within the bloc at 0.43, with exchange rate volatility

Fig. 16.2 The relationship between exchange rate volatility and intra-trade in SACU. (Source: Authors)

highly peaked at 0.04. This can be attributed to the aftermath of the global financial crisis and member- states execution of expansionary monetary policies. (South Africa Reserve Bank, 2011/2012; AfDB, 2018).

In 2007, intra-trade peaked high at 0.1 in line with rising exchange rate volatility at 0.02. This can be attributed to a depreciation of the U.S. dollar. In 2009, intra-trade peaked at 0.04, with exchange rate volatility rising at 0.04 in 2010. This can be attributed to the aftermath of the global financial crisis coupled with the depreciation of the U.S. dollar (Abban & Ofori-Abebrese, 2019). Also, intra-trade and exchange rate volatility peaked high at 0.04 and 0.03, respectively in 2017.

In some trading periods, exchange rate volatility and intra-trade were negatively related. For example, in the year 2003, exchange rate volatility was highly peaked at 0.052 and low peaked intra-trade at 0.04. This can be attributed to interest rates and inflation being relatively high (South Africa Reserve Bank, 2011). Also, 2005 recorded an exchange rate volatility low peaked at 0 and intra-trade highly peaked at 0.07. In 2008, exchange rate volatility was peaking to 2010 at 0.04, with intra-trade low peaked at 0.025 due to the international financial crisis coupled with power crises. In 2011, intra-trade was high at 0.05, and exchange rate volatility peaked low at 0. This can be attributed to South Africa increasing its exports by 80% of intra-trade, culminating in 16% of trade in the bloc (IMF, 2013). Furthermore, 2013 recorded highly peaked exchange rate volatility at 0.04 and low peaked intra-trade at 0.01. This can be attributed to budget constraints, administrative and corruption-related issues, thereby reducing the volume of trade (Templeton, 2017). Also, 2015 recorded a highly peaked intra-trade at 0.03 and low peaked exchange rate volatility of 0.01. This can be attributed to slow global economic recovery, persistent drought, declining commodity prices, and subdued world merchandise trade with policy uncertainty (SACU, 2017).

Results for the Proposed Common Currency on Trade

The study estimates the effect of the proposed common currency on trade, and the results are presented in Table 16.6

In Table 16.6, the GDP estimation coefficient is 1.683, which is statistically significant at the 5% significance level. If the coefficient is interpreted as semi-elastic, a 1% increase in GDP will increase the trading volume by 0.017%. This finding is not surprising, especially as higher GDP facilitates trade in subregions. The results are consistent with Alesina et al.

Table 16.6 Proposed common currency on trade

Variables	Coefficients	Standard errors
GDP	1.683**	0.6632502
GDP per capita	1.637	1.11855
Distance	0.152	2.086502 1
Border	-0.527	0.971615
Colonizer	0.606 *	0.3539668
Incolo	1.068***	0.2302132
Common currency	0.505	0.6972794
Exchange rate volatility	0.941 **	0.476104
Exchange rate peak	0.282 ***	0.1022529
Cons	-28.79406 ***	11.00541

Note: *, ** and *** represent rejection of null hypothesis at 10%, 5% and 1%. Authors' Estimates

(2005) who argues that economic scale is important for trade with other countries. In support of this, Vijayasri (2013) stipulates that countries produce relatively large amounts of certain raw materials in order to exchange with other countries what cannot be produced with existing resources. As a country produces more, economic activity increases along GDP, leading to further trade effects.

GDP per capita has the expected positive sign but statistically insignificant to trade with a coefficient of 1.637. This result shows that other relevant factors not specified in the model had an insubstantial impact on trade. Distance is found to positively affect trade with an estimated coefficient of 0.152 but statistically insignificant. The result was startling but logically plausible because countries in the sub-region are geographically close to one another. The results indicate that as distance increases, the trade cost increases, reducing the level of trade among member states. The result confirms Bausinger et al. (2015) report that the proximity of member-states facilitates trade.

Border is found to have a negative impact on the level of trade in SACU. The estimated coefficient of -0.527 and statistically insignificant. The result is surprising but logically plausible due to countries' intense trade with South Africa than other SACU members. The World Bank (2015) attributes this to the many borders not operating on a 24 days/7 days a week basis and the adverse effects of border clearance which poses delays at the main corridors of SACU, and its effect on trade.

This implies that artificial impediments have been mounted at the borders that compound trade costs.

Countries that share the same colonizer are found to have a positive effect on trade. The estimated coefficient is 0.606 and significant at 10%. Thus, countries trade based on the current strive of ameliorated conditions due to established colonial trade links and memberships of international organizations through treaties with colonizers. SACU countries sharing colonial ties substantially reduced the trade cost (Grynberg & Motswapong, 2012; Kagochi & Durmaz, 2018). Incolo is a variable that represents a member of the union colonized the other. It is found to have a positive effect on trade and is significant at 10%. The result is not startling because South Africa was Namibia's major trade partner within the union, according to the UNCTAD database.

Having a common currency is found to have a positive and but insignificant impact on trade, with an estimated coefficient of 0.505. The result demonstrate the positive effect of adopting a common currency and that it stimulates trade by reducing transaction costs. This result matches the conclusion drawn by Rose (2000a) that adopting a common currency increases trade flows within countries. Theoretically, adopting a common currency ensures greater integration using political, social, economic, and cultural to attenuate ills in the trade bloc.

Exchange rate volatility also has a positive and significant effect on trade in the sub-region. The estimated coefficient is 0.941 and statistically significant at 5%. Again, interpreting as semi- elasticity, exchange rate volatility is associated with an increased trade of about 0.009%. According to the findings, exchange rate plays a far more expected role in the level of trade in the sub-region. Thus, when exchange rate volatility is low, trade increases among member states since it reduces the cost of trading, indicating that the exchange rate stimulates trade in the sub-region due to the practice of the currencies fixed to the South African Rand and the financial market serving as a buffer for the volatility of the Rand. The result attests to the reason for being the most successful REC in Africa. However, adopting a common currency is superlative to practicing pegged currency due to greater transparency and intense trading within countries than merely trading among countries.

Furthermore, the exchange rate peak is found to have a positive and significant effect on trade. The estimated coefficient is 0.282 at 1% level of significant. The result indicates that the exchange rate was low peaked for most trading periods in the years under study. This partly accounts for the relatively high level of trade among member states compared to other African countries in other trade blocs. The high or low peak captures the unpredicted variation of exchange rate volatility. The adverse effect of volatility on exports is greater the higher the value of the unpredicted factors. The higher the volatility (on exports high peak), the greater the adverse effect on the level of exports (Serenis & Tsounis, 2014; Panda & Mohanty, 2015).

Results for Trade Potential in the SACU

The study seeks to determine whether countries are over-trading or under-trading empirically (Table 16.7).

The negative mean value depicts that countries in the SACU have the potential to trade and, therefore, currently are under trading. Countries will be trading more based on their economic and geographic fundamentals in this context. The result shows there are impediments to trade in SACU.

CONCLUSIONS AND RECOMMENDATIONS

Africa records low intra-regional trade, and many efforts have been made to encourage the regional blocs to trade among themselves to facilitate the continent's growth. The study's main objective was to estimate the effect of adopting a common currency on intra-regional trade in the Southern Africa Customs Union and the Economic Community of West African Countries. The study further estimated whether countries were overtrading or under-trading among themselves. The study adopted the Poisson Pseudo Maximum Likelihood (PPML) estimates.

The results show that increases in GDP and per capita GDP enhance trade in the ECOWAS sub- region. Distance is revealed to have a negative effect on trade, indicating that as distance increases, the cost involved in trading increases, therefore reducing trade among member states.

Table 16.7 Trade potential in SACU

Variable	Observation	Mean	Standard deviation	Minimum	Maximum
Trade potential	126	−2.7808	9.7008	−6.6309	9.3208

Note: The Minimum and Maximum depict the range for trading. Authors' Estimates

Countries sharing the same colonizer are found to trade more among themselves and their colonial master, reducing trade in the sub-region. Language also reveals that countries speaking the same language (WAEMU for French and WAMZ for English) trade among themselves. The use of common currency is found to have a strong positive and significant impact on trade. The result shows that when exchange rate volatility is high, the level of trade declines among member states and that the exchange rate was highly peaked for most trading periods in the years under study. The border could not explain the variations in trade. It is also revealed that adopting a common currency will lead to trade creation in the sub-region. However, trade potential in the sub-region is found to be minimal.

Per the findings on the effect of the proposed ECOWAS currency union on intra-regional trade, the study proposed that the ECOWAS sub-region has an incentive to adopt a common currency by achieving the nominal convergence criteria. In line with the findings of the proposed ECOWAS currency union's impact on intra-regional trade, this study suggests that ECOWAS subregions have an incentive to adopt a common currency by meeting nominal convergence criteria. ECOWAS should focus on providing technical assistance to all Member States to facilitate the convergence criteria of the policies implemented. Exchange rate fluctuations have been found to adversely affect trade in subregions. The introduction of a common currency will eliminate exchange rate fluctuations and inflation distortions between countries. In this context, the focus of ECOWAS should be on the stability of the common currency being introduced. Therefore, ECOWAS needs to focus on financial market development as it can reduce currency volatility by indexing all financial assets in a common currency and building a financial market buffer. Financial institutions are supposed to be quoted in a common currency. This gives potential investors confidence in the financial markets of various ECOWAS countries.

ECOWAS needs to advise countries on the need to monetize their budget deficits. This will devaluate the currency and increase national debt repayment obligations by adhering to the proposed policies implemented by the central bank. In addition, countries must comply with fiscal convergence standards to ensure a sustainable monetary union.

Furthermore, the results show that trade resulting from a common currency has a trade-creating effect in the sub-regions. Therefore, ECOWAS needs to take steps to reduce the outflow of FDI and limit the outflow of financial assets from subregions. In this context, the benefits of joining a monetary union will be fully enhanced. In addition, ECOWAS needs to establish an institution to address trade-related issues between Member States.

Finally, the potential for trade in subregions is assessed as minimal, suggesting that the outlook for trade in subregions is large and needs to develop. The results showed that the countries are undertrading. The focus of ECOWAS should be on the removal of trade and non-trade barriers through the formation of a monetary union. It is known that the home currency functions as a trade barrier due to fluctuations in exchange rates. A currency union is a means of eliminating the effects of exchange rate fluctuations and ensuring price transparency.

The Poisson Pseudo Maximum Likelihood (PPML) estimates for the SACU sub-region showed that GDP, GDP per capita, colonizer, exchange rate volatility, and peak showed a positive impact on trade whereas distance and border had a negative impact on trade. The study showed that countries fixing their currencies to the South African Rand had a significant impact on trade due to the positive exchange rate volatility coefficient.

In this background, adopting a common currency will stimulate trade, but a greater portion of the trade will be due to greater trade potential and a pool of non-members in the SADC. However, a common currency will ensure greater price transparency, market integration, and diversification; therefore, countries should adopt a currency union with a common policy. The study showed that more trade potential could be unleashed when a common currency is adopted in the trade bloc. Also, the estimates showed that countries are trading below their geographic and economic fundamentals; therefore, adopting a common currency can have a greater effect on trade in the sub-region. The study recommends that countries adopt currency unions with a common policy to effectively unearth more trading potentials. The authorities should judiciously engage in a road map towards the diversification of the economies. Also, the study recommends that SACU prioritize infrastructural development, notably transportation. Finally, the study underpins the essence of sound political, social and cultural environment in ensuring the economic well-being of member-states. This indicates that there are impediments to trade in the sub-region. The use of a common currency and coordination of economic policy can be a means by which trade potential in the sub-region can be harnessed.

REFERENCES

Abban, S., & Ofori-Abebrese, G. (2019). *The prospect of ECOWAS currency union on intra-regional trade* (MPRA paper 102226). University Library of Munich.
African Development Bank Group. (2018). *Annual report 2018.* http://www.afdb.org/fileadmin/uploads/afdb/Documents/Generic-
Alesina, A., Spolaore, E., & Wacziarg, R. (2005). Trade, growth and the size of countries. In *Handbook of economic growth* (Vol. 1, pp. 1499–1542). Elsevier.
Amoah, D. (2013). *Feasibility study of a single currency for West African.*
Anokyc, M., A., & Imran S. C. (2014). The currency union effect on intra-regional trade in Economic Community of West African States (ECOWAS). *Journal of International Trade Law and Policy, 13*(2), 102–122. https://doi.org/10.1108/JITLP-04-2013-0008
Bausinger, M., Bertlesmann-Scott, T., Charalambides, N., Slabbert, J., & Van Heerden, F. (2015). Overcoming Barriers to Supply Chain Integration in SACU. World Bank Working Papers December 2015.
Bhowmik, D., & Sen, R. K. (2013). Economic integration in SACU through common currency. *The Indian Economic Journal, 61*(3), 358–380.
Bobková, B. (2012). *Gravity model estimation using panel data-is logarithmic transformation advisable?* Univerzita Karlova, Fakulta sociálních věd.
Crowley, P. M., Garcia, E., & Quah, C. H. (2013). *Is Europe growing together or growing apart?* (Bank of Finland Research discussion paper, 33).
Eichengreen, B., & Irwin, D. A. (1996). *The role of history in bilateral trade* (Working paper 5565). National Bureau of Economic Research.
Ethier, W. (1973). International trade and the forward exchange market. *The American Economic Review, 63*(3), 494–503.
Gagnon, J. E. (1993). Exchange rate variability and the level of international trade. *Journal of International Economics, 34*(3–4), 269–287.
Glick, R., & Rose, A. K. (2002). Does a currency union affect trade? The time-series evidence. *European Economic Review, 46*(6), 1125–1151.
Grynberg, R., & Motswapong, M. (2012). SACU revenue sharing formula: towards a developmental agreement. No 32, Working Papers from Botswana Institute for Development Policy Analysis.
International Monetary Fund. (2013). *Promoting a more secure and stable global economy.* International Monetary Fund Annual Report 2013, ISBN 9781475515398/2227-8915.
Kagochi, J., & Durmaz, N. (2018). Assessing RTAs inter-regional trade enhancement in Sub-Saharan Africa. https://doi.org/10.1080/23322039.2018.1482662.
Kamara, M. S. H. (2015). *An analysis of the proposed currency union of the Economic Community of West African States (ECOWAS).* Doctoral dissertation, University of Leeds.
Kaplan, S. (2006). West African integration: A new development paradigm? *Washington Quarterly, 29*(4), 81–97.

Kenen, P. (1969). The theory of optimum currency areas: An eclectic view. *Monetary Problems of the International Economy, 45*(3), 41–60.
Komárek, L. and Horvath, R. (2002). Optimum Currency Area Theory: A Framework for Discussion about Monetary Integration. Economic Research Papers 269460, University of Warwick - Department of Economics.
Masson, P. R. (2008). Currency unions in Africa: Is the trade effect substantial enough to justify their formation? *The World Economy, 31*(4), 533–547.
McKinnon, R. I. (1963). Optimum currency areas. *The American Economic Review, 53*(4), 717–725.
Mensah, I. (2015). Monetary and economic union in West Africa: An analysis on trade. *International Journal of Business and Economic Sciences Applied Research (IJBESAR), 8*(2), 87–118.
Micco, A., Stein, E., & Ordoñez, G. (2003). The currency union effect on trade: Early evidence from EMU. *Economic Policy, 18*(37), 315–356.
Mundell, R. A. (1961). A theory of optimum currency areas. *The American Economic Review, 51*(4), 657–665.
Ncube, M., Brixiova, Z., & Meng, Q. (2014). *Can intra-regional trade act as a global shock absorber in Africa?* Williams Davidson Institute Working Paper. Number 1073.
Ngwenya, M. (2015). The promotion and protection of foreign investment in South Africa: a critical review of promotion and protection of Investment Bill 2013 (Doctoral dissertation).
Ofori-Abebrese, G. (2006). The eco and economic development of West Africa. *Journal of Science and Technology (Ghana), 26*(2), 124–136.
Osabuohien, E. S., & Efobi, U. R. (2013). Africa's money in Africa. *South African Journal of Economics, 81*(2), 292–306.
Panda, S., & Mohanty, R. K. (2015). Effects of exchange rate volatility on exports: Evidence from India. *Economic Bulletin, 35*(1), 305–312.
Patroba, H., & Nene, M. (2013). *Is SACU ready for a monetary union?* South African Institute of International Affairs.
Qureshi, M., & Tsangarides, C. (2009). Exchange rate regimes and trade: Is Africa different? In *Growth and institutions in African development*.
Rametsi, T. S. (2015). *Is southern African custom union an optimum currency area?* Doctoral dissertation.
Rose, A. K. (2000a). One money, one market: The effect of common currencies on trade. *Economic Policy, 15*(30), 08–45.
Rose, A. K. (2008). Is EMU becoming an optimum currency area? The evidence on trade and business cycle synchronization. University of California, Berkeley working paper, mimeo.
Rose, A. K., & Van Wincoop, E. (2001). National money as a barrier to international trade: The real case for currency union. *American Economic Review, 91*(2), 386–390.
Rose, A. (2000b). One money, one market: Estimating the effect of common currencies on trade. *Economic Policy, 15*(April), 7–45.

SACU (2017). 2017 Annual Report, Implementing a common agenda towards regional integration in Southern Africa.
Sercu, P., & Vanhulle, C. (1992). Exchange rate volatility, international trade, and the value of exporting firms. *Journal of Banking & Finance, 16*(1), 155–182.
Serenis, D., & Nicholas, T. (2012). *A new approach for measuring volatility of the exchange rate.* http://www.researchgate.net/publication/252322730_
Serenis, D., & Tsounis, N. (2014). *Exchange rate volatility and aggregate exports: Evidence from two small countries* (ISRN Economics, 2014).
Settles, J. D. (1996). *The impact of colonialism on African economic development.*
Silva, J. S., & Tenreyro, S. (2006). The log of gravity. *The Review of Economics and Statistics, 88*(4), 641–658.
Silva, J. S., & Tenreyro, S. (2011). Further simulation evidence on the performance of the Poisson pseudo-maximum likelihood estimator. *Economics Letters, 112*(2), 220–222.
South African Reserve Bank. (2011). *Annual economic report.* http://static.pmg.org.za/docs/111012sarbrep_0.pdf
Southern African Reseve Bank. (2017). *Promoting the economic well-being of South Africans.* http://resbank.onlinereport.co.za/2017/index.html
Tchokote, J., Uche, M. E., & Agboola, Y. H. (2015). Impact of exchange rate volatility on net- export in selected west African countries. *AshEse Journal of Economics, 1*(4), 57–73.
Templeton, F. (2017). *Aspiration requires commitment.* Franklin Resources Inc. Annual Report, Frank Templeton Investment. http://www.franklintempleton.com/forms-literature/download/FSS1-A
Torres, C., & van Seters, J. (2016). *Overview of trade and barriers to trade in West Africa* (European Centre for Development Policy Management discussion paper, 195).
UNCTAD (2018). Trade and Development Report 2018.
Vavrek, Š. (1996). Of thesis: Estimation methods of gravity models. *International Economics, 40*(1–2), 23–39.
Vavrek, Š. (2018). Of thesis: Estimation methods of gravity models. *International Economics, 40*(1–2), 23–39.
Vijayasri, G. V. (2013). The importance of international trade in the world. *International Journal of Marketing, Financial Services & Management Research, 2*(9), 111–119.
Viner, J. (1950). Full employment at whatever cost. *The Quarterly Journal of Economics, 64*(3), 385–407.
Vrňáková, I., & Bartušková, H. (2013). Is euro area an optimal currency area and what barriers could obstruct its future development? *Economic Studies & Analyses/Acta VSFS, 7*(2).
World Bank (2015). "An Analysis of Issues Shaping Africa's Economic Future." Africa's Pulse Volume 11. Washington, DC.

CHAPTER 17

A Single Currency for Africa: Challenges and Possibilities

Augustin Ntembe

INTRODUCTION

African countries established the Organization for Africa Unity (OAU) in 1963 to promote unity and solidarity among African states, promote socio-economic development to achieve better lives for Africa's peoples, and integrate the continent. The prospect of a common African currency was envisioned at the creation of the OAU. With the launching of the African Union in 2002, the idea became a possibility as African leaders made it one of the key goals of the union (Masson & Pattillo, 2004a, 2004b, 2004c). Several institutions have been created to move forward this vision of a single African currency and economic integration but have largely failed to materialize into concrete structures because of ideological differences and financial structures that are highly entangled (Ekekwe, 2009). However, the successful launching of a single European currency, the Euro, and the economic benefits accruing to European member countries so far has reignited Africa's desire for a single currency.

A. Ntembe (✉)
Bowie State University, Bowie, MD, USA
e-mail: nntembe@bowiestate.edu

© The Author(s), under exclusive license to Springer Nature Switzerland AG 2022
A. A. Amin et al. (eds.), *Monetary and Financial Systems in Africa*,
https://doi.org/10.1007/978-3-030-96225-8_17

Many questions remain to be answered regarding the African context. Do African countries perform better when they use national currencies or when they surrender their monetary policy independence to a monetary union? If African countries form a monetary union, will such a union correspond to an optimum currency area? The theory of optimal currency area provides the necessary and sufficient criteria for creating a single currency but is it relevant to the African context? The most frequently advanced argument against a single currency for Africa is that the continent's economies will not satisfy the optimum currency criteria or attain macroeconomic convergence. However, the growth in international trade in the last few decades and rapid integration of world economies raises questions regarding the relevance of national currencies and redirects attention towards the transaction benefits of common currencies.

This chapter examines the existing literature on single currencies for relevant theoretical and empirical considerations. Thus, the chapter begins with background information on the creation of a single African monetary union and a single currency, evaluates the literature and findings from the research on the creation of the single African currency, and examines the costs and benefits of a single currency union. Finally, a way forward for monetary integration in Africa is proposed based on the options available to African monetary authorities and the specificities of African economies.

HISTORICAL BACKGROUND

In May 1963, twenty-eight African leaders met in Addis Ababa, Ethiopia, to sign the Charter of the Organization of African Unity (OAU), which inter-alia was to foster unity and promote solidarity among the newly independent African states. The signing of the Charter of the OAU was a stepping stone towards greater cooperation among African nations. The Charter called for the respect of the sovereignty and the territorial integrity of each member state (Elias, 1965). The creation of the OAU saw the emergence of the Casablanca Group, which advocated for a federal model similar to the United States of America as opposed to the Monrovia, which believed that independent African states could cooperate and live in harmony with each other without resorting to political federation and integration (Ekwealer & Mtshali, 2018).

The Casablanca group led by Kwame Nkrumah of Ghana and Julius Nyerere of Tanzania advanced arguments for the newly independent nations to unite. However, Nyerere supported that such an arrangement should emerge from a gradual formation of regional bodies across the continent (Simura & Asuelime, 2017). Dr. Nkrumah believed that his proposal would bring unity and prosperity to Africa (Banienuba, 2013). A united Africa would undoubtedly establish a common currency, central bank, and foreign trade policy. However, the proponents of the Casablanca Group were viewed as radicals and extremists as opposed to the proponents of the Monrovia Model that favored a coalition based on the European model (Ta'a, 2014; Ekwealer & Mtshali, 2018). Nevertheless, the type of African unity advocated by the Monrovia Group that allows for a loose coalition between the newly independent states prevailed due to significant backing by the newly independent states and Europe.

Ghanaian Leader Kwame Nkrumah in his iconic speech during the inaugural ceremony of the OAU suggested the creation of the United States of Africa. Some African leaders supported the vision of a united Africa, but most feared that such a move could dissolve the different countries' territorial integrity and sovereignty, especially those who fought hard to gain independence.

Thus, ideological differences among countries and the desire of some countries to remain tied to the interests of their colonists, such as some former French colonies, made it difficult for full integration between African countries (Ekwealer & Mtshali, 2018).

The OAU summit held in Lagos, Nigeria, in July 1980 was organized to address the issue of neo-colonialism in Africa and craft a new path for Africa. A key concern for the continent's development was the dependence on exports of primary products and a need to promote the continent's industrialization process. Therefore, the summit also proposed the establishment of the African Economic Community (AEC) based on the African Common Market (Martin, 1993, p. 70). The proposal set the AEC to become operational by 2000. The African Economic Community seeks to (1) to promote the economic, social, and cultural development of Africa, (2) integrate the African economies leading to increased economic self-reliance; (3) harness and develop Africa's human and material resources; (4) promote cooperation to raise the standard of living and enhance economic stability; (5) foster peaceful relations among member states; and (6) contribute to the progress, development, and economic integration of the continent.

The objectives set at the treaty were to be achieved mainly through trade liberalization between member states by (1) abolishing customs duties and non-trade barriers and the eventual creation of a free trade area,

(2) harmonize policies across member states in areas of agriculture, industry, transport, communication, energy, finance, science, and technology; (3) removal of obstacles to the free movement of people, goods, services, capital and (4) the establishment of a common market (Naldi & Magliveras, 1999). The Lagos Plan of Action was concretized in the Abuja Treaty to create the African Economic Community. The AEC Treaty was signed on June 3, 1991, in Abuja, Nigeria, and entered into force in May 1994 (Marinoz, 2014). The treaty was to be implemented in six stages for 34 years, culminating in creating the African economic and monetary union and a common currency (Marinoz, 2014).

The desire for the United States of Africa was again resurrected by the Libyan leader Colonel Muammar Gaddafi and President Robert Mugabe of Zimbabwe, who took up the mantle and became post-independence proponents of the push for a united Africa (Ekwealer & Mtshali, 2018). The Libyan leader vigorously led this idea before his demise in 2011. To Ghadaffi, a United Africa as federated states with one currency, one passport, and one army will lead to a strong Africa that is competitive internationally. Gaddafi showed his support for a united Africa when he disbursed financial resources towards achieving the plan. However, Ghadaffi's fast-track proposal for the United States of Africa, based on federated states organized in a federalist and demographic framework, was received with opposition from some countries, notably Nigeria, Kenya, and Zambia (Ekwealer & Mtshali, 2018).

African Economic Community Treaty

The modalities for establishing the African Economic Community (AEC) are provided in Article 6 of the Abuja Treaty. The AEC will progress via six stages spread over not exceeding thirty-four years (34). Specific activities shall be assigned and implemented concurrently (Ofodile, 2015) during each stage. The first stage consists of strengthening existing regional communities and establishing new ones where they do not exist. This stage will last for a period not exceeding five (5) years and should last until 1999.

By the time the treaty came into force, there were four Regional Economic Communities (RECs) in Africa, and since then, new communities have been created (See Fig. 17.1 and Table 17.1). A decision was arrived at in 2006 that apart from the above communities, the AU will no longer accept any other community as a building block of the African

Economic Community (Marinoz, 2014). Instead, the AU strategy towards monetary integration promotes and strengthens regional monetary unions, which will later merge to create a single African Central Bank and currency.

A successful unification of currencies in Africa will depend on the ability of the African Union to develop and strengthen the existing regional communities as proposed in the Abuja Treaty. However, the problem facing RECs in Africa is that many countries belong to more than one REC, such as Angola, Botswana, Burundi, Demographic Republic of Congo, Malawi, Mauritius, Namibia, Seychelles, Swaziland, Rwanda, Zambia, and Zimbabwe (see Table 17.1). In addition, different communities have timetables for harmonizing trade policies and eliminating tariff and non-tariff barriers, which creates a considerable obstacle to integration.

During the second stage, which will take eight (8) years, the RECs will stabilize tariffs and non- tariff barriers to regional and intra-community trade. Concurrently, sectoral integration at a regional and continent-wide level in

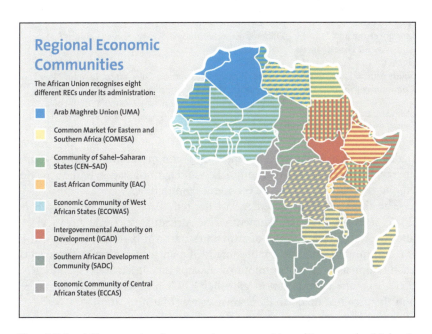

Fig. 17.1 African regional economic communities. (Source: de Melo & Brown, 2018)

Table 17.1 Membership in regional communities

Regional community	Member countries
Arab Magreb Union (AMU)	Algeria, Libya, Mauritania. Morocco and Tunisia
Community of Sahel-Saharan States (CEN-SAD)	Benin, Burkina Faso, C.A.R., Chad, Comoros, Cote d'Ivoire, Djibouti, Egypt, Eritrea, Gambia, Ghana, Guinea, Guinea Bissau, Kenya, Libya, Mali, Mauritania, Morocco, Niger, Nigeria, Sao Tome, Senegal, Sierra Leone, Somalia, Sudan, Togo, Tunisia
Common Market for Eastern and Southern Africa (COMESA.)	Burundi, Comoros, DR Congo, Djibouti, Egypt, Eritrea, Eswatini, Ethiopia, Kenya, Libya, Madagascar, Malawi, Mauritius, Rwanda, Somalia, Seychelles, Sudan, Tunisia, Uganda, Zambia, Zimbabwe
East African Community (EAC.)	Burundi, Kenya, Rwanda, Tanzania, South Sudan, Uganda
Economic Community of Central Africa (ECCAS.)	Angola, Burundi, Cameroon, C.A.R., Chad, Congo, Dr Congo, Equatorial Guinea, Gabon, Sao Tome
Economic Community of West African States (ECOWAS.)	Benin, Burkina Faso, Cabo Verde, Cote d'Ivoire, Gambia, Ghana, Guinea, Guinea Bissau, Liberia, Mali, Niger, Nigeria, Senegal, Sierra Leone, Togo
Intergovernmental Authority on Development (IGAD.)	Djibouti, Eritrea, Ethiopia, Kenya, Somalia, South Sudan, Sudan, Uganda
South African Development Community (SADC)	Angola, Botswana, Comoros, DR Congo, Eswatini, Lesotho, Madagascar, Malawi, Mauritius, Mozambique, Namibia, Seychelles, South Africa, Tanzania, Zambia, Zimbabwe

Source: African Trade Statistics 2020 Yearbook

trade, agriculture, finance, transport and communication, industry, and energy. Finally, there will be coordination and harmonization of the activities among the existing and future economic communities.

The third stage, expected to last for ten years and to be realized by 2017, includes the establishment of an African Free Trade Area (AfTA) and the gradual elimination of tariff and non-tariff barriers to trade within the community, and the establishment of a customs union at the level of each regional economic community. Except for UMA, IGAD, and CEN-SAD, to some extent, almost all other RECs have completed this stage, and the progress made so far is satisfactory (Marinoz, 2014).

Stage four, scheduled to be accomplished for a period not exceeding two (2) years, include the coordination and harmonization of tariff and non-tariff systems among RECs with the view to establishing a continent-wide customs union through the adoption of a common policy in areas such as agriculture, transport and communication, industry, energy, and scientific research. Furthermore, monetary, financial, and fiscal policies will be harmonized during this stage. In addition, the creation of the Tripartite Free Trade Area between the Common Market for Eastern and Southern Africa (COMESA), Southern African Development Community (SADC), and East African Community (EAC) in 2008 to abolish trade barriers between each other was a positive step and progress towards the economic integration of the continent.

The fifth stage will be implemented for a period not exceeding four (4) years and will establish an African Common Market. Also, a common policy will be adopted in several areas, including agriculture, transport, communications, industry, energy, and scientific research, harmonizing monetary, financial, and fiscal policies; the application of the free movement of persons within the AECs.

The final stage is expected not to exceed five (5) years and includes the consolidation and strengthening of the African Common Market structure. The process involves the free movement of people, goods, capital, and services; the integration of all the sectors, namely economic, political, social, and cultural; the establishment of a single domestic market and a Pan-African Economic and Monetary Union; and the sixth stage will culminate in setting up the African Central Bank and the creation of a single African Currency. The fifth and sixth stages are yet to make any progress so far but will witness the establishment of a Pan-African Parliament. An African Monetary Union will be set up during the sixth and final stage, and a single African Central Bank and currency will be created.

The question that remains is whether African countries need to satisfy convergence criteria for optimum currency to launch the single currency. Two opposing views on the practicality of a single African currency have emerged. One is that the plan is ambitious and is not pragmatic. The other is that a common currency has the potential for a strong value given the world's dependence on African commodities. A discussion of the optimum currency area in the next section will provide a perspective of African economies with regards to convergence criteria.

Is Africa an Optimum Currency Area? A Theoretical Perspective

Developed from the seminal work of Mundell (1961) and extended by McKinnon (1963), the Optimal Currency Area (OCA) provided theoretical foundations for the empirical work and new developments that laid the framework in the creation of the single European Monetary Union.

The optimum currency area provides a set of criteria that a country must meet to gain membership in a currency union. The first criteria are openness to trade and intraregional trade. The criteria proposed by McKinnon (1963) suggests that countries that are open to international trade do not need to worry about adhering to a single currency union and losing an exchange rate. The reason is simply that an exchange rate is no longer an adjustment tool for open economies because changes in the nominal exchange rate will leave the real exchange rate unaffected due to changes in domestic prices (Jager & Hafner, 2013).

Intra-regional trade is critical for product integration and economic integration (Jager & Hafner, 2013). It can improve the competitiveness of the continent's industry through economies of scale and high productivity. Intra-African trade is able to reinforce the product value chain and help transfer knowledge and technology across countries through spillover effects (Kimenyi & Routman, 2012). In addition, intra-regional trade can spur infrastructure development and thus attract foreign direct investment. It should be underlined here that Africa's infrastructure is in despair but critical in accelerating economic growth. The desire for African countries to increase intra-Africa trade can spur infrastructural development. However, intra-regional trade in Africa was only 10 percent in 2010. Besides, most African exports went to more advanced nations. As a result, intra-African trade as a percentage of total trade was only 17 percent in 2017.

Although trade intra-African trade is slowly ticking up, the low trade among African countries is partly due to low income compared to levels in Europe (69%), Asia (59%), and North America (31%) (Masson, 2006a, 2006b). Nevertheless, African trade was projected to increase by about 15 to 25%, depending on the liberalization efforts after the African Continental Free Trade Area (AfCFTA) became operational (Songwe, 2019). African countries signed the AfCFTA Agreement in 2018 which commits African countries to remove tariffs on 90 percent of goods and progressively liberalize trade on services and remove other trade barriers, thus creating a single market for the free movement of goods and services (Songwe, 2019). The successful implementation of trade liberalization efforts will make Africa the most extensive free trade area globally.

Kenen (1969) suggests that diversity in a nation's product mix was more relevant to forming an optimum currency area, and the absence of diversification in a nation's product mix could decrease revenue if there is a negative demand shock that affects exports. Kenen (1969) further argued that a well-diversified economy has a diversified export sector, and the effect of a positive shock in one industry will cancel out the effect of a negative shock in another industry resulting in macroeconomic stability. Such economic diversification would allow the economy to make trade changes compared to a single-product economy and could tolerate small costs associated with abandoning their national currencies to benefit a single currency.

Songwe and Winkler (2012) have opined that trade diversification is critical as it allows countries to resist changes in demand resulting from economic downturns in importing countries and price cuts. Export diversification can also allow countries exporting commodities to shift to high value-added products and services. African reliance on the sale of primary products to the benefit of industrialized nations hinders diversification and intra-African trade. Small manufacturing and semi-transformation of primary products might serve as a good starting point to promote trade diversification and industrialization.

The second criteria for an OCA are labor mobility and wage flexibility. Mundell (1961) suggests that countries open to factors and labor mobility were critical for forming an optimum currency area. The main cost of monetary integration is losing monetary policy independence for member countries to smooth out business cycles and stabilize the economy. High wage flexibility and labor mobility will allow countries joining a monetary union to have less difficulty adjusting to shifts in demand than countries with their national currencies and are prone to using devaluations or revaluations as tools for economic stabilization.

If labor were highly mobile, it would be possible for the economy to adjust quickly to shocks. As Mundell suggested, labor could migrate from regions facing depression to those that are prospering. McKinnon and Mundell agreed that the presence of labor mobility between regions provides the rationale for the formation of a common currency area. Furthermore, countries joining an economic union with similar economic structures combined with a low degree of economic specialization will reduce the vulnerability to asymmetric shocks. Also, economies that are similar in size, openness, level of economic development, and share proximate geographical area are likely to gain more from monetary integration than those that are dissimilar.

Since the birth of the European monetary union, economists have developed more interest in the OCA theory (Tavlas, 1993, p. 663). The new optimum currency theory has explored different issues mainly, those relating to the effectiveness of the monetary policy, credibility of monetary policy, correlation and variation of shocks, labor market institutions, and many others. While this chapter is not intended to explore the different theoretical constructs, the peculiarity of African economies and African political landscape require much resolve on the part of African political leaders and policymakers to strengthen economic and political institutions and to ensure that there is political stability in addition to meeting up to some extent with criteria developed in the theories.

CAN AFRICAN ECONOMIES CONVERGE?

The Constitutive Act of the African Union, ratified by member states in Lomé, Togo on July 11, 2000, proposed the formation of an African Monetary Union through the integration of regional monetary zones and the establishment of an African Monetary Fund, and the African Central Bank. A coherent implementation of the six stages of the African Economic Community is similar to the five degrees of economic integration identified by Balassa (1961). Balassa's stages include the setting up of a free trade area, a customs union, a common market, an economic union, and finally, economic integration, which also cumulates in the formation of a monetary union and the harmonization of monetary and fiscal policies administered under one supranational authority (Ekekwe, 2009). The African Union's strategy for economic and monetary integration is to promote the integration of regional economic communities to enable them to develop strong economic blocs. However, regional integration is hindered by many shortcomings, including limited mobility of labor and people, infrastructure in despair, and weak institutional structures compared to Europe.

Countries that form a monetary union and thus an optimum currency area must have a widely diversified production and export base and possess similar characteristics (Baldwin, Wyplosz, 2006). Export diversification is critical since highly diversified countries are less susceptible to economic shocks. Another question regarding the desirability of a single currency in Africa is whether they can adequately deal with asymmetric shocks. Masson and Pattillo (2002) analyzed shocks that affect African countries and concluded using empirical evidence that African economies have highly heterogeneous production structures and face asymmetric shocks that could exacerbate the challenges of forming a monetary union.

A challenge of a single currency to most African countries is establishing a central bank that is more independent and imposes more discipline over fiscal policies than national central banks (Masson, 2006a, 2006b). A key objective of macroeconomic policy is to maintain internal balance, achieve full employment, and keep inflation at the lowest level. The countries will accomplish macroeconomic goals during recessions through expansionary monetary policies, while contractionary policies will be employed during high inflation. With a monetary union, member economies will lose their ability to deal with such situations and would be hesitant to join monetary unions where there are divergences in external and asymmetric shocks with especially key members of the monetary union (Ekekwe, 2009). Differences in the handling of fiscal policies by different economies with different political agendas and goals can ultimately heighten inflation in the currency area. The situation will have varying impacts on nations, with some losing and some gaining. Some countries already have a stable and well-developed currency could adversely be affected by joining a poorly managed single currency with high inflation (Ekekwe, 2009).

BENEFITS OF A SINGLE AFRICAN CURRENCY

There is a resurgence of interest in analyzing currency unions as a form of monetary arrangement. The renewal of interest in currency unions has largely been attributed to the European single currency experience. Europe has successfully launched the Euro, which has stimulated interest in other regions, including Africa. The benefits from a common currency arise mostly from creating trade linkages. Adopting the single currency for African countries' regions can reinforce regional integration and solidarity among nations, and a single currency within a region promotes trade and economic growth (Collier, 1991). Also, inflation would largely be controlled since money printing is not a financing option for nations with a single currency. This benefits from employing productivity and better economic strategies to manage budget deficits (Ekekwe, 2009). The economy's long-term macroeconomic stability resulting from the common monetary union and the central bank provides better fiscal control mechanisms to control inflation.

The efficient implementation of the single currency can offer Africa a wide range of benefits. First, the single currency could enhance competition among nations leading to reforms that foster greater cooperation among nations. Second, the adoption of a single currency in Africa could improve the management of African economies through fiscal prudence that would lead to macroeconomic stability and improvement in international reputation. Third, creating a monetary union may improve central banks' monetary policies, which tend to face significant pressure to finance government deficits, thus producing high inflation and depreciating currencies. Thus, participation in a single currency that insulates the central bank from government pressures will reinforce central bank independence and greater stability and fiscal discipline.

Countries could become more competitive, leading to greater productivity, efficiency in allocating resources, and better economic policies and job growth. A common central bank and single currency could potentially reduce business costs, the movement of resources and people across the region, and more stable political systems and governments. A large monetary union is likely to internalize more trade, and because of a single currency, all trade will become domestic trade between a heterogeneous group of countries (Alesina & Barro, 2002).

Although trade within African regions tends to be a small portion of total trade, adopting a single currency can increase intra-African trade. However, consistent with the gravity model, countries will trade more with richer countries with higher per capita incomes requiring that African countries trade more with European nations, North America, and Asia than within African countries. Table 17.2 shows the distribution of African Union trade by economic regions in millions of US dollars. The table shows the share for intra-African Union trade not exceeding 25% in any years under consideration.

Costs of Monetary Integration in Africa

Considered highly successful, monetary integration in Europe did not come without obstacles and missteps. The process of replacing national currencies with a common European currency (the EURO) was besieged with uncertainties. African countries are plagued with severe fiscal

Table 17.2 African Union trade by economic regions-imports (millions USD)

Intra-African Union Trade, millions US dollars

	2013	2014	2015	2016	2017	2018	2019
Total AU imports	621,828.3	638,170.5	592,117.5	508,071.7	510,782.7	572,253.2	560,465.5
Intra AU imports	97,626.6	95,028.2	81,244.2	61,789.4	61,986.0	74,732.4	70,432.7
Share of intra-AU imports	15.7	14.9	13.7	12.2	12.1	13.1	12.6
Total AU Exports	575,188.5	554,621.5	401,821.0	348,671.3	429,551.1	491,107.2	465,920.8
Intra AU exports	104,503.3	106,491.1	95,302.0	82,191.8	84,083.2	98,565.5	91,819.7
Share of Intra AU exports %	18.2	19.2	23.7	23.6	19.6	20.1	19.7

Source: AFRICA TRADE

problems and fragile monetary institutions compared to European economies. Certainly, African countries will take decades to create such an institution if the Europeans with more developed and stable bureaucracies took over fifty years to achieve a single common currency. The monetary union would undoubtedly be an enormous challenge for African nations. Furthermore, ideological differences between African countries are visible and present significant obstacles to adopting a common currency for the continent.

African economies are characteristically weak, and African countries have unstable political systems. The motivation for a common currency and monetary has been to promote regional solidarity and cooperation between the nations. African nations would, through such arrangements, be able to negotiate trade arrangements as a block bilaterally with Europe, the United States, or Asia. However, what is unknown is whether a common currency or a monetary union will reinforce the strength of African economies, given that such currency could be poorly managed or subject to continual depreciation and will tend to affect all nations. Furthermore, adopting a common currency will imply that African countries will have to give up the ability to respond to asymmetric shocks through monetary policy response. African countries need to have identical response production and export structures to adapt to these shocks (Masson & Pattillo, 2004a, 2004b, 2004c).

Collier's (1991) suggestion that membership to the existing monetary unions in Africa is not associated with an increase in trade among nations but attribute the low inflation in the Franc C.F.A. franc zones to French support through the French Treasury, which guarantees the convertibility of the currency with the use of the operations account. African countries will face obstacles from the start; thus, developing the right model for a single currency will certainly be achieved. The criticisms of the African single currency project and the prophetic declaration of its infeasibility and doom by the West is rooted in the fear that the agenda would be a threat to the West if Africa were to rise as a major economy like the EU and China (Simura and Asuelime (2017).

The calculated attempt to discredit the Lagos Plan of Action through the World Bank's Berg Commission Report in 1981 attributed Africa's economic woes to internal structural problems, external factors, and domestic policy inadequacies. The structural adjustment programs implemented in Africa in the 1980s and early 1990s to address the purported problems plaguing the structures of African economics were unsuccessful. Should Africa follow its path? The response is a resounding yes, even if Africans have structural and political differences compared to the West.

Africa's Single Currency Strategy

Although satisfying the optimal currency criteria is not a guarantee for the successful launching of a single currency for African countries, increases in asymmetric shocks might increase the cost of giving up the dual adjustment mechanisms of exchange rate movements and interest rate changes. However, these costs can be reduced by allowing for free movement of factors within the region that can help reduce the inflation and unemployment trade-off that would otherwise be eliminated through adjustments in exchange rates or interest rates. Also, increasing the flexibility of nominal prices and wages may reduce the need for an exchange rate adjustment to restore external balance and reduce the loss created by a move to monetary integration.

The free movement of resources and people across Africa is critical for successfully implementing the African monetary union single currency. Thirty-two member states of the African Union (AU) have adopted the Protocol to the treaty on the Establishment of the African Economic Community Relating to the Free Movement of Persons, Right of Residence, and the Right of Establishment in January 2019. The roadmap for the implementation of the treaty has also been signed. However, in addition to the low pace of signature and ratification of the Protocol on Free Movement of Persons, some AU member countries still have restrictive visa regimes which restrain cross-border crossings. Furthermore, armed conflicts in some parts of the continent, the free movement of people has been perceived as posing security threats.

Promoting free trade via regional economic unions could foster integration across the continent. Prominent among the initiatives for the implementation of free trade is the ratification of the African Continental Free Trade Area (AfCFTA), which kicked off in January 2021, having been ratified by 35 out of the 55 African Union members. The AfCFTA will bring together 1.3 billion people across 55 countries with a combined gross domestic product of US$3.4 trillion (World Bank, 2020). The kick-off of the AfCFTA is a strong realization of one project of the 2063 Agenda put in place by the AU for the economic integration of Africa. Agenda 2063 is the continental roadmap that includes "inclusive growth and sustainable development" and an "integrated continent." Also, furthering regional integration in infrastructure, transport, and communication provides greater economic integration in the continent.

The consensus is that regional integration across Africa offers enormous benefits for economic growth and the potential for a single currency. The successful kickoff of the AfCFTA is a sign that things are seemingly moving in the right direction. Economic and monetary integration will offer Africa a chance to expand the markets for products made in Africa, lower transaction costs, and provide these countries with the means to negotiate better trade agreements and coordinate macroeconomic policies. However, AU member countries must demonstrate the political will to implement good plans and programs. A lot needs to be done to improve infrastructure, and binding measures should be implemented to resolve conflicts and promote political stability, good governance, and accountability.

Measuring Regional Integration in Africa

The African Union relies on regional integration to achieve the goals established in the Abuja Treaty for Economic and monetary integration in Africa. Accordingly, the African Union has used two different indices to measure integration in regional economic communities. The measures are critical because the AU relies on regional integration to attain continent-wide economic and monetary integration.

The most recent African Regional Integration Index (ARII) published in 2019 by the African Union Commission and the United Nations Economic Commission for Africa includes the regional integration index for five dimensions: trade, productivity, macroeconomic, infrastructural, and free movement of people. These dimensions are the hallmarks of African Economic and monetary integration. The ARII compares countries within regional communities and others across the regions and also measures the state of regional integration of the continent. The success of creating an African Central Bank depends on the successful integration of the five dimensions. It should be noted that Regional integration is critical for African integration.

Regional integration will expand markets and trade, enhances cooperation, mitigate risks, and foster socio-cultural cooperation and regional stability.

Although there are differences in performance among member countries of the different regional communities, the index provides average scores and the standard deviations of the different dimensions of integration. The Southern African Development Community (SADC) has a low overall integration score (0.337). The region's performance was low among six dimensions except for the free movement of people (0.490) and macroeconomic integration, where its performance was moderate (0.422). The Economic Community of West Africa (ECOWAS) has a moderate average score of 0.425. The Economic Community of Central Africa (ECCAS), based on an average index of 0.442, is moderately integrated. The Intergovernmental Authority on Development (IGAD) is also moderately integrated with an overall score of 0.438. The Sahel Saharan States (CEN-SAD), with an average overall score of only 3.77, is less integrated. The Arab Maghreb Union (AMU) is moderately integrated with an average score of 0.488. The Common Market for Eastern and Southern Africa (COMESA) has a low average score of 0.367 but can improve. With an overall score of 0.537, the East African Community is relatively integrated and performs well in all the dimensions. The Intergovernmental Authority on Development (IGAD) has an average integration score of 0.38 and is moderately integrated (Table 17.3).

Table 17.3 Overall Regional Integration Scores Ranks

Country	Regional integration	Trade integration	Productive integration	Macroeconomic integration	Infrastructural integration	Free movement of people
COMESA Average	0.367	0.445	0.328	0.365	0.317	0.385
ECOWAS Average	0.425	0.438	0.22	0.469	0.298	0.733
SADC Average	0.337	0.34	0.239	0.422	0.214	0.49
AMU Average	0.488	0.481	0.449	0.571	0.509	0.438
IGAD Average	0.438	0.444	0.321	0.423	0.48	0.54
CEN-SAD Average	0.377	0.377	0.256	0.441	0.302	0.508
ECCAS Average	0.442	0.357	0.323	0.684	0.373	0.469
EAC Average	0.537	0.44	0.434	0.66	0.555	0.664

Source: African Regional Integration Index Report 2019

The African Union has also developed another framework known as the Multidimensional Index of African Regional Integration Index (AMRII). The AMRII was put in place because monetary integration in Africa should start from integrating regional economic unions. The frameworks should evaluate the progress made at respective regional communities, highlight the achievements, and identify weaknesses, challenges, and opportunities of the integration process in Africa to implement the Abuja Treaty and the Agenda 2063 (African Union, 2020). As envisaged in the Abuja Treaty, African monetary integration should begin by realizing regional economic integration, establishing the African Economic Community, and eventually an African Central Bank with a common currency.

Table 17.4 provides an overview of monetary integration based on the 2020 Multidimensional Index of African Regional Integration Index (AMRII) results. The indicators used to evaluate monetary integration show that the East African Community (EAC), the Economic Community of West African States (ECOWAS), and the Common Market for Eastern and Southern Africa (COMESA) have adopted a convergence program and have established a monetary institute, the rest of the communities are yet to implement measures towards monetary integration in their respective regional communities.

While the achievement of the dimensions highlighted in the Abuja Treaty is critical for the successful implementation of the single African currency, the treaty provides that the African Economic and Monetary Union was to be set up no later than 2018. The process would be done by consolidating the African Common Market and creating an African Monetary Fund, an African Central bank, and an African Parliament. These institutions have not been set up yet but are in progress. The criteria for monetary integration have still not been achieved as of 2020. As the implementation of the Abuja Treaty is a stage-by-stage process, the African Union has put in place mechanisms to monitor and evaluate the progress made so far at the level of RECs in the implementation of the treaty. A total of 33 indicators have been developed for each of the eight dimensions for integration. The Abuja Treaty and Agenda 2063 provides guidelines that would guide the continent towards integration (African Union, 2020).

Although many obstacles mar regional integration in Africa, the African Continental Free Trade Area (AfCFTA) entered into force at the beginning of 2021 and will likely be a game-changer if the business climate

Table 17.4 Monetary Integration in African: Overview

	EAC	ECOWAS	COMESA	SADC	ECCAS	IGAD	AMU	CEN-SAD
Regional Economic Community Currency convertibility	Yes	No	No	No	No	No	No	No
Adoption of a Convergence Programme	Monetary cooperation program adopted and multilateral monitoring mechanism functional	Monetary cooperation program adopted and multilateral monitoring mechanism functional	Monetary cooperation program adopted and multilateral monitoring mechanism functional				No	No
Establishment of a Monetary Institute	East African Monetary Institute in 2001 (EAMI.)	West African Monetary Institute (WAMI.)	COMESA Monetary Institute (CMI)	No	No	No	No	No

Source: AUC, 2020

Table 17.5 Intra-regional economic trade in total African trade (2016)

Community	Billions $ US.	Share in total African trade %	Intra-regional tariff rates %
SADC	34.7	84.9	3.8
CEN-SAD	18.7	58.4	7.4
ECOWAS	11.4	56.7	5.6
COMESA	10.7	59.5	1.89
AMU	4.2	51.8	2.6
EAC	3.1	48.3	0.00
IGAD	2.5	49.0	1.80
ECCAS	0.8	17.7	1.86

Source: UNCTAD, 2019: Facts & Figures

improves and African countries embrace free and fair trade. From 2015–2017, intra-African trade was only 2% compared to 47% for America, 61% for Asia, 67% for Europe, and 7% for Oceania, respectively (UNCTAD, 2019). The share of intra-regional trade as a total of African trade show widespread differences among regional communities with more profound levels of integration in SADC (84.9%), followed by COMESA (59.5%). The lowest level of integration was in ECCAS, with only 17.7% of intra-regional trade in total African trade (Table 17.5).

Summary and Conclusion

The Abuja Treaty that established the African Economic Community outlines six stages that will lead to establishing a common currency for Africa by 2028. The strategy proposes creating new regional economic unions and strengthening existing ones that will eventually merge into a larger continental union having a Central Bank and a single currency. The chapter has highlighted membership benefits to a continent-wide monetary union and the challenges facing Africa's regional integration process. Political considerations and interests are critical in this process, and effective initiatives need to identify the different aspirations and interests of the African people. The African Union should monitor and track commitments made towards regional efforts.

For obvious reasons, regional monetary integration in Africa has not increased trade among countries that adopted common currencies at regional levels, such as the FCFA countries. The major trading partners for all African countries are the advanced nations. Besides, some of the countries participating in currency unions in Africa are among the poorest in the continent, highlighting that currency unions have not brought any development to Africa. Lack of political commitments towards economic integration, instability, and poor infrastructure are some of the challenges to development in the continent. Thus, prominent economists and policy advisers have expressed doubt about the effectiveness of promoting currency unions and regional economic groupings to achieve the goal of a single currency for Africa. Given the diverse nature of African countries, monetary integration and a common currency may not be effective when some countries have to bail out low-performing nations that do not practice fiscal discipline as a goal. Furthermore, it should be clear that large economies like Nigeria and South Africa with different trade shocks would adversely affect monetary policy, which will tend to penalize other economies (Masson, 2006a, 2006b).

The success of the European single currency demonstrates that regional economic integration could successfully bring countries together to pursue a common purpose. As with the European case, some countries faced challenges at the level of macroeconomic stability but were eventually able to get their policies right. Africa is not Europe and must address all the challenges facing these countries, especially at the political level, higher transaction costs, infrastructural neglect, poor governance, and instability. These challenges can be overcome if African countries demonstrate political will and commitments to implement the plans while surrendering some form of economic policy sovereignty to the institutions of the African Monetary Union.

Furthermore, the AU could create regional monetary zones in each region and expand unions like the WAEMU to include other countries in ECOWAS and the Central African Economic and Monetary Union to include other members of ECCAS. The AU could then merge these unions. Although the approach might take longer to accomplish the goal to establish the AMU and the Single African currency by 2028, it could be an alternative among fewer options. Despite the challenges, hopes have heightened since the recent start of the African Continental Free Trade Area in January 2021. The successful launching of the AfCFTA is a sign that things are seemingly moving in the right direction.

REFERENCES

African Union. (2020). *African trade statistics 2020 yearbook*.
Alesina, A., & Barro, R. B. (2002, May). Currency Unions. *Quarterly Journal of Economics*, 409–436. A recent restatement of OCA theory.
Balassa, B. (1961). *The theory of economic integration*. George Allen and Unwin.
Baldwin, R., & Wyplosz, C. (2006). The economics of European integration, Chapter 15. Fiscal Policy and The Stability Pact.
Banienuba, S. (2013). Where is Nkrumah's United States of Africa 50 years on? https://www.pambazuka.org/pan-africanism/where-nkrumah%E2%80%99s-united-states-africa-50-years (accessed 28.01.2019)
Collier, J. L. (1991). On the first year of German monetary, economic and social union. *Journal of Economic Perspectives*, 5(4), 179–186.
de Melo, J., & Brown, E. (2018). *Working with the grain of African Integration* (Briefing note No. 106). ECDPM.
Ekekwe, N. (2009). Toward single african currency: A necessity of prior convergence of African regional economies. *African Union Commission Policy Brief*, 2, 7–10. https://au.int/sites/default/files/documents/29926-doc-congress_article_volume_2.pdf
Ekwealer, C. T., & Mtshali, K. (2018). The United States of Africa and the conundrums. *Journal of African Foreign Affairs*, 5(1), 25–39.
Elias, T. O. (1965). The Charter of the Organization of African Unity. *The American Journal of International Law*, 59(2), 243–267. Cambridge University Press.
Jager, A., & Hafner, K. A. (2013). The optimum currency area theory and the EMU. *Intereconomics*, 48(5), 315–322. https://doi.org/10.1007/s10272-013-0474-7
Kenen, P. B. (1969). The optimum currency area: An eclectic view. In R. A. Mundell & A. K. Swoboda (Eds.), *Monetary problems of the international economy*. University of Chicago Press.
Kimenyi, M. S., Lewis, Z. A., Routman, B., Page, J., Smith, J., Kamau, A., & Adewuyi, A. O. (2012). Accelerating Growth through Improved Intra-African Trade. African Growth Initiative at Brookings, 1–32.
Marinoz, E. (2014). The history of African integration – A gradual shift from political to economic goals. *Journal of Global Economics*, 6(4), 74–86.
Martin, L. (1993). International and domestic institutions in the EMU process. *Economics and Politics*, 5(2), 125–144.
Masson, P. (2006a). *Trade and currency unions in Africa*. Available at https://www.gtap.agecon.purdue.edu/events/Conferences/2006/documents/Masson_PPT
Masson, P. (2006b). New monetary unions in Africa: A major change in the monetary landscape? *International Economics*, CEPII research Center, Issue 3Q, 87–105.

Masson, P., & Pattillo, C. (2002). Monetary union in West Africa: An agency of restraint for fiscal policies? *Journal of African Economies, 11*(September), 387–412.

Masson, P., & Pattillo, C. (2004a). A single currency for Africa? Probably not, but the selective expansion of existing monetary unions could be used to induce countries to improve their policies. *Finance & Development.*

Masson, P., & Pattillo, C. (2004b, December). A single currency for Africa? *Finance and Development Magazine, 41*(4).

Masson, P., & Pattillo, C. (2004c). *The monetary geography of Africa.* Brookings Institution.

McKinnon, R. I. (1963). Optimum currency areas author. *The American Economic Review, 53*(4), 717–725. https://www.jstor.org/stable/1811021

Mundell, R. (1961). Theory of optimum currency areas. *American Economic Review, 51,* 657–665. The original OCA theory.

Naldi, G. J., & Magliveras, K. D. (1999). The African economic community: Emancipation for the African states or yet another glorious failure. *North Carolina Journal of International Law and Commercial Regulation, 24*(3).

Ofodile, U. E. (2015). Protocol on the establishment of the African Monetary Fund & Statute of the African Monetary Fund. *International Legal Materials, 54*(3), 507–531. https://doi.org/10.5305/intelegamate.54.3.0507

Simura, B., & Asuelime, L. E. (2017). BREXIT from the European Union: What lessons for the African Union integration? *Journal of African Union Studies, 6*(1), 25–38.

Songwe, V. (2019). Intra-African trade: A path to economic diversification and inclusion. Coulibaly, Brahima S..: Foresight Africa: Top Priorities for the Continent in, 97–116.

Songwe, V., & Winkler, D. (2012). *Exports and export diversification in Sub-Saharan Africa: A strategy for post-crisis growth.* Brookings Institution.

Ta'a, T. (2014). Pan-Africanism: A historiographical analysis. *EJSSLS, 1*(1), 63–77.

Tavlas. (1993). The 'new' theory of optimum currency areas. *The World Economy, 16*(6), 663–685.

Union, A. (2020). Decision on the African Continental Free Trade Area (AfCFTA). African Union, Addis Ababa, Ethiopia.

United Nations Conference on Trade and Development. (2019). Economic Development in Africa Report 2019: Made in Africa: Rules of Origin for Enhanced Intra-African Trade. UN.

World Bank. (2020). *The African continental free trade area: Economic and distributional effects.* World Bank. https://openknowledge.worldbank.org/handle/10986/34139 License: CC BY 3.0 IGO.

PART V

Conclusion: The Way Forward

CHAPTER 18

Conclusion: Currency Regimes and Monetary Integration in Africa, the Way Forward

Regina Nsang Tawah, Augustin Ntembe, and Aloysius Ajab Amin

INTRODUCTION

This book has provided an overview of monetary arrangements in Africa and assessed the effectiveness of the different monetary and financial systems in the development of African economies. The book has brought out salient points on the conduct of monetary policies, banking and capital market development, and monetary and economic integration in the continent in relation to trade expansion, economic growth, and development. No doubt, Africa is fast becoming the nexus of global growth. As the McKenzie Global Institute's 2016 report puts it, Africa is becoming the

---

R. N. Tawah • A. Ntembe (✉)
Bowie State University, Bowie, MD, USA
e-mail: RTawah@bowiestate.edu; nntembe@bowiestate.edu

A. A. Amin
Clayton State University, Morrow, GA, USA
e-mail: AloysiusAmin@clayton.edu

© The Author(s), under exclusive license to Springer Nature Switzerland AG 2022
A. A. Amin et al. (eds.), *Monetary and Financial Systems in Africa*,
https://doi.org/10.1007/978-3-030-96225-8_18

next new frontier of global investment and economic opportunities. These investments could benefit from the enormous amounts of Africa's natural resource endowments. Currently, the continent counts six of the ten fastest-growing economies globally (Signé and Gurib-Fakim, 2019).

Furthermore, the African Economic Outlook (2021) reported that Africa's GDP at current US dollars, which was $1.9 trillion in 2010, is estimated at $2.5 trillion by the end of 2021 (31.6% increase in growth). Therefore, the favorable economic outlook will enable Africa to create business opportunities to generate $5.6 trillion by 2025. However, sustained growth and improvement in economic indicators will require improvements in macroeconomic reforms, better macroeconomic management, and increased investment in infrastructure. All these require the mobilization of financial resources, through an efficient monetary and financial system in the continent.

African economies have been surprisingly more resilient to macroeconomic shocks than other regions of the world. The impact of the 2007–2009 financial crisis and the COVID-19 pandemic has been less severe in Africa. Gross domestic product increased steadily in Africa between 2017 and 2019, surpassing that in the Euro area, Latin America, and the Caribbean, and emerged as the second fastest-growing region globally (African Export-Import Bank, 2020). Harnessing financial resources towards development and implementing prudent monetary and macroeconomic policies that guarantee stability in the financial sector is critical to growth and development. Therefore, the ongoing project on monetary and economic integration in Africa will be critical in moving the continent forward.

Monetary Policies Across Africa

Monetary policy in Africa has become more orthodox; but, it is fraught with difficulties arising from sometimes political interference. Nevertheless, African countries, particularly those participating in monetary unions and those with well-managed fixed exchange regimes, have maintained a degree of relative price stability. Moreover, these countries have equally built financial markets undistorted by internal political meddling and thus contrast sharply with countries that have suffered from price volatility with high inflation.

Price stability is the core of the monetary policy frameworks of central banks in Africa. However, countries cannot have a monetary policy that focuses only on price stability but rather should be an objective tied to other monetary policy objectives. For example, in Ghana and Tanzania, the price stability objective has effectively kept inflation low and stable. However, competency questions arise under the inflation targeting regime because the monetary authorities set frequently missed targets (Chap. 2). This scenario raises concerns about the limitation of management in the conduct of monetary policy in some African countries. Conversely, in Tanzania, the monetary policy objective of price stability has been successful (Chap. 3). Furthermore, monetary policy interventions in Sierra Leone have been found to play a significant role in economic growth with increases in credit to the private sector as a leading transmission mechanism (Chap. 4).

Financial Institutions

Although the financial system in Africa has improved tremendously over the last few decades, financial markets are, to a large extent, underdeveloped, thus limiting access to financial instruments and services that are critical for African growth and development. Africa's financial integration with global markets is limited with less financial depth than other world regions. Financial integration and cooperation between African countries could go a long way to expand financial inclusion, thus increasing access to financial services. Monetary integration and prudent fiscal and monetary policies, together with the viability of the financial system, can provide the necessary funding for African development.

However, the challenge has been to encourage funding to businesses irrespective of their capital structure and size. The effect of minimum bank capital on the financing of businesses in the Economic and Monetary Community of Central Africa (EMCCA) region, for example, indicates commercial banks' reluctance to finance agriculture, and small and medium-sized enterprises. Therefore, regulatory authorities need to develop ways to encourage a higher level of funding these sectors from banks. The level of funding from financial institutions, particularly banks, depends on the development of the banking sector, which depends inter alia, on governance, interest rates, bank liquid reserves, and bank asset ratio.

Africa's economic performance is below its potentials partly because of underdeveloped and thin capital markets despite some progress in the bonds market. Furthermore, these shallow capital markets constrain the continent's development efforts. African capital markets have great potentials, but with challenges including low capitalization, and short lists of participating companies in the stock exchanges. Developing this potential will require a conducive macroeconomic environment that affects the size and structure of capital markets, well developed financial sector, and a legal and institutional environment that could boost capital markets development. African countries should implement the right policies to speed up the development of capital markets. These measures can support monetary policy, diversify the financial portfolio options, and create secondary markets to boost investment and development.

Monetary and Economic Integration

Macroeconomic stability and shocks can significantly affect monetary policy and the financial market. Therefore, the choice of monetary institutions and policies can play a significant role. Monetary arrangements in Africa began with state-led regulations and bank control but have evolved with implications on Africa's monetary policy performance. The changes that have taken place over time have been influenced by the diversity of African economies and political orientations. For example, countries under colonial rule started with currency boards, which was the case for most British colonies.

Currency boards provided stability to the colonial currency, given its link to the currency of the colonial master. Currency boards eliminated inflation risk through prudent currency issues. However, as the currency was highly controlled, it hindered structural economic change in the colonies and only served the interest of the colonizers. The system allowed for an overly rigid colonial currency. The rigidity of currency boards and the absence of monetary independence implied that policymakers were less flexible in using monetary policy to support development efforts and economic stability. The colonies having currency boards were restricted from typical central bank functions. Unlike colonies under British rule, African countries under French colonial rule were imposed the French Colonial African franc (Colonies Françaises d'Afrique) by a decree of the French Government in December 1945 (African Department Study Group, 1969). The French colonial currency was created to foster economic integration and facilitate control and complete dominance in the colonies' economic, administrative, and political spheres that have lasted till date (Pigeaud, Sylla, & Fazi, 2020).

Driven by post-colonial nationalist aspirations, domestic shocks arising from fiscal pressures, currency boards gradually ceded to the printing press regime. The regime allows countries to accommodate shocks with expansionary monetary policy (Honohan & O'Connell, 1997; Ncube, 2008). Countries such as the Democratic Republic of Congo, formerly known as Zaire, Burkina Faso, Liberia, Sierra Leone, Guinea Bissau, and Uganda, experienced this regime in the 1980s and the 1990s. Although the printing press regime was characterized by an automatic response of prices and exchange rates to macroeconomic shocks, the regime represents the most inflationary means of deficit financing.

Rationing regimes have been typical in controlled economies and were commonplace in 1970 for most countries that practiced this type of regime, such as Ghana, Sudan, Uganda, Burkina Faso and extended to the first half of the 1980s in Mozambique and Zimbabwe (Ncube, 2008). In these economies, prices or quantities did not allow to adjust to clear markets (Honohan & O'Connell, 1997). Most African countries imposed extensive control of prices and foreign exchange as part of macroeconomic policy between the late 1960s through the mid-1980s. Rationing regimes maintained fixed exchange rates, and macroeconomic shocks were accommodated by way of rationing. A common way to finance government deficits was by channeling banking resources, that has the tendency of crowding out the private sector.

The fourth type of monetary regime that falls between the rationing regime and the market-clearing regime is the credit ceiling regime. In this regime, commercial banks face a ceiling on the credits that they could generate. Here, the government has limited access to borrowing, and monetary policy typically uses interest rates and exchange rates as targets. Because interest rates are controlled, the response to macroeconomic shocks is different from when the market determines credit. Finally, the market-clearing regime represents a purely market-orientated central bank and financial system. In this system, the government borrows from the central bank at a market rate just like other banks. Thus, the institutional arrangements discourage monetary expansion by the government. Unfortunately, only a few countries in Africa have reached this stage. Some of these include Ghana, Kenya, Zimbabwe, and The Gambia.

With the dismantling of the monetary zones created by all other European colonial powers during the decolonization process, France moved to consolidate the link of the financial institutions of her former colonies to the French franc after independence. This consolidation allows for more African participation in decision-making while maintaining the Operations Account at the French Treasury. The arrangement led to the creation of two central banks: Banque centrale des états de l'Afrique de l'ouest (BCEAO) and the Banque centrale des états de l'Afrique équatoriale et du Cameroun (BCEAEC). In addition, the headquarters of the two central banks were initially in Paris but were moved to Africa, and the latter was renamed Banque des états de l'Afrique centrale (BEAC).

It is clear that the CFA franc is a colonial currency and the monetary dependency arising from the arrangement is that the capitalist CFA franc and credit-debit relations empowers and enriches France and has weakened and impoverished the African CFA franc countries. Thus, the long-lasting colonial monetary arrangement between France and CFA franc zone former colonies is that of exploitation. Moreover, France has maintained this repression and elite cooptation to deal with African leaders that seek more autonomy (Koddenbrock & Sylla, 2019).

The CFA franc cooperation arrangement is not beneficial to Africa as it allows France to control economic, financial, and political decisions in these countries. In addition, the fact that the CFA is tied to the Euro backed by France would presumably not be a danger to the French public budget that could destabilize the European Union, thanks to the operations account that each CFA franc zone country maintains at the French treasury. However, because the CFA franc is pegged to the Euro, the currencies are subjected to restrictive rules regarding inflation, public debt, and public deficit. The target of the African CFA franc central banks is to have price stability and a targeted rate of inflation that is not allowed to exceed three percent. Such a fixed target often leads to deflationary outcomes that are not good for the long-term growth of African economies (Koddenbrock & Sylla, 2019). Despite the longevity of the CFA franc arrangement, the zone remains a producer of raw materials with limited financial opportunities for the development of the private sector and financing economic activities (Chap. 9).

Thus, the France-Afrique monetary relationship poses difficulties for the African countries to restructure their economies. For instance, commercial banks operating in the CFA franc zone are reluctant to finance local small and medium enterprises (SMEs) in favor of big companies predominantly French-owned (Chap. 7). Policies to encourage the funding of local SMEs should be put in place and supported at the level of institutions, with the leaders working in tandem with the banks to determine the level of funding that is adequate. Furthermore, the monetary and financial system should play an important role in financing economic activities. The system should encourage and support structural transformation with changes in the production structure of African economies, diversify production, and promote regional trade. However, these changes must be accompanied by changes in the monetary and financial systems for the continent's benefit.

Despite the relatively stable prices, low inflation, and monetary integration in the franc CFA monetary communities, experience has been that the West and Central African CFA franc zone economies lag behind other developing countries (IMF, 1998; Chang, 2000). Nevertheless, the CFA franc zone's monetary authorities and the French government have praised the low inflation and the fixed peg. Monetary authorities and decision-makers view the relatively low inflation as an advantage of the currency, although the distribution of wealth arising from the monetary arrangement largely favors France (Koddenbrock and Sylla, 2019). Also, the effect of the strong Euro compared to the US dollar discourages African agricultural producers who become bankrupt because primary products are less competitive in the face of a strong Euro. Consequently, the structural transformation of African economies is hindered because of the loss of revenue from their primary source of income which is agriculture.

With the limitations of the CFA franc union, monetary integration in Africa based on the CFA franc zone model is not a likely option. Critics of the African monetary union have argued that the challenges facing the new continent-wide monetary union are enormous. The African continent consists of small open economies that require flexibility in choosing exchange rate regimes (Monga, 2020). However, the extent of the challenges will depend on the form of the exchange rate regime. Indeed, the single currency will probably not be pegged to any world currency that will compromise external competitiveness. Although inflation is mainly low under the CFA franc regime, monetary arrangements with France do not favor these countries that are exporters of unprocessed primary products. Currency pegs such as the franc CFA could lead to problematic outcomes (Chang, 2000). In the circumstance, if the CFA franc zone were to experience a rise in production costs, member countries would be hit with a deterioration in their competitiveness relative to France and vis-à-vis other countries if the then French franc and now the Euro appreciated relative to the other currencies (IMF, 1998 in Chang, 2000).

Critics also add that the two CFA franc zones have operated for over seven decades but participating countries do not meet the optimal currency criteria for joining a monetary union. Consequently, the optimum currency area criteria would not apply for Africa, and decisions based on the criteria are irrelevant for African integration. The African monetary union plan is widespread and enormous. Masson and Pattillo (2004) have argued that the diversified nature of African economies could suffer from asymmetric shocks because of weak governance, which could pressure the central banks to finance deficits through expansionary monetary policies. This flexibility is no longer possible in a monetary union where policy is entrusted to a supranational body. Masson and Pattillo have also argued that peer pressure within a monetary union could induce countries to improve their policies. Thus, the doubt regarding the success of the single African currency is unwarranted.

It is important to underline here that not all European members of the Euro met the criteria when the single currency was launched. Over time, countries adjusted their policies to align with the required criteria. Economists were more or less divided when the Euro was launched, with many arguing that binding the economies to a single currency was a mistake. Milton Friedman, for example, predicted a downturn that could disrupt the new currency. For the single African currency to be successful, each of the economies needs to have a certain level of economic development to prevent it from crashing in the case of a crisis or shocks. Individually, these countries will be unable to use monetary policy instruments. The single currency is rigid, and policy authorities would not use this option to address economic problems. This is an extreme free market theoretical position, which does not take into consideration market failure, public good with the issue of economies of scale that can result from greater integration of economies.

Hence, African governments must agree to a strong shared commitment to regional integration independent of foreign intervention or influence. Such integration must be inspired by a common African purpose. Ongoing efforts at integration in Africa should continue to address forcefully challenges faced by various countries regarding conflicts, strengthen political institutions and improve economic infrastructure. These would provide a more favorable environment for prudent fiscal discipline, and monetary and financial policies that foster the continent's growth and prosperity. Improved institutions and infrastructure expand productive capacity and enable the free movement of products and people.

Trade, Competitiveness and Monetary Integration

The African Continental Free Trade Area (AfCFTA) became operational in January 2021, and with a population of 1.35 billion people and a combined GDP of $3.4 trillion, Africa is projected to be the largest free trade area in the world when it is fully implemented. The AfCFTA requires countries to reduce trade and non-trade barriers to allow for the free movement of products, and people with rights to live, establish and invest in any part of the continent. Also, differences in the exchange rate regimes across the continent are likely to result in heterogeneous responses to price changes and other shocks that could lead to disparities in growth rates. Consequently, challenges to African exchange rate regimes have been at the center of doubts and misgivings about the success of the proposed African central bank and the single currency in dealing with differences in exchange rate regimes.

African countries are taking necessary steps towards having monetary integration at sub-regional and continental levels with the aim of establishing a single continental currency—the newly launched AfCFTA is a precursor of the African Monetary Union and common currency, which by all indications is nearing fruition. The building block for the new supra structure is promoting integration at the level of the current regional groupings. Successful implementation of the initiative is projected to lead to macroeconomic stability and low inflation across Africa.

The free movement of resources as a result of the AfCFTA will improve the competitiveness of African businesses. The recent introduction of the Pan-African Payments and Settlement System (PAPSS) platform accelerates payments on cross-border transactions and reduces dependence on the dollar and Euro. Also, the doubt associated with the choice of exchange rate regimes and monetary policies will be eliminated through monetary integration (Masson & Milkiewicz, 2003). The successful launching of the AfCFTA and the PAPSS are signals for progress towards building the African Monetary Union.

Currently, African countries are lagging the Europeans with respect to the real effective exchange rate, export-gross domestic product ratio, and export-import ratio, but outperform on the technological development index. Conditional convergence appeared thus satisfied, raising the hope for a brighter future. However, the trade financing gap constrains trade within Africa and the rest of the world. The African Union or countries can set up a development finance institution to facilitate and support trade with infrastructure development. This solution should entail setting up rapid emergency facilities coupled with risk mitigation instruments earmarked to support banks.

The convergence criteria emphasized especially with respect to the European single currency will certainly not hold for Africa because of the differences in the structures of African economies. One of the arguments in support of macroeconomic convergence is monetary stability achieved by CFA zone countries even when they do not meet the criteria. Betting on convergence as a panacea to monetary integration in Africa is shortsighted. Notwithstanding, African countries should continue to achieve the convergence criteria, including political and macroeconomic stability, prudent and responsible macroeconomic policy with a robust policy of credit access expansion. The fact that countries will lose the monetary policy flexibility to address severe macroeconomic problems would require that member countries, especially those with weak economies, are supported. Also, political stability and institutional discipline would be critical for monetary integration. Regional conflicts and political strife must be addressed with inclusive participation of the people in the political process at the level of the respective countries.

Continental Monetary and Financial Pillars

The continent has in place pillars for growth and development. These include the abundance of natural and human resources, a promising information technology sector, ongoing efforts for economic and monetary integration at the level of regions, and the African Union efforts to dismantle trade barriers. Compared to other regions, African economies are structurally weak, despite high growth rates in countries such Botswana, Kenya, Ghana, South Africa, Djibouti, Morocco, and Libya. African economies have low diversification and depend principally on the production and export of primary products. The latter leaves African economies with low resource wealth relative to that of countries with developed manufacturing sectors.

Rapid economic growth is historically connected to industrialization and the latter is associated with technological advancement. Manufacturing industries generate forward and backward linkages and thus huge opportunities for business services, retailers, and suppliers. Recent trends indicate that Africa is experiencing an industrial renaissance although its average percentage share of employment in manufacturing is only 8.4

(Signé & Johnson, 2018; de Vries et al., 2021). The surge in manufacturing is predominantly fueled by small firms that produce mostly resource-based products for the domestic market rather than for exports. The AfCFTA offers African businesses an opportunity to expand, access to markets and increased competitiveness. The African Continental Free Trade Area also creates an enabling environment for the diversification of African manufacturing, ease much of the external shocks common with primary commodities production and exports and thus help countries to satisfy an important criteria for monetary integration.

The opportunities arising from free trade fuel the quest to develop an enabling infrastructure. A propitious infrastructure allows the building of industries and diversifies African economies. The key to successful implementation of an efficient development strategy for the continent depends on the availability of financing. Hence developing innovative and cohesive monetary and financial system to finance industry and trade is critical. The African continent is embracing financial technology such as cryptocurrency, digital money and mobile banking that is providing flexibility and inclusion in the financial system.

The current economic and monetary integration in Africa provides opportunities to take advantage of the low labor cost and mobility, natural and human endowments to boost investments in manufacturing. African leadership must take the lead to provide an attractive environment to investors and this should include good infrastructure and favorable regulatory and institutional arrangements. However, infrastructural development is a costly undertaking that can possibly be relaxed through public financing, public-private partnerships financing and appropriate alignment of monetary and financial policy.

Africa is in need of a solid financial infrastructure capable of generating the required resources to finance investment, boost manufacturing and intra-African trade. These initiatives are achievable through favorable monetary and financial policies that strengthen and expand the banking and financial sector. Presently, Africa is experiencing a growth in pan-African banking (PABs) that is enhancing competition in the delivery of banking services. Although in its infancy, PABs are enhancing the cross – border integration of payments and settlement system in Africa (Stijns, 2015).

The progress and experience made so far towards regional integration across the African continent provide the incentive for a greater union with all the advantages accruing from these arrangements. The advantages from large scale and scope provide African economies with the opportunity for accelerated development and the increased benefits from a larger financial system. Integration at regional level serves as the pillars of monetary integration in Africa and will provide the momentum for successful integration at the continental level.

Figure 18.1 provides an overview of the process of forming the African Monetary Union which we believe is the path forward for the achievement of the plan set forth at the Abuja conference that established the pathway to the formation of a single currency for Africa. It is noteworthy that efforts are gearing up at regional level for a continental single currency. For example in West Africa, the ECOWAS is working towards a common currency (Eco) that will bring together members of the West Economic and Monetary Union (WAEMU) and the non CFA franc participating countries. In the SADC region, an integrated regional electronic settlement system (SIRESS) became operational in 2013 with all member countries except Madagascar participating. The South African Custom Union (SACU) is planning to create a common market area that will include SADC members with the aim of creating a common currency unit. East African economic community signed a monetary union protocol in 2013 which included a provision to create an East African Central Bank and a single currency. Despite challenges at the level of the different

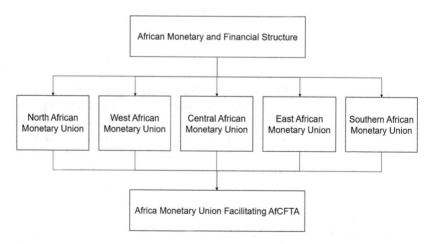

Fig. 18.1 One monetary and financial system. (Source: Authors' construction)

regions, African countries supported by the African Union are forging ahead with the process.

Conclusion

Evidently, the regional monetary unions will provide the structure necessary for monetary integration at the continental level. Developments at the regional levels received a boost from the launching of the AfCFTA in January 2021. The AfCFTA is an economic and global game changer for African economies and it has the potential of raising the global share of African economies in world trade as long as African countries continue to implement the necessary policies to ensure long term peace and security and remove any remaining supply-side constraints that affect development. Policy in Africa has been dictated from either its former colonial masters or international lending agencies. These policies often are not based on the African realities and perspectives. Critics have raised the concern that the African Union projects articulated at the Abuja Summit were cosmetic and far-fetched given record failures in similar initiatives across Africa. The current AU agenda and projects are on track to a record success despite the challenges. The African leadership has a critical role to play in this endeavor. The aspiration of the African people and the desire for accelerated development require African countries to take their destiny into their hands. Monetary and financial integration of the continent is critical for the way forward.

References

African Department Study Group. (1969). Financial arrangements of countries using the CFA Franc (Accords financiers des pays dont la Monnaie et le franc CFA) (Ordenamiento Financiero de Los países que utilizan el franco CFA). *Staff Papers (International Monetary Fund), 16*(2), 289–389. https://doi.org/10.2307/3866436

African Economic Outlook. (2021). *From debt resolution to growth: The road ahead for Africa*. The African Development Bank Group.

African Export-Import Bank. (2020). *African trade report 2020: African trade report 2020. Informal cross-border trade in Africa in the context of the AfCFTA*. Afreximbank.

Chang, R. (2000). *Regional monetary arrangements for developing countries*. Rutgers University.

de Vries, G., Mensah, E. B., Kruse, H., & Sen, K. (2021). *Many African countries had a surprise manufacturing surge in 2010s – It bodes well for the years ahead.* UNU-WIDER. Extracted on the October 16, 2021 from https://theconversation.com/many-african-countries-had-a-surprise-manufacturing-surge-in-2010s-it-bodes-well-for-the-years-ahead-155405.

Honohan, P., & O'Connell, S. A. (1997). *Contrasting monetary regimes in Africa* (International Monetary Fund working paper).

International Monetary Fund. (1998). *The west African economic and monetary union: Recent developments and policy issues* (Occasional paper 170). IMF.

Koddenbrock, K., & Sylla, N. (2019). *Towards a political economy of monetary dependency: The case of the Franc CFA* (MaxPo discussion paper, No. 19/2). Max Planck Sciences Po Center on Coping with Instability in Market Societies (MaxPo), Paris.

Masson, P. R., & Milkiewicz, H. (2003). Africa's Economic Morass—Will a Common Currency Help? *Policy Brief #121*. Washington, D.C.: The Brookings Institution.

Masson, P., & Pattillo, C. (2004). A single currency for Africa? *Finance & Development*, International Monetary Fund.

Monga, C. (2020). *Africa Isn't ready for currency unions.* Project Syndicate.

Ncube, M. (2008). *Financial systems and monetary policy in Africa.* African Economic Research Consortium.

Pigeaud, F., Sylla, N., & Fazi, T. (2020). *Africa's last colonial currency: The CFA Franc story.* Pluto Press. https://doi.org/10.2307/j.ctv1g6q8w3

Signé, L., & Gurib-Fakim, A. (2019). *The high growth promise of an integrated Africa.* Brookings Institute.

Signé, L., & Johnson, C. (2018). *The potential of manufacturing and industrialization in Africa trends, opportunities, and strategies.* African Growth Initiative at Brookings.

Stijns, J.-P. (2015, July). Pan-African banks: Stylized facts and results of a pilot survey. In J.-P. Stuns & D. Revoltella (Eds.), *Recent trends in banking in Sub-Saharan Africa – From financing to investment.* European Investment Bank.

INDEX

A
Abrigo, M. R., 154
Adverse selection, 13, 151
Africa, 144, 145
African Financial Community (CFA), 145, 155, 156
Agents, 144–148, 153, 159–163
Assets, 148
Asymmetric information, 13, 20

B
Bank-based financial system, 10–12
Bank capital, 150, 151
Bank capital of the channel theory, 150
Banking development, 28, 217, 226, 227, 231, 232, 234, 235
Banking system, 11–13, 23, 24, 26, 46, 64, 70n3, 84, 91, 119, 120, 144, 146–149, 191, 219, 242, 285
Bank of Central African States (BEAC), 155
Bank reserves, 148
Basel, 150
BCEAO, 222, 224, 225, 324n3, 426
Benefits and risks, 33–35
Billions, 145
Blockchain technology, 32, 33
British heritage, 28
Broad-based industrialization and development, 4

C
Capital, 147, 148
Capitalization, 150
Capital market development, 28, 29, 239, 248, 250–253, 255, 256, 285, 295, 308, 310, 421
Capital markets, 11–13, 17, 24, 28, 29, 200, 202, 211, 239, 240, 244–246, 250, 255, 285, 297, 311, 355, 356, 423, 424

[1] Note: Page numbers followed by 'n' refer to notes.

Capital ratio, 148
Central African Banking Commission (COBAC), 155
Central Bank (CB), 3, 5, 7–9, 13–17, 25, 31–35, 43, 44, 46, 49, 51, 52, 60, 61, 64, 82, 88, 98, 110, 120, 127–129, 173, 180, 188, 189, 193–202, 207, 211, 223–225, 228, 331, 399, 401, 404, 410, 412, 414, 432
Central bank digital currency (CBDC), 33–35
Central Bank of West African Countries (BCEAO), 129, 135, 188, 189, 193, 195, 198, 201, 205
Central banks, 405, 406, 422, 425, 426, 428, 429
Challenges, 30, 97, 278, 279, 347, 395
Channel, 147–150
Channels of transmission, 12–17
Continental Monetary and Financial Pillars, 430–433
Control of corruption, 28, 226, 227, 231–235, 326
Cooke ratio, 148
Credit institutions, 147–150, 155
Credit offer, 150, 151
Credit ratio, 148, 149
Crypto assets, 31
Crypto tokens, 31
Cyber security, 35

D
Decentralized virtual currency, 31
Developing financial deepening, 10
Development, 145, 150
Digital currency, 7, 33
Digital technology, 7
Diversified financial system, 12

E
Eco, 27, 97, 115, 116, 123–139, 373, 432
Economic agents, 144–148, 153, 159–163
Economic capital, 150
Economic financing, 147, 149, 163, 164
Economic growth, 4, 5, 8, 9, 11–14, 16, 17, 20, 21, 24, 26, 28, 44, 53–55, 57–60, 64, 66, 69, 82, 86, 87, 92, 99, 113, 151, 169, 171, 178, 180, 185, 186, 201, 204, 208, 209, 217, 218, 225, 239–256, 263, 264, 285–288, 308, 309, 322, 326, 348, 352, 356, 365, 382, 402, 405, 410, 421, 423, 430
Economic integration, 29, 30, 98, 109, 115, 118, 121, 174, 210, 261–263, 279, 331, 370, 395, 397, 401, 402, 404, 409, 410, 412, 415, 421, 422, 424
Equity, 145

F
Financial access, 21, 23, 28, 34
Financial assets, 5–7, 85, 389
Financial efficiency, 8, 15–17
Financial institutions, 3–5, 7, 8, 11, 13, 17, 24, 31–33, 35, 36, 64, 146, 149, 151, 180, 200, 201, 204, 217, 223, 226, 228, 234, 242, 288, 344, 355, 361, 423, 425
Financial instruments, 5, 32, 246, 423
Financial integrity, 36
Financial markets, 4–6, 9, 10, 12, 14–17, 23, 34, 84, 86, 108, 147, 195, 200, 202, 245, 285, 286, 389, 422, 423
Financial resources, 144

Financial sector, 148
Financial services, 5, 7, 19, 22, 35, 84, 100, 222, 234, 263, 286, 423
Financial system, 5, 17, 432
Financing, 144–152, 159, 163, 164, 166
Financing the economy, 151, 152, 246
Forms of money, 7, 36
Fragmented, 36
France, 149, 150
Funds, 146, 148, 150

G
Gossé, J. B., 151
Guillaumin, C., 151

H
Heuvel, S. J., 148

I
Inflation (INF), 4, 8, 9, 14–17, 25–27, 44–61, 65–68, 71, 74–76, 78, 79, 82, 85–87, 89–92, 98, 100, 109, 110, 114, 118, 120, 137, 169, 175–178, 186, 193, 200, 201, 207, 225, 226, 229, 231, 232, 234, 245, 250, 251, 267, 269, 320, 321, 372, 384, 385, 389, 405, 406, 408, 409, 422–424, 426, 427, 429
In need of funding, 146, 148
Institution, 144
Intermediation, 146

L
Legal, 8, 10, 11, 32, 33, 35–36, 64, 84, 108n6, 130, 186, 187, 225, 245, 424

Lending funds, 150
Lending rate, 68, 229
Levieuge, G., 150
Levin-Lin-Chin (LLC), 158
Liability, 148
Loans, 147–150
Love, I., 154

M
Macroeconomic convergence, 26, 99, 101–103, 106, 107, 109, 110, 114, 118, 119, 265, 371, 373, 430
Macroeconomic performance, 25, 63, 315, 326
Managing cybersecurity, 35
Market, 148
Market-based financial system, 10–12
Market Breadth, 248–250
Market capitalization, 29, 180, 246–248, 250–253, 256, 293–295, 297, 299, 301–310
Market liquidity, 11
Minimum bank capital (CBM), 146, 147, 154, 155, 158, 159, 161, 162
Modeling, 151
Monetary and financial systems, 3, 4, 180, 185, 421, 422, 427
Monetary policy, 4, 8, 9, 12–14, 16, 17, 24–26, 28, 29, 33–35, 43–61, 63–79, 81–92, 98, 108, 114–118, 125, 126, 129, 130, 134, 138, 147–149, 169, 182, 193, 198, 200–202, 208, 210, 221, 223–225, 265, 311, 316, 321, 324n3, 325, 372, 396, 403, 404, 408, 415, 421–425, 428–430
Monetary systems, 24

Monetary unions, 4, 25, 29, 97, 114–116, 131, 139, 173, 174, 181, 265, 271, 272, 315, 316, 320, 321, 328, 336, 339, 340, 398, 399, 404, 405, 408, 422, 432, 433

Money, 5–10, 12–14, 21, 22, 31–36, 46–48, 51, 52, 64–66, 68–70, 73, 75, 76, 78, 79, 82, 86, 87, 90, 92, 101, 103, 116, 121, 180, 189, 192, 193, 195, 196, 198, 199, 202, 218, 224, 243, 405, 431

Moral hazard, 13, 14, 17, 20, 23

O

Operational risk, 35
Organization of the economy, 5
Osborne, M., 159

P

Panel, 149, 152, 154
Payment systems, 33, 108, 109, 115, 120
Positive impact, 159
Potential benefits, 7
Price stability, 8, 9, 15–17, 25, 43–47, 49–51, 54, 60, 64, 65, 75, 78, 82, 86, 113, 137, 199, 208, 225, 331, 422, 423, 426
Price volatility, 4, 32, 52, 422
Public banking, 239, 244
PVAR, 153, 154

R

Regulation, 147–149
Regulatory agencies, 5, 7
Regulatory and supervisory bodies, 8
Regulatory capital, 150, 151
Regulatory quality, 28, 226, 227, 231–233, 235, 326

Risk, 148–150
The rule of law, 28, 151, 202, 226, 227, 232, 234, 235, 326

S

Shock, 148, 149, 164
Short-term credit, 154
Stock exchange, 64, 202, 240, 245–247, 285, 310
Synchronized infrastructure, 35

T

Technological change and economic transformation, 19
Total Effective Rate (TEG), 154, 158–160, 165
Transforming the economies, 4
Transforms currencies, 7
Transmission channel, 26, 88, 89
Tri-sector macroeconomic model, 18

U

Uncertainty, 148
Union, 149

V

Variable, 165
Vector Autoregressive (VAR), 151, 152
Virtual currency, 31, 33
Volume, 147, 151

W

Wood, D., 148

Z

Zone, 163, 164

Printed in the United States
by Baker & Taylor Publisher Services